HOW EUROPE'S ECONOMIES LEARN

How Europe's Economies Learn: Coordinating Competing Models

Edited by

EDWARD LORENZ
and
BENGT-ÅKE LUNDVALL

OXFORD
UNIVERSITY PRESS

OXFORD
UNIVERSITY PRESS

Great Clarendon Street, Oxford ox2 6DP
Oxford University Press is a department of the University of Oxford.
It furthers the University's objective of excellence in research, scholarship,
and education by publishing worldwide in

Oxford New York

Auckland Cape Town Dar es Salaam Hong Kong Karachi
Kuala Lumpur Madrid Melbourne Mexico City Nairobi
New Delhi Shanghai Taipei Toronto

With offices in

Argentina Austria Brazil Chile Czech Republic France Greece
Guatemala Hungary Italy Japan Poland Portugal Singapore
South Korea Switzerland Thailand Turkey Ukraine Vietnam

Oxford is a registered trade mark of Oxford University Press
in the UK and in certain other countries

Published in the United States
by Oxford University Press Inc., New York

British Library Cataloguing in Publication Data
Data available

Library of Congress Cataloging in Publication Data
Data available

Typeset by SPI Publishing Services, Pondicherry, India
Printed in Great Britain
on acid-free paper by
Biddles Ltd., King's Lynn, Norfolk

ISBN 0-19-920319-9 978-0-19-920319-2
1 3 5 7 9 10 8 6 4 2

Acknowledgements

The two editors met for the first time in 1994 at a conference in Austria. Since then we have worked together on and off with several project proposals, projects, and papers. Our common concern has been to enhance our understanding of knowledge-based economic dynamics by integrating organization theory and political economy with economics of innovation. We see this book as an important step forward in this respect. All the contributions come from scholars who, while being experts in their own field of research, share our ambition to cross borders between disciplines when these get in the way for understanding important socio-economic phenomena.

This book brings together contributions from a number of high-quality, Europeanwide, socio-economic projects in the areas that are normally kept separate: knowledge management, labour markets and education and training systems, the economics of innovation, and the political economy of state systems. The chapters were specifically commissioned for a series of workshops and conferences organized in the context of the Loc Nis project (Labour, Organization and Competence in National Innovation Systems), an 'Accompanying Measures' project under the European Union's Sixth Framework programme (Contract No. HPSE-CT-2001-60004). To make sure that we end up with a coherent volume, each chapter has been discussed at several gatherings and, as well, exposed to several rounds of editing.

One of the most positive aspects of the Sixth Framework programme is that it is much more open to experimental and interdisciplinary socio-economic research than similar national programmes. The 'Accompanying Measure' type of project has the further specific advantage, without counterpart in national funding systems, that it gives an opportunity to integrate results from different specific projects. We are grateful to the Commission for giving us this unique opportunity to draw upon rich and diverse sources of insights when working out this synthesis on how Europe's economies learn. Specifically we want to thank Ronan O'Brien and Virginia Vitorino from the Commission for the way they have been coaching our work.

The vision developed here has benefited from all the participants in the Loc Nis exercise, including several that do not appear as contributors to the book. We would like to express our thanks not only to all the authors but also to Lars Aagaard, Lars Erik Andreasen, Laura Balbo, John Barber, Nick Boreham, Benjamin Coriat, Patrick Deiss, Ina Drejer, Reinder van Duinen, Per Eriksson,

Lars Espersen, Charles Equist, Peter Fisch, Francesco Garibaldo, Nathalie Greenan, Rik Huyts, Paul Huyts, Birgit Kjølby, Wilhelm Krull, Crystal Lane, Kurt Larsen, Christian Lebas, Reinhard Lund, Franco Malerba, Jonathan Michie, Riel Miller, Alejandro Naclerio, Lars Beer Nielsen, Jens Nyholm, Erkki Ormala, Bjarne Palstrøm, Alaisdair Reid, Anna Rogaczewska, Isi Saragossi, Gerd Schienstock, Roland Schneider, Esko Olavi Seppælæ, Keith Smith, Peter M. Smith, David Soskice, Marianne van der Steen, Lennart Svensson, John Sweeney, and Frank Wilkinson.

A special thanks to Michael Storper who, besides taking part in seminars, gave us the idea for the title of the book at a late Parisian dinner. We would also like to thank David Musson, Stephen Rehill, and Matthew Derbyshire of Oxford University Press for their assistance at the different stages of commissioning and preparing the volume for publication.

Contents

PART III. EDUCATION SYSTEMS AND SCIENCE–INDUSTRY LINKS

PART IV. MULTI-LEVEL GOVERNANCE AND POLICY OPTIONS

List of Figures

List of Tables

List of Boxes

List of Contributors

Bessy, Christian, CNRS Research Fellow, Ecole Normale Supérieure de Cachan, France.

Cappelen, Ådne, Director of Research, Statistics Norway, Norway.

Cohendet, Patrick, Professor, Department of International Business, HEC School of Management, Canada.

Dosi, Giovanni, Professor, Laboratory of Economics and Management (LEM), Sant'Anna School of Advanced Studies, Italy.

Ho, Mei H. C., Doctoral Candidate, Eindhoven Centre for Innovation Studies, Eindhoven Technical University, The Netherlands.

Labini, Mauro Sylos, Doctoral Candidate, Laboratory of Economics and Management (LEM), Sant'Anna School of Advanced Studies, Italy.

Lam, Alice, Professor of Organization Studies, School of Management, Royal Holloway University of London, UK.

Lanciano-Morandat, Caroline, CNRS Research Fellow, Laboratory of Economics and Labour Sociology (LEST), University of Aix-en-Provence, France.

Llerena, Patrick, Professor, Office for Theoretical and Applied Economics (BETA) University Louis Pasteur, France.

Lorenz, Edward, Professor, University of Nice-Sophia Antipolis, France.

Lundvall, Bengt-Åke, Professor, Department of Business Studies, Aalborg University, Denmark.

Mailhot, Chantale, Associate Professor, Department of International Business, HEC School of Management, Canada.

Nielsen, Peter, Associate Professor, Aalborg University, Denmark.

Nohara, Hiroatsu, CNRS Research Fellow, Laboratory of Economics and Labour Sociology (LEST), University of Aix-en-Provence, France.

Rodrigues, Maria João, President, European Commission's Advisory Group for Social Sciences and Professor, University Institute, Portugal.

Schaeffer, Véronique, Assistant Professor, Office for Theoretical and Applied Economics (BETA) University Louis Pasteur, France.

Tomlinson, Mark, Lecturer, Birmingham Business School, University of Birmingham, UK.

Tylecote, Andrew, Professor, Management School, University of Sheffield, UK.

Valeyre, Antoine, CNRS Research Fellow, Centre for Employment Studies (CEE), France.

Verdier, Eric, CNRS Research Director, Laboratory of Economics and Labour Sociology (LEST) University of Aix-en-Provence, France.

Verspagen, Bart, Professor, Department of Technology Management, Eindhoven Technical University, The Netherlands.

Whitley, Richard, Professor of Organizational Sociology and Director of Research, Manchester Business School, University of Manchester, UK.

List of Abbreviations

BERD—business enterprise R&D

BRR—benefit replacement rate

CEA—Nuclear Energy Centre

CME—coordinated market economies

CNES—National Centre for Space Research

CNET—National Centre for Telecommunications Research

CNRS—National Centre for Scientific Research

DGA—General-Directorate for Armaments

DUI—doing, using and interacting

ECJ—European Court of Justice

EPL—employment protection legislation

EPO—European Patent Office

ERA—European Research Area

ETUC—European Trade Unions Confederation

EUROLICS—European Observatory of Learning, Innovation and Competence Building Systems

GDP—gross domestic product

GNVQs—General National Vocational Qualifications

HERS—higher education and research system

HRST—human resources for science and technology

ICT—information communication technology

ILM—internal labour market

ITB—Industrial Training Boards

IUT—Instituts Universitaires de Technologie (University Institutes of Technology)

JPO—Japanese Patent Office

LIS—Luxembourg Income Study

LME—liberal market economies

MCA—multiple correspondence analysis

MENRT—Ministère de l'Education Nationale et de la Recherche (Ministry of National Education and Research)

NSF—National Science Foundation

NSI—national system of innovation

NVQ—National Vocational Qualification

OJT—on-the-job training

OLMs—occupational labour markets

OST—Observatoire des Sciences et des Techniques

SBIR—small business innovation research

SBTC—Skill biased technical change

SBU—Strategic Business Unit

STI—science, technology, and innovation

SYS—Stanford-Yale-Sussex

TECs—Training Enterprise Councils

TLOs—technology licensing offices

UD—union density

USPTO—US Patent and Trademark Office

1

Understanding European Systems of Competence Building

Edward Lorenz and Bengt-Åke Lundvall

1.1. INTRODUCTION

Over the last decade there has been a growing consensus among policymakers all over the world that knowledge has become of great importance for wealth creation and that innovation is an important driver of economic growth. International competitiveness is no longer seen primarily as a question of low wages and currency rates. In OECD countries, it has been generally realized that a national strategy focusing on relative cost advantage is doomed to fail in a context of an increasingly global competition where major economies, such as China and India, enter markets both for manufacturing and for services on a big scale. The gap in wage costs is too big to be closed by wage policies. Currency policies have proved to be of limited relevance for the competitiveness of a national economy. Even big changes in currency rates— as the current devaluation of the US dollar illustrates—do not have the expected dramatic effect on market shares.[1]

These insights were reflected in the Lisbon declaration where the goal was set for Europe to become 'the most dynamic and competitive economy' of the world. Competitiveness was linked explicitly to 'dynamic efficiency', to the knowledge base of the economy and to the innovation system. But the shift from a static to a more dynamic perspective on competitiveness has been far from complete. While innovation policy has become more visible in the public discourse, those responsible for 'general economic policy' have remained faithful to the credo of standard economics and to the more static views on policy and institutions inherent in this perspective.

This book aims at bringing the understanding of the dynamic interplay between knowledge creation, learning, and innovation on the one hand, and the economic performance and competitiveness of Europe on the other, some further steps ahead. It contributes with new items to the agenda for European socio-economic research and new theoretical foundations for European policymaking. There is a growing concern that the objectives set in the Lisbon process will not be reached. Some ascribe this to the unwillingness of European policymakers to pursue radical structural reforms aiming at freeing up market forces in the economy. The alternative view behind this book is that this perspective is too simplistic and that a deeper and fuller understanding of how Europe's economies learn should lead to institutional reforms that combine the flexibility of markets with collective responsibilities and investments in collective infrastructure.

The Lisbon declaration presents Europe as 'one economy', and there is a tendency to compare this economy with the economies of Japan and the US in benchmarking exercises. Standing alone such a perspective is seriously misleading. It needs to be complemented with an understanding of the fundamental differences between Europe's economies. It might have value as signalling a normative agenda for Europe but when it is mistakenly used as analytical concept, things go wrong. General prescriptive policy at the European level must take into account the systemic differences between the countries in Europe.

In what follows we start by summarizing some of the evidence assembled in this volume to characterize this diversity across European nations. We then present an evolutionary framework for analysing the links between national systems' capacity to innovate and their institutional arrangements at the levels of labour markets, financial systems, and education and training systems. We conclude by considering how diversity in Europe's socio-political systems has shaped and constrained processes of institutional change at both the national and EU levels. We argue that it is only by giving due recognition to these socio-political differences that progress will be made in establishing more 'Europe' in the areas of science, technology, and innovation.

1.2. DIVERSITY IN EUROPEAN SYSTEMS OF COMPETENCE BUILDING

One major difference between standard economics and industrial dynamics/ evolutionary economics is that history and institutions matters. The 'innovation system' concept signals that the economic structure and the current institutional set-up, both with historical roots, need to be analysed and understood in order to set policy priorities. Comparative studies which aim to define and transplant generally valid 'best-practice' are not useful, while 'learning by comparing' different systems may be useful in order to understand the characteristics of each single system (Lundvall and Tomlinson 2002).

If used in a naive way, international benchmarking where countries are ranked according to a number of 'good' variables such as amount of R&D or frequency of research collaboration between public and private may be harmful. It is not helpful to aim at getting to the top in every single category in the 'scoreboard' and doing so is no guarantee that a system is promoting wealth and welfare. Used intelligently, with an understanding of the systemic features of the national economy, benchmarking may provide useful insights as to where, when, and how to intervene with public policy and with attempts to redesign institutions.

Tomlinson's chapter takes a first step in developing this more intelligent and systemic approach to benchmarking. By breaking down simple indicators, like R&D spending, and combining them with other measures, he develops composite measures that provide a representation of learning styles across Europe that is at odds with the effort to pick winners and losers. Countries that are ahead according to certain indicators may be behind according to others. For example, if we examine the trend in the intensity of private–public research links over the 1980s and 1990s, a sort of cyclical effect can be observed for many countries with the general trend being an increase in intensity except for the US. If we then plot GDP growth against the measure of private–public links, we find that the US ranks low in terms of linkage intensity but has healthy growth rates, the UK ranks high in terms of links but has relatively low growth rates, and Ireland ranks high on both scales.

Complex trends and relations such as these belie any attempt to identify a best-practice model to which all European nations should be encouraged to converge. The point here, as Tomlinson observes, is not to argue that European nations cannot learn from each other, but rather that policy needs to be situated relative to local context. Valuable lessons can be learned from benchmarking-type exercises, but this should not get in the way of local strengths in a futile attempt at destroying what makes a nation or region different.

A similar point about the need to frame policy from recognition of the diversity of European systems emerges from Ho and Verspagen's analysis of processes of knowledge diffusion across Europe. While they find strong empirical support for the view that national borders do hinder knowledge spillovers, they also identify a number of 'higher-order' regions which play a central role in the diffusion of knowledge across national borders within the EU. Most countries according to their data have regions which serve as gatekeepers, transferring knowledge from abroad into its own country. This may occur because of their exceptional ability to attract multinationals and to extract knowledge from them, thus promoting cross-national knowledge flows.

Such regional diversity need not be seen in a negative light relative to European integration and the construction of a European Research Area (ERA) in particular. Rather, it means that the ERA should be characterized as a network composed of parts which differ. Policy should take into account the differences among regions, and knowledge diffusion policies in particular should take into account the existence of a number of higher-order regions that serve as hubs.

In the current concern that objectives of the Lisbon process will not be realized, it is often forgotten that the Lisbon declaration was more than a call for greater competitiveness. In fact, it set the goal for Europe, 'to become the most competitive and dynamic knowledge-based economy in the world capable of sustainable economic growth with more and better jobs and greater social cohesion' (Rodrigues, this volume, p. 387). Combining competitiveness with other features defined a distinctively European trajectory to the knowledge-based economy.

A special problem with the knowledge-based economy is that it may create growing inequality in terms of income and earnings distribution (Lundvall 2002; Rodrigues, this volume). Cappelen's chapter provides up-to-date empirical evidence on changes in wage dispersion for OECD countries. There is, of course, a vast literature on this and the tendency towards increased wage dispersion in the US and the UK and to a lesser extent in Canada and Australia for the 1980s and the early 1990s has been documented. This same difference in trend between the Anglo-Saxon countries and other OECD countries is partially confirmed through 1990s, and if we compare levels of dispersion in 2000 or 2001, it is possible to distinguish three groups of nations: the Anglo-Saxon countries with relatively high dispersion, the Continental European nations with intermediate levels, and the Nordic European nations with relatively low levels of dispersion.

While there is no systematic relation between the level of dispersion and the relative unemployment rates for skilled and unskilled labour, Cappelen does identify a negative correlation between wage dispersion and measures of labour market regulation including the degree of coordination in collective bargaining. Further, there is a considerable overlap between those nations characterized by both low dispersion and high levels of bargaining coordination and the group of nations that Lorenz and Valeyre (this volume) identify as intensive users of 'learning' forms of organization.

Cappelen concludes by suggesting that institutional arrangements across Europe have mediated in different ways the appropriation of productivity gains associated with increased investments in knowledge creation. In the deregulated labour market settings of the Anglo-Saxon nations, the accent has been on private appropriation of gains and inequality has increased. In the Continental European and Scandinavian nations, labour markets are relatively regulated and the accent on private public partnerships and strong firm linkages has resulted in lower levels of inequality. These, albeit tentative, conclusions bolster the view developed in this volume that innovation dynamics are tightly connected to the characteristics of socio-political systems and, in particular, to the mechanisms whereby the benefits and costs of change are redistributed. The following section develops a general framework in this light.

1.3. AN EVOLUTIONARY FRAMEWORK FOR ANALYSING HOW ECONOMIES LEARN

1.3.1. Building on the NSI Framework

While the national system of innovation (NSI) concept signals that both the economic structure and the institutional set-up need to be analysed in order to set policy priorities, it is obvious that different authors mean different things when referring to a NSI. Some major differences have to do with the focus of the analysis and with how broad the definition is in relation to institutions and markets.[2]

Authors from the US with a background in studying science and technology policy tend to focus the analysis on 'the innovation system in the narrow sense'. They regard the NSI concept as a follow-up and broadening of earlier analyses of national science systems and national technology policies (see for instance the definition given in Mowery and Oxley 1995: 80). The focus is on the systemic relationships between R&D efforts in firms, science and technology (S&T) organizations, including universities and public policy.

Freeman (1987) developed a more organizationally grounded concept that took into account national specificities in the way firms organize innovative activities. He emphasized, for example, how Japanese firms increasingly used 'the factory as laboratory'. Researchers at Aalborg (Lundvall 1985; Andersen and Lundvall 1988) also developed a concept of innovation systems where there are other major sources of innovation than science. Innovation is seen as reflecting interactive learning taking place in connection with ongoing activities in production and sales. Therefore, the analysis takes its starting point in the process of production and the process of product development assuming, for instance, that the interaction with users is fundamental for product innovation.

None of these approaches, however, gave sufficient attention to the broader set of institutions shaping competence building in the economy such as labour markets, the education and training system, and their relation to systems of corporate governance. Nor did they consider the broader connections between these institutional subsystems and national political cultures and welfare regimes. A major concern of this volume is to build on established work in the NSI tradition to develop a broader and more integrated understanding of national systems of competence building. Moreover, the wider perspective developed in this volume seeks to give due attention to the role played by informal experienced-based learning in determining the pace and 'style' of innovation. This is seen as complementary to more formal processes of learning based on investments in R&D and on firms' capacities to absorb external sources of codified scientific knowledge.[3]

In order to capture this wider set of interactions in a dynamic perspective, we introduce an evolutionary framework for analysing how economies learn. The framework links up three levels: transformative pressures, capabilities to innovate, and the way different national systems redistribute the costs and benefits of change. Without taking into account the relations between these different levels and how they are connected to different institutional subsystems, it is difficult to judge the impact of different specific forms of innovation policy on the welfare of citizens. For Europe as a whole, getting these broader settings to converge is a much greater and more difficult challenge than diffusing specific best-practice innovation policies.

The starting premise in the framework is that globalization, deregulation, and information technology have resulted in an acceleration of economic change. The assumption is that competition in OECD countries has changed so that now a bigger share of the labour force than before are required to participate in frequent processes of learning and forgetting. This idea is summed up in the notion of 'the learning economy'.[4]

In a globalizing learning economy, even big national systems are increasingly exposed to *transformation pressure*. The transformation pressure will affect the population of firms in two ways. On the one hand, firms will be created and destroyed, and on the other, surviving firms will change in terms of organization, technology, and capability. At the level of the labour market, this process will be reflected in dynamics where workers will gain, lose, or change jobs while learning and forgetting skills and competences.

A crucial characteristic of a national system is how it responds to an increase in transformative pressure. The *capability to innovate and to adapt* will reflect systemic features having to do with how easy it is to establish interactive learning within and across organizational borders (social capital) and with the preparedness to take risks (entrepreneurship). Organizational capabilities and the competence structure of the workforce play an important role. Social cohesion may be an important factor behind social capital while it might get in the way of entrepreneurship.

The mechanism for *redistribution of costs and benefits emanating from change* differs between national systems. In the Anglo-Saxon countries, the basic idea is that individuals should carry as much as possible of both benefits and costs. In the Nordic countries, universal tax financed welfare systems redistribute in favour of individuals that lose their job or become handicapped. The more conservative systems in place in Continental European countries tend to redistribute through employment-tied public insurance systems. In Southern Europe, where systems of social protection are relatively weak, the family can still play an important role as redistributing mechanism.

Figure 1.1 below builds on the framework developed in Archibugi and Lundvall (2000) to link transformation pressure to the capacity to innovate and to the distribution of costs and benefits of change. One view is that processes of globalization and the diffusion of ICT will result in a progressive convergence of national systems and innovative styles and performance. The alternative view developed in this book is that capabilities to innovate and to adapt reflect systematic differences in national institutional arrangements at the levels of the science and technology system, labour markets, education and training, and finance. These institutional subsystems will impact on how knowledge is developed and used within organizations, and these organizational differences in turn will have a bearing on innovation pace (fast or slow) and innovation style (incremental or radical).

But national differences in innovation systems need to be seen in an even broader perspective. Europe's economies differ in terms of their political cultures and social welfare systems, and these differences are fundamental for how the different national economies respond to transformation pressure. This is partly because of the way feedbacks from the distribution of costs and benefits affect the capacity to innovate and to adapt. An uneven distribution may create a negative attitude to change among those who mainly register the costs and if there are high degrees of insecurity among individuals, they will tend to oppose change. This is one of the reasons why social cohesion is crucial for the learning economy. But a redistribution of income that is too ambitious may lead to weak economic incentives and hamper individual entrepreneurship. We should therefore expect to find different (more or less participatory) modes of innovation in national systems with different redistribution strategies, and this is confirmed by comparative work on national

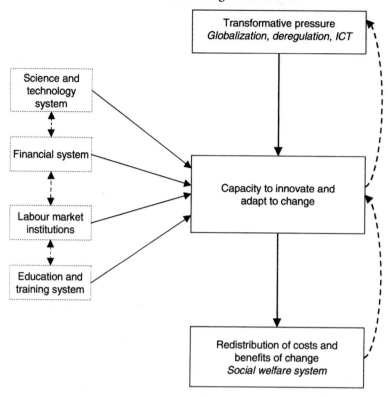

Figure 1.1. A model linking transformation pressure to the capacity to change and to the distribution of the costs and benefits of change

innovation and learning systems (Amable, Barré, and Boyer 1998; Lorenz and Valeyre, this volume; Whitley, this volume).

A second kind of feedback mechanism goes from the ability to innovate to transformation pressure. An increase in innovative capacity tends to stimulate entrepreneurship and the building of more flexible organizations. This implies a selection of people and institutions that are more change oriented, and this further increases transformation pressure.

1.4. UNDERSTANDING CAPACITIES TO INNOVATE

If we open up the 'black box' of firm-level knowledge use and development, we can characterize types of knowledge along two main axes: individual versus collective or dispersed; and explicit versus tacit or implicit. This gives rise to a four-way taxonomy of knowledge types which may be more or less developed in different organizational forms (Lam and Lundvall, this volume). Knowledge that is embodied in the individual employee and thus relatively portable (e.g. professional or skilled craftsman) but nonetheless has significant tacit elements based on practical problem-solving experience tends to characterize what Mintzberg (1979) refers to as 'the operating adhocracy'. More dispersed or collectively embodied knowledge of a highly tacit and firm-specific character correspond to 'the J-form' organization (Japanese firm) as described by Aoki (1986). Knowledge in the 'machine bureaucracy', which operates on the basis of formal hierarchies and a breakdown of work into detailed jobs, is both explicit and dispersed or collective. Individually embodied knowledge that is codified according to established professional standards corresponds to the 'professional bureaucracy'. In comparison with the two organizational forms with high levels of tacit knowledge, work in the machine and professional bureaucracies tends to be highly standardized.

These different organizational forms can be expected to give rise to different rates and styles of innovation. Innovation rates can be anticipated to be relatively high in the operating adhocracy and the J-form compared to the two bureaucratic forms of organization. However, the operating adhocracy tends to surpass the J-form in terms of radical innovations. This is because of the greater scope the operating adhocracy offers experts to autonomously explore novel solutions to problems and because of the ease of reconfiguring the mix of competences due to competences being individually embedded and hence portable on the labour market.

The empirical evidence for the Danish economy presented in Nielsen and Lundvall (this volume) provides support for the postulated link between organizational form and rate of innovation. Danish firms adopting organizational practices characteristic of the operating adhocracy or the J-form (e.g. delegation of functions, extensive horizontal communication, high levels of investment in human resource development) have a higher probability of innovating a new product or service than firms using more hierarchical practices characteristic of the 'machine bureaucracy'.

Limited/narrow	Fast/incremental	Fast/radical
Machine bureaucracy Professional bureaucracy	J-form organization	Operating adhocracy

Figure 1.2. Rate and style of innovation
Source: Lam and Lundvall (this volume, p. 125).

Developing empirical indicators of the degree to which innovations are radical as opposed to incremental is more problematic than developing innovation rate indicators. The distinction is often seen as corresponding to the degree to which innovations are competence destroying as opposed to competence enhancing. However, survey manuals, such as the *Oslo Manual*, which establishes conventions for the European Community's innovation surveys, do not propose guidelines for measuring this distinction. A related distinction that has been measured in European survey instruments is between innovations that are 'new to the market' and innovations that are 'new to the firm'. Strictly speaking, this is not identical with the radical–incremental distinction, since introducing a 'new to the firm' innovation that was originally developed elsewhere may require the firm to make radical changes to its mix of competences. The new to the market/new to the firm distinction does capture some of what the radical–incremental distinction aims to represent, since developing innovations that are new to the market depends on the firm's capacity to explore new knowledge.

The empirical evidence presented in Lorenz and Valeyre (this volume) for the fifteen member states of the EU in 2000 supports the view that 'the operating adhocracy' form of organization is superior in terms of developing new for the market innovations. Their empirical analysis distinguishes between two organizational forms with strong learning dynamics, what they refer to as the 'autonomous learning' forms and the 'lean' forms. The former (which corresponds to the operating adhocracy) can be distinguished from the latter (which corresponds to the J-form) by the lesser importance of team forms of work organization and by the higher levels of autonomy that employees exercise in their work. The empirical analysis (see Figure 6.4; p. 153) shows that the relative importance of 'new to the market' innovations tends to be higher in those nations where the autonomous learning forms of organization are overrepresented compared to the EU average. For example, the UK, which is characterized by a relatively weak development of the learning relative to the lean forms of organization, stands out for the low importance of new to the market innovations relative to those that are merely new to the firm.

1.4.1. Institutional Frameworks

The four-way classification of firms and types of knowledge can be connected to differences in labour markets and education and training systems. Education systems can be distinguished according to whether they are narrow 'professional oriented' or broad 'competence-based', and labour markets can be distinguished according to whether they take the form of occupational labour markets (OLMs) characterized by high levels of mobility, or internal labour markets (ILMs) characterized by relatively stable employment and well-structured internal career paths. This gives rise to a four-way classification of 'models of competence building', which may be more or less developed in different nations. Thus, the combination of ILMs and narrow professional oriented education and training provides a favourable institutional setting for the 'machine bureaucracy' forms of organization, while ILMs combined with relatively broad competence-based training systems provide support for the J-form organization. The presence of OLMs in combination with broad competence-based training underpins the 'operating adhocracy', while the 'professional bureaucracy' tends to flourish where OLMs are combined with narrower professional-oriented training (Lam and Lundvall, Figure 5.4, p. 125).

As Lam and Lundvall stress, the taxonomy is a set of ideal types and it is implausible that any national economy could be adequately characterized in terms of one of the pure models. This is so not only because hybrid arrangements can be found but also because the institutional conditions supporting particular types of organizations and innovation trajectories may have a regional as well as national base. This latter point applies to the operating adhocracy whose capacity for radical innovation is based on the way its members combine formal knowledge with tacit knowledge derived from a rich practical experience of problem-solving. Such organizations are under pressure to bureaucratize because of the difficulties they face in accumulating and transferring tacit knowledge. This explains why such firms often tend to flourish in regional settings where localized networks of firms provide the necessary 'social capital' for the efficient transfer of tacit knowledge in an inter-firm career framework.

These considerations help to explain the fact that the UK economy overall performs so poorly in terms of radical or 'new to the market' innovation. The

	Occupational labour market	Internal labour market
Narrow professional education system	Professional bureaucracy (narrow innovation)	Machine bureaucracy (slow/limited innovation)
Broad competence-based education system	Operating adhocracy (radical innovation)	J-form organization (incremental innovation)

Figure 1.3. Labour markets, education systems, and organizational models
Source: Lam and Lundvall (this volume, p. 125).

operating adhocracy tends to be found in a few isolated contexts, such as the cluster of high-technology firms around the University of Cambridge, where there is an active process of inter-firm mobility of entrepreneurs, consultants, and researchers. Outside of these high-tech clusters, the UK institutional framework, with a weak system of vocational training that is more suitable for the requirements of standard jobs than those requiring creative problem-solving, tends to support the development of bureaucratic forms of organization or possibly hybrid arrangements combining features of the machine bureaucracy and the J-form (see Bessy, this volume). The evidence of Lorenz and Valeyre (this volume) is largely consistent with this interpretation of the UK innovation system.

The taxonomy also provides a way of understanding the very wide diffusion of the operating adhocracy forms of organization in the Scandinavian countries (see Lorenz and Valeyre, this volume, p. 149). As a number of authors have observed (Amable 2003; Lundvall 2002), these nations can be distinguished from the Continental European nations by the way relatively weak levels of employment protection are combined with systems of social protection that reduce the costs and risks of job changes. These institutional arrangements favour the development of relatively high levels of labour market mobility which, when combined with well-developed systems of vocational and continuous training, promote the wide adoption of the forms of cooperation and learning within and between firms characteristic of the operating adhocracy.

As Maskell (1998) observes for the case of Denmark, these conditions favour the development of a set of localized capabilities that are tacit and hard to imitate for outsiders. However, in comparison to Sweden and Finland, or the high-tech clusters in the UK for that matter, Denmark stands out for its relatively 'low-tech' industrial specialization and for an innovation style that is more incremental than radical. This arguably reflects distinctive features of its science and technology system including a predominance of small firms specialized in low-technology manufacturing sector and less well-developed links between universities and industry (Lundvall 2002).

1.4.2. Corporate Governance and Innovation Style

The taxonomy on innovation systems developed here, based on a differentiated understanding of how knowledge is used and developed within firms, can be linked up with the framework developed by Tylecote (this volume) and Tylecote and Conesa (2004) to provide an understanding of the relation between systems of corporate governance (shareholder vs. stakeholder), organizational forms and innovative style. The starting point here is the common observation that shareholder systems are more supportive of radical innovation than stakeholder systems, since shareholder systems are conducive to a rapid redeployment of assets that might be resisted by 'insiders' in stakeholder systems. This suggests that shareholder systems are highly complementary to the operating adhocracy forms of organization in supporting radical innovation.

This line of argument needs to be qualified by taking into account another feature which bears on the suitability of different forms of corporate governance: *visibility*. Overall, stakeholders (family shareholders, banks, other firms, employees) can be expected to have superior firm perceptiveness than outside shareholders, and thus are in a superior capacity to judge whether the firm should be funded, and to monitor progress (Tylecote and Conesa 2004). This suggests a degree of complementarity between stakeholder systems and the operating adhocracy forms of organization that depend on significant tacit elements of knowledge which are difficult to observe and monitor for outsiders. A further feature of innovation which bears on the suitability of different forms of corporate governance is *appropriability*. Tacit knowledge which is embodied in the employee moves with the employee, and it is impossible for the firm to assert ownership over it. Thus, it is important to enfranchise such employees as stakeholders.

As Tylecote observes (pp. 189–90), neither of the classic stereotypical forms of corporate governance (shareholder or stakeholder) appear to be equipped to exploit the full potential of the new forms of organization which mobilize both codified and non-codified knowledge in non-standard creative work settings. Tylecote argues that the future may then lie with hybrid systems that combine some of the features of shareholder and stakeholder capitalism. The key actor in these hybrid systems are the 'new institutional' shareholders with considerable industry-specific expertise that can use proportionately small holdings as a basis for engaging management. Along with shareholding employees, engaged institutional shareholders are characterized by their concern for long-term profits. However, based on an overview of current development in Europe, it seems clear that the simple presence of these actors is not enough to bring about changes in corporate governance. It also depends on the extent to which a nation's culture and tradition predisposes shareholder engagement and employee participation.

The way we have classified innovation systems here has some elements in common with other classifications and notably with the 'varieties of capitalism' approach (Hall and Soskice 2000). This is based on a dichotomous distinction between liberal market economies (LME) and coordinated market economies (CME). LME are characterized by fluid or active labour markets and a reliance on the general educational system to supply industry with employees whose skills are general hence transferable. Overall, the institutional arrangements discourage investments in specific and hence non-redeployable assets. In CME, well-developed vocational training systems provide employers with industry-specific skills, and relatively secure employment encourages employees to invest in complementary firm-specific skills. The institutions of LME (e.g. the UK) are seen as favourable to achieving the rapid reconfiguration of competences which radical innovation requires, while the institutions of CME (e.g. Germany) support incremental innovation.

The parsimonious nature of the varieties of capitalism framework makes it an extremely powerful tool for comparative systems analysis, and its ability to provide insight into many of the observed differences among nations has been demonstrated. One way in which the approach developed here differs is in opening up the 'black box' of knowledge management to provide a more differentiated account of types of knowledge and learning within firms. This has the advantage of providing insight into some current developments that are difficult to account for within the varieties of capitalism framework, such as the strong performance of such CME as Finland and Sweden in high-tech sectors characterized by radical technological change, or the limited capacity of the UK economy as a whole for developing fundamentally new product and processes. It also provides a basis for analysing the southern European nations where the combination of a relatively weak science base and the use of more bureaucratic forms of work organization accounts for the more incremental nature of innovation dynamics.

1.5. STATES, SOCIO-POLITICAL SYSTEMS, AND PROCESSES OF INSTITUTIONAL CHANGE

The firm-centred approach developed above helps explain how institutionalized variation promotes or inhibits the adoption of specific organizational forms related to differences in innovation rate and style. It also suggests that there are alternative models for generating different types of innovation which may lead to societal comparative advantage in different industrial sectors.

One obvious limitation of the approach is that it takes a nation's institutional framework, or what Hall and Soskice (2000) call its coordinating institutions, as given. Yet as a number of the contributions in this volume demonstrate, institutional arrangements in EU nations have changed considerably over the last decade or so. Tylecote, for example, discusses the emergence in the EU of hybrid forms of corporate governance falling somewhere between the shareholder model traditionally associated with the UK or the

US, and stakeholder forms as traditionally practised on the continent. Dosi et al. and Cohendet et al. (this volume) discuss and analyse the impact of changes in the institutional arrangements that have governed the generation of scientific knowledge and the relations between science and industry for much of the twentieth century. The chapters by Cohendet et al., Verdier, Luciano-Morandat and Nohara, and Bessy analyse changes in the role of universities and in education and training systems more generally. Whitley explores the relations between state structures and the development of distinctive and homogeneous innovation systems and draws conclusions for the impact of multi-level EU governance on national and regional innovation systems. Rodrigues as well as Lundvall and Lorenz analyse the relation between EU multi-level governance and the characteristics of national systems in order to gain insight into the factors which have held back the process of EU integration. They agree in arguing that greater attention needs to be given to national differences and strategies in making progress towards achieving the goals laid-out in the Lisbon process. Lundvall and Lorenz in particular argue that a more explicit recognition of the differences that exist in socio-political systems and the characteristics of national welfare systems is fundamental to understand and promote institutional change at the European level.

The chapters in the book thus attest to the evolving and diverse nature of the institutional subsystems in Europe that shape corporate behaviours and capacities for innovation. While accounting in general for the changes in institutional set-ups goes beyond the scope of this volume, the chapters cited above do offer elements of an explanation. They point to the need to move away from the firm-centred approach that we have emphasized above and to focus more squarely on the actions of governments in relation to the characteristics of socio-political systems. The point here is not to ignore the contribution of enterprises to processes of institutional change, but rather, as Hall and Soskice (2000) have observed, to give recognition to the fact that changing the collective rules that shape corporate behaviours typically requires government intervention to introduce legislation supportive of the new institutional arrangements.

The capacities of governments in these respects are sharply constrained by the characteristics of the socio-political system and notably by the interests and the degree of organization of key socio-political groups. One reason for this, as Amable (2003: 68) observes, is that governments will be reluctant to introduce changes that threaten the interests of dominant socio-political groups. Correspondingly, institutional changes in which these powerful groups have little interest often prove easier to bring about. However, it may also be the case that governments are constrained in what they can achieve because the relevant socio-economic groups, such as employers or labour, are poorly organized. As Whitley (this volume) observes, weak collective organization can prove an obstacle to institutional changes calling for new forms of cooperation in cases where there are problems of free-riding that can only be solved through the ability of peak organizations to coordinate individual behaviours, possibly by imposing sanctions on members who deviate from the new rules of the game.

1.5.1. Science-Industry Links Promoted by Public Policy

These points are illustrated in various ways by the chapters of the book focusing on changes in science-industry links and more generally on the transformation of European education and training systems. For example, the chapters by Dosi et al. and Cohendet et al. detail the considerable changes that have occurred over the last two decades in the 'open science institutions' that have governed the generation of science and the relations between science and industry for much of the twentieth century. The classical system that was fully developed in the decades following the Second World War is character-ized by a science-base that is largely the product of publicly funded research with the knowledge produced by that research being largely open and avail-able for potential innovators to use (Nelson 2004). Underlying this system was a distinctive organization and culture consisting of a scientific commu-nity largely relying on self-governance and peer evaluation and committed to 'an ethos of disclosure of research results driven by "winner takes all" precedence rules' (Dosi et al., this volume, p. 208).

As the two chapters document, important areas of science are now much more under the sway of market mechanisms in Europe than used to be the case, and this is reflected in the growing attractions of a new model of the 'entrepre-neurial university' inspired by an at best imperfect understanding of how US research universities operate. The key elements of this emerging model, which can be observed to varying degrees across Europe, are the progressive substitu-tion of private for public funding, increased private appropriation of publicly funded research, and an increased emphasis on strategic alliances between universities and industry including the development of hybrid organizations within networks of heterogeneous actors (universities, public laboratories, private consultants, etc.) capable of responding to an increasing demand for interdisciplinary research projects on the part of firms.

While the authors recognize that none of these developments are entirely new, they also point to the key role of government policies at the national and EU levels in promoting change. Legislation that has framed the commercial-ization of research in higher education establishments in the US, such as the Bayh-Dole Act, has been used as a model in several EU countries, including the UK, Finland, Austria, and France. EU programmes have been framed within a perspective that gives priority to user needs, interactions with industry and achieving concrete results in a short time span. Relatively small amounts of funding have been set aside for fundamental research within universities. The Sixth Framework Programme, as the authors observe, calls for focusing European R&D investments in the fields likely to generate, in the medium term, profits for economy and society and relies on new instruments certain of which (e.g. networks of excellence) explicitly preclude using EU funds for research.

Both chapters raise important questions about the desirability of these changes for the longer-term technological and innovative performance of European nations. Dosi et al., while recognizing the diversity of performances across Europe, provide evidence that Europe as a whole has made little progress in closing the gap relative to the US in terms of technological capability. They argue that relative weak technological performance is due not to the absence of university-to-industry transfer mechanisms but rather to the failure of European firms to exploit the available opportunities reflecting their weak absorptive capacities.

1.5.2. European Diversity in Education Systems and Knowledge Development

While the chapters by Dosi et al. and Cohendet et al. focus on certain trends that are common to many EU nations, the papers by Luciano-Morandat and Nohara, Verdier, and Bessy move in for a closer inspection of the differences that exists across Europe. Luciano-Morandat and Nohara provide a detailed international comparison of one dimension of changing university–industry links: the mode of production and deployment of Ph.D.s within industry. The evolving labour market mechanisms within which Ph.D.s operate constitute one aspect of what the authors refer to as a new 'intermediate labour market' between academia and industry characterized by the co-production of resources and competences. As such it is a facet of the more general strengthening of university–industry links described by Cohendet et al.

While new hybrid labour market arrangements are common to the countries examined, one can identify national differences in the way groups and interests are organized. For example in France, where formal research systems are organized into relatively strong hierarchies of prestige and resources tend to be concentrated in a small number of elite institutions, not only is there relatively little career mobility across different segments of the research system but academic and industrial careers tend to remain separate (see Whitley, this volume, p. 359). This contrasts with the situation in the UK where the diversity and competition between universities and research establishments generate considerable mobility, at least in the early stages of Ph.D. careers. Another effect can be seen in terms of the precariousness of employment, with civil service status stabilizing the situation of young university or public sector scientists in France, while relatively long selection processes result in a precarious situation for young scientists in the UK and Germany.

Verdier's discussion of developments in France over the last two decades brings out in a quite striking manner the links between specific features of the French socio-political system, the evolving nature of its education and training system, and the performance characteristics of its innovation system. Prior to the 1990s, a distinguishing feature of the French system was the role played by the upper levels of the French civil service coming from the elite engineering schools and the civil service college (ENA) to conduct State-led technology policy based on their control of the larger enterprises that were nationalized in 1945 and in 1981. These arrangements underpinned France's state coordinated mission-oriented innovation model directed to the production of complex high-technology products. Further, the combination of an elitist and narrow professional educational system combined with the weight of ILM structures helps, as the taxonomy of Lundvall and Lam suggests, account for the traditional importance of bureaucratic forms of work organization in France that were poorly adapted to competing on the basis of a capacity for incremental innovation in such established technology areas as vehicles, electrical engineering, and iron and steel.

As Verdier observes, from the 1990s these same elite networks benefited from their privileged position in the 'worlds' of finance, major industrial groups and state administrations to mobilize resources in the interests of new management structures that were relatively autonomous from the State and more adapted to competing on the basis of incremental innovation. Key to this restructuring were the privatizations beginning in 1986 and the considerable development of new human resources based on the expansion of third-level education which increased its production of specific vocational qualifications. One result was a segmented workforce characterized by a marked split between operating personnel with few qualifications and often precarious work situations and a younger cohort of technical personnel with permanent positions. On these bases a distinctively French version of 'diversified quality production' emerged, characterized by a relatively hierarchical organization of work (Coutrot 1998).

At the same time other features of the French innovation system connected to the dominant role played by these elite networks proved an obstacle to establishing technological excellence in new sectors, such as biotechnology and ICT, characterized by more radical innovation. Publicly financed R&D in these sectors is massively non-pluralistic, and the large industrial groups that receive the lion's share of government R&D credits (OST 1999) are reluctant to recruit university Ph.D.s and show a continued preference for recruiting their research personnel from the ranks of engineers coming out of the elite 'grandes écoles'. The combination of a polarized R&D system and the inability of industry to make full use of the science and technology human resources produced by the university system helps to account for the absence in France of a dynamic of technological exploration and risk-taking of the sort generated by small-sized start-ups.

While Verdier's chapter illustrates the way the interests of dominant groups set limits on the types of institutional reforms that are attempted, Bessy's analysis of the failure of the attempted reform of the UK vocational training system illustrates how government policies can flounder on the weak collective organization of key socio-political groups. The National Vocational Qualification (NVQ) system introduced in the 1980s to replace traditional apprenticeship was a 'modular' system designed around the principles of identifying certain general attributes of jobs that are common to different industrial and work settings and certifying the acquisition of competences acquired through on-the-job training at different stages of an employee's career. One of the goals was to increase labour market mobility and thus increase flexibility in terms of firms' ability to reconfigure their competences. Another goal was to promote lifelong learning by allowing for continuous updating of skills while limiting the risks of exclusion of adult workers lacking initial training in a particular occupation or field.

Bessy argues that these goals have remained largely unmet due to the fact that the organization of vocational training is de-connected from the collective organization of employers and workers. On the one hand, in the absence of such collective employer coordination, there is a marked tendency for competences and certification to be highly firm-specific which goes contrary to the goal of increased inter-firm mobility. On the other hand, in so far as the system validates the acquisition of general competences and analytical abilities of the sort provided by the general education system (e.g. general problem-solving skills, communication skills, etc.), it runs the risk of reproducing the patterns of exclusion that are characteristic of the general education system.

1.5.3. Multi-Level Governance and European Policy Challenges

Similar points about the way the characteristics of the socio-political system limit what governments can accomplish are developed in Whitley's chapter focusing on the relation between EU multi-level governance and national-level governance. First, he shows how state structures are a principal factor generating different degrees of homogeneity of actors and strategies across nation states for the basic reason that states play a central role in establishing the rules and mechanisms that regulate capital and labour markets and the education and training system. Nation states differ in the degree of cohesiveness of these basic institutional mechanisms and in the degree to which they standardize behaviours and strategies throughout the country.

For example, a relatively high degree of homogeneity may be anticipated in corporatist state settings where employers, professional associations, and labour organizations cooperate in the establishment of standardized skill formation systems that integrate state schools with employer-provided training. 'Arm's-length' states, such as the US, on the other hand, focus on establishing the rules of the competitive game in which varied actors are free to pursue their objectives. The organization of labour tends to be left open and subject to capital market constraints leaving employers considerable freedom to determine strategy. Thus, one can anticipate greater heterogeneity of corporate behaviours and strategies and more diversity in sectors and regional innovation patterns in these settings.

Such diversity is of capital importance when we consider the implications of EU multi-level governance for national and regional innovation. As Whitley observes (p. 371), 'the EU is less sovereign and autonomous in terms of setting the collective and operational rules governing innovative activities than most, if not all, European governments'. This limits its ability to establish a pan-European innovation policy by establishing rules of the game for firms and other groups that dominate existing and diverse national ones. Establishing strong EU institutions governing public science systems and technology policies would require, 'the support of key transnational actors such as strong European industrial associations and research organizations who could dominate national ones' (p. 371).

The policy chapters by Rodrigues and by Lundvall and Lorenz similarly point to the impact of national diversity on the process of EU integration and the construction of an EU innovation system. In an overview of the Lisbon strategy, Rodrigues describes how multi-tiered EU governance has relied on the 'open-method of coordination' calling for different modes of governance and different types of policy instruments depending on the nature of the problem and the policy field. Governance modes range from integration through directives (e.g. the single market) to looser and more contextualized forms of cooperation and coordination based on the development of framework strategies and the identification of common objectives (e.g. social inclusion or lifelong learning). In her view, at this phase in the process the main problem in terms of making progress towards the goals of the Lisbon strategy is that many member nations simply do not have well-defined national strategies for implementation. The key question for each member state, then, will be how to adapt the European agenda to its specific industrial and institutional context.

Lundvall and Lorenz in their concluding policy chapter start by referring to the current impasse following the no-vote on the European constitution in France and the Netherlands. This presented an image of Europe in disarray, torn between the classical ideological poles of pro-state and pro-market, and behind this are actual differences in how state and market combine in the governance of the economy. They go on to identify the links between national welfare regimes and labour market structures while the latter, as the taxonomy developed in the first part of this introduction showed, can be linked to innovation style and rate. Their broad conclusion is that different welfare systems support different modes of learning and innovation. Correspondingly, the current political impasse bodes ill for polices designed to establish more 'Europe' in the areas of science and technology and innovation.

The chapters by Rodrigues and by Lundvall and Lorenz converge in arguing that it is only by recognizing the systemic difference that exists across EU nations that further progress will be made in achieving the goals set out by the Lisbon process. Lundvall and Lorenz in particular argue for giving explicit recognition to the differences in systems of social protection that are all to often hidden under loose concepts such as 'structural reform'. In order to push the debate forward, they suggest that the Danish model may serve not so much as a best-practice benchmark for reform but as heuristic device pointing to possible ways forwards in resolving the tension between market and state regulation. This is most apparent in the area of the labour market where the Danish system, more than other systems, is characterized by 'flexicurity' consisting in a combination of low levels of employment protection and relatively high levels of unemployment protection.

1.6. RESEARCH AGENDA FOR THE FUTURE

1.6.1. The Need for a Sustained Holistic Effort to Understand Competence-Building Systems at the European Level

As we observed in the acknowledgements, this book is the outcome of a major interdisciplinary effort—the Loc Nis project, organized as an 'accompanying measures' project under the European Union's Sixth Framework Programme. The Loc Nis project explicitly set out to engage in disciplinary 'trespassing' by combining and incorporating research tools and results from domains that are normally kept separate: management research on knowledge use and development at the level of organizations; research in the field of education and training systems, research on the economics of innovation, and the political economy of state systems.

The set-up of the project made it a kind of test ground for how to organize interdisciplinary socio-economic research in Europe and its specific research agenda overlapped with the specific programme in the Sixth Framework Program on knowledge-based development and social cohesion. We believe that this volume demonstrates the value of the approach and has provided new insights regarding emerging patterns of industrial dynamics and their implication for policy.

On the background of the chapters in this book we could point to a multitude of specific research issues that require further efforts in order to enhance our understanding of the learning economy and of national systems of innovation and competence building. There is a clear need for both fundamental and applied research focusing on the links between modes of learning at the level of the firm and the characteristics of the wider institutional setting, including education systems, labour markets, and systems of social protection. The empirical understanding of learning and knowledge in working life calls for the development of new indicators and new survey tools. These are especially difficult to develop in relation to international comparative research.

But rather than going into detail with these challenges that we believe can be responded to within the context of the Seventh Framework Program, we will end this introduction by emphasizing the need to develop *a new instrument* for socio-economic research in the European context. The research effort needed when it comes to understand the importance of the co-evolution and transition of the specific national systems of innovation and competence building in Europe calls for such new instruments. It is not realistic to establish such an understanding within the framework programmes in their current form. The traditional model with multinational teams in projects or networks with limited lifespan cannot solve the task.

We believe that the time has come to establish several national and one 'European Observatory of Learning, Innovation and Competence Building Systems' (EUROLICS) with a permanent staff of highly qualified academic scholars with expertise in different fields, including economics, management, education, labour market, innovation, corporate and public governance, as well as social policy. The focus should be on experience-based as well as on science-based learning, and it should study competence building in high-tech as well as low-tech sectors. The aim should be to develop a deeper understanding of how Europe's economies learn and to work out the theoretical and practical implications.

Such observatories should aim at understanding the systemic features of each economy and thereby they could support policy learning at the national and the European level while constituting a necessary complement to the current efforts to develop benchmarking in specific policy areas. One of the tasks would be to define bottlenecks and mismatches within each national system as well as national institutional set-ups that create friction among European systems. A European strategy for further integration would use such insights to build a sustainable strategy and to avoid conflicts rooted in mutual ignorance about national systemic differences.

NOTES

1. For those with a short memory, it is useful to point out that these insights were developed only over the last two decades. When the OECD ad hoc working group on science, technology, and international competitiveness came with a report presenting innovation as a key to competitiveness and criticizing the idea of 'wage-cost competitiveness' in 1984, it was so controversial that it did not get into print. (Lundvall was member of the group and Chris Freeman, as expert, contributed to its work with a paper where the concept of NSI was mentioned for the first time—see Lundvall 2005.)
2. To a certain degree, these differences in focus reflect the national origin of the analysts. In small countries such as Denmark, as in developing countries—a major concern of Freeman—it is obvious that the competence base most critical for innovation in the economy as a whole is not scientific knowledge. Incremental innovation, 'absorptive capacity' and economic performance will typically reflect the skills and motivation of employees as well as inter- and intra-organizational relationships and characteristics. Science-based sectors may be rapidly growing but their shares of total employment and exports remain relatively small.
3. Elsewhere we refer to these two partially complementary types of learning as STI (science, technology, innovation) learning and DUI (doing, using, and interacting) learning. See Jensen et al. (2005).
4. The idea that organizations and even national economies 'learn' is controversial. Without engaging in any fundamental philosophical debate about methodological individualism, we will argue that it is useful to apply a perspective where collective learning is possible. In the case of national systems, aggregate learning might be defined in terms of the processes of transformation and selection of institutions, firms, and individuals.

REFERENCES

Amable, B. (2003). *The Diversity of Modern Capitalism*. Oxford: Oxford University Press.

—— Barré, R., and Boyer, R. (1997). *Les systémes d'innovation a l'ére de la globalization*. Paris: Economica.

Andersen, E. S. and Lundvall, B.-Å. (1988). 'Small National Innovation Systems Facing Technological Revolutions: An Analytical Framework', in C. Freeman, and B.-Å. Lundvall, (eds.), *Small Countries Facing the Technological Revolution*. London: Pinter Publishers, pp. 1–31.

Aoki, M. (1986). 'Horizontal vs. Vertical Information Structure of the Firm', *American Economic Review*, 76(5): 971–83.

Archibugi, D. and Lundvall, B.-Å. (2000). *The Globalizing Learning Economy*. Oxford: Oxford University Press.

Council of the European Union (2000). *Conclusions of the Lisbon European Council*, Council of the European Union SN 100/00, 23–24 March.

Coutrot, Th. (1998). *L'entreprise néolibérale, nouvelle utopie capitaliste?* Paris: La Découverte.

Freeman, C. (1987). *Technology Policy and Economic Performance: Lessons from Japan*. London: Pinter Publishers.

Hall, P. and Soskice, D. (2000). *Varieties of Capitalism*. Oxford: Oxford University Press.

Jensen, M., Johnson, B., Lorenz, E., and Lundvall, B.-Å. (2004) 'Absorptive Capacity, Forms of Knowledge and Economic Development', Paper presented at the Annual Globelics Conference. Beijing, China.

Lorenz, E. and Valeyre, A. (2005). 'Organisational Innovation, Human Resource Management and Labour Market Structure: A Comparison of the EU-15', *The Journal of Industrial Relations*, 47(3): 424–42.

Lundvall, B.-Å. (1985). *Product Innovation and User-Producer Interaction*. Aalborg, Denmark: Aalborg University Press.

—— (2002). *Innovation, Growth and Social Cohesion: The Danish Model*. Cheltenham, UK: Edward Elgar.

—— (2005). 'Why the New Economy Is a Learning Economy', DRUID Working Paper.

—— and Tomlinson, M. (2002). 'International Benchmarking as a Policy Learning Tool', in M. J. Rodriguez (ed.), *The New Knowledge Economy in Europe: A Strategy for International Competitiveness with Social Cohesion*. Cheltenham, UK: Edward Elgar.

Maskell, P. (1998). 'Learning in the Village Economy of Denmark. The Role of Institutions and Policy in Sustaining Competitiveness', in H. J. Braczyk, P. Cooke, and M. Heidenreich (eds.), *Regional Innovation Systems. The Role of Governance in a Globalized World*. London: UCL Press, pp. 190–213.

Mintzberg, H. (1979). *The Structuring of Organizations: A Synthesis of the Research.* Englewood Cliffs, NJ: Prentice-Hall.

Mowery, D. and Oxley, J. (1995). 'Inward Technology Transfer and Competitiveness: The Role of National Innovation Systems', *Cambridge Journal of Economics*, 19: 67–93.

Nelson, R. (2004). 'The Market Economy and the Scientific Commons', *Research Policy*, 33: 455–71.

Observatoire des Sciences et des Techniques (OST) (1999) 'La compétitivité technologique de la France', Annexe 1, *Rapport de Mission sur la Technologie et l'innovation*, Ministère de l'Économie, des Finances et de l'Industrie, Paris.

Tylecote, A. and Conesa, V. (2002). 'Corporate Governance, Innovation Systems and Industrial Performance', Paper presented at the First Loc Nis Workshop, Maison de la Chimie, Paris.

Part I

Diversity in European Systems of Competence Building

2

Do National Systems Converge?

Mark Tomlinson

2.1. INTRODUCTION

There has been much debate in recent years about the question of the convergence of economic systems. This has taken on a new importance in European economies in the light of European integration. Not least with the accession of ten new countries to the Union. The more recent debates have to some extent blurred the discussion about convergence and what it actually means.

The chapter proceeds as follows. First of all, after a general discussion of the importance of convergence, different definitions of convergence will be briefly explored. While it is not possible here to go into all the details and nuances of the debates, the concept of convergence will be set within the context of the European Commission's enduring fascination with international benchmarking and the use of various uni-dimensional indicators and league tables to assess the progress of member states (e.g. the Innovation Scoreboard or 'Trendchart').

Second, the chapter explores a possible alternative approach that is rooted firmly within the systems of innovation model (Lundvall 1992; Nelson 1993; Edquist 1997). This approach will attempt to create composite indicators using multivariate statistical techniques and OECD time series data. New 'systemic' indicators representing different learning styles within national systems will then be traced over time. This will enable us to see whether there is convergence or divergence of learning styles within the EC rather than between monolithic single indicators such as productivity growth or per capita income, etc. These results are preliminary and meant to illustrate the usefulness of the technique rather than produce final definitive answers.

With a multidisciplinary spirit, indicators not normally combined together will be explored to try and begin a debate about the nature of the European project and the role of indicators in policy learning. This ultimately would involve simultaneously combining indicators from education, labour markets, industrial performance, science, and health, etc.—in other words, all aspects of the different competence-building systems within the European community. Only a modest beginning is adumbrated below.

National systems of innovation differ for all sorts of reasons. For example, education and training is connected to people and competence building and these systems, being for the most part nationally specific, have evolved in different ways within Europe. Some of these aspects of innovation systems are closed and nationally determined while some aspects are more open to globalizing forces (such as science and technology). The combinations of different levels of sophistication of nationally specific competence-building systems and the differing exposure to the intensity of global aspects of innovation will affect different countries in different ways. It is possible to combine measures of these different facets of innovation systems into more useful and balanced indicators.

2.2. DOES IT MATTER IF NATIONAL SYSTEMS CONVERGE OR DIVERGE?

The conceptualizations of convergence and divergence raise several policy issues with respect to national innovation systems. If differences in performance can be identified between nations, it seems only natural that convergence to some ideal optimum state of play should be encouraged. This seems particularly relevant when it comes to issues of national income, income distribution, or poverty alleviation, for example. So the issue of 'catching up' with one's neighbours seems almost a natural objective to many policymakers.

When it comes to international trade, policy is still influenced by ideas of comparative advantage where it is supposed that any sort of specialization in exports (of almost any kind) will have positive effects for any nation state. However, it could be argued that it is better to concentrate on specialization on specific sectors that induce high levels of learning and innovation rather than predominantly low technology/low learning sectors (Lall 2001). The bulk of world trade is now becoming dominated by high-technology sectors. Developing countries that have successfully implemented high-technology strategies in this respect seem to have done better (such as the Asian tigers). Developing countries following low-technology specialization seem to have done rather badly, although it is far from clear whether this should be seen as a general rule. Denmark, for instance, stands out as a system that has historically done very well out of traditional and 'low-tech' sectoral specialization (Lundvall 2002).

Another aspect of policymaking when it comes to thinking about aspects of European integration and convergence is the idea that there is a best-practice strategy whereby particular policies and approaches can be copied from one state to the next. Especially since the Lisbon Summit in 2000 the idea that there should be this type of policy benchmarking has become very popular. Unfortunately this approach is anathema to the systems of innovation framework because the context that policy and strategy exists within will differ in different countries. What may be a best practice in one context cannot be blindly copied into another with much hope of success (Lundvall and Tomlinson 2000, 2002). Institutions and routines may be transferable from one system to another, but only in very specific and simple cases will this be successful.

Accordingly, it is not generally logically consistent to be in favour of convergence with respect to NSI. Systems that apparently perform well on one measure of 'success' (such as R&D expenditure) may perform badly on another (such as patents or growth). This happens for various institutional and other complex reasons which cannot be disentangled very easily. Furthermore, if reasons are forthcoming, these reasons will not necessarily be the same in other national contexts which have apparently similar set-ups.

It may be that Europe's biggest strength is actually the variety of its institutions and systems and this should warn us against the dangers of too much convergence. Moreover, there are certain models that perform very well when a narrow number of indicators are chosen to measure success (such as the US or so-called Anglo-Saxon model—flexible labour markets, low-labour security, and lack of welfare benefits). But in Europe we have a choice and can adopt a model where we take different indicators into account, such as provision of universal health care, education for its own sake, a shorter working week or whatever. Different European countries can also choose to adopt different indicators to each other when it comes to assessing the success of their own systems. This naturally flies in the face of the current thinking around international benchmarking, which emphasizes 'naming and shaming' and league tables.

2.3. THE CONCEPT OF CONVERGENCE

Since the debates surrounding the introduction of a common European currency, the concept of convergence has become much more confused. In the UK, it is often now meant to refer to some set of criteria (the chancellor, Gordon Brown's five economic tests) that will indicate that the UK economy is sufficiently in line with the rest of Europe to allow entry to the Euro and the abandonment of Sterling. However, before this the concept had a long history in economic thought stretching back to at least the 1950s. Godinho and Mamede (1999: 7) suggest a typology of different approaches to the concept where there are roughly three different versions:

First of all there is 'unconditional convergence' where more backward economies are expected to converge with more advanced ones. This was put forward initially in the work of Gershenkron (1962) and Posner (1961). The same conclusions are drawn to some extent by traditional growth theorists as well as being in line with a neoclassical trade model. These studies tend to imply that technological or economic backwardness can be a virtue; e.g. lagging economies can benefit from more advanced ones by imitating technological advances developed in the latter (see e.g. Gomulka 1971). Thus, there is a tendency to converge. Variations might include the neoclassical model where labour will flow to where wages are higher while simultaneously capital flows in the opposite direction.

Second, there is the idea of 'conditional convergence'. This is most obviously advocated by scholars such as Abramovitz (1986, 1994). These scholars argue that social capabilities allow certain countries to mobilize resources, but not others. Therefore, some countries can catch up if the conditions are right, but this is not unconditional. Economists such as Pavitt (1985) also argued along similar lines where a certain degree of technological accumulation had to take place for countries to catch up with their rivals. This accumulation process is not possible everywhere.

The third variant is termed 'divergence'. This set of theories argues that there are tendencies for economies or regions to diverge rather than converge. Some economic geographers argue, for example, that there are economies of agglomeration which tend to concentrate resources in particular places such as labour supply, supply of inputs, and localized knowledge spillovers. This can create industrial cores without there necessarily being any catching up in the periphery. Rather, further polarization is a distinct possibility.

According to Godinho and Mamede (1999), the general consensus on convergence in the EU is that there has been a strong tendency to converge in the post-war period until around the 1970s. From the early 1970s to the mid-1980s this tendency slowed and since then there has been little or no regional convergence at all. These studies generally use measures such as income per capita or productivity to measure convergence patterns. In what follows we take a different approach and create multidimensional systemic indicators and see whether these reveal patterns of convergence or divergence.

In the evolutionary economics tradition diversity is regarded as a key to new combinations and to enhance innovative capacity; and ultimately growth. This diversity is actually necessary in order to reveal the potential options within the system and, through the process of competition, to eventually figure out a better way forward for the system. This implies that capitalist economic dynamics actually may be seen as a process of convergence and divergence within certain fields at different times. National borders may sometimes be regarded as barriers to convergence since the options available are to a degree interlocked with other variables within the national system. The following analysis shows that there is a great deal of diversity within the EC (or OECD countries for that matter) whichever of the systemic indicators is chosen for analysis.

2.4. DATA AND METHODOLOGY

The data come from the OECD Main Science and Technology Indicators (OECD 2002). This has been used to create a main database of twenty-five countries with indicators of science and technology from the years 1981 to 2001. The indicators include things such as business enterprise R&D (BERD), public and private R&D, number of scientists in the labour force, as well as growth figures and other economic performance statistics.

There are several time series, but many are incomplete and so many of the countries and/or particular observations drop out of the analysis. The seventeen countries ultimately remaining in the analysis below are shown in Table 2.1.

Several variables were chosen to represent different aspects of the innovation systems of these countries. These are shown in Table 2.2 (the numbers refer to the OECD variable number in the database). These variables were included in a factor analysis to try and reduce several complex indicators of learning systems within nations into a reduced set of systemic indicators that reflect different coherent strategies within each NSI. They include R&D statistics (e.g. business R&D measures, labour market statistics such as the number of researchers in the system, R&D collaboration figures, public sector research, etc.).

Table 2.1 Countries in overall analysis

Australia
Austria
Canada
Denmark
Finland
France
Germany
Greece
Ireland
Italy
Japan
Norway
Portugal
Spain
Sweden
UK
USA

2.5. RESULTS OF FACTOR ANALYSIS

The factor analysis of the seventeen countries revealed six interpretable factors which explained 85 per cent of the variance (the full analysis is shown in Figure 2.1):

1. The first factor relates to the general intensity of mainly private R&D measures. It combines levels of GERD, business and industrial R&D, number of business researchers, and HERD. It is also negatively associated with the percentage of GERD financed by government. We refer to this factor as a 'general R&D intensity' factor.
2. This factor associates government-financed research in business R&D, and defence R&D. It is negatively associated with BERD financed by industry. This most likely represents levels of research in defence and areas such as the medical technologies sector, financed mainly by government. It is therefore referred to as the 'public/defence' research factor below. It is interesting to note that this spending is negatively correlated with industry-funded BERD, suggesting that countries where industry BERD is low tend to compensate for this by using public money to finance research and defence.
3. This factor represents the growth of the various research expenditure types, which are all correlated with each other. It combines the growth rates of GERD, BERD, and GOVERD thus representing a fairly general growth in research spending within the economy. We refer to this as the 'R&D growth' factor.

Table 2.2 Variables in factor analysis

2. GERD as a percentage of GDP
3.a. GERD—Compound annual growth rate (constant prices)
4. GERD per capita population (current PPP $)
13. Percentage of GERD financed by industry
17. Percentage of GERD performed by the business enterprise sector
18. Percentage of GERD performed by the higher education sector
19. Percentage of GERD performed by the government sector
24. BERD as a percentage of GDP
25.a. BERD—Compound annual growth rate (constant prices)
29. Business Enterprise researchers per thousand industrial employment
35. Percentage of BERD financed by industry
36. Percentage of BERD financed by government
46. HERD as a percentage of GDP
48. Percentage of HERD financed by industry
53. GOVERD as a percentage of GDP
54.a. GOVERD—Compound annual growth rate (constant prices)
55. Percentage of GOVERD financed by industry
60. Defence Budget R&D as a percentage of Total GBAORD
62.d.2. Civil GBAORD for non-oriented research programmes as a percentage of Civil GBAORD
65.b. Number of patents granted by the USPTO (priority year)

4. This factor includes government R&D and civil GBAORD and represents some level of government-financed research without necessarily being applied. This is referred to as the 'government research' factor.
5. This factor appears to represent levels of industry-linked public research as it includes both HERD and GOVERD financed by industry. This is therefore referred to as the 'public–private research' factor.
6. This is associated with levels of higher education (HE) research as a percentage of GERD in HE and HERD as a percentage of GDP. It is referred to as the 'HE research' factor. Note that the loadings on this factor are both negative. To ease interpretation the scores on this factor have been converted into positives (i.e. a high positive value indicates a high level of HE research).

2.6. USING THE FACTORS TO LOOK AT EUROPEAN DIVERSITY

Once we have the six factors we can create scores for each factor by country and year that we have the sufficient time-series data available for and compare the trends in the changes of the factors over time. Some of these graphs for western European countries are shown below (the US is also included as a

			Component			
	1	2	3	4	5	6
2. GERD as a percentage of GDP	0.912					
3.a. GERD—Compound annual growth rate (constant prices)			0.941			
4. GERD per capita population (current PPP $)	0.910					
13. Percentage of GERD financed by industry	0.792					
17. Percentage of GERD performed by the business enterprise sector	0.831					
18. Percentage of GERD performed by the higher education sector	−0.457					−0.798
19. Percentage of GERD performed by the government sector	−0.856					
24. BERD as a percentage of GDP	0.938					
25.a. BERD—Compound annual growth rate (constant prices)			0.849			
29. Business enterprise researchers per thousand industrial employment	0.914					
35. Percentage of BERD financed by industry		−0.897				
36. Percentage of BERD financed by government		0.873				
46. HERD as a percentage of GDP	0.741					−0.512
48. Percentage of HERD financed by industry					0.696	
53. GOVERD as a percentage of GDP				0.811		
54.a. GOVERD—Compound annual growth rate (constant prices)			0.589		−0.420	
55. Percentage of GOVERD financed by industry					0.781	
60. Defence budget R&D as a percentage of total GBAORD	0.472	0.752				
62.d.2. Civil GBAORD for non-oriented research programmes as a percentage of civil GBAORD				0.833		
65.b. Number of patents granted by the USPTO (priority year)	0.648					

Figure 2.1. Full factor analysis results after Varimax rotation of principle components

reference to what is commonly considered a 'benchmark' country). Clearly, some factors show divergent patterns in styles within western Europe.

Taking the general R&D factor (Figure 2.2), we see that there are generally increases for all countries over time with the US in the lead, but there is no clear pattern of convergence or divergence. For example, France, Ireland, Germany, and the UK seem to be converging, whereas the US is stretching away. Italy and Spain appear to be lagging behind the others. This shows a common enough pattern. It is well known that the US is some way ahead of Europe in terms of its general capacity to spend money on R&D. This is taking place while the southern European countries are lagging behind the rest of Europe in this respect. Ireland is proving an exception in the sense of a small country doing relatively more R&D than before. Hence, Ireland is shown to be

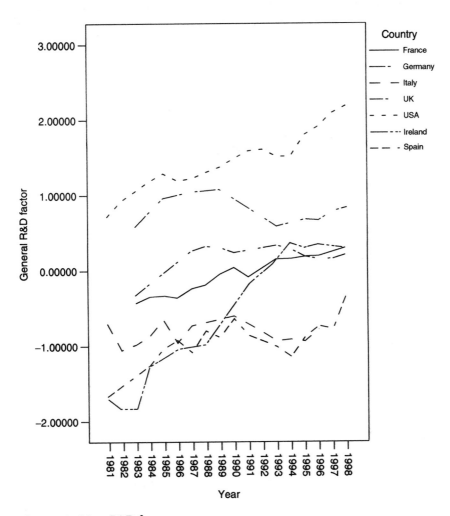

Figure 2.2. Mean R&D factor

very similar to Spain and close to Italy in the 1980s, but by the late 1980s, it has shifted up to the paths of Germany, France, and the UK.

In terms of the government research factor (Figure 2.3), it is France that is in the lead by some distance. And if anything this factor shows divergence. The gaps between the countries seem to be widening over time, with the US now at the bottom of the league. Some countries show increasing trends in the 1990s (e.g. the UK and Ireland) and some show decline (such as France, US, and Germany). The overall trend appears to be a slow decline which is perhaps symptomatic of less government financial interest in business research. Again, the US is interesting in that, if taken as a benchmark nation, other European countries should also be decreasing government involvement with business

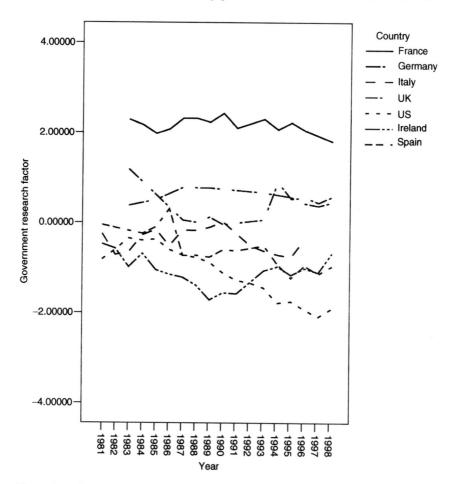

Figure 2.3. Government research factor

R&D. Where the trend is different in Europe is in the public–private research area.

The public–private research factor (Figure 2.4) seems to show some sort of cyclical effect in many countries, but the general trend appears to be increasing for all countries except the US. Again, no clear patterns in terms of convergence or divergence appear to be taking place, but there are several countries that have shown high increases in the late 1990s. Here it seems to be Ireland and the UK that are leading the way, but apart from the US, no country shows a real declining trend over the last twenty years. Again, the US model comes out as governed by a completely different set of dynamics when it comes to R&D trends when looked at in this light. And once

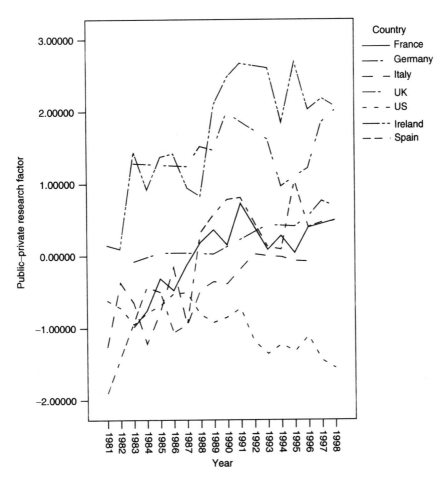

Figure 2.4. Public–private research factor

again some countries seem to be converging within Europe and some seem to be stretching away from others.

The HE research factor (Figure 2.5) shows a clear case of divergence in the 1990s with almost all countries with a declining trend. It seems that in the 1980s there was not much difference between the countries shown, but in the 1990s large differences started to appear. Here countries like Spain and Italy are clearly declining faster than the others. Ireland and the US seem to be leading countries. So although the US model seems to be one of declining public–private linkages and declining government finance of business oriented R&D, it is still doing relatively well in the funding of HE research, whereas many European countries

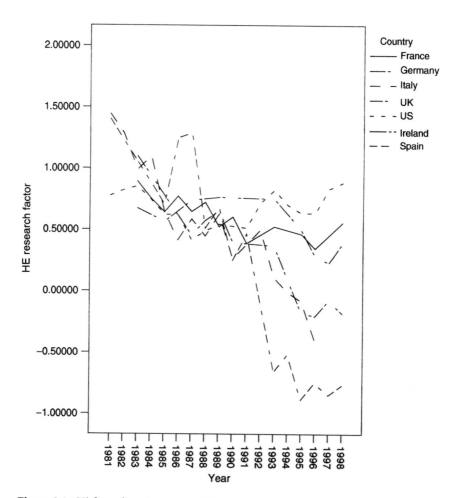

Figure 2.5. Higher education research factor

seem to be letting this aspect of the innovation system slide. So the models discussed in Cohendet et al. (this volume) whereby in a Mode 2 world, these linkages between public–private and government–business such as the triple helix are seen as the new way forward might not be the happening to a great extent in the US according to these figures. Rather, the US government continues to push resources at HE research, but is not on the whole increasing the intensity of public–private linkages or the funding of business R&D.

2.7. LEARNING STYLES AND GDP GROWTH

Another way of exploring different innovation styles and trajectories is to plot various factors against GDP growth. GDP growth has been used as a trad-itional indicator of convergence and divergence for many years. It seems only natural that some exploration of the way the factors here relate to growth is called for. Some examples of this are shown below. The same countries used in the previous analysis are shown again. Figure 2.6 shows GDP growth against the general R&D factor. Here we can see that Ireland and the US appear to occupy quite different parts of this space. Ireland is stretching away in terms of growth in the 1990s while its score on the general R&D factor has remained roughly the same. The US, on the other hand, has increased its score quite markedly but has not seen the huge impact on GDP growth that Ireland has which was starting from a much lower base and has had very high increases in foreign direct investment.

Figure 2.7 shows the growth figures plotted against the R&D growth factor. There does appear to be a positive correlation between R&D growth factor scores and GDP growth. But again Ireland seems to be an exceptional case presumably because of the huge distortions in the economy caused by the impact of inward (mainly US) investment in certain key industries such as computer manufacturing. Looking at the trajectory of the Irish economy here shows that from 1994–8 Ireland was increasing GDP growth while decreasing its R&D growth factor score.

Finally, Figure 2.8 shows the GDP figures plotted against the public–private factor scores. Here we see again that Ireland is in a different situation; there is no sense of convergence or divergence here. If anything different countries appear to just cluster in different parts of the space. So the US seems to have very low scores on the factor, but healthy growth rates, while the UK has high scores on the factor, but relatively low-growth rates. In fact, if we take Ireland out of the equation it would imply a *negative* relationship between the public–private research factor and growth. This does not

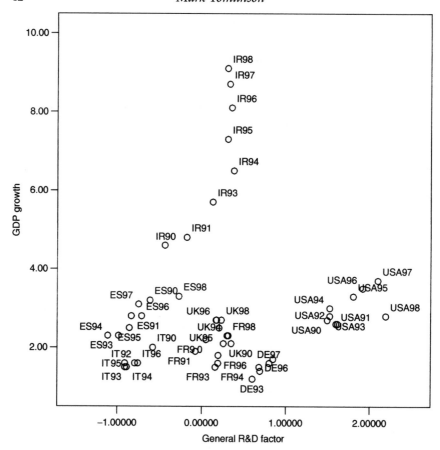

Figure 2.6. General R&D and GDP growth

necessarily mean that there is anything wrong with public–private linkages, but perhaps too much is being expected of them in the European context.

2.8. USING THE FACTORS TO REVEAL THE EXTENT OF EUROPEAN DIVERSITY

A final examination of converging and diverging innovation styles can be revealed by plotting factor scores against each other. Figure 2.9 shows the first and last observations in each time series for the same countries but plotting the general R&D factor against the public–private research factor. It is

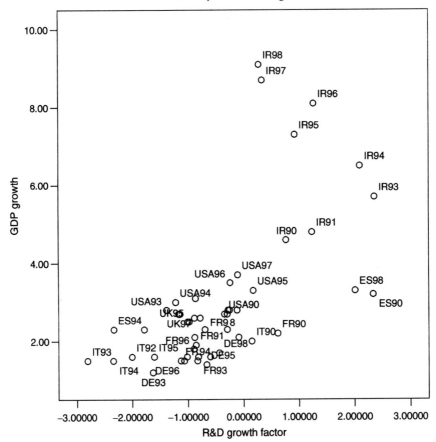

Figure 2.7. R&D growth and GDP growth

evident from this that most European countries are heading roughly in the same direction, but the US is once more revealed to be on a completely different trajectory (increasing R&D intensity in general, but decreasing public–private research intensity). European countries seem to be increasing both, but not achieving the high growth rates of the US.

Figures 2.9 and 2.10 show a more complex picture by plotting the public–private research factor against the public/defence factor and the R&D growth factor. Here the different countries shown are on quite different trajectories. There is no sense using this approach that any of the countries could be said to be 'converging' or 'diverging'. Clearly, a much more diverse and complex picture arises that reveals that if these factors represent learning or innovation styles in any sense, the different contexts of each country make a great deal of

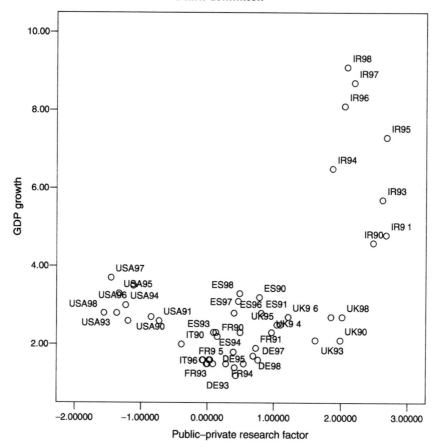

Figure 2.8. Public–private research and R&D growth

difference in terms of the way resources for the innovation system are generated and allocated.

2.9. CONCLUSIONS

This chapter has made a tentative step towards analysing what might be termed systemic indicators. Rather than using simple univariate indicators that can give a crude and misleading picture of overall innovative performance or resource allocation, these composite indicators aim to strike a balance by combining data from a variety of sources in a more statistically sophisticated way (in this case, factor analysis).

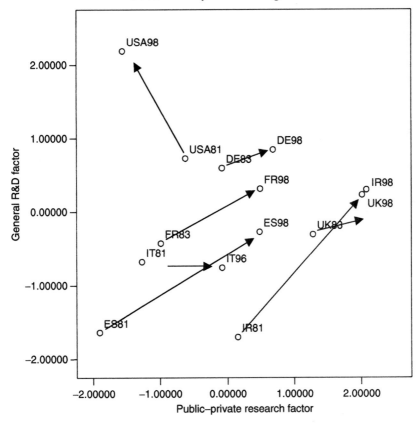

Figure 2.9. R&D and public–private research

The factors have been interpreted as representing learning or innovation styles and have then been used to show whether any sense of convergence or divergence in the economies of Europe can be demonstrated. It is clear that there is a great deal of diversity in western Europe with respect to these factors. There are also no consistent patterns of convergence or divergence whichever styles we decide to explore. Clearly, the context in which innovation takes place can have quite different consequences in terms of the way innovation or learning styles are combined, or the way adopting these styles in any way affects performance (measured using indicators such as GDP growth). Different countries within Europe are clearly often on quite different and complex trajectories as far as innovation is concerned.

These results further undermine the attempts by European countries to benchmark innovative performance using simple indicators such as R&D

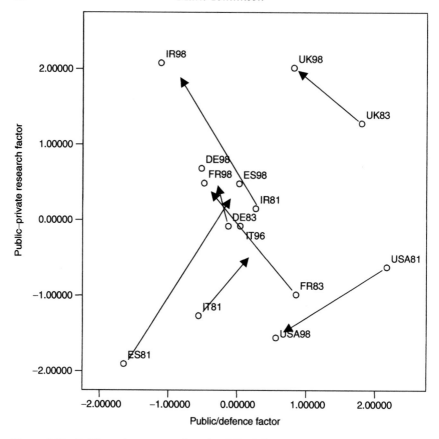

Figure 2.10. Public–private research and public/defence

spending. Clearly, different types of R&D spending are associated with quite
different goals and policies at national level. Once these R&D figures are broken
down and analysed, or combined with other indicators of innovative effort, it is
impossible to say which trajectories would suit which countries better than
others. A one-size-fits-all policy is quite inappropriate. Also the impact or
association of R&D intensity with growth or other factors is different in
different countries and this has to be taken into account. The type of naive
benchmarking (see Lundvall and Tomlinson 2000, 2002) often debated uncrit-
ically within the European community is clearly at odds with these findings.

The differences between Europe and the US also raise important issues
about the European project. The data reveal that the US government support
for academic research seems to be outstripping any push towards increasing
industry–academic linkages or business R&D supported by the state. This

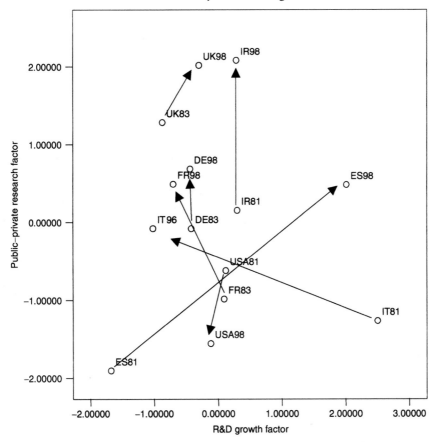

Figure 2.11. Public–private research and R&D growth

bolsters the point made by Cohendet et al. elsewhere in this volume that the US model is misrepresented when it is used in Europe to support policies for a progressive substitution of private for public funding of research. Rather, the US institutional framework corresponds more with Pavitt's advocacy of an open science policy (Pavitt 2000) in Europe, but this would result in a drastic change in the present science and technology systems of the EC. The US academic system also has its problems and 'even if we consider the US model has been successful, this does not mean we take the US model in its entirety as the reference model for European universities' (Cohendet et al., this volume).

The Lisbon strategy (Rodrigues, this volume) uses benchmarking as a technique and as the US is often held up as *the* benchmark there is a danger that in exploring data like that presented here it is easy to fall into the trap of trying to copy the 'US model'. But, as Rodriguez points out, the so-called 'open method of coordination' is much more than simple benchmarking. The purpose of the open method is not to create a simple ranking of European countries, but to infuse a European dimension to political choices and guidelines about what we want Europe to become. These guidelines include the maintenance of European diversity and subsidiarity. In this sense European nations can try to agree on which areas to converge and which areas to keep separate. This also includes the noble ambition of maintaining and enhancing social cohesion.

Europeans have choices and do not have to blindly follow others who are supposed to be ahead of the game in some sort of catch-up race. It is to be hoped that more imaginative use of available indicators such as those presented here and the creation of new indicators that take into account a wider array of socio-economic dimensions will have its place in the open method of coordination. This chapter has hopefully demonstrated that there is a great deal of diversity of learning and innovation styles at work in Europe and to try to converge on a common model would appear to be sheer folly. We can learn valuable lessons from the US, but we should not let this get in the way of European strengths in a futile attempt at destroying what makes us different.

REFERENCES

Abramovitz, M. (1956). 'Resources and Output Trends in the United States Since 1870', *American Economic Review*, 46: 5–23.

—— (1986). 'Catching up, Forging Ahead and Falling Behind', *Journal of Economic History*, 46(2): 385–406.

—— (1994). 'The Origins of the Postwar Catch-up and Convergence Boom', in J. Fagerberg, B. Verspagen, and N. Von Tunzelmann, (eds.), *The Dynamics of Technology, Trade and Growth*. Aldershot, UK: Edward Elgar, pp. 21–52.

Edquist, C. (ed.) (1997). *Systems of Innovation: Technologies, Institutions and Organizations*. London: Pinter Publishers.

Gerschenkron, A. (1962). *Economic Backwardness in Historical Perspective*. Cambridge: Cambridge University Press.

Godinho, M. and Mamede, R. (1999). 'Technological Convergence in Europe: What Are the Main Issues?' Mimeo, Technical University of Lisbon, Lisbon.

Gomulka, S. (1971). *Inventive Activit, Diffusion, and the Stages of Economic Growth*. Århus, Denmark: University of Århus Press.

Lall, S. (2001). *Competitiveness, Technology and Skills*. Cheltenham, UK: Edward Elgar.

Lundvall, B.-Å. (ed.) (1992). *National Innovation Systems: Towards a Theory of Innovation and Interactive Learning*. London: Pinter.

—— (2002). *Growth, Innovation and Social Cohesion: The Danish Model*. Cheltenham, UK: Edward Elgar.

—— and Tomlinson, M. (2000). 'Learning-by-Comparing—Reflections on the Use and Abuse of International Benchmarking', in G. Sweeney (ed.), *Innovation, Economic Progress and the Quality of Life*. Cheltenham, UK: Edward Elgar, pp. 120–36.

—— —— (2002). 'International Benchmarking as a Policy Learning Tool', in Maria Joao Rodriguez (ed.), *The New Knowledge Economy in Europe: A Strategy for International Competitiveness with Social Cohesion*. Cheltenham, UK: Edward Elgar, pp. 203–31.

Nelson, R. R. (ed.) (1993). *National Innovation Systems: A Comparative Analysis*. Oxford: Oxford University Press.

OECD (2002). *Main Science and Technology Indicators*. Paris: OECD.

Pavitt, K. (1985). 'Technology Transfer Among the Industrially Advanced Countries', in N. Rosenberg and C. Fristack (eds.), *International Technology Transfer: Concepts, Measures and Comparisons*. New York: Praeger.

—— (2000). 'Why European Funding of Academic Research Should Be Increased: A Radical Proposal', *Science and Public Policy*, 27(6): 455–60.

Posner, M. V. (1961). 'International Trade and Technical Change', *Oxford Economic Papers*, 13: 323–41.

3

The Role of National Borders and Regions in Knowledge Flows

Mei H. C. Ho and Bart Verspagen

3.1. INTRODUCTION

One key issue of national systems of innovation is that knowledge does not easily flow between them. In the European context, this may be seen as a crucial aspect hindering the effective application of knowledge in an economic way. With many different national systems of innovation present in the (recently enlarged) Union, a lack of scale economies with regard to knowledge may easily become an issue. At the same time, however, diversity may enhance system performance.

Our main research question in this chapter is how the diffusion of knowledge is affected by the partitioning of the European innovation system (a term that we do not intend to indicate homogeneity) into smaller national systems. To this end, we conceptualize the European innovation system as a set of interconnected regions, where the regions are partitioned into national systems of innovation. We then apply methodologies from social network analysis to analyse the partitioned network of regions.

At a theoretical level, we argue that the regional level of analysis is especially useful to identify linkages (knowledge flows) between separate national systems of innovation. This line of argument is summarized in the next section. Specifically, we introduce the notion of a higher order regional innovation system, a term we borrow from Cantwell and Janne (1999) and Cantwell and Iammarino (2001), to describe a special type of region that manages to connect disparate national systems of innovation. Our empirical analysis is aimed at conceptualizing a method to identify these higher order regional systems, and to apply this to our dataset.

Section 3.3 summarizes the existing empirical literature on the role of borders and regions in knowledge flows. We focus on summarizing the quantitative (econometric) literature that uses the same type of indicators as we use in our empirical analysis (patent citations).

Our database and methodology is shortly summarized in Section 3.4. Section 3.5 presents the empirical findings, first in terms of descriptive statistics, then in terms of descriptive network analysis, and finally in terms of an analysis aimed at identifying the higher order regional innovation systems in Europe. The line of argument and findings is summarized in the concluding section, which also shortly discusses policy implications.

3.2. SYSTEMS OF INNOVATION AND NATIONAL BORDERS

The notion of a system of innovation was introduced in a national context. Since the seminal contributions of Freeman (1986), Lundvall (1992), and Nelson (1993), the concept of a National System of Innovation (NSI) has become the prime vehicle for analysing knowledge interactions in the national context. The concept of an innovation system arises from the idea that innovation is to an important extent a collective phenomenon, in which multiple actors contribute to a final outcome. The network of interaction between these actors is the most important subject of study in the innovations systems literature. In this network, the set of actors (e.g. firms, customers, policymakers, public research institutes, and universities), the institutions with which they work and which they create, and the (absence of) interaction between the actors contribute to the final result.

The idea that all major elements of an innovation system are influenced to an important extent by national factors, leads the way for the concept of a NSI. Actors may be influenced by national borders because they operate to an important extent in a local context (e.g. for a typical firm, a majority of customers and suppliers are domestic firms), or, in the case of non-private actors, they are financed and governed by national policymakers (public research institutes or universities). Rules and regulations, both as laid down in formal law and less formal institutions, are also deeply dependent on the national context, both because of cultural heritage and because of legal jurisdictions.

Thus, the early literature on innovation systems stressed that these systems may differ deeply between countries. Based on a detailed descriptive research strategy, differences between these national systems may be revealed, and causal factors behind differences in national performance with regard to innovation (and ultimately economic performance) may be identified. Although the notion of a 'global best-practice' system of innovation will be considered as alien to the theory by most contributors, the idea that some systems of innovation may yield better outcomes than others is surely one of the motivations for the development of the literature.

However, the notion of a system of innovation has also been fruitfully applied to the regional level. The basic idea here is the same. Actors in the innovations process, their pattern of interaction, and institutions may all be argued to be specific to a region. For the case of a regional system of innovation (e.g. Morgan 2004), strong local interactions may result from the tacit nature of knowledge. Thus, in order to benefit from knowledge flows (e.g. learning from public research institutes, universities, or other firms), it may be necessary to be located closely to that partner. Also, especially for larger countries, it may be argued that cultural backgrounds, and associated to this, informal rules of the game of institutions may be more characteristic for the regional level than the national level.

In this chapter, we embrace both the notions of a NSI and that of a regional system of innovation. We argue that one may usefully speak of both types of system, and that the two interact with each other. More specifically, our first working hypothesis is that interactions between knowledge actors are relatively strong both at the national level and at the regional level. In the next section, we summarize the econometric evidence based on patent statistics that supports this hypothesis, and we also illustrate the phenomenon using our own dataset in the subsequent section.

Based on this point of departure, we argue that regional systems of innovation may play a crucial role in facilitating interaction between national systems of innovations. As the background for this line of reasoning, we draw on the notion of a 'higher order regional system of innovation', a concept that was introduced by Cantwell and Janne (1999) and Cantwell and Iammarino (2001). In their work, a higher regional system is defined as a region in which knowledge intensity is high, and in which a broad range of knowledge activities, rather than a narrow specialization, is represented.

Our own definition of a higher order regional system is different, but it draws on ideas that are present in Cantwell and Janne (1999) and Cantwell and Iammarino (2001). We use the concept to describe a region that plays a pivotal role between distinct national systems of innovation, because it transfers knowledge between them. We may think of a region that attracts foreign multinational firms, who bring with them specific knowledge from the national system in which they originate. Through interaction with local firms in the foreign region, this knowledge may be (partly) transferred to the host region, and from there it may diffuse into the NSI of that country. The chain may also run backward, when the foreign multinational absorbs knowledge from the host region, and transfers this back to the home location.

Multinational firms may be considered as an important vehicle to such knowledge flows, but they are not the only one. International collaboration between researchers is another vehicle, especially so in the (semi-)public sector. Interaction that is less directly related to knowledge, such as international and inter-regional trade, may also contribute to knowledge flows, albeit in a less direct way.

Our second hypothesis, which we put to the test in the empirical part of this chapter, is that there exist a limited number of regions that are responsible for the majority of knowledge flows that occur between national systems of innovations. We use social network theory to make operational this hypothesis, and test it using data on patents and patent citations.

3.3. REGIONS, NATIONAL BORDERS AND KNOWLEDGE SPILLOVERS

In this section, we review the empirical evidence in favour of our first working hypothesis, i.e. that knowledge interactions and knowledge flows are more intensive within than between systems of innovation, both when viewed at the level of an NSI, and at the level of a regional system of innovation. There are two crucial theoretical inputs to this hypothesis. The first one comes from the field of geography, and argues that knowledge activities and knowledge spillovers tend to be concentrated in geographical space. A long tradition of literature argues in favour of this idea (see Caniëls 1999 for an overview). One may both draw on traditional agglomeration theory, and specific theories of knowledge to explain this phenomenon.

From the point of view of agglomeration theory, knowledge development activities (such as R&D) can be expected to concentrate in an area where there is a common resource pool, such as skilled workers with a specific expertise, or a public research institute, or university. This common resource pool may act as a vehicle for knowledge spillovers between the firms that it attracts, for example, because workers move between firms, or because researchers in a university participate in the same professional networks as private researchers. Knowledge theory adds to this the idea of tacit knowledge (e.g. Johnson, Lorenz, and Lundvall 2002). Tacit knowledge, as opposed to codified knowledge, is not easily transferable, and in many cases requires face-to-face contact. Obviously, such transfer is facilitated by short geographical distances, although in the age of transcontinental flights and advanced electronic communication, it is not entirely impossible at longer distances.

The idea of geographically concentrated knowledge activities and spillovers was put to the test in a seminal paper by Jaffe, Trajtenberg, and Henderson (1993). They used patent citations as an indicator of knowledge spillovers.[1] For a sample of US patents, they found that patent citations were more likely to occur between two patents that originated from the same region (they used both US states and smaller geographical units). By controlling for the pre-existing pattern of agglomeration of patents, they were able to show convincingly that this finding is the result of knowledge interaction being stronger at short distances. Maurseth and Verspagen (2002), although using a different statistical approach and European patents rather than US patents, were able to show that the same finding holds for European regions. They included data on most countries in the EU, and used a sample of approximately 125 regions, defined both at the NUTS-2 and -3 levels. Breschi and Lissoni (2001) are critical of these findings, and they argue that the observed citations are often related to market exchange of technology (e.g. universities contracting research to firms) rather than pure spillovers.

This finding, which has given rise to a rather elaborate literature on the spatial nature of knowledge spillovers, first of all points to the importance of a regional system of innovation. However, because the statistical evidence also indicates that knowledge flows relatively intensely between nearby regions, it is also related to the idea of an NSI. Nearby regions are obviously found more often within a single country than between different countries. However, there is also additional evidence on the role of national systems of innovation. Country borders play a crucial role in this. In the model by Maurseth and Verspagen (2002), country borders are represented as an explanatory variable in the form of dummies. Their model takes the number of patent citations between two regions as the dependent variable. The dummy indicating that two regions are within the same country comes out positive and significant. They also include an additional dummy indicating whether or not the two regions share the same language, and also this comes out as a positive and significant influence on knowledge spillovers. Although some languages (German, French, and Dutch) are shared between more than one country in the sample of Maurseth and Verspagen (2002), languages are obviously related to NSI. Concluding on their results, Maurseth and Verspagen (2002: 540) state 'that citations within countries are from 18 to 154 per cent more numerous than between countries', and that '[h]aving the same language increases the knowledge flows between two regions by up to 28%' (p. 541).

Similar findings are obtained for US patents by Jaffe and Trajtenberg (1996: 12677), who investigate the extent two which US patents are cited within and outside the national borders of the US. They estimate a model of the number of citations made to a patent over a longer period of time, and distinguish between domestic (US) citations, citations from Canada, and citations from Europe. Cited patents are always patents originating from US universities or public research institutes. The model that they estimate postulates the amount of knowledge diffusing from patent documents as initially growing with time, but after a peak the total amount of knowledge that diffuses declines.

The most striking aspect of their findings with regard to geographical borders, is that knowledge diffusion within national borders is quite different from the diffusion across nations. As their analysis shows, patents granted to US applicants are much more likely to cite previous US patents than patents granted to applicants in other countries. The frequency of citation from the US is almost twofold the frequency of citation from other countries.

But this localization effect is not constant in time. The effects of national borders are growing in the immediate period after the publication of the cited patent, but decrease over time. In other words, the effects of national borders fade over time. Their analysis also suggests that countries that are at a larger cultural and/or geographical distance from the US experience a stronger negative border effect. Canada, as a US neighbour shows the highest frequency to cite US patents, followed by Europe and Japan.

The empirical econometric literature on patent citations thus seems to confirm the importance of borders for knowledge flows. Based on this, we further examine how national border impact on knowledge interactions across European countries.

3.4. DATA AND METHODOLOGY

3.4.1. Data

We rely on patents and patent citations as indicators of knowledge activities and knowledge spillovers. It is well known that patents only represent a small part of technology and knowledge. Many inventions are not patented. Besides this, patents, and citations, are imperfect indicators even of the knowledge that is embodied in them. Griliches (1990) provides a survey of the main advantages and disadvantages of using patent statistics. Despite these well-known problems, we use patent statistics as the sole indicator in this chapter.

Patent documents contain a detailed description of the patented innovation. In addition to the name and address of the innovator and the applicant, patent documents also contain references to previous patents, that is, patent citations. The legal purpose of the patent references is to indicate which parts of the described knowledge are claimed in the patent, and which parts other patents have claimed earlier. From an economic point of view, however, the assumption is that a reference to a previous patent indicates that the knowledge in the latter patent was in some way useful for developing the new knowledge described in the citing patent. This is the line of reasoning offered in Jaffe, Trajtenberg, and Henderson (1993) for US patents. The detailed case study by Jaffe et al. (2000) on a limited sample of patents concludes that patent citations are a 'valid but noisy measure of technology spillovers'.

We use citations between European patents as a measure of knowledge flows. Data on patents and patent citations in Europe are obtained from the European Patent Office (EPO) (Bulletin CD and REFI tapes). There is one major difference with regard to citations between the European and US patent datasets. This concerns the requirements to the applicant with regard to describing the state-of-the-art of knowledge in the field by means of a list of references (citations). In the US Patent and Trademark Office (USPTO) system the applicant, when filing a patent application, is requested to supply a complete list of references to patents and non-patent documents. In the EPO system, the applicant may optionally supply such a list. In other words, while in the US this is a legal requirement and non-compliance by the patent applicant can lead to subsequent revocation of the patent, in Europe it is not obligatory. As a result applicants to the USPTO 'rather than running the risk of filing an incomplete list of references, tend to quote each and every reference even if it is only remotely related to what is to be patented. Since most US examiners apparently do not bother to limit the applicants' initial citations to those references which are really relevant in respect of patentability, this initial list tends to appear in unmodified form on the front page of most US patents' (Michel and Bettels 2001: 192). This tendency is confirmed by the number of citations that on average appear on USPTO patents. Michel and Bettels report that US patents cite about three times as many patent references and three-and-a-half times as many non-patent references compared to European patents. Citations on EPO patents, on the other hand, might suffer from the problem that they are mostly added by the examiner, and thus only an indirect indication of knowledge actually used by the inventor.

Still, it is obvious that a citation link in the European case can be seen as an indicator of technological relevance. Moreover, citations in the European system may indicate potential spillovers. Although this potential may not have been realized in all cases, it is reasonable to assume that since patents are public knowledge, professional R&D laboratories would have a reasonable knowledge about existing patents in their field. This is why we argue that European patent citations are a useful indicator of knowledge flows.

It should be emphasized that knowledge flows are a much broader concept than is captured by patent citations (US or European). In terms of the distinction introduced by Griliches (1979), patent citations focus on a specific form of pure knowledge spillovers. Rent spillovers, which reflect the fact that intermediate input prices do not embody completely the product innovations or the quality improvements resulting from R&D activities, are completely left out. Even within the category of pure knowledge spillovers, patent citations (to the extent that they are related to spillovers) are only a part of the complete story. For example, in order for patent citations to take place, both the spillover-receiving and spillover-generating firms must be actively engaged in R&D and apply for (European) patents.

In addition, patents are an ultimate example of codified knowledge, because they require an exact description of technological findings according to legally defined methods. One may assume, however, that the codified knowledge flows of patent citations go hand-in-hand with more tacit aspects of knowledge flows. According to the 'knowledge conversion' model by Nonaka and Takeuchi (1995) there is a strong interaction between codified and tacit knowledge during the creation of new technological assets. Tacit knowledge can therefore be converted into some forms of codified knowledge that can be incorporated in patent documents.

Our primary data source is the EPO database on patent applications. We select all patent applications, whether they have been granted, rejected (or withdrawn), or are still under review. We collect data for two separate periods: 1994–6 and 1985–7. In both cases, the cited patents are limited to the first year of the period, while citing patents may come from all three years. We use the so-called priority date of a patent to attribute it to a year.

Patents are limited to those originating from a set of European regions (documented precisely in the appendix). A patent is attributed to a region on the basis of the inventors' addresses. On the basis of the postal code of the address, we are able to attribute the address to one of the regions in our sample (for a basic description of the methodology to do this, see Caniëls 1999). When more than one inventor is listed on the patent, we use a fractional counting method (i.e. the patent is 'distributed' over all the regions listed). In this way, we are able to attribute the patent to the region where the actual research took place, as opposed to the headquarters of the applicant firm. In case of citations, both the cited and citing patents are attributed to regions, and in this way we are able to set up an indicator of citation flows between regions. Our dataset includes more than 120 European regions for two different periods. The dataset of 1994–6 includes 127 regions whereas the data-set of 1985–7 contains 126 regions. Some regions have been excluded because they have no patents (this was the case for Portuguese regions).

The indicator of citations flows between regions is calculated as follows. We start by setting up a square matrix of dimension n, which is the number of regions. Each cell in the matrix shows the number of patent citations between the two regions in the column and row. Note that because patent citations have a direction (citing and cited region), the matrix is not symmetric. We denote this matrix by C, where c_{ij} (the elements of the matrix) is the number of patents originating from region i cited by region j. We also have a vector R representing the number of patents originating from the region. Finally, we construct a matrix F by dividing each element of C by the element of R corresponding to the column (spillover receiving) region, i.e. $f_{ij} = c_{ij}/r_j$. Note that f is not restricted to be smaller than 1, because a patent usually makes more than 1 citation. The natural lower boundary for f is 0.

F captures the importance of a particular region as a knowledge input for the reporting region. This is the consequence of dividing the elements of C by the element of R corresponding to the column of C. This is an arbitrary choice, and an alternative is to divide by the element of R corresponding to the row of C. This would yield an indicator of the importance of various receiving regions in the total spillover originating from a particular region. We leave an analysis of such an indicator for a future study.

3.4.2. Methodology

Our methodology draws, first of all, on social network analysis. The matrix F represents a network, in which the regions are the nodes, and the citations the links between them. Some nodes are connected directly to each other (when they cite each other's patents), others may not be. The crucial assumption behind social network analysis is, however, that even when two nodes (regions) are not directly connected to each other, they may be indirectly connected. For example, consider the case where Region A is connected to Region B, but not to Region C, and Region B is connected to Region C. Knowledge may still flow from A to C, when B acts as an intermediary. This assumption of indirect linkage underlies all of our analyses.

From the toolbox of social network analysis (see Wasserman and Faust 1994 for an overview), we first draw on the theory of brokerage (Gould and Fernandez 1989).[2] This is a method of classifying relationships between triangles of nodes (such as the example of Regions A, B, and, C above) in a network in which the nodes are classified in groups. In our case, the regions belong to countries, which are the groups in our analysis. Brokerage roles are classified into five types, which depend on the groups that have been linked by the brokerage. We use only three of the five types, by the nature of the problem that we are interested in. These three types are gatekeeper, representative, and liaison.[3] Each of these types represents a specific way in which a regional system of innovation may transfer knowledge between national systems of innovation. The precise definitions of the brokerage types are given in Table 3.1.

A related concept, also prominent in the social network analysis literature, is the notion of a structural hole (Burt 1992; Brass and Burkhardt 1993; Powell, Koput, and Smith-Doerr 1996; Gulati 1998). This starts from the idea that nodes in a network may be able to influence network resources if they are situated centrally in the network (i.e. connected to many other nodes). In particular, Burt (1992, 1997) proposed the concept of a structural hole and emphasized that nodes that have links to other nodes in different groups of the network are relatively influential. Note that in terms of the definitions in Table 3.1, all of the underlined regions in the second column reach out to different groups in the network, and thus satisfy Burt's definition.[4] Nodes that act like a bridge between groups in the network will absorb and transmit crucial information through the network. In other words, in terms of our research question, the regions that we are interested in (those that connect NSI), will play crucial brokerage roles for facilitating knowledge interactions, and will tend to be situated in the central part of network.

The structural holes view of networks leads us to use below three indicators, which are all derived from Burt (1992). The first of these is Effective Network Size of a region. When computed for region k, this measure starts from the network of all regions that are directly connected to k (the ego-network of k). The effective network size of k is the number of nodes in this network (not counting k itself) minus the average number of connections each node has. The idea behind this is that connections that k has to regions that it is already indirectly connected to are redundant, and therefore do not

Table 3.1 The three brokerage types used in the analysis

Definition of brokerage types	Relationships between groups
1 A *gatekeeper* absorbs knowledge from other countries and passes it on to home country regions	$A->\underline{B}->B$
2 A *representative* diffuses knowledge from home country regions to regions in foreign countries	$A->\underline{A}->B$
3 A *liaison* enhances knowledge interactions between other countries	$A->\underline{B}->C$

Note: The definitions apply to the underlined region in the second column.

contribute to the effective network of k. The second indicator, Constraint of region k, is related to this. It measures the degree to which region k is connected to regions that are already connected to the other regions in k's ego-network. The last measure, Hierarchy, measures how much the Constraint value depends on a single other region (node in the network).

3.5. EMPIRICAL RESULTS

3.5.1. Descriptive Statistics: Density of Interaction Within and Between National Systems of Innovation

We first look at the density of interaction within national systems of innovation and between them. In other words, we partition matrix F into parts that represent linkages between regions in each single country, and a part corresponding to linkages between regions in different countries. In order to calculate density of the partitions in the matrix, we recode all values of F into a binary value, where all positive values are transformed to a 1. Density is then calculated as the number of all cells in the partition containing a 1 divided by the total number of cells in the partition.

The hypothesis that knowledge interactions are hindered by national borders corresponds to the statistical null-hypothesis that the density is higher in the partitions of the matrix that correspond to within-country interaction. In order to examine this, we apply a one-factor ANOVA table, and document the basic descriptive statistics in Figure 3.1. The complete density matrices are shown in the appendix.

The density within countries is much higher than the density between countries. This is confirmed in the ANOVA analysis in Table 3.2 (p-values <0.0001), which thus supports our first hypothesis of relatively strong interaction within national borders. Figure 3.2 shows the values of the within-country densities in the two periods (the density of the total matrix, taking into account both within- and between-countries, is equal to 0.12 and 0.10, respectively for the 1980s and 1990s). Except for Spain, Portugal, and Greece (the latter only in the 1980s), the densities reported in Figure 3.2 are all higher than average density in the complete matrix. The three reported countries are an exception to this general rule, indicating that their national systems of innovation, at least as measured by our indicator of patent citations, are less interactive than the others. This seems to be a result of the fact that one condition for intensive knowledge interaction between the regions within the same country to be picked up by our method, is that the country has a sufficient level of patents.

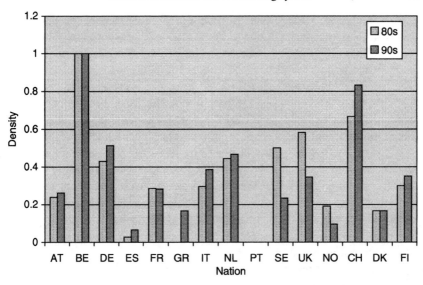

Figure 3.1. Density of interactions within national systems of innovations

In addition, we find a significant difference of density between the two periods. Using a *t*-test statistic, it is shown that the density in the 1990s is significantly smaller than the density in the 1980s (P < 0.005).[5] As Figure 3.1 shows, however, the trend of increasing density is not observed for all countries. For example, the within-NIS density of Sweden, the UK, and Norway has decreased sharply from the 1980s to the 1990s, whereas other countries do not change very much. The reductions in these countries are the main source for the whole-network density decrease.

Table 3.2 ANOVA analysis for density of interaction

(I) 1984–6

Source of variation	SS	Df	MS	F	p-Value
Treatment (between groups) Within-NIS vs. between-NISs	0.81289	1	0.81289	407,5185	0.0000
Within groups	444,825	223	0.019947		
Total	526,114	224			

(II) 1995–7

Treatment (between groups) Within-NIS vs. between-NISs	0.982302	1	0.982302	7,075,346	0.0000
Within groups	309,601	223	0.013883		
Total	4,078,312	224			

The results on densities can be graphically illustrated by means of the network plots in Figures 3.2 and 3.3. These graphs were produced in the Netdraw module of Ucinet, using a spring-embedding algorithm. This is a heuristic method that tries to plot the network in 2D space in such a way that nodes that have strong interaction are plotted closely to each other. The method is heuristic in the sense that it does not (necessarily) provide an 'optimal' layout of the network, but it does convey the main nature of the interaction between nodes.

The different shades of the nodes show the different nationalities of the regions. We find that the nodes with the same shades seem be closer together than the nodes with different shades, again an indication of stronger within-border interactions. The individual interactions between the regions are not easy to identify due to the large clutter of lines in the graph. In the appendix, we provide similar figures where we leave out lines of relatively small weight (low value of the cells in matrix F).

In summary, the results clearly show the importance of borders, and hence national systems of innovation, in determining knowledge flows (patent citations) between regions in Europe. Country borders hinder knowledge flows. Nevertheless, the matrix F also shows selected interactions between regions that are not part of the same country. These specific interactions will be the subject of the analysis below, when we try to identify the 'higher order regions' that act as brokers between the national systems of innovation of Europe. We start by a graphical representation of these linkages, limiting ourselves, for the moment, to the country level.

In order to do this, we select the 'strong linkages' between countries and document them in network graphs similar to Figures 3.2 and 3.3. As a benchmark, we use for each country the within-country density. We then select links to other countries by comparing the within-country density to the density in the partition of matrix F corresponding to links with a particular (other) country. In case the density of this partition is higher than the within-country density, the link with this country is included in the graph. As an example, consider the within-country density of Italy in the 1990s, which is approximately equal to 0.4. Looking at the partition of the matrix that represents linkages between Portugal and Italy, it is found that this has higher density than 0.4, and hence the link from Italy to Portugal is included in the network plots in Figures 3.4 and 3.5. Figures 3.4a and 3.5a display the strong linkages to *diffuse* knowledge whereas Figures 3.4b and 3.5b include the stronger linkages to *receive* knowledge.

The networks in the diffusing part of the graphs (Figures 3.4a and 3.5a) are relatively sparse. Not many countries are present in these graphs. This indicates that in terms of 'sending' spillovers, most countries do not have many

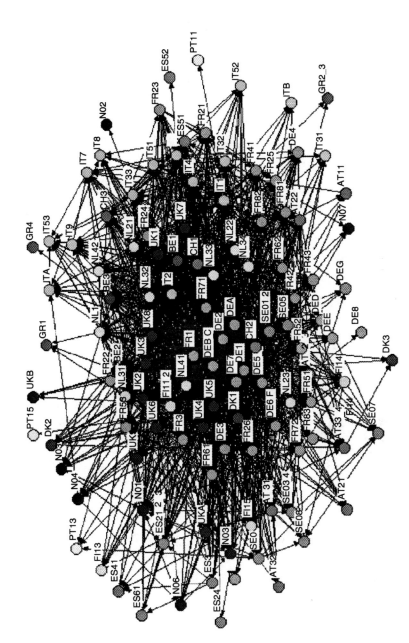

Figure 3.2. The knowledge flows network in the 1980s

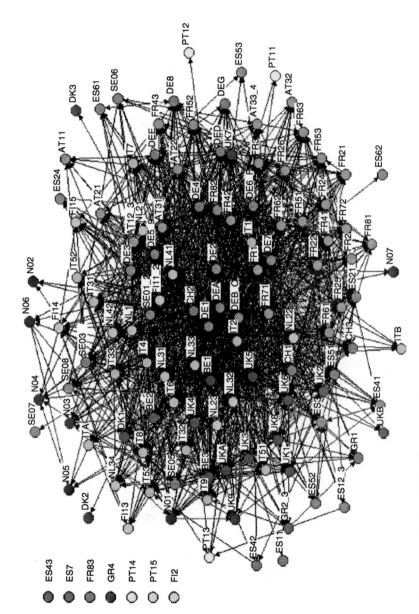

Figure 3.3. The knowledge flows network in the 1990s

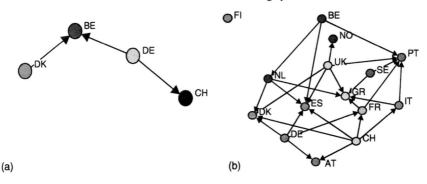

Figure 3.4. Strong linkages between countries, 1980s

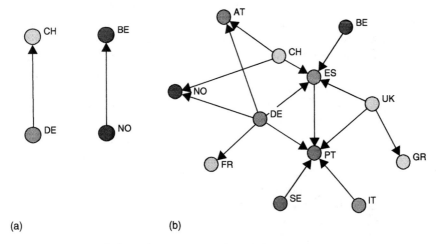

Figure 3.5. Strong linkages between countries, 1990s

specific 'targets'. Of the relationships found in the 1980s, we find that Germany diffuses relatively strongly to its neighbour countries Belgium and Switzerland (but not its three other neighbours in the sample, the Netherlands, Austria, and Denmark). The link to Switzerland survives in the 1990s.

The figures that represent relatively strong receiving links (Figures 3.4b and 3.5b) are less sparse. Here the most notable part is the central positions of the Southern European countries that have relatively few patents (Spain, Portugal, and Greece). These countries attract important (relative to their own technology effort) spillovers from the main European technological leaders, such as Germany, Switzerland, the UK, and Sweden. But we also find that some highly developed countries, such as France and the Netherlands, have relatively high knowledge inflow from other highly developed countries, for example. Germany or Belgium. Together, the graphs in Figures 3.4 and 3.5 clearly show that there are some 'preferential' linkages between national systems of innovation. How regional innovation systems play a role in these will be the topic of the remainder of the empirical analysis of this chapter.

3.6. IDENTIFYING HIGHER ORDER REGIONAL SYSTEMS OF INNOVATIONS

The brokerage analysis is aimed at identifying the triangles of regions that were explained in Table 3.1. For each region in the sample, we simply count the number of times it is present as a gatekeeper, representative, or liaison in one of these triangles. We then report in Table 3.3 for each country the region with the highest score for gatekeeper and representative (in a limited number of cases, there are two regions with the same score on top of the country lists). Remember that these two brokerage roles are crucially related to the knowledge flowing in and out of the country to which the region belongs (a gatekeeper transfers knowledge from abroad into its own country, a representative transfers knowledge from its own country abroad).

The first finding is that most countries indeed have regions within their borders that act as a gatekeeper or representative. Only a few countries, Denmark, Greece, and Portugal, have no regions to play (one of) these two brokerages roles. Second, it is striking that quite often, the same region is at the top of the list of both brokerage roles at the same time. This is the case in Austria (1980s and 1990s), Belgium (1980s and 1990s), Spain (1990s), France (1990s), Greece (1990s), Italy (1980s and 1990s), Sweden (1980s and 1990s), the UK (1980s and 1990s), Norway (1980s), Switzerland (1990s), and Finland (1980s and 1990s). This points to a tendency for the two brokerage roles of representative and gatekeepers to be complementary. Third, there is a tendency for regions to be on top of the two lists in both periods, pointing to persistence in the brokerage roles over time. In every country, there is at least one region that appears both in the part of the table for the 1980s and the part for the 1990s.

Liaisons are regions that connect two foreign systems of innovation. They receive knowledge from one country, and pass it on to a different country, in the same triangular relationship that was considered in the previous two brokerage roles. Table 3.4 lists the fifteen regions that are most active as liaison in both periods. Overall, there is a large tendency for the same regions that were already prominent in Table 3.3 to be also present in Table 3.4. Only six regions that were not in Table 3.3 are now listed in Table 3.4. In other

Table 3.3 Most important gatekeepers and representatives for each country

(a) 1980s

	Gatekeeper		Representative	
AT	Niederösterreich	(AT12_3)	Niederösterreich	(AT12_3)
BE	Brussels Hfdst. Gew	(BE1)	Brussels Hfdst. Gew	(BE1)
DE	Hessen	(DE7)	Bayern	(DE2)
ES	Madrid	(ES3)	Baleares	(ES53)
FR	Rhone-Alpes	(FR71)	Île De France	(FR1)
GR	—		—	
IT	Lombardia	(IT2)	Lombardia	(IT2)
NL	Zuid-Holland	(NL33)	Noord-Brabant	(NL41)
PT	—		—	
SE	Stockholm & Östra Mellansverige	SE01_2	Stockholm & Östra Mellansverige	SE01_2
UK	South East /North West	UK5/8	South East	UK5
NO	Akershus, Oslo	NO1	Akershus, Oslo	NO1
CH	Jura, Geneva Neuchâtel, etc.	CH1	Berne, Zurich, etc	CH2
DK	Hillerød, Helsingør, København	DK1	—	—
FI	Uusimaa, Etelä-Suomi	FI11_2	Uusimaa, Etelä-Suomi	FI11_2

(b) 1990s

AT	Niederösterreich/ Steiermark	AT12_3/ AT22	Steiermark	AT22
BE	Brussels Hfdst. Gew	BE1	Brussels Hfdst. Gew	BE1
DE	Bayern/Baden-Württemberg	DE2/DE1	Nordrhein-Westfalen	DEA
ES	Madrid	ES3	Madrid	ES3
FR	Île de France	FR1	Île de France	FR1
GR	Kentriki Ellada and Attiki	GR2_3	Kentriki Ellada and Attiki	—
IT	Lombardia	IT2	Lombardia	IT2
NL	Zuid-Holland	NL33	Noord-Brabant	NL41
PT	—	—	—	—
SE	Stockholm & Östra Mellansverige	SE01_2	Stockholm & Östra Mellansverige	SE01_2
UK	South East	UK5	South East	UK5
NO	Østfold, Busekrud, Vestfold, Telemark	NO3	Akershus, Oslo	NO1
CH	Berne, Zurich, etc.	CH2	Berne, Zurich, etc.	CH2
DK	Hillerød, Helsingør, København	DK1	—	—
FI	Uusimaa, Etelä-Suomi	FI11_2	Uusimaa, Etelä-Suomi	FI11_2

words, the regions listed so far tend to play multiple brokerage roles, and thus play an important role in facilitating knowledge flows in the network. Furthermore, many regions are present in Table 3.4 for the 1980s and the 1990s, indicating that they maintain a strong position over the whole

Table 3.4 Regions ranked on score on liaison role

1980s	Region	Liaison value	1990s	Region	Liaison value
1 UK—South East	UK5	802	BE—Brussels Hfdst. Gew	BE1	674
2 CH—Berne, Zurich, etc.	CH2	693	UK—South East	UK5	640
3 DE—Hessen	DE7	592	CH—Berne, Zurich, etc.	CH2	594
4 IT—Lombardia	IT2	507	FR—Île de France	FR1	450
5 DE—Baden-Württemberg	DE1	487	DE—Bayern	DE2	418
6 BE—Brussels Hfdst. Gew	BE1	451	IT—Lombardia	IT2	385
7 UK—North West	UK8	439	NL—Zuid-Holland	NL33	266
8 SE—Stockholm and Östra Mellansverige	SE01_2	420	DE—Nordrhein-Westfalen	DEA	263
9 CH—Jura, Geneva Neuchâtel, etc.	CH1	407	FI—Uusimaa, Etelä-Suomi	FI11_2	255
10 DK—Hillerød, Helsingør, København	DK1	383	DE—Rheinland-Pfalz and Saarland	DEB_C	223
11 NL—Zuid-Holland	NL33	376	FR—Rhone-Alpes	FR71	182
12 DE—Bayern	DE2	348	DE—Bremen and Niedersachsen	DE5_9	173
13 UK—East Anglia	UK4	345	DE—Hessen	DE7	171
14 FR—Rhone-Alpes	FR71	298	BE—Vlaams gewest	BE2	147
15 NL—Noord-Holland	NL32	294	IT—Emilia Romagna	IT4	139

Note: Regions printed in bold do not appear in Table 3.3.

period. Another peculiarity is the presence of a large number of regions from Germany, especially in 1990s.

We now proceed to perform a more formal analysis of the different roles that regions play in the knowledge network of Europe, with the aim to identify the higher order regional systems of innovation which play an important role in connecting the European national systems of innovation.

We enter the three indicators based on the structural holes theory, and the three brokerage indicators into a factor analysis, the results of which are shown in Table 3.5. The datasets in the 1980s and 1990s both extract two factors with a high (>86 per cent) portion of the variance accounted for. Moreover, the factor loadings for these two factors are similar in both periods. The first factor loads high on effective size of the network and all three brokerage variables. Hence, we term this factor 'network standing' to indicate that it measures in a broad sense the centrality of a region in the knowledge network. This factor measures the importance of the region's position in the network as well as its abundance of network resources and technological information. The second factor loads high on the two remaining indicators, network constraint and hierarchy, is called 'network constraints'. This factor

Table 3.5 Exploratory factor analysis, factor loadings

Indicators	Factor 1 'Network standing'		Factor 2 'Network constraint'	
	1980s	1990s	1980s	1990s
Effect-size	0.943	0.936		
Representative	0.908	0.934		
Liaison	0.905	0.883		
Gatekeeper	0.806	0.806		
Hierarchy			0.981	0.981
Constraints			0.950	0.953

Note: Only value >0.4 has been reported in the table.

essentially measures the extent to which a region has difficulties in obtaining resources from the knowledge network.

The factor score on the network standing factor turns out to have a rather peculiar distribution. We calculate the range between the maximum and minimum values on this factor score. It turns out that only nine (in the 1980s) or ten (in the 1990s) regions occupy the upper half of this range. This indicates that the distribution over regions of this factor score is rather skewed, with only a small number of regions taking the leading positions, and a large pack of regions that act as followers at quite some distance from the leaders. The regions occupying the upper half of the distribution for the two periods are listed in Table 3.6.

The method that has been used to identify higher order innovation systems in this way is admittedly an inductive method. It is not based on objective,

Table 3.6 Higher-order innovation systems as defined by factor sores on the 'network standing' factor

1980s		Factor score	1990s		Factor score
UK5	UK—South East	4.38	FR1	FR—Île de France	4.64
IT2	IT—Lombardia	3.10	UK5	UK—South East	3.92
FR1	FR—Île de France	2.98	IT2	IT—Lombardia	3.43
FR71	FR—Rhone Alpes	2.81	DE2	DE—Bayern	2.73
DE7	DE—Hessen	2.62	DEA	DE—Nordrhein-Westfalen	2.52
DE1	DE— Baden-Württemberg	2.22	BE1	BE—Brussels Hfdst. Gew	2.25
DE2	DE—Bayern	2.20	DE1	DE—Baden-Württemberg	2.08
UK8	UK—North West	2.13	FR71	FR—Rhone Alpes	2.06
CH2	CH—Berne, Zurich, etc.	1.77	CH2	CH—Berne, Zurich, etc.	1.96
			NL33	NL—Zuid-Holland	1.91

pre-specified, quantitative criteria. However, the basic variables going into the analysis (based on brokerage and structural holes) are rooted in the theory of innovation systems, and the factor analysis performed on these indicators does adequately summarize the empirical patterns. But the cut-off of the range of factor scores at one half of the total range is arbitrary, and as a result the list of regions obtained in Table 3.6 is in no sense the final answer to the question of which are the higher order regional innovation systems in Europe. The list may be made longer or shorter, according to how strict one would like to make the definition.

Taking the arbitrariness of the cut-off point for granted, we look at which regions are found on the list in Table 3.6. A prominent feature is again the persistence of the regions in the two decades. The top-3 of the two lists consists of the same regions in both periods, although the order in which they appear has been changed. A total of six regions are found on the lists of both periods. Furthermore, one may indeed say that many of the regions on the lists are more or less expected, because these regions are rather well-known as industrial and technological centres. Germany, the UK, and France appear as the dominating countries, each with more than a single region on the lists. Although Germany has the largest number of regions on the lists overall, it does not have a region in the top-3 of either list.

Summarizing, our analysis has used social network theory to identify the regions of Europe that play a crucial role in linking together the European national systems of innovation. We arrive at a list of nine or ten regions that can be said to take this role.

3.7. CONCLUSIONS AND DISCUSSION

Based on a broad-brush interpretation of the theory of innovation systems, we have argued that national borders play an important role in constraining knowledge spillovers between countries. This is confirmed by our empirical results, which have been based on an, admittedly, selective indicator calculated using patent citations. Patent citations have been taken as an indicator of knowledge spillovers between regions and the countries they belong to. Knowledge flows are more intensive within countries than between countries.

Our argument then proceeded to mark a special role of a selected set of regions, the so-called higher order regional innovation systems of Europe, in linking together the national systems of innovation. Regional systems were argued to be especially prone to play this role because knowledge does not easily flow over large distances. Regions that are able, for example, to attract foreign multinationals and extract spillovers from them, may be key players in facilitating international knowledge spillovers. These key regions act as a knowledge centre for other regions nearby (in the same country).

Using tools from social network analysis and multivariate analysis, we were able to identify for two different periods (in the 1980s and in the 1990s) a list of regions that may be characterized as such higher order regional innovation systems. It turns out that the list is small (depending on the period, nine or ten regions), and that the same regions tend to figure on the list in both periods. We argue that these regions are the central hubs of the European innovation system. The top-3 of the lists in both periods features the areas around Paris, London, and Milan. Knowledge flows in the European innovation system at large depend crucially on these hubs, as they shorten greatly the distance between the receiving regions at the end of their spokes.

Our analysis is mainly descriptive, in taking a specific view on the nature of interaction between national and regional innovation systems, and applying this to paint an impressionistic map of the European innovation system. But our results bear implications for policy discussions, for example, on the notion of a European Research Area (ERA). In our view, such an ERA must be characterized as a network in which there are parts that differ greatly in terms of their density and global connectivity. In our view, it may well be argued that different policies must be designed for higher and lower order regional systems. While the emphasis in lower order systems may well be on local performance—something that is the current focus on many initiatives related to knowledge, technology, and innovation in the Structural Funds and other regional policies—the higher order systems require a different policy emphasis. Their role as hubs is crucial for the performance of the system as a whole, and therefore policies aimed at (far-reaching) diffusion are more appropriate here.

Two lines of further research may contribute to the refinement of such policy recommendations. In the first place, a more detailed formal theory is necessary to outline the network nature of knowledge flows in the European innovation system. One may think of recent advances in network models of knowledge flows (e.g. Cowan and Jonard 2004) as a way to apply quantitative theory to the field of innovation systems. Our results and methodology may become more refined when insights from such models are applied. Second, we may use the information in our dataset on sectoral specialization of innovative efforts in regions. Because knowledge flows unevenly between sectors, sectoral specialization patterns may well be related to the network position that a region has. This is also in line with the work by Cantwell and Janne (1999) and Cantwell and Iammarino (2001) on higher order regional innovation systems.

NOTES

1. Our review of the empirical literature will be limited to the key contributions using formal quantitative methods, and patents and patent citations as the indicator of knowledge activities. This is closest to our own methodology.
2. All calculations involving social network analysis are made using UCINET 6.0 (Borgatti, Everett, and Freeman 2002).
3. The other two roles, consultant and coordinator, involve links between two regions in the same country, and are therefore not of prime interest to our research problem.
4. This illustrates the similarity between the concept of brokerage and the notion of structural hole.
5. In order to compare the density in two periods, equal sample size is required. For the dataset in 1990s, we ignore the region PT12. The t-statistics is -2.662 (p-value < 0.005), indicating that the density in the 1990s (0.1055) is significantly smaller than the density in the 1980s (0.1228).

REFERENCES

Borgatti, S. P., Everett, M. G., and Freeman, L C. (2002). *Ucinet for Windows: Software for Social Network Analysis*. Cambridge, MA: Analytic Technologies.

Brass, D. J. and Burkhardt, M. E. (1993). 'Potential Power and Power Use: An Investigation of Structure and Behaviour', *Academy of Management Journal*, 36(3): 441–70.

Breschi, S. and Lissoni, F. (2001). 'Knowledge Spillovers and Local Innovation Systems: A Critical Survey', *Industrial and Corporate Change*, 10: 975–1005.

Burt, R. S. (1992). *Structural Holes: The Social Structure of Competition*. Cambridge, MA: Harvard University Press.

—— (1997). 'The Contingent Value of Social Capital', *Administrative Science Quarterly*, 42(2): 339–66.

Caniëls, M. C. J. (1999). *Regional Growth Differentials*. Ph.D. thesis, Maastricht University, Maastricht, Universitaire Pers Maastricht.

Cantwell, J. and Iammarino, S. (2001). 'EU Regions and Multinational Corporations: Change, Stability and Strengthening of Technological Comparative Advantages', *Industrial and Corporate Change*, 10(4): 1007–37.

—— and Janne, O. (1999). 'Technological Globalization and the Innovative Centres: The Role of Corporate Technological Leadership and Locational Hierarchy', *Research Policy*, 28(2–3): 119–44.

Cowan, R. and Jonard, N. (2004). 'Network Structure and the Diffusion of Knowledge', *Journal of Economic Dynamics and Control*, 28: 1557–75.

Freeman, C. (1986). *Technology Policy and Economic Performance: Lessons from Japan.* London: Pinter.

Gould, J. and Fernandez, J. (1989). 'Structures of Mediation: A Formal Approach to Brokerage in Transaction Networks', *Sociological Methodology,* 19: 89–126.

Griliches, Z. (1979). 'Issues in Assessing the Contribution of Research and Development to Productivity Growth', *The Bell Journal of Economics,* 10: 92–116.

—— (1990). 'Patent Statistics as Economic Indicators: A Survey', *Journal of Economic Literature,* 28: 1661–707.

Gulati, R. (1998). 'Alliance and Networks', *Strategic Management Journal,* 19: 293–317.

Jaffe, A. B. and Trajtenberg, M. (1996). 'Flows of Knowledge from Universities and Federal Laboratories: Modelling the Flow of Patent Citations over Time and Across Institutional and Geographical Boundaries', *Proceedings of the National Academy of Sciences,* 93: 12671–77.

—— Trajtenberg, M. and Henderson, R. (1993). 'Geographic Localization of Knowledge Spillovers as Evidenced by Patent Citations', *Quarterly Journal of Economics,* 108: 577–98.

—— Trajtenberg, M. et al. (2000). 'The Meaning of Patent Citations: Report on the NBER/Case-Western Reserve Survey of Patentees'. NBER Working Paper No. 7631.

Johnson, B., Lorenz, E. and Lundvall, B.-Å. (2002). 'Why All This Fuss About Codified and Tacit Knowledge?', *Industrial and Corporate Change,* 11: 245–62.

Lundvall, B.-Å. (1992). *National System of Innovation—Towards a Theory of Innovation and Interactive Learning.* London: Pinter.

Maurseth, P. B. and Verspagen, B. (2002). 'Knowledge Spillovers in Europe: A Patent Citations Analysis', *The Scandinavian Journal of Economics,* 104(4): 531–45.

Michel, J. and Bettles, B. (2001). 'Patent Citation Analysis. A Closer Look at the Basic Input Data from Patent Search Reports', *Scientometrics,* 51: 185–201.

Morgan, K. (2001). 'The Learning Region: Institutions, Innovation and Regional Renewal', *Regional Studies,* 31(5): 491–503.

Nelson, R. R. (1993). *National Innovation Systems. A Comparative Analysis.* Oxford: Oxford University Press.

Nonaka, I. and Takeuchi, H. (1995). *The Knowledge-Creating Company.* Oxford: Oxford University Press.

Powell, W., Koput, K., and Smith-Doerr, L. (1996). 'Interorganizational Collaboration and the Locus of Innovation: Networks of Learning in Biotechnology', *Administrative Science Quarterly,* 41(1): 116–45.

Wasserman, S. and Faust, K. (1994). *Social Network Analysis: Methods and Applications.* Cambridge: Cambridge University Press.

APPENDIX

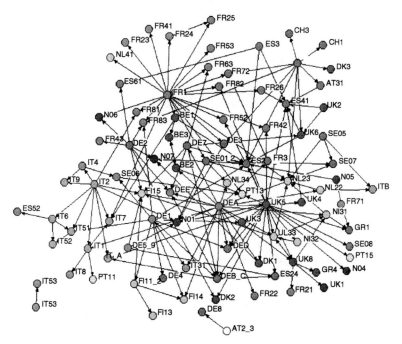

Figure A.3.1. Knowledge flows network in 1980s (simplified network)

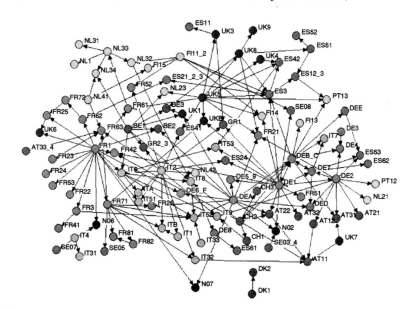

Figure A.3.2. Knowledge flows network in 1990s (simplified network)

Table A.3.1 Regions used in the analysis
For the following countries/regions, the NUTS classification has been used:

Austria		France	
AT11	Burgenland	FR1	Ile de France
AT12+AT13	Niederösterreich	FR21	Champagne-Ardenne
AT21	Kärnten	FR22	Picardie
AT22	Steiermark	FR23	Haute-Normandie
AT31	Oberösterreich	FR24	Centre
AT32	Salzburg	FR25	Basse-Normandie
AT33+AT34	Tirol and Vorarlberg	FR26	Bourgogne
		FR3	Nord-Pas-De-Calais
Belgium		FR41	Lorraine
BE1	Brussels Hfdst. Gew	FR42	Alsace
BE2	Vlaams Gewest	FR43	Franche-Comte
BE3	Region Wallonne	FR51	Pays de la Loire
		FR52	Bretagne
Germany		FR53	Poitou-Charentes
DE1	Baden-Württemberg	FR61	Aquitaine
DE2	Bayern	FR62	Midi-Pyrenees
DE3	Berlin	FR63	Limousin
DE4	Brandenburg	FR71	Rhone-Alpes
DE5+DE9	Bremen and Niedersachsen	FR72	Auvergne
DE6+DEF	Hamburg and Schleswig-Holstein	FR81	Languedoc-Roussillon
D E7	Hessen	FR82	Provence-Alpes-Côte d'Azur
DE8	Mecklenburg-Vorpommern	FR83	Corse
DEA	Nordrhein-Westfalen		
DEB+DEC	Rheinland-Pfalz and Saarland	**Greece**	
DED	Sachsen	GR1	Voreia Ellada
DEE	Sachsen-Anhalt	GR2+GR3	Kentriki Ellada and Attiki
DEG	Thüringen	GR4	Nisia Aigaiou, Kriti
Spain		**Italy**	
ES11	Galicia	IT1	Nord Ovest
ES12+ES13	Asturias and Cantabria	IT2	Lombardia
ES21+ES22+ES23	Pais Vasco, Navarra and Rioja	IT31	Trentino-Alto Adige
ES24	Aragon	IT32	Veneto
ES3	Madrid	IT33	Friuli-Venezia Giulia
ES41	Castilla-Leon	IT4	Emilia-Romagna
ES42	Castilla-La Mancha	IT51	Toscana
ES43	Extremadura	IT52	Umbria
ES51	Cataluna	IT53	Marche

(*Continued*)

Table A.3.1 (*Continued*)

Spain			Italy	
ES52	Valenciana		IT6	Lazio
ES53	Baleares		IT7	Abruzzo-Molise
ES61	Andalucia		IT8	Campania
ES62	Murcia		IT9	Sud
ES7	Canarias		ITA	Sicilia
			ITB	Sardegna

Netherlands				
NL1	Noord-Nederland		**United Kingdom**	
NL21	Overijssel		UK1	North
NL22	Gelderland		UK2	Yorkshire and Humberside
NL23	Flevoland		UK3	East Midlands
NL31	Utrecht		UK4	East Anglia
NL32	Noord-Holland		UK5	South East
NL33	Zuid-Holland		UK6	South West
NL34	Zeeland		UK7	West Midlands
NL41	Noord-Brabant		UK8	North West
NL42	Limburg		UK9	Wales
			UKA	Scotland
Portugal			UKB	Northern Ireland

Portugal	
PT11	Norte
PT12	Centro
PT13	Lisboa E Vale Do Tejo
PT14	Alentejo
PT15	Algarve

Sweden	
SE01+SE02	Stockholm and Östra Mellansverige
SE03+SE04	Småland and Sydsverige
SE05	Västsverige
SE06	Norra Mellansverige
SE07	Mellersta Norrland
SE08	Övre Norrland

For the following countries, a national classification has been used:

Norway based on Fylken	
NO1	Akershus, Oslo
NO2	Hedmark, Oppland
NO3	Østfold, Busekrud, Vestfold, Telemark
NO4	Aust-Agder, Vest-Agder, Rogaland
NO5	Hordaland, Sogn og Fjordane, Møre of Romsdal
NO6	Sør-Trøndelag, Nord-Trøndelag
NO7	Nordland, Troms, Finnmark

Switzerland based on Cantons

CH1	Jura, Neuchâtel, Fribourg, Vaud, Geneva
CH2	Argovia, Appenzell Inner-Rhodes, Appenzell Outer-Rhodes, Basel-Country-Basel-Town, Berne, Glarus, Lucerne, Nidwalden, Obwalden, St. Gallen, Schaffhausen, Schwyz, Solothurn, Thurgovia, Uri, Zug, Zurich
CH3	Valais, Ticino, Grisons

Denmark based on postal regions

DK1	Hillerød, Helsingør, København
DK2	Fyn, Sjaelland ex. Hillerød, Helsingør, København
DK3	Jylland

Finland based on postal regions

FI11_12	Uusimaa, Etelä-Suomi
FI13	Itä-Sumoi
FI14	Väli-Suomi
FI15	Pohjois-Suomi
FI2	Ahvenanmaa/Åland

Table A.3.2 A summary of national densities

Nations	1980s	1990s
AT (Austria)	0.2381	0.2619
BE (Belgium)	1.0000	1.0000
DE (Germany)	0.4295	0.5128
ES (Spain)	0.0275	0.0659
FR (France)	0.2854	0.2814
GR (Greece)	0.0000	0.1667
IT (Italy)	0.2952	0.3857
NL (Netherlands)	0.4444	0.4667
PT (Portugal)	0.0000	0.0000
SE (Sweden)	0.5000	0.2333
UK (United Kingdom)	0.5818	0.3455
NO (Norway)	0.1905	0.0952
CH (Switzerland)	0.6667	0.8333
DK (Denmark)	0.1667	0.1667
FI (Finland)	0.3000	0.3500
Network mean	0.1228	0.1039

Table A.3.3 Network density

1980s

	AT	BE	DE	ES	FR	GR	IT	NL	PT	SE	UK	NO	CH	DK	FI
AT	**0.2381**	0.0000	0.044	0.0204	0.0455	0.0000	0.0857	0.0143	0.0000	0.0238	0.039	0.0204	0.1429	0.0952	0.0571
BE	0.0476	**1.0000**	0.1538	0.0476	0.2424	0.0000	0.2222	0.4667	0.0833	0.0000	0.4545	0.1429	0.1111	0.0000	0.2667
DE	0.3626	0.4359	**0.4295**	0.0824	0.3497	0.0000	0.2718	0.4231	0.0000	0.3462	0.3916	0.1868	0.4615	0.2051	0.2462
ES	0.0102	0.0000	0.0055	**0.0275**	0.0032	0.0000	0.0143	0.0071	0.0000	0.0119	0.026	0.0000	0.0238	0.0000	0.0000
FR	0.0649	0.2576	0.0874	0.0195	**0.2857**	0.0152	0.0909	0.1318	0.0114	0.0606	0.1736	0.0519	0.1667	0.1364	0.0818
GR	0.0000	0.0000	0.0000	0.0000	0.0000	**0.0000**	0.0000	0.0000	0.0000	0.0000	0.0000	0.0000	0.0000	0.0000	0.0000
IT	0.0571	0.1111	0.0872	0.0238	0.0818	0.0222	**0.2952**	0.0800	0.0167	0.0778	0.097	0.0381	0.2000	0.0889	0.0800
NL	0.0857	0.3667	0.0846	0.0357	0.1318	0.0333	0.1400	**0.4444**	0.0000	0.1333	0.2000	0.0429	0.1667	0.2333	0.0600
PT	0.0000	0.0000	0.0000	0.0000	0.0000	0.0000	0.0000	0.0000	**0.0000**	0.0000	0.0000	0.0000	0.0000	0.0000	0.0000
SE	0.0952	0.0556	0.1282	0.0119	0.1061	0.0556	0.1111	0.1333	0.0417	**0.5000**	0.1212	0.119	0.0000	0.1111	0.1667
UK	0.1169	0.4848	0.2587	0.1039	0.2397	0.0606	0.2000	0.3455	0.0455	0.1667	**0.5818**	0.2078	0.3636	0.3333	0.1636
NO	0.0000	0.0476	0.0110	0.0204	0.0000	0.0000	0.0095	0.0000	0.0000	0.0714	0.039	**0.1905**	0.0000	0.0000	0.0000
CH	0.4286	0.5556	0.3846	0.0714	0.4394	0.0000	0.3778	0.4333	0.0000	0.2778	0.4242	0.1429	**0.6667**	0.3333	0.2000
DK	0.0952	0.2222	0.0513	0.0000	0.0152	0.0000	0.0889	0.1333	0.0000	0.0000	0.0303	0.1429	0.0000	**0.1667**	0.0667
FI	0.0286	0.1333	0.0615	0.0143	0.0455	0.0000	0.0267	0.0800	0.0000	0.1667	0.0000	0.0571	0.1333	0.1333	**0.3000**
AT	**0.2619**	0.1905	0.0659	0.0204	0.0455	0.0000	0.0762	0.0429	0.0000	0.0238	0.0000	0.0000	0.0000	0.0476	0.0286

BE	0.1429	**1.0000**	0.2564	0.0952	0.197	0.1111	0.3778	0.4000	0.0000	0.1667	0.2424	0.0000	0.3333	0.1111	0.1333
DE	0.3736	0.4103	**0.5128**	0.1429	0.2832	0.0769	0.2872	0.2538	0.0462	0.1795	0.3147	0.1099	0.5128	0.1026	0.2000
ES	0.0000	0.0238	0.0165	**0.0659**	0.0065	0.0000	0.0238	0.0000	0.0143	0.0000	0.0195	0.0000	0.0000	0.0000	0.0000
FR	0.0714	0.0909	0.1154	0.0519	**0.2814**	0.0000	0.0909	0.1409	0.0000	0.0455	0.1033	0.0325	0.1364	0.0152	0.0273
GR	0.0000	0.0000	0.0000	0.0000	0.0000	**0.1667**	0.0222	0.0000	0.0000	0.0000	0.0000	0.0000	0.0000	0.0000	0.0000
IT	0.1048	0.1333	0.1026	0.0429	0.0667	0.0667	**0.3857**	0.0600	0.0133	0.0444	0.0545	0.019	0.0889	0.0222	0.0000
NL	0.0857	0.3000	0.1000	0.0214	0.1318	0.0000	0.0933	**0.4667**	0.0000	0.0000	0.1000	0.0429	0.1333	0.1000	0.0800
PT	0.0000	0.0000	0.0000	0.0000	0.0000	0.0000	0.0000	0.0000	**0.0000**	0.0000	0.0000	0.0000	0.0000	0.0000	0.0000
SE	0.1667	0.0556	0.0897	0.0238	0.0530	0.0000	0.0556	0.0833	0.0333	**0.2333**	0.197	0.1667	0.0556	0.1111	0.2000
UK	0.1429	0.2727	0.1399	0.0779	0.1570	0.2424	0.1455	0.2091	0.0364	0.0152	**0.3455**	0.0649	0.2121	0.0606	0.1091
NO	0.0000	0.1905	0.022	0.0000	0.0000	0.0000	0.0190	0.0000	0.0000	0.0000	0.013	**0.0952**	0.0476	0.0476	0.0000
CH	0.3333	0.3333	0.2821	0.1667	0.2576	0.0000	0.3111	0.2000	0.0000	0.1111	0.1818	0.0952	**0.8333**	0.1111	0.0667
DK	0.0476	0.0000	0.0000	0.0238	0.0000	0.0000	0.0000	0.0667	0.0000	0.0556	0.0303	0.0476	0.0000	**0.1667**	0.0000
FI	0.0857	0.0000	0.1385	0.0143	0.1091	0.0000	0.0933	0.1000	0.0000	0.1000	0.0909	0.0571	0.1333	0.0667	**0.3500**

4

Differences in Learning and Inequality[1]

Ådne Cappelen

4.1. INTRODUCTION

It has become commonplace to say that *knowledge* is the most important resource in modern economies. Estimates of national wealth often end up with a share of total wealth due to human capital in the order of two-thirds or three quarters of total wealth. Knowledge is accumulated through *learning*. In the learning economy the core processes are related to producing, distributing, and using knowledge according to OECD (1996*a*). The knowledge-based economy means, '... economies which are directly based on the production, distribution and use of knowledge and information. This is reflected in the trend in OECD economies towards growth in high-technology investments, high-technology industries, more highly skilled labour and associated productivity gains' (OECD 1996*a*: 229).

This chapter addresses the relationship between knowledge and learning and the income distribution in the OECD countries since 1980. Why do we expect any relationship between learning and income distribution? One simple microeconomic reason could be that people with more skills or knowledge are better paid than the average worker. When there is skill upgrading in a country this may lead to a more unequal distribution. However, this will only be the case if there is increased demand for these skills. If not, the skill premium may fall and the income distribution may in fact become more equal. Another reason is the classical argument put forward by Kuznets (1955). An increase in economic growth is often caused by structural change in the economy with a new sector growing much more rapidly than the economy as a whole. The growth of the ICT sector is a recent example. As a consequence demand for certain skills increases rapidly and so will the wages paid for these skills by the new sector. Initially this increases dispersion of wages. However, as supply of these skills increases and a much larger share of the labour force is employed by the new sector often at the net expense of more traditional sectors, inequality may fall. Thus, initially growth goes hand-in-hand with more inequality while in a more mature stage growth and equality is taking place at the same time. This is one explanation behind the traditional Kuznets curve that depicts an inverted U-shaped curve between the income level and inequality.

As indicated by the quotation from OECD above, OECD countries (as well as many non-OECD countries) are characterized by more investments in high-tech goods and software than before. This has led many observers to talk about a 'new economy'. Furthermore, OECD countries have deregulated both product and labour markets during the last two decades or have been subject to structural reforms. In addition, many markets are subject to globalization that has affected factor prices. Thus, skills may become obsolete or at least the market remuneration of these skills may be influenced by more competition in both factor and product markets. So, although the growth of high-skilled labour is an important feature of most or all OECD countries, this growth has taken place alongside a number of other important changes in these countries. Thus, the combined effect on the income or wage distribution is far from easy to determine.

The relation between learning and knowledge formally resembles how real investments accumulate into real capital in national accounting. However, learning is socially, geographically, and institutionally embedded in more complicated ways than the 'physical' accumulation of capital. Knowledge may according to Lam and Lundvall (this volume) be seen as either individualized or collective and either as explicit or tacit. Thus, learning is not only an individual activity but also an activity that takes place at different institutional levels, within firms, bureaucracies, and even at the various societal levels. Knowledge formation as well as knowledge remuneration varies with institutions. In economies such as the US and UK (cf. Whitley, this volume, and Lam and Lundvall, this volume) the labour market is characterized by high mobility and focus on private ownership of knowledge. Thus, there are strong incentives to codify collective forms of knowledge in these countries given the limited long-term cooperation between firms. In economies where there is broad-based public education and training and more of a focus on public–private partnership as well as stronger firm linkages and strong unions, collective knowledge is more likely to take a tacit form. Finally, in economies where the state is more important and labour markets are dominated by large corporations and long-term employment contracts (Japan), collective knowledge is mobilized again mainly in firm-specific tacit forms. The way knowledge is institutionally embedded and how labour markets are organized in different economies, may thus affect earnings and income equality.

In the following section I present updated empirical evidence on changes in the distribution of income and wages in many OECD countries. Next, a simple model of the labour market is presented and used to organize the discussion of factors that may influence wage dispersion. Then I refer to a number of studies that have presented different interpretations of these empirical features before I conclude.

4.2. TRENDS IN EARNINGS INEQUALITY AMONG OECD COUNTRIES

There is by now a vast literature on the distribution of earnings as well as the wider question of income inequality among OECD countries (cf. Gottshcalk and Smeeding 1997; Atkinson 1999; Förster and Pearson 2002 to mention just a few). The literature on growth theory as well as empirical growth studies are also concerned with the relationship between growth and inequality (cf. Aghion, Caroly, and Garcia-Peñalosa 1999 for a survey). In this section I draw on these studies and others to present the highly diverse historical experience of various OECD countries when it comes to their distribution of income and more narrowly the earnings distribution.

When analysing distribution of income there are many important data issues that need to be taken into account before comparisons between countries or even within countries over time can be made with some reliability. Let me briefly address some of these issues. In Förster and Pearson (2002) income is measured as total disposable income mainly by using income statistics for tax purposes at the household level and they adjust for household size by using equivalent scales. This is useful for some purposes but I argue not necessarily for the purpose of studying the relationship between learning and inequality. Economic and social changes will influence how households are formed and dissolved but these changes vary much between countries and over time and may have little to do with learning, earnings, and productivity. The number of children will also affect this measure of distribution. Inequality may increase or decrease due to changes in the tax system (say taxation of capital income) or transfers that are not linked to learning. Inequality may be affected by working hours by adult household members that have to do with factors unrelated to how learning and knowledge is remunerated.

Similarly, if one chooses to study earnings inequality a number of data issues are worth considering before making any comparison between countries. Are we to use annual or weekly earnings that are affected by working time that may change between countries and over time? If we use annual earnings, should we focus only on full-time workers in order to avoid too large an influence of differences in working hours and how do we make this adjustment consistent between countries? Would it be best to focus on hourly wage rates since these are what workers face as parameters when they decide how much labour to supply? Perhaps are there restrictions or barriers to 'pure' labour supply decisions that we should take into account? I shall not try to answer these questions here, but they are forwarded simply to make us aware of some difficult data issues that need to be dealt with in order to make comparisons between countries and over time as I do in this chapter.

An alternative to a pure statistical exercise is instead to estimate individual wage equations (Mincer equations) that explicitly try to measure how education, work experience, and other factors closely linked to knowledge are rewarded in the economy. If say the educational premium (How much does the wage rate increase if you spend one more year in formal education?) increases over time, are we then to conclude that knowledge is rewarded more generously than before? What if there is a simultaneous decline in the experience reward (How much more are you paid if you work another year?) so that on the job training or 'learning by doing' is less rewarded?

There is no agreed upon method or best practice available when studying income distribution. The purpose of each study and sometimes simply data availability will to a large extent determine the method that is most relevant. I begin discussing changes in the distribution of income in general and not earnings specifically. The reason for this is that the distribution of disposable income is perhaps more relevant for discussions of social cohesion than focusing solely on the earnings distribution which more easily can be related to differences in skills and learning.

4.2.1. Household Distribution of Disposable Income

A number of studies have discussed changes in the distribution of income within OECD countries over time as well as between these countries at any time. There are various measures available as mentioned earlier, but I focus on the Gini coefficient as supplied by the Luxembourg Income Study (LIS) in February 2004. The advantage of using these figures is that they have been compiled and adjusted in order to make them more suitable for comparisons between countries and over time. I focus on the period from around 1980 and as far as recent figures go. It is generally accepted that during the 1970s there were tendencies in most countries for income inequality to decline or at least be stable. Even in a country like the US where inequality has increased in recent decades, inequality decreased or was stable during the 1970s. This seems to have changed in recent decades and many observers relate this change to those factors that the OECD suggests characterize the learning economy.

The main trends are shown in Figure 4.1a, 4.1b, and 4.1c. The LIS figures are for various years and are simply interpolated. As is evident from the figures there are no common trends in inequality between countries over time. Many countries have a rather stable income distribution while in some countries there is increasing inequality. We do not observe a downward trend in inequality for any country.

Let me comment briefly the development for each country. In Australia there is a steady increase in inequality. Percentile ratios (also supplied by LIS but not reported here) show that it is mainly the bottom part of the distribution that has become more unequal. In Canada the distribution of income is fairly stable but with more inequality during the second half of the 1990s. As for Australia, it is the bottom end of the distribution that has changed. In the US increased inequality took place in the first half of the 1980s and during the first half of the 1990s with a large increase at the bottom end of the distribution in the early 1980s but not thereafter. In the UK increased inequality took place during the whole of the 1980s but not much change thereafter. There was a large increase in inequality at the bottom end of the distribution. For Austria, Belgium, Denmark, France, Germany, Ireland, the Netherlands, and Norway the distribution of income has been

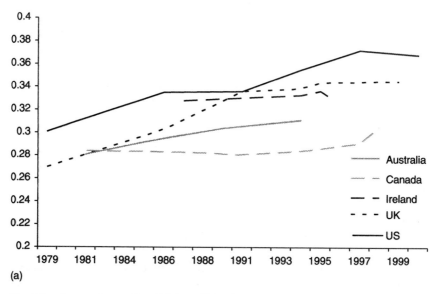

(a)

Fig. 4.1a. Income inequality (Gini coefficient)

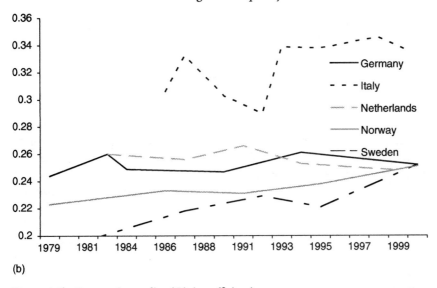

(b)

Figure 4.1b. Income inequality (Gini coefficient)

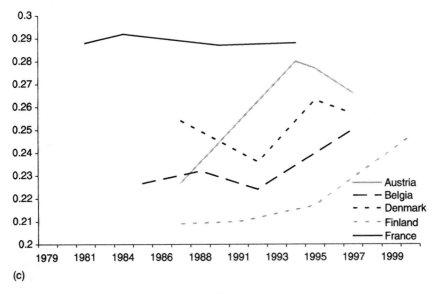

(c)

Figure 4.1c. Income inequality (Gini coefficient)

quite stable. In Finland we observe a fairly stable income distribution but some sign of increased inequality recently. Finally, in Sweden there has been an increase in inequality in particular during the latter half of the 1990s.

To sum up, there are quite diverse country experiences when it comes to changes in the distribution of income. Clearly some Anglo-Saxon countries have experienced some marked increases in inequality, while continental Europe has not, or at least the increase in inequality began much later. Anglo-Saxon countries also have a more unequal income distribution than most other European countries. These 'facts' are well known to students of income distribution and are reported by Gottschalk and Smeeding (1997). In the OECD study by Föster and Pearson (2002) also using comparable data from different countries, they conclude that the tendency for a more polarized distribution within each country started in the Anglo-Saxon countries in 1980s and was followed by a similar tendency in many continental European countries in the 1990s.

The empirical studies referred to above also show that market incomes have become more unequally distributed. In spite of the fact that government transfers and taxation contribute more towards equality than before (again as a general trend not a feature of all OECD countries) the change in the distribution of market incomes outweighs this phenomenon. The main contributor to this change is more unequal distribution of earnings across households (cf. Förster and Pearson 2002: 22). They show that one important reason for this is what they call employment polarization; at the household level, total number of hours worked is more unequally distributed than before. There are more households where both adults work full time and fewer where only one adult works and there are also more households where both adults are workless. The high level of unemployment during the 1980s and 1990s has clearly contributed to this polarization. However, we cannot infer that a more unequal distribution of household earnings implies a more unequal remuneration of skills. Let us therefore look at the distribution of wage rates in order better to assess the relationship between learning, wages, and distribution.

4.2.2. The Distribution of Wages

OECD (1996b) presents data on the distribution of earnings for a large number of OECD countries from around 1980 and until the early or mid-1990s. The data are presented as the ratio of the earnings level of the upper ninth decile (D9) to the median and the ratio between the median to the lower level of the first decile (D1). The data are for full time workers and presented for male and female workers separately. In order to simplify, I concentrate on the total D9/D1 ratio in this chapter. The OECD figures show a strong trend toward greater inequality of wages in the UK and US but not in other countries. The increase in earnings dispersion in these two countries applies to both sexes as well as to the upper and lower parts of the distribution so it is pervasive.

The increase in wage inequality in the US has been the subject of a number of studies reviewed by Gottschalk and Smeeding (1997) and others. In order to narrow down possible sources of increased inequality many studies have focused on male earnings for full-time workers. The standard findings in this literature are that there was a large increase in returns to education in the US during the 1980s as well as an increase in returns to experience. Finally, there was also an increase in wage inequality within specific groups even after adjusting for education and experience. All these findings seem to indicate that the remuneration of formal learning and on the job training as well as unidentified personal characteristics have increased and thus contributed to increased dispersion of wages.

According to Gottschalk and Smeeding (1997) only the UK experienced an increase in wage inequality similar to that of the US among OECD countries. Both Canada and Australia showed a clear tendency towards higher wage inequality but less than in the US and UK, while France, Japan, the Netherlands, Sweden, and Finland formed a group of countries with quite small increases in inequality and also starting a bit later than in the other countries. Only Germany and Italy showed no increase in inequality according to this summary of many studies of wage inequality. Among these countries only Sweden and the UK showed a clear tendency for the wage distribution to become more unequal due to returns to education. Returns to experience produced more inequality in Australia, Canada, France, the Netherlands, and the UK. Finally within group inequality increased in Australia, Canada, Sweden, and the UK.

All in all there seems to be a consensus in the literature based on evidence from the 1980s and early 1990s that wage inequality increased substantially in Anglo-Saxon countries based on increased wage premiums for education and experience as well as within group inequality. For many other OECD countries tendencies were not so clear. But no country shows systematic signs of less wage inequality, as was the case in several countries during the 1970s. In this respect the evidence on wage inequality is quite similar to that on income inequality based on household disposable income as referred to earlier. I discuss the possible causes of the increase in wage inequality later.

It is more difficult to establish what has happened to recent developments in wage dispersion because there is no comprehensive single database that is up to date on this issue. What I have done is to update the figures in Table 3.1. of OECD (1996*b*) as far as other sources are available mainly by linking or calibrating more recent data to the OECD data in order to avoid any breaks. The main source of information is an updated version of the OECD earnings database that has data until 2001 for some countries. Additional sources are

Atkinson (1999), Barrett, Fitzgerald, and Nolan (2000), Phelps (2000). As far as these data go, they indicate that the qualitative features found by Gottschalk and Smeeding (1997) are somewhat modified.

According to recent data (the ratio between the upper earnings limit of the ninth and first decile) shown on Figure 4.2a there is still some increase in wage dispersion going on in the US, but the increase in the dispersion during the 1990s is much less than during the 1980s. For the UK there is hardly any increase in wage inequality at all during the 1990s. While the wage dispersion in Australia did not change much until the mid-1990s, there is an increase in inequality during the latter half of this decade. Wage dispersion is clearly falling in Japan and Canada during the 1990s after having increased some-what during the 1980s. In South Korea the large decrease in wage inequality during the latter half of the 1980s seems to have come to a halt in the 1990s. So the two East-Asian countries have, if anything, enjoyed stable or even a more equal distribution of wages since the early 1980s. The experience of the English-speaking countries is more varied and it seems difficult to claim they follow similar patterns of development. The US development is in fact an outlier both in terms of the level of inequality and in its trend.

Moving to continental Europe (cf. Figure 4.2b), wage dispersion in France is quite stable or has been slightly reduced during the latter half of the 1990s. Also in Germany the wage distribution is quite stable if we do not regard the last observation as indicating a change in development. The same goes for Austria while the Italian development is hard to interpret with a large decrease in wage inequality during the 1980s and a similar but more rapid increase in the early 1990s. The wage dispersion in the Netherlands was quite stable from the mid-1980s to mid-1990s (cf. Figure 4.2c), but there is a jump from 1994 to 1995 that may be due to data problems (linking various sources) but could otherwise be interpreted to indicate an increase in wage dispersion during the 1990s.

Developments in some Nordic countries are also shown in Figure 4.2c. Finland is an interesting case from the perspective of the 'new economy' because the country is relatively intensive in terms of the development and production of ICT goods. Here, if anything, wage inequality has fallen during the 1990s; a decade that most observers regard as the heydays of globalization and ICT-driven technological change. Norway has hardly experienced any change in wage dispersion during the last two decades. In Sweden, on the other hand, there has clearly been a moderate increase in inequality for some time. By international standards dispersion is still very low in all Nordic countries (there are no data for Denmark for the 1990s but wage dispersion during the 1980s was similar to that of Sweden and Norway).

For the US, the UK, and Sweden inequality is on the increase both at the top and lower end of the distribution. In Australia there has been a

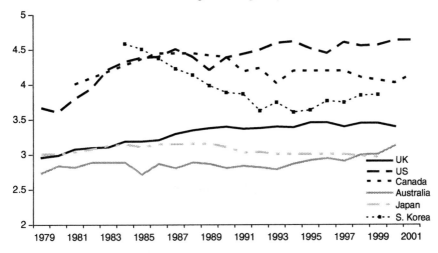

Figure 4.2a. Earnings inequality (the ratio D9/D1)

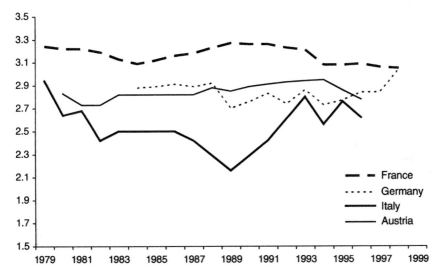

Figure 4.2b. Earnings inequality (the ratio D9/D1)

compression of the wage distribution in the low-income end but an increase at the top. This tendency of less inequality at the lower end of the distribution but more inequality at the upper end is apparent in many countries such as Finland, Germany, and Japan. For France and Austria the decline in dispersion

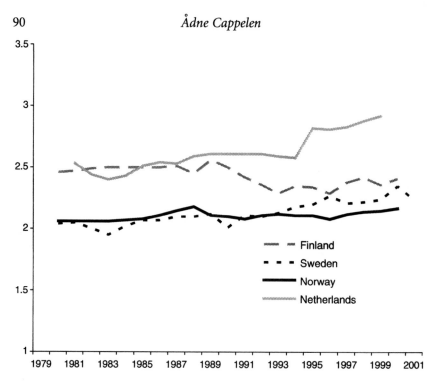

Figure 4.2c. Earnings inequality (the ratio D9/D1)

is mainly due to lower inequality at the lower end of the earnings distribution. Using the OECD earnings database, a more detailed investigation of different parts of the earnings distribution suggests that the experience of various countries is quite varied and no consistent pattern emerges. Thus, the picture that emerges from Figures 4.2a–c of no common trend in the earnings distribution is even more pronounced when looking at the distribution in more detail. I now turn to the question of how to interpret this diverse picture.

4.3. THE SKILL PREMIUM IN A MODEL WITH IMPERFECT LABOUR MARKETS

In this section, I present a simple and partial model of the labour market in order to structure my discussion of factors that may explain the changes in wage dispersion presented above.

Assume that demand for skilled labour (N_s) relative to unskilled labour (N_{us}) depends negatively on relative wages for these two groups (W_s/W_{us}) and positively on technical change represented by a shift variable (t)

$$\frac{N_s}{N_{us}} = f\left(\frac{W_s}{W_{us}}, t\right). \tag{4.1}$$

By definition employment equals labour supply (S) minus unemployment (U), hence relative employment may be written as

$$\frac{N_s}{N_{us}} = \frac{1 - u_s}{1 - u_{us}} \frac{S_s}{S_{us}}, \tag{4.2}$$

where the us are unemployment rates. Combining equations (4.1) and (4.2) and defining s as the share of skilled labour in the total labour force, we have:

$$\frac{1 - u_s}{1 - u_{us}} = (s^{-1} - 1)f\left(\frac{W_s}{W_{us}}, t\right). \tag{4.3}$$

According to equation (4.3) a positive shift in t due to technical change that results in more demand for skilled workers at the expense of unskilled (so-called skill-biased technical change or SBTC hereafter), the skill premium will have to increase if relative unemployment is to be constant unless there is an increase in the share of skilled persons in the labour force denoted by s in (4.3). Note that it is relative unemployment rates and not their absolute difference in per cent that matters for this result according to this model.

Assume further that wage formation can be described by wage curves (cf. Layard, Nickell, and Jackman 1991 for each skill category)

$$W_s = PQg_s(u_s, u), \, g'_{s1}, g'_{s2} < 0, \tag{4.4}$$

$$W_{us} = PQg_{us}(u_{us}, u), \, g'_{us1}, g'_{us2} < 0, \tag{4.5}$$

where u_s and u_{us} are the skill-specific unemployment rates and where u is the average unemployment rate, P is producer price, and Q is average labour productivity by sector. Thus, the wage equations state that in the long run the labour share of value added depends negatively on both skill-specific and average unemployment. The wage curve representation encompasses several theories on wage setting.[2] Solving for relative wage rates, and assuming that the effects of the average unemployment rate are the same for both skill groups (cf. Bjørnstad et al. 2002) yields:

$$\frac{W_s}{W_{us}} = g\left(\frac{u_s}{u_{us}}\right), \ g' < 0. \tag{4.6}$$

According to (4.6) there is a negative relationship between relative wages and relative unemployment rates for skill groups. If wages are affected by education-specific unemployment rates, the skill premium adjusts to skill mismatch. However, if there is no such effect, skill mismatch is likely to prevail, at least until supply adjusts accordingly. The exact degree of labour market flexibility depends on the parameters, the substitution possibilities, and the price elasticities. Notice also that demand shifts, such as SBTC, affect wage inequality only through skill mismatch in the long run in this model. This assumption is plausible when the labour force is endogenous. Layard, Nickell, and Jackman (1991, ch. 6) show that only supply-side factors, such as costs of attaining education, affect relative wages and unemployment. In steady state, the skill premium is equal to the cost of attaining that skill.

Figure 4.3 illustrates the determination of relative wages and relative unemployment according to equations (4.3) and (4.6). SBTC will shift the demand curve for labour implying an upward shift in the curve marked equation (4.3) to a higher skill premium and lower unemployment for skilled persons. A relative increase in the share of skilled persons in the labour force (increase in *s* in equation (4.3)) results in a downward shift in (4.3) and leads to lower skill premium and higher relative unemployment for skilled persons. We can also interpret the shift parameter as indicating what happens if there is

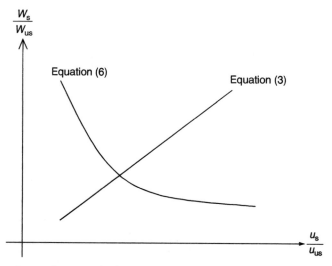

Figure 4.3. Determination of relative wages and unemployment rates

a change in the structure of demand by skills due to changes in industry structure. If one industry uses relatively more unskilled labour and experiences a negative shock of some kind, the relative demand for unskilled will decline even for a given level of relative wages. Through market forces this will change both relative wages and unemployment rates. According to this model, a more skilled labour force will reduce the wage premium for the skilled. Thus, learning as such is negatively related to wage inequality. Only when the change in demand for skills due to say technological change is increasing faster than the upgrading of the labour force, will relative wages for skilled workers increase.

According to equations (4.3) and (4.6), relative unemployment rates for skilled and unskilled as well as relative wage rates are both determined by the skill composition of the labour force (s) and the shift parameter for technological change (t). It is fairly straightforward to show that this shift parameter also can be interpreted to capture changes in international trade and as such pickup changes in relative product prices due to say increased competition from low income countries. In this case, we may think of the unskilled employed mainly in one sector and the skilled in another. The standard interpretation is, on the other hand, that in the macrosector both types of labour are employed and there is substitution between them. I stick to the technological change interpretation as this is by and large considered to be the most relevant explanation for wage dispersion. This is due to the fact that changes in the skill composition seem to have taken place in nearly all sectors of the economy so it can be interpreted as a common shock to all sectors and not as a sector-specific shock.

If we focus on the technological change explanation as the most relevant one for explaining why wage dispersion has increased in some but not all countries (cf. Figures 4.2a–c), how can the model presented be helpful? First of all, I argue that it is reasonable to regard SBTC as a common shock to all countries studied here. The degree of the shock may vary somewhat between countries but it is a common shock to most sectors in all countries. According to the model presented earlier, only changes in the skill structure of the population may offset the effects of SBTC. Consequently, in those countries where a parallel upgrading of skills has taken place alongside changes in technology we should expect to see less inequality. So what do we know about changes in the skill structure in the countries included in the figures earlier?

In Table 4.1, I show the share of the population between 25 and 64 years that has attained the highest type of education (tertiary) for some of the countries discussed earlier. For other countries included in Figure 4.2a–c, no comparable figures were found for a sufficiently long period so they are not included here. The figures in the table show very large differences in educational levels

Table 4.1 Share of population in per cent that has attained tertiary (type A) education

Country	1981	1989	1994	1998	2001
Australia	missing	10	14	17	19
Canada	12	15	17	18	20
UK	8[1]	9	12	16	18
US	22	24	25	27	28
Austria	missing	6	5	6	7
France	7	7	9	11	12
Italy	missing	6	8	9	10
Finland	8[2]	10	11	13	15
Norway	7	11	17	24[3]	28
Sweden	11	13	13	13	17

Notes: [1]1984. [2] 1982. [3]1997.
Sources: OECD (1997, 2000, 2003).

by country with the US ranking highest but with Norway catching up during the 1990s. Also Canada has a high level and Australia and the UK are rapidly increasing their levels of education during the 1990s too. Many EU countries have fairly low levels of their population between 25–64 years with tertiary education according to the OECD. Both Germany and Belgium (not included in the Table because of lack of consistent data) have relatively low levels in 2001, while the Netherlands are similar to Canada.

According to the model presented earlier, it is the *change* in the education level that is relevant in 'explaining' *changes* in the wage distribution. The levels of education will be reflected in the industry structure of countries and are as such part of the comparative advantage created by countries, although it may of course also affect the levels of wage dispersion. Let us, therefore, relate changes in education levels to what has happened to changes in wage dispersion taking as our basic starting point SBTC in all countries. In Australia there has been a large increase in the share of the population with higher education thus possibly counteracting SBTC. Australia has no large change in wage dispersion. Also Canada has increased its educational level although not by as much as Australia. It is hard to relate changes in wage dispersion in Canada with the upgrading of skill according to Table 4.1. For the UK, the increase in education was moderate during the 1980s and wage dispersion increased while there was less increase in dispersion during the 1990s when educational levels increased more rapidly which fits well with our partial model presented earlier. For the US, there was also less increase in the share of the population with the highest education during the 1980s than during the 1990s, again in line with how the model would predict a larger increase in dispersion in the 1980s than later given a constant rate of SBTC. For Austria there is little change in dispersion as well as in education that is not in line with what you would expect in light of SBTC. For France the increase in the educational level is moderate and the decline in dispersion is accordingly unexplained. The increase in dispersion in Italy during the 1990s may partly be explained by the lack of increase in educational level. In Finland there has been a large increase in the level of education although from a fairly low level in line with slightly falling wage dispersion. For Norway there has been a dramatic increase in educational levels and no increase in dispersion. One would nearly have expected a decline in dispersion given this change in educational levels. For Sweden the increase in dispersion could be explained by a fairly modest increase in higher education. Thus, taking all countries together, the figures in Table 4.1 seem to indicate some relevance of the model presented in which countries with substantial upgrading of their educational level have experienced less increase in wage dispersion and even a decline. But there are deviations from this story so there is obviously a need for refining our argument. I turn to this in a moment.

It has been argued by Krugmann (1994) and others that in many European countries the unskilled have been made unemployed by rigid wage bargaining institutions due to SBTC, while in the US this shock has been absorbed by changes in relative factor prices (or wages). Figure 4.4 shows that there is no such simple relationship present in aggregate data for the countries I study. In fact there is hardly any correlation between wage dispersion and relative unemployment rates for skilled and unskilled. On the vertical axes I show the wage dispersion (D9/D1) in the last year available according to Figures 4.2a–c and the ratio u_s/u_{us} in 2001 according to OECD (2003). Even if we change the figure by using the difference and not the ratio of unemployment rates, the no correlation story is valid. This is also the case if we use total unemployment; there is simply no (partial) correlation between dispersion and unemployment between countries.

So far I have not referred to changes in institutional factors that may influence the bargaining position of the parties involved in wage negotiations. These variables are in fact suppressed in the wage equations (4.4) and (4.5) and affect the location of equation (4.6) in Figure 4.3 and thus relative wages. According to the literature on wage determination and wage inequality (cf. Blau and Kahn 1996; Wallerstein 1999; and Nunziata 2001) institutional variables that affect the outcome of bargaining are trade union bargaining power and the degree of coordination in wage bargaining. Trade union bargaining power is related to:

- the proportion of employees covered by collective agreements and union membership;

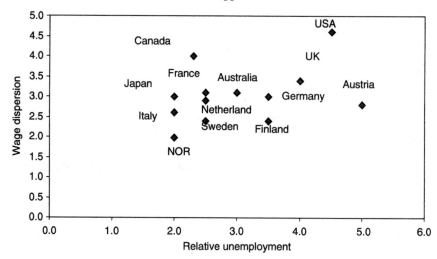

Figure 4.4. Wage dispersion and relative unemployment rates

- labour market regulation and employment protection;
- unemployment benefits or the benefit replacement rate (BRR) that affects 'outside options'; and
- the minimum wage that can act as a floor to wage bargaining.

The degree of coordination in wage bargaining is related to a number of institutional factors among which the degree of centralization of wage bargaining is found to be of great significance. Here one distinction is between systems where wages are largely negotiated at the plant level (the US, Canada, and the UK) while in many European countries wages are often negotiated at the industry level while the Nordic countries and the Netherlands (since the 1982 Wassenaar Agreement) have traditionally had significant additional national coordination and periodically direct governmental interference at the macro level, (cf. Wallerstein 1999). Interestingly EU countries with a relatively high degree of coordination in wage bargaining also belong to the group of countries with a relatively high share of so-called learning organization (cf. the chapter by E. Lorenz and A. Valeyre in this volume). Several estimates of wage bargaining coordination exist in the literature, and it is not obvious how one best should measure an institutional factor. I have chosen a measure of coordination developed by Wallerstein (1999) that applies to most countries in my sample. If we relate this qualitative variable to wage dispersion in the same way as in Figure 4.4, we get a picture of a possible link between coordination and dispersion as in Figure 4.5. From this

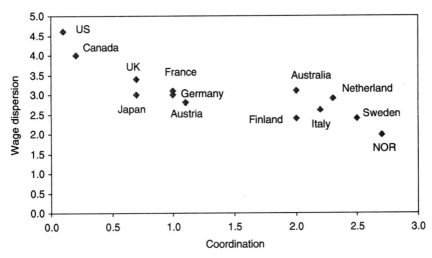

Figure 4.5. Wage dispersion and bargaining coordination

figure we clearly see a negative relation between wage dispersion and the degree of coordination in wage bargaining. The US and Canada have hardly any coordination in wage bargaining and large wage dispersion while in the Scandinavian countries on the other hand there is much more coordination and less dispersion.

Let me now try to explain *changes* in dispersion using changes in those institutional factors affecting wage bargaining that I listed above and data supplied in Nunziata (2001). For the US, there has been little change in coordination. However, the unemployment BRR declined somewhat during the 1980s (but not the 1990s) and union density (UD) declined during the 1980s but stabilized later. Also the minimum wage declined markedly during the 1980s, a fact we return to in the next section. Thus, there are some changes in institutions that may explain the increase in dispersion during the 1980s for the US. Noticeably, these factors changed much less during the 1990s when also dispersion was more stable. A similar story can be told for the UK where also wage coordination measured by the proportion of employees covered by collective agreements declined during the 1980s. Thus, here there are strong reasons to believe that institutional changes have lead to increased dispersion in the UK. For Australia, the degree of coordination was reduced during the first half of the 1990s, which fits well with the moderate increase in dispersion that we observe in Figure 4.2a from 1993 and onwards. For Canada, there are few changes in institutions except for the minimum wage that relative to average earnings has developed inversely to dispersion; falling markedly from the late 1970s until 1986 (cf. OECD 1997), and increasing thereafter very much the opposite direction of earnings inequality according to Figure 4.2a. For Japan, there is hardly any change in the institutional factors and inequality.

For France, the institutional variables show a diverse picture. The BRR has declined along with UD but coordination has increased somewhat. From Figure 4.2b we see that dispersion has not changed much. For Germany, BRR declined recently along with UD. This should lead to more inequality and that is what we observe during the second half of the 1990s, but changes are small. For Austria, there are in general small changes. For Italy, the institutional indicators point in different directions. According to Wallerstein (1999) coordination has been reduced recently and this may explain the large increase in dispersion during the early 1990s.

In Finland, both BRR and UD have increased and this may explain the slight reduction in dispersion according to Figure 4.2c. For Norway, there is little change in institutional factors and hardly any change in dispersion. In Sweden wage coordination has been reduced and this might explain the increase in dispersion. UD has on the other hand increased while BRR shows an inverted U-shape. For the Netherlands, coordination has been stable and BRR has increased somewhat, but here there is a strong decline in the minimum wage that may explain the upward trend in inequality.

My summary of the country evidence is that changes in institutional variables seem to fit well with the observed changes in wage dispersion across countries. Thus it is a more likely candidate for explaining the diverse experience of the OECD countries when it comes to changes in wage dispersion than a common technological shock like SBTC. In addition, changes in educational attainment help explain why some countries have been more successful in mitigating the effect of SBTC on wage dispersion.

4.4. A CLOSER LOOK AT SOME COUNTRY STUDIES

Let me now refer to some recently published country studies that can add to our knowledge on wage dispersion and skills. Let me start with a recent study of the US, where the debate on wage dispersion and the causes for its increase over time have been vivid for many years. Card and DiNardo (2003) argue against the current dominating view that SBTC is the most important factor that can explain the rising wage inequality in the US (and elsewhere). Using several sources of information and arguing for the use of hourly wage rates for all workers and not annual earnings for full-time male workers, Card and

DiNardo conclude that in the US it was only during the 1980s that wage dispersion increased and in particular in the early part of the 1980s. Looking at men and women separately, there is some tendency for wage dispersion to increase for women. Note that these data are not the same as those in the OECD earnings database which shows a moderate increase in dispersion also during the 1990s (cf. Figure 4.2a). So it matters which wage measure is used. This should of course make us more careful when concluding because it is far from obvious which to choose.

Card and DiNardo (2003) also show that the education premium as measured by the college/high school wage ratio, has been quite stable during the 1990s. In particular, for men there is hardly any change in the ratio while there was a large increase (more than 10 percentage points) during the 1980s and again mostly during the early part of the decade. For women there was an increase during the 1980s similar to that for men, but also an increase in the ratio during the 1990s, although only half of the absolute increase of the 1980s. The reason for the large increase in the education ratio for both men and women was that the younger cohort of college-educated persons increased their relative wages compared to others. During the 1990s there had been more stability in the dispersion also controlling for age. So the education premium increased much during the 1980s in particular for younger people and this indicates that formal skills or knowledge were relatively better remunerated than before. However, this feature did not continue at least not at the same pace during the 1990s. Finally, looking at the residual in Mincer-type wage equations (i.e. after taking into account education, age (or experience), gender, and race), the same pattern of changes in wage dispersion occurs—an increase in dispersion during the 1980s and little change thereafter.

Having established these empirical features of the wage dispersion in the US (in addition to a number of other facts that we shall not consider in detail here), Card and DiNardo (2003) argue quite convincingly that in order to explain the increase in dispersion in the 1980s but stability in the 1990s, it is in particular relevant to look at which of the explanatory factors survive when taking the features of both decades into account. They argue that SBTC is much less convincing as the main explanatory factor in the US because productivity change due to increased production and use of computers cannot have been slower during the 1990s than during the 1980s. In fact when looking at aggregate productivity figures for the US economy, there is no increase in productivity growth in the 1980s compared to the 1970s. However, such an increase in productivity growth took place during the 1990s but then no increase in wage dispersion occurred. Thus the timing of SBTC and aggregate productivity growth does not match and neither does the timing of SBTC and changes in wage dispersion. What is then a reasonable explanation? According to Card and DiNardo (2003) reduced minimum wages is the 'culprit' in particular because the timing fits well. Real minimum wages fell during most the 1980s and quite dramatically from 1979 to 1984 (by 33 per cent) but the fall continued during the whole decade while it changed little during the 1990s. A simple regression of the D9/D1 wage gap on the log of real minimum wages explains most of the changes in this dispersion from 1973 to 2000 according to the authors. There are other studies concluding similarly, in particular DiNardo, Blau and Kahn (1996), Fortin, and Lemieux (1996), Lee (1999), and recently by Teulings (2003).

So while much of the early literature on what explained the increasing wage dispersion had concluded that this was mainly due to SBTC, more recent evidence seems to question this conclusion. Instead a larger role for institutional factors and changes in these factors may be called for. The main problem with the hypothesis that large reductions in the minimum wage level caused the increased dispersion in the US is that although it may well explain increasing wage dispersion at the bottom end of the wage distribution, it is unclear why falling minimum wages affects the upper tail of the distribution (i.e. the 90/50 gap).

A recent study for the UK by Gosling (2003) is based on data much in line with those in Figure 4.2a. The growth in high incomes (the 90th percentile) has been larger than the growth in low incomes (the 10th percentile) but with an interesting difference between men and women. Income growth for low-income (unskilled) women has been much larger than for men. Also when controlling for education, Gosling finds that the educational premium for men has been increasing but not for women; in fact, it seems like the male education premium is converging towards the female premium. This can explain why wage inequality among men has been increasing as more men have acquired more skills through more human capital or education while this has not been the case for women in the UK. However, when comparing with the US, a different picture emerges, as there it is among the well-educated women that wages have been increasing most. This leads Gosling to conclude that there must be institutional differences in the labour market between the two countries that explain the different outcomes.

Let us now move to Norway, a Nordic country where there is generally a more equal distribution of incomes as well as earnings. A recent study by Hægeland and Kirkebøen (2004) shows that very moderate changes in the wage dispersion have taken place in Norway since 1980. There was compression of the wage structure during the 1970s but really no clear trend during the 1980s. However, during the 1990s and in particular during the boom in the latter half of the decade, inequality increased somewhat. This increase took place only at the upper half of the distribution, that is full-time workers in top deciles have become relatively richer than before. During the first (and second) half of the 1980s the compression of the wage structure continued in the lower part of the distribution while inequality increased in the upper part. These changes can be decomposed into changes in skill premiums (due to education and experience), changes in the distribution of these characteristics, and unobserved characteristics and premiums. An interesting result in the study by Hægeland and Kirkebøen (2004) in our context is that they find no systematic change in skill premiums from 1980–2000 that can explain why there has been a moderate increase in wage inequality in Norway. There is more systematic evidence indicating that given existing skill premiums, education and experience have changed in order to produce a moderate increase in inequality. In addition, unobserved skills and prices have contributed to more inequality. This result is also found in earlier studies for the US and Sweden. This increased within group inequality (i.e. after adjusting for sex, education, experience, sector, and region) may indicate that wage determination has become more market oriented and less centralized or influenced by unions than before. An obvious reason for this—at least in the private sector—is that sectors of the Norwegian economy where unions traditionally have not been very strong have been expanding more than sectors that are traditionally union strongholds. Thus, the increase in wage inequality in Norway over the last twenty years is not related to increased premiums for skills or by learning.

To sum up these three country studies they all show fairly stable educational wage premiums with the premium for UK men as the obvious outlier. Thus at least recent evidence point to the possibility that increased formal learning can take place without increased wage inequality. One reason may of course be that the supply of more educated people has increased sufficiently to match the increase in demand. In my view the argument in Card and DiNardo (2003) that technological change during the 1990s cannot have been less than during the early 1980s is very convincing. For the US labour productivity increased more during the 1990s than during the 1980s. This was even more so in Norway, while the opposite seems to be the case in the UK. In fact, it is quite difficult to find any stable or systematic relationship between economic growth and inequality (cf. Banerjee and Duflo 2003 for a recent study). Comparing the change in earnings distribution according to Figure 4.2a–c and the change in labour productivity growth according to Table 1.A1.1 in OECD (2002) between the 1980s and 1990s simply leaves you confused. By further comparing these changes using the data for 1970s when income inequality in general was on the decline in the OECD area and productivity growth generally higher than during the 1980s, simply adds to this confusion.

4.5. SUMMARY AND DISCUSSION

From the mid-1990s (labour) productivity growth in the US increased markedly compared to previous decades when productivity growth was slow. In the Euro area the picture is quite the opposite with dismal growth more recently but rapid growth during the 1980s and early 1990s. Much of the increase in US growth is due to the production and use of ICT. The rapid growth of the ICT sector in the US is partly due to new ways of measuring output of industries producing new capital goods of higher quality.[3] Freeman (2004) suggests that microelectronics is the key factor behind a new long wave in the world economy, cf. while others are sceptical as to the effect that the ICT revolution has on the overall economy (Gordon 2000). Even if there is no general agreement on the size of the impact of ICT on the economy, there is hardly any disagreement that it has changed and is changing production at the firm level as well as household consumption. It makes earlier knowledge obsolete and creates the need for acquiring new knowledge and learning. The change in the structure of the economy with uneven growth in productivity between sectors also affects labour markets and challenges previous institutions and systems of wage bargaining (Acemoglu et al. 2001). Thus, there are reasons to believe that the economic effects of the ICT revolution may potentially be far-reaching and widespread including effects on the distribution of earnings.

The main empirical findings of this chapter are the following:

- There are no systematic changes in income distribution or wage dispersion among OECD countries during the last two decades. Some countries have experienced increasing inequality while this is not the case for many others, in particular when it comes to earnings inequality. There is a tendency for inequality to increase less during the 1990s than during 1980s. In some countries there is even falling wage inequality more recently.
- The evidence on inequality suggests that technological change and SBTC in particular is only one of many factors contributing to more inequality. Institutional changes and differences may be more important in studying the relation between inequality and skills than technological change. It is difficult to find any systematic link between changes in inequality and productivity growth among OECD countries.

- There is no correlation between wage inequality and unemployment differences across countries. The claim that high rates of unemployment of the unskilled is caused by rigid relative wages needs to be modified to say the least. There is strong evidence, both within and between countries, that those institutional factors that influence wage bargaining—both at the national and at firm level—also have effects on wage inequality.
- Wage dispersion has increased less or is even absent in countries where an increasing proportion of the population has attained tertiary education. In many EU countries the level of education is relatively low compared to most OECD countries. Both in order to promote growth and avoid increasing inequalities, these countries should focus more on stimulating education. In this sense more learning is good both for growth, equality and social cohesion.

If we relate these observations on earnings inequality to institutional differences between countries we may perhaps shed new light on our findings. In most Anglo-Saxon countries (US, UK, Australia, but not Canada) earnings inequality has increased. This phenomenon has been studied extensively and the standard view is that this change in distribution is mainly due to specific changes in technology. But in addition labour markets have been deregulated in these countries and are also characterized by high mobility and the focus is on private ownership of knowledge. Expenditures on higher education are high and increasing and so is productivity. The results of this productivity growth have been individually appropriated and inequality has increased.

In some Asian countries (Japan and South Korea) there has not been much increase in wage dispersion (rather the opposite). Labour markets in these countries are much influenced by large corporations and knowledge is more collective in nature. Thus productivity improvements are distributed to many and inequality has not increased.

In many continental EU countries labour markets have not been much deregulated although some structural reforms have been carried out. In these countries there is more focus on private–public partnership and strong firm linkages and strong unions where tacit knowledge is harder to remunerate individually. Thus there is less increase in inequality in spite of a rapid growth in labour productivity during the 1980s and first half of the 1990s. According to the chapter by Lorenz and Valeyre in this volume, many of these countries also have a high share of learning organizations.

Finally, in most Nordic countries labour markets are still quite regulated and bargaining coordinated (but with some deregulation in Sweden) and there is less change in inequality (again with Sweden as the exception) in spite of high productivity growth.

So, even if countries should face similar productivity shocks, their institutions vary both at the firm level as well as at the industry and macro-levels. These institutional differences are probably important for explaining why the changes in productivity have been distributed so differently between countries during the last decades with large increases in inequality as a result in some countries but not in others.

NOTES

1. I am indebted to Torbjørn Hægeland and the editors for comments on an earlier draft.
2. Competitive labour market, bargaining between labour unions and firms, and efficiency wages, see Blanchflower and Oswald (1994).
3. A seminal contribution to the methodological change in output measurement is Gordon (1990).

REFERENCES

Acemoglu, D., Aghion, P., and Violante, G. I. (2001). 'Deunionization, Technical Change, and Inequality', *Carnegie-Rochester Conference Series on Public Policy*, 55: 29–64.

Aghion, P., Caroly, E., and Garcia-Peñalosa, C. (1999). 'Inequality and Economic Growth: The Perspective of the New Growth Theories', *Journal of Economic Literature*, 37: 1615–60.

Atkinson, A. (1999). 'Is Rising Income Inequality Inevitable? A Critique of the Transatlantic Consensus', 1999 WIDER Annual Lecture, Oslo, Mimeo.

Banerjee, A. V. and Duflo, E. (2003). 'Inequality and Growth: What Can the Data Say?', *Journal of Economic Growth*, 8: 267–99.

Barrett, A. M., Fitzgerald, J., and Nolan, B. (2000). 'Earning Inequality, Returns to Education and Immigration into Ireland', CEPR Discussion Paper No. 2493.

Bjørnstad, R., Cappelen, Å., Holm, I., and Skjerpen, T. (2002). 'Past and Future Changes in the Structure of Wages and Skills', Documents 2002–4, Statistics Norway.

Blanchflower, D. G. and Oswald, A. (1994). *The Wage Curve*. Cambridge, MA: MIT Press.

Blau, F. D. and Kahn, L. M. (1996). 'International Differences in Male Wage Inequality: Institutions versus Market Forces', *Journal of Political Economy*, 104: 791–837.

Card, D. and DiNardo, J. E. (2002). 'Skill-Biased Technological Change and Rising Wage Inequality: Some Problems and Puzzles', *Journal of Labor Economics*, 20: 733–83.

DiNardo, J. E., Fortin, N., and Lemieux, T. (1996). Labor Market Institutions and the Distribution of Wages, 1973–1992: A Semi-parametric Approach', *Econometrica*, 64: 1001–44.

Förster, M. and Pearson, M. (2002). 'Income Distribution and Poverty in the OECD Area: Trends and Driving Forces', *OECD Economic Studies*, 34: 7–40.

Freeman, C. (2004). 'Income Inequality in Changing Techno-Economic Paradigms', in E. S. Reinert (ed.), *Globalizing Economic Development and Inequality*. Cheltenham, UK: Edward Elgar, pp. 243–58.

Gordon, R. J. (1990). *The Measurement of Durable Goods Prices*. Chicago: University of Chicago Press.

—— (2000). 'Does the "New Economy" Measure Up to the Great Inventions of the Past?', *Journal of Economic Perspectives*, 14: 49–74.

Gosling, A. (2003). 'The Changing Distribution of Male and Female Wages, 1978–2000: Can the Simple Skills Story Be Rejected?', CPER Discussion Paper No. 4045.

Gottschalk, P. and Smeeding, T. M. (1997). 'Cross-National Comparisons of Earning and Income Inequality', *Journal of Economic Literature*, 35: 633–87.

Hægeland, T. and Kirkebøen, L. (2004). Utdanning, lønn og næring, mimeo, Statistisk sentralbyrå, Oslo.

Krugman, P. (1994). 'Past and Prospective Causes of High Unemployment', *Economic Review*, 79: 23–43.

Kuznets, S. (1955). 'Economic Growth and Income Inequality', *American Economic Review*, 45: 1–28.

Layard, R., Nickell, S., and Jackman, R. (1991). *Unemployment, Macroeconomic Performance and the Labour Market*. Oxford: Oxford University Press.

Lee, D. S. (1999). 'Wage Inequality During the 1980s: Rising Dispersion or Falling Minimum Wages?', *Quarterly Journal of Economics*, 114: 977–1023.

Luxembourg Income Study (2004). http://www.lisproject.org/keyfigures/ineqtable.htm

Nunziata, L. (2001). 'Institutions and Wage Determination: A Multi-Country Approach', mimeo. Oxford: Nuffield College.

OECD (1996a). *The Knowledge-based Economy*. Paris: OECD.

—— (1996b). *Employment Outlook*. Paris: OECD.

—— (1997). *Employment Outlook*. Paris: OECD.

—— (2000). *Education at a Glance*. Paris: OECD.

—— (2002). *Economic Outlook*. Paris: OECD.

—— (2003). *Education at a Glance*. Paris: OECD.

Phelps, E. S. (2000). 'The Importance of Inclusion and the Power of Job Subsidies to Increase It', *OECD Economic Studies*, 30: 85–109.

Teulings, C. N. (2003). 'The Contribution of Minimum Wages to Increasing Wage Inequality', *Economic Journal*, 113: 801–33.

Wallerstein, M. (1999). 'Wage-Setting Institutions and Pay Inequality in Advanced Industrial Societies', *American Journal of Political Science*, 43: 649–80.

Part II

Organization, Labour Markets, and Corporate Governance

5

The Learning Organization and National Systems of Competence Building and Innovation

Alice Lam and Bengt-Åke Lundvall

5.1. INTRODUCTION

There is a growing understanding that knowledge is at the core of economic development. This is reflected in OECD publications referring to the *knowledge-based economy* (OECD 1996a, 1996b; Foray and Lundvall 1997). Here we prefer to define the present stage as a 'learning economy'. Knowledge has always been at the core of economic development, and it is not obvious that there has been a radical change in 'the amount of economically useful knowledge'. The useful stock of knowledge is not the sum of all knowledge that was ever created in the history of mankind. A lot of knowledge has been lost in a process of creative destruction.

The last decades have been characterized by an acceleration of both knowledge creation and knowledge destruction (EIRMA 1993; Carter 1994). Information and communication technology (ICT) has made a lot of information more easily accessible to a lot of people, but it also has made many skills and competencies obsolete. What is really new is the high rate of change and, as we discuss below, this acceleration of the rate of change is perhaps the most important impact of the wide use of ICT. What constitutes success in the current market economy for individuals, firms, regions, and national economies is rapid learning and forgetting (because old ways of doing things often get in the way of learning new ways).

In this new context the learning capability of firms located in the domestic economy becomes a major concern for national governments and, vice versa, the national infrastructure supporting knowledge creation, diffusion, and use becomes a concern for management and employees. To get the two to match and support each other becomes a prerequisite for economic success for firms as well as for the national economy. The new economy gives new responsibilities to both business and governments. One of the major objectives of this chapter is to demonstrate that societal institutions, which may exist at the national or regional levels, shape the types of organizational learning predominating at the level of the firm.

The analysis presented in this chapter illustrates the logic of institutionalized variation in patterns of learning and innovation. It also discusses how such variation may enable, or constrain regions or countries to create organizational forms needed for generating the types of innovation associated with different technologies or industrial sectors. The chapter argues that tacit knowledge, which is difficult to create and transfer in the absence of social interaction and labour mobility, constitutes a most important source of learning and sustainable competitive advantage in an increasingly globalized knowledge-based economy. Learning builds on trust and social capital. Institutions that are able to imbue these elements into firms and markets encourage interactive learning and are more likely to produce strong innovative capabilities.

5.2. TOWARDS A LEARNING-BASED THEORY OF THE FIRM

There is a gap between the normative, management-oriented literature on learning organizations on the one hand and theoretical contributions regarding the theory of the firm on the other. In the first category, we find strong recommendations to focus on the management of knowledge but these recommendations are sometimes based on a rather limited perspective. They reflect correctly that firms need to give more attention to their capacity to learn and to manage knowledge, but in order to promote their ideas, they tend to abstract from the wider set of activities and functions related to good performance. In theories of the firm, considerations of knowledge and learning are either absent or integrated in a somewhat static way. It might be worthwhile to consider how this gap could be narrowed in order to make the management literature more comprehensive and the theories of the firm more relevant.

In what follows we will indicate how the original contribution by Penrose (1959) on the resource-based theory of the growth of the firm can be developed into a learning-based theory of the firm. The fact that firms and management teams search and learn is taken into account by Penrose

(1959: 76–80 *et passim*).[1] In her model it is the competence of management and the human resources it controls that set the limits for growth. It is implicit in the analysis that it is more time-consuming and costly to develop this core of knowledge than to acquire other types of (tangible) resources.

If we bring this analysis to its logical conclusion we end up with *a learning-based theory of the firm*. If it is correct that the limits to growth (Penrose assumes that in practical terms the objectives of growth and profit are inseparable, 1959: 30) are set by the competence of the management team and the costs of extending this team, the *increase in competencies* becomes the most important strategic objective. Or, as formulated by Senge (1990), 'the only enduring source of competitive advantage is the ability to learn'.

It is interesting to note that recent contributions by Penrose (1959, 1995) and Richardson (1996, 1997) also indicate the need for such a more dynamic (learning-based) theory of the firm. In the new foreword to her classical text, where she brings together and comments on what seem to be the most important new developments since she published her own work, Penrose points to the contribution by Loasby (1991) and his emphasis on how management construct 'research programmes' that make it possible for individuals to learn without threatening the coherence of the firm. The most recent contributions by Richardson (1996, 1997) have typically presented theoretical and empirical analysis of processes of knowledge creation in highly dynamic sectors.

5.2.1. Three Basic Functions of the Firm

It is useful to specify the basic functions of the firm into three categories:

- Allocating scarce resources (statics)
- Exploiting underutilized resources by entering into new activities (first-order dynamics)
- Speeding-up learning and creating new competencies (second-order dynamics)

The three functions are at the focus of three different theories of the firm—neoclassical, resource-based, and learning-based theories of the firm. But real firms have to take all the three functions into account. The firm will reallocate its resources if there is a (substantial) change in relative factor prices. To exploit underutilized resources and to use the existing knowledge base, in connection with the introduction of new products, is also an important part of the strategy of firms. But, in the long run, the success and growth of the firm will depend on its capability to build new competencies.

It is also important to note that there are trade-offs between the three functions. A strictly 'optimal' use of all resources (with no x-inefficiency) will leave too little slack for flexible adaptation and for growth endeavours. A growth pattern characterized by a 'harmonious' combination of 'similar' activities may hamper the learning capability by reducing the diversity on which learning processes thrive (see below on this point).

The three functions may take on different weight in different parts of the economy. In those parts of the economy that are stable in terms of techno-logical opportunities and user needs, we might find firms that successfully focus on the static allocation function. In other parts where the rate of change is dramatic, the third function becomes the central concern of management.[2]

One aspect of the learning economy is that there is a general movement within firms that gives stronger emphasis to the third function, and this is why there is a demand for the management literature on how to implement learning organizations and knowledge management. But, of course, knowledge management strategies have to take into account the other two functions as well. Firms still have to be concerned about their allocation of existing resources and about growth on the basis of its existing competencies.

5.2.2. Building Learning Organizations and Integrating Strategies of Competence Building at the Level of the Firm

The theoretical considerations discussed above have their correspondence in management considerations. Management is constantly in a situation where it has to consider alternative ways of creating and using competence eman-ating from different sources. These choices have to do both with human resource development (HRD) and with the degree of vertical integration of tasks. The competence of the work force will reflect a combination of hiring/firing decisions and investment in internal training and learning. Takeovers and mergers is one way to get access to individual and collective knowledge pools while a positioning in networks or in strategic alliances is another. Knowledge management needs to have an integrated and coherent approach to the use of these different sources. An *integrated competence building strategy* is needed and such a strategy should take into account how to combine the three different major sources of competence building: internal competence building, hiring and firing, and network positioning (see Figure 5.1).

Firms differ in how strongly they emphasize each of these elements both between and within national innovation systems. Japanese firms have emphasized internal competence building while most hi-tech firms in Silicon Valley depend on learning through high inter-firm mobility of employees

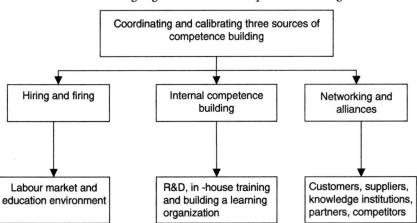

Figure 5.1. Knowledge management in the learning organization

within the industrial district. In Denmark, the institutional set-up of the training system and the labour market supports networking firms and high mobility in the labour market, making it attractive for firms to locate in 'industrial districts'. Below we develop a taxonomy of organizational strategies and national systems that bring such differences into focus.

As we see there is no single optimal strategy in this respect. What is a good practice will depend on sectoral and regional contexts. Under all circumstances, the diagram gives a first hint that there is a connection between the knowledge management style of the firm and education and labour market institutions. It is important when designing public training and labour market reforms to be aware of the behaviour of firms in this respect and to balance the needs of the firms to social needs. The aim of reform should be to shape framework conditions in such a way that firms get strong incentives to contribute to competence building without undermining social cohesion in society at large.

5.2.3. The Generic Trends Towards Learning Organizations

An extensive literature shows that there is a strong synergy between the introduction of *new forms of organization* and the performance and innovative capacity of the firm (Gjerding 1996; Lorenz and Valeyre, this volume; Lund and Gjerding 1996; Lundvall 1999; Lundvall and Nielsen 1999). Establishing the firm as a learning organization characterized by decentralized responsibility, teamwork, circulation of employees between departments, and investment in training has a positive impact on a series of performance variables. Flexible firms are characterized by higher productivity, by higher rates of growth and stability in terms of employment, and they are more innovative in terms of new products. Research also shows that success in terms of innovation is even greater when such a strategy is combined with active networking in relation to customers, suppliers, and knowledge institutions.

While there are generic tendencies reflecting the movement towards a learning economy, different types of organizations learn and manage knowledge differently. During the past decade, a large literature has discussed new organizational models and concepts designed to support organizational learning and innovation (see Lam 2004). These models include 'high performance work systems' or 'lean production' (Womack, Jones, and Roos 1990), pioneered by Japanese firms in the automobile industry; and the 'N-form corporation' (Hedlund 1994) and 'hypertext organization' (Nonaka and Takeuchi 1995). Concepts such as 'cellular forms' (Miles et al. 1997), 'modular forms' (Galunic and Eisenhardt 2001), and 'project-based networks' (DeFillippi 2002) reflect the growth of flexible and adaptive forms of organization with a strategic focus on entrepreneurship and radical innovation in knowledge-intensive sectors of the economy. These studies highlight the different ways in which firms seek to create learning organizations capable of continuous problem-solving and innovation. Very few studies explain the nature of the learning processes underpinning these structural forms, the types of innovative competences generated, and the wider institutional context within which this organizational learning is embedded.

One of the major points in this chapter is to demonstrate how the national (or regional) context shapes the forms of organizational learning predominating at the level of the firm. In the next section we start from the now widely diffused concept 'the national system of innovation (NIS)' and discuss how it can be both extended and deepened by putting competence building of people and organizations at the centre of the analysis.

5.3. TOWARDS A CONCEPT OF NATIONAL SYSTEMS OF COMPETENCE BUILDING AND INNOVATION

The concept of NSI goes back to Friedrich List (List 1841). The analysis of national systems developed by List took into account a wide set of national institutions, including those engaged in education and training as well as infrastructures, such as networks for transportation of people and commodities (Freeman 1988). The modern revival of the concept some 12–15 years ago gave rise to different more or less broad (often implicit) definitions of innovation systems.

The US approach (Nelson 1988, 1993) linked the concept mainly to high-technology industries and put the interaction between firms, the university system and national technology policy at the centre of the analysis. Freeman (1987), in his analysis of Japan, introduced a broader perspective that took into account national specificities in the organization of firms—he emphasized for instance how Japanese firms increasingly used 'the factory as a laboratory'. The Aalborg approach (Lundvall 1985; Andersen and Lundvall 1988) also took the broader view: it looked at NSI as rooted in the production system, and it also emphasized the institutional dimension, where institutions where defined theoretically as norms and rules (Johnson 1992). Porter (1990) brought in regimes of competition as important dimensions of national systems.

But none of these approaches gave education, training, and labour markets the central role that they deserve. The education systems and labour markets are nationally constituted, and it is obvious that they play a key role in competence building and thereby in shaping the foundation for innovation processes. There are national specificities in the formation of skills and in the national labour dynamics as well as economic and cultural barriers to the free movement of labour across national borders. There are important changes taking place that increase the international mobility of highly skilled labour, but there is little doubt that 'human capital' and labour remains the least mobile of the resources used in the production process.

There have been some broader approaches that give more attention to the role of labour markets and training in national systems. Starting from a different tradition that, historically, has put less emphasis on technical innovation and more on macroeconomic dynamics, regulation school economists have been among the first to introduce the human resource dimension when pursuing comparative analyses of national systems (Amable, Barré, and Boyer 1997). Also, in the parallel work on 'national business systems' pursued by Whitley (1996 and this volume) and others there is an emphasis on national specificities in HRD systems and labour markets.

5.3.1. Innovation Systems—Three Alternative Perspectives

We can thus identify at least three different ways of delimiting the innovation system. The first is the innovation system as rooted in the R&D system, the second is the innovation system as rooted in the production system, and the third is the innovation system as rooted in the production and human resource development system. There are several reasons why the last perspective is to be preferred.

Several OECD countries that are characterized by a low-tech specialization in production and exports are among the countries in the world with the highest GNP per capita. To focus on the rather small part of the economy engaged in formal R&D activities would give very limited insights regarding the growth potential for these countries. This is true for most small OECD countries and for developing countries. It may be argued that the 'made in America' study (Dertoutzos, Lester, and Solow, 1989) and the 'made in France' study (Taddei and Coriat 1993) indirectly have demonstrated that this wider perspective has relevance even for the big OECD countries.

A second reason has to do with the fact that empirical studies especially at the regional level (see Gelsing 1992 and Jensen 1992) only partially support the original hypothesis in Lundvall (1985) about innovation systems as primarily constituted by inter-firm, user–producer relationships. It is an obvious alternative to broaden the perspective on regional and national systems and to see them as constituted also by a common knowledge base embedded in local institutions and embodied in people living and working in the region.

The final and perhaps the most important reason for taking the broader view has to do with the basic assumption presented above about the present era as dominated by a 'learning economy'. This hypothesis points to the need to give stronger emphasis to the analysis of the development of human and organizational capabilities. In the national education systems people learn specific ways to learn. In labour markets they experience nation-specific incentive systems and norms about what kinds of knowledge are the most valuable. Again this will have an impact on how they learn. This is a theme that is addressed in the next section.

5.4. KNOWLEDGE, ORGANIZATION, AND SOCIETAL INSTITUTIONS

The knowledge creation and learning capabilities of firms cannot be separated from specific organizational forms and societal institutions (Lam 1997, 2000a). Here, we develop a typological framework linking the micro and macro levels to explain the links between learning patterns, organizational forms, and societal institutions. It highlights the importance of education and training systems, and types of labour markets as the key societal institutions shaping organizational forms and the learning capabilities of firms.

Education and training shape the social constitution of 'knowledge', and thus provide the basis of qualification, work status, and job boundaries. As such, they influence the relative status and importance of different types of knowledge, and the nature of their interaction. The types of labour market determine the locus of learning, the incentives for developing different types of knowledge, and define the boundaries and social framework within which individual learning interacts with collective learning. These institutional features interact with organizational structures and processes to generate different types of knowledge, patterns of learning, and innovation.

The analysis seeks to link together the literature on knowledge and learning with that on organizational forms and NSI. In order to cover these fields, normally treated separately, a number of simplifying assumptions have to be made. However, we believe that this integrated approach has great heuristic value both for theoreticians who tend to be locked in into more narrow fields of analysis and for practitioners who may also tend to focus too myopically either on the organizational or at the societal level.

5.4.1. Characterizing Knowledge

The knowledge of the firm can be analysed along two dimensions: the epistemological and ontological. The former concerns the modes of expression of knowledge, namely, Polanyi's distinction (1962, 1966) between explicit and tacit knowledge. The latter relates to the locus of knowledge which can reside at the individual or collective levels. These two dimensions give rise to four different forms of organizational knowledge: 'embrained', 'embodied', 'encoded', and 'embedded' knowledge (see Figure 5.2):

Embrained knowledge (individual and explicit) is dependent on the individual's conceptual skills and cognitive abilities. It is formal, abstract, or theoretical knowledge. It is typically learnt through reading books and in formal education. Embrained knowledge enjoys a privileged social status within Western culture. The high-occupational status of science compared with engineering reflects this.

	Individual	Collective
Explicit	Embrained knowledge	Encoded knowledge
Tacit	Embodied knowledge	Embedded Knowledge

Figure 5.2. Knowledge types

Embodied knowledge (individual and tacit) is action oriented; it is the practical, individual types of knowledge on which Polanyi (1962, 1966) focused. It is learnt through experience and training based on apprenticeship relations. Embodied knowledge is also context specific; it is 'particular knowledge' which becomes relevant in light of the practical problem solving experience (Barley 1996).

Encoded knowledge (collective and explicit) is shared within organizations through formal information systems—any member of the organization who knows the code can easily get access to relevant databases through the use of IT. Encoded knowledge is formed in making explicit as much as possible of tacit knowledge. This is well-illustrated by the principles of Scientific Management which attempt to codify worker experiences and skills into objective scientific knowledge.

Embedded knowledge (collective and tacit) is built into routines, habits, and norms that cannot easily be transformed into information systems. Embedded knowledge is produced in an interaction among different members of the organization, and it may be supported by storytelling and processes aiming at making members of the organization share its cultural norms. Embedded knowledge is relation specific, contextual, and dispersed. It is an emergent form of knowledge capable of supporting complex patterns of interaction in the absence of written rules.

5.4.2. Characterizing Organizations

All organizations potentially contain a mixture of knowledge types, but their relative importance differs. Organizations may be dominated by one type of knowledge rather than another. To each of the knowledge forms there corresponds an ideal type organization. We distinguish four ideal typical organizational forms, using two dimensions: the degree of standardization of knowledge and work, and the dominant knowledge agent (individual or organization) (see Figure 5.3). These different organizational configurations vary in their ability to mobilize tacit knowledge, resulting in different dynamics of learning and innovation.

5.4.2.1. *Professional Bureaucracy and Embrained Knowledge*

Professional bureaucracy (based upon individual and standardized knowledge) refers to a hierarchical complex organization where individual experts are highly specialized and where they operate within narrowly defined fields

	Individual	Organization
Standardized work	Professional bureaucracy (embrained knowledge)	Machine bureaucracy (encoded knowledge)
Non-standardized work	Operating adhocracy (embodied knowledge)	J-form organization (embedded knowledge)

Figure 5.3. Organizational types

of knowledge. Such organizations may be especially efficient when the environment is stable and the need for high degree of professional precision is necessary to avoid big negative risks. However, its learning focus tends to be narrow and constrained within the boundary of formal specialist knowledge. Tacit knowledge is circumscribed and contained; it plays a limited role in a professional bureaucracy. Professional bureaucracies are not innovative, and they will get into serious crisis when faced with radical change in the environment.

5.4.2.2. Machine Bureaucracy and Encoded Knowledge

Machine bureaucracy (with a knowledge base that is collective and standardized) refers to an organization where the dominating principles are specialization, standardization, and control. This is an organizational form that is well suited for mass production in a stable environment. It may be said to be the ideal type of Fordist production where principles of Taylorist management are predominating. There is a clear dichotomy between the 'execution' and 'conception' of knowledge. The managers are the key agents responsible for translating individual knowledge into rules and procedures and for filtering information up and down the organizational hierarchy. A large part of tacit knowledge is naturally lost in the translation and aggregation process. It is a structure designed to deal with routine problems but is unable to cope with novelty or change.

5.4.2.3. 'Operating Adhocracy' and 'Embodied Knowledge'

Operating adhocracy (the knowledge base is individual and non-standardized) is a highly organic form of organization with little standardization of knowledge or work process. It relies not only on the formal knowledge of its members, but draws its capability from the diverse know-how and practical problem-solving skills embodied in the individual experts. It has a strong capacity for generating tacit knowledge through experimentation and interactive problem-solving. Organizations engaged in providing non-standard, creative, and problem-solving services directly to the clients, such as professional partnerships, software engineering firms, and management consultancies, are typical examples. In these organizations, formal professional knowledge may play only a limited role; a large part of the problem-solving activities has very little to do with the application of narrow standardized expertise and more to do with the experience and capacity to adapt to new situations. Tacit knowledge is generated through interaction, trial-and-error, and experimentation. It is a very flexible and innovative form of organization. Its weakness has to do with the problems of reproducing what has been learnt into an organizational memory and with a high degree of vulnerability when it comes to individuals leaving the organization.

5.4.2.4. *J-Form Organization and Embedded Knowledge*

The J-form organization (with a knowledge base that is collective and non-standardized) derives its capability from knowledge that is 'embedded' in its operating routines, team relationships, and shared culture. Its archetypal features are best illustrated by some of the big knowledge-intensive Japanese firms (Aoki 1988; Nonaka and Takeuchi 1995). It combines the stability and efficiency of a bureaucracy with the flexibility and team dynamics of an adhocracy. One fundamental characteristic is that it allows an organic, non-hierarchical team structure to operate in parallel with its formal hierarchical managerial structure. Shared values and organizational culture form the environment where interaction across functions and divisions take place in a systematic manner. This is an adaptive and innovative form of organization. It has a strong capacity to generate, diffuse, and accumulate tacit knowledge continuously through 'learning-by-doing' and interaction. It is good at generating incremental and continuous innovation. However, learning in the J-form organization is also potentially conservative. Its stable social structure and shared knowledge base may block radical innovation.

5.4.3. Characterizing National Systems of Competence Building and Innovation

The relative dominance of different knowledge types, and the ability of an organization to mobilize tacit knowledge as a source of learning are powerfully influenced by the wider societal and institutional factors. Here, we focus on education and training systems and labour market organizations as key institutional features shaping the knowledge and learning pattern of firms. Our implicit argument is that these institutional aspects and patterns of learning within firms are inter-dependent and they constitute a subsystem within the wider national system. There is a process of mutual adaptation between knowledge types, organizations, and institutions. Other national institutions such as the capital market also affect learning within firms but in a less direct way, and the process of mutual adaptation is less obvious.

5.4.3.1. Education and Training Systems: Narrow 'Professional-Oriented' vs. Broad 'Competence-Based'

On the education and training dimension, national systems can vary according to the relative importance they attach to different types of knowledge (e.g. formal academic knowledge vs. practical skills), the level of formal professional control over the nature and content of high-level expertise, and the distribution of competence among the entire workforce. A narrow 'professional-oriented' system is characterized by the dominance of formal academic knowledge, a high degree of professional control over training programmes, and an uneven two-tier distribution of competence: a well-developed higher education system for the professional elites while the majority of the workforce is poorly trained. Such a system gives rise to a narrow conception of knowledge, and the expertise acquired tends to be highly specialized and distant from problem-solving practices. For example, the system in the UK and US can be described as narrow professional oriented. It displays a strong bias towards academic education and attaches little social status and economic credibility to practical skills which acts as a disincentive for investment in this area. As a result, there is a widespread lack of formal intermediate skills and qualifications among the general workforce in these two countries (Buechtemann and Verdier 1998). Such a system creates a bias in the use of human capital and labour market polarization. It is associated with a bureaucratic form of work organization. The wide disparity in the educational backgrounds and skill levels between the different categories of the workforce generates knowledge discontinuities and social distance within firms. It reinforces the domination of formal knowledge over tacit skills.

In contrast, a broad competence-based education and training system recognizes the value of both academic education and vocational training. It is characterized by a widespread and rigorous general and vocational education for a wide spectrum of the workforce. Such a system is more conducive to a decentralized mode of work organization. A more even distribution of competence among the workforce provides a better basis for interactive learning and the cultivation of tacit knowledge as a source of organizational capability. The cases of Germany, Japan, and also Denmark are illustrative (Koike 1995; Kristensen 1996; Soskice 1997). The systems in these countries accord relatively high-social status to 'practical experience', and recognize it as a source of competence and qualification. This encourages investment in vocational training which has resulted in a good supply of intermediate skills. This enables firms to organize work in a more cooperative and decentralized manner, conducive to the transmission and mobilization of tacit knowledge.

5.4.3.2. *Labour Markets and Careers: Occupational vs. Internal Labour Markets*

Labour market institutions constitute another important dimension of national systems of competence building. They influence the knowledge base and learning capabilities of the firm in three main ways. First, these determine the extent to which expertise is developed outside or within the firm, and hence the relative importance of formal education and training institutions vis-à-vis employers in defining the knowledge base of the firm. Second, they determine career mobility and incentives for individual workers and the capability of the firm in acquiring and accumulating different types of knowledge. And third, they shape the individual's career and social identity and define the boundaries of learning. A broad distinction can be drawn between systems where careers take place through job shifts in an occupational labour market (OLM) and where the typical career is connected to a firm-based internal labour market (ILM). The former implies a higher degree of market control over skills and competence criteria, and hence a stronger tendency towards formalization and codification of knowledge across firms. In contrast, the latter allows a greater degree of individual firm control over the definition of expertise, leading to a lower level of standardization of expertise around formal knowledge.

5.4.3.3. *Occupational Labour Market*

An OLM offers a relatively high scope for job mobility. Knowledge and learning are embedded in an inter-firm career. Formal education and training play a much greater role in generating directly relevant occupational competence. The type of qualifications generated can be highly task-specific based on standardized, advanced 'packaging' of knowledge and skills (e.g. craft-oriented training or professional education). Alternatively, it can be a broad-based general education that can be adapted and applied across a wide variety of work settings and tasks. The former approach assumes that the task environment is relatively stable and the knowledge required can be codified and pre-packaged in initial training programmes. The latter, in contrast, rests on the notion that the task environment is uncertain and the knowledge required is fluid and emergent. It cannot be easily bundled into occupations or codified in advance, and hence requires a broad-based initial qualification to enable individuals to pursue a more varied and flexible approach to continuous learning.

In an OLM, knowledge and skills are owned by and embodied in the individuals; they are personal property for career advancement. The transparency and transferability of the knowledge acquired is of paramount importance for inter-firm career mobility. Such career mobility relies on effective signals: dependable information about the type and quality of skills and knowledge that individuals have. This can be based either on public certification (institutional signals), or peer group recognition (information signals). The former approach works well provided that the knowledge and skills required can be easily identified and codified, i.e. bundled into specific occupations with a distinctive set of tasks or problems to which these skills and knowledge are applied. In situations where the tasks are highly fluid and unpredictable, and the knowledge used contains a large tacit component, institutional signals become insufficient and unreliable. This is because tacit skills cannot be easily codified; they can only be revealed through practice and work performance. Their transfer will have to rely heavily on social and professional networks based on shared industrial or occupational norms. In other words, the efficient transfer and accumulation of tacit knowledge in an OLM requires the support of a 'containing social structure', for example, the formation of a community-based OLM based on localized firm networks and industry clusters (Saxenian 1996). Social networks facilitate the 'marketability' of cumulative personal tacit skills.

Learning within an OLM tends to be person centred and market oriented. It is rooted in the individual's professional and career strategy, and characterized by a greater degree of autonomy and latitude in the boundary and domains of learning. This can potentially enlarge the knowledge base of the firm and stimulate radical innovation. Moreover, firms operating in an OLM are able to reconstitute their knowledge base through hiring and firing. This allows them to respond flexibly to shifting market requirements and technological changes.

5.4.3.4. Internal Labour Market

Internal labour markets are characterized by long-term stable employment with a single employer and career progression through a series of interconnected jobs within a hierarchy. Knowledge and learning are embedded in an intra-firm career; a large part of the knowledge and work-related skills is generated through firm-specific on-the-job (OJT) training. Formal knowledge acquired through education serves only as an entry qualification and provides the basis upon which work-related skills are built within the firm. The nature of the work organization and careers determines the quality and boundaries of learning through OJT. Where jobs are narrowly defined and careers are organized around hierarchies of jobs with tiered boundaries based on formal entry qualifications as in the case of a machine bureaucracy, OJT will tend to be narrow and job-specific. In contrast, an ILM can also be organized around broadly defined jobs and a continuous career hierarchy based on a common ranking system (e.g. the case of Japan). Progression to upper level positions is achieved, in this case, through accumulation of a wide range of skills and organizational experience. Formal knowledge plays only a limited role in defining competence criteria and entry to senior positions; the key emphasis is on the long-term accumulation of firm-specific skills and practical experience. OJT is broad-based and linked systemically with career progression. This increases the variety of experience and facilitates the generation of tacit knowledge. Job rotation also serves an important socialization function and helps to reduce social distance between different categories of the workforce. The close integration of OJT with career progression also gives individuals a strong incentive to accumulate knowledge through practical experience. The career hierarchy becomes a device for tacit knowledge creation and learning.

Learning within an ILM tends to be organization-oriented and self-reinforcing. It evolves along the internal requirements of the firm, and is rooted in a firm-based career and organizational identity. The stability of personnel within an ILM facilitates the retention and accumulation of knowledge. Firms may display a strong capacity for incremental innovation and focus on developing a distinctive core competence.

5.4.3.5. Four Contrasting Societal Models of Competence-Building System

The education and labour market dimensions are inextricably linked, and there is an institutional logic defining their specific configurations. The interaction between these institutions gives rise to four contrasting 'societal models' of competence-building systems (see Figure 5.4). The term societal requires some qualification. It is used in a broad sense to point out the effect of institutional environments on ways of organizing knowledge and learning rather than simply to emphasize national distinctiveness. The institutional environment may exist at the national, regional, or sector levels.

	Occupational labour market (OLM)	Internal labour market (ILM)
Narrow 'professional-oriented' education and training	Professional model (Professional bureaucracy, embrained knowledge) Narrow learning inhibit innovations	Bureaucratic model (Machine bureaucracy, encoded knowledge) Slow learning, limited innovation
Broad 'competence-based' education and training	Occupational community model (Operating adhocracy, embodied knowledge) Dynamic learning, radical innovation	Organizational community model (J-form organization, embedded knowledge) Cumulative learning, incremental innovation

Figure 5.4. Societal models of competence-building systems and their innovative potentials

The *professional model* refers to an economy where the education and training is governed by professions and education institutions and where the typical career is one of moving between different employers. It is one where practical experience has a low status while codified and scientific knowledge is regarded as very important. Broad segments of the population have insufficient training. In this context there will be a predominance of hierarchical forms of organizations. Learning will be narrow and takes place mainly among those who have already a strong formal education background. The professional model is most likely to be found in Anglo-American countries where the norms of 'professional specialization' and 'elitism' remain deeply rooted.

The *bureaucratic model* is one where careers take place inside firms but where hierarchies are stable and connected with formal training and access to codified knowledge. It seeks to control and eliminate tacit knowledge, and its capacity to innovate is very limited. The bureaucratic model prevails in economies or firms which seek to sustain competitive advantage through standardization and price-based competition.

The *occupational community model* is one where there is high inter-firm mobility in the context of a region. Inter-firm mobility fosters social and professional networks. Education and training institutions may be well connected with professional networks and with firms in the region. Italian industrial districts and Silicon Valley are examples of this kind of model. This kind of context is highly flexible and promotes continuous innovation as well as radical innovation. The occupational community is an institutional pre-requisite for fostering and sustaining the innovative capability of the 'oper-ating adhocracy'. In a 'boundaryless' open labour market, the operating adhocracy will be under pressure to bureaucratize because of difficulties in accumulating and transferring tacit knowledge. The tacit knowledge creating capability of the operating adhocracy can only be sustained if it operates as a member of localized firm network. Such networks of social relationships provide the 'social capital' and 'information signals' needed to ensure the efficient transfer of tacit knowledge in an inter-firm career framework (Saxenian 1996).

The *organizational community* model is characterized by a broad-based egalitarian education system and with careers that take place inside the firm. Training takes place inside firms or in activities organized by the firm. This kind of context is well suited to promote permanent incremental innovation, but it might be difficult to start up completely new activities in such an environment. It might be combined with financial systems that give priority to existing firms. Japan represents a typical example of this model.

Of course, what has been presented is a set of ideal types and in reality none of the categories are pure. The typology is a heuristic tool. It helps us to understand how institutionalized variation in learning and innovation may allow, or constrain firms to create different organizational forms and related innovation trajectories. It also suggests that there are alternative models for generating different types of innovation which may lead to societal compara-tive advantage in different industrial sectors.

5.5. LOOKING FOR GOOD PRACITCES OF LEARNING ORGANIZATIONS: ALTERNATIVE SOCIETAL MODELS

One fundamental characteristic of the learning economy is the rapid pace of change and acceleration of knowledge creation. Although the use of IT enhances the incentives and possibility to codify knowledge, the rapid pace of knowledge advancement has also created immense barriers to codification. The limit of codification is especially obvious in skills and knowledge trans-mission in labour markets.

In the high-skills sector, knowledge is now moving too rapidly to be encoded and institutionalized into a stable set of occupations. Traditional institutional signals, for example, occupational qualifications, have severe limits in providing dependable information about the quality and contents of skills (Lam 2000*b*). Codification is indeed too slow a process for the transmission of rapidly evolving knowledge. The high rate of change and growing complexity of knowledge required for innovation has reinforced the importance of tacit knowledge and collective learning in the knowledge economy.

The above analysis suggests that both the 'organizational' and 'occupational community' models are favourable to the creation and transmission of tacit knowledge. However, the different labour market structures generate some significant contrasts in their learning and innovation patterns. The occupational community model operates within a more open and fluid labour market which permits extensive hiring and firing, risk taking, and the development of human resources in a 'competency destroying' environment. In other words, it facilitates the diffusion of tacit knowledge within a broader boundary and varied contexts. It encourages experimentation and entrepreneurial behaviour and has the potential to achieve radical innovation.

In contrast, the organizational community model derives its competitive strength from the cultivation of firm-specific core competence. It allows the accumulation of tacit knowledge within the boundary of the firm, and the continuous combination and recombination of firm-specific product and process technology with industry technology. Firms within the organizational community may develop a strong orientation to pursuing an incremental innovation strategy and do well in established technological fields. The strong emphasis on 'competence preservation' within organizations, however, inhibits the creation of active labour markets, and thus makes it difficult for firms to renew their knowledge base and compete successfully in rapidly developing new fields.

The sections that follow examine three concrete examples to illustrate the theoretical argument developed in this chapter. The divergent innovation trajectories pursued by Japanese and US firms in the high-technology sectors give the most vivid illustration of the contrasts between the organizational and occupational community model of learning and innovation. The example of Denmark provides another interesting example of an innovation system with characteristics of the occupational community model that differs from the high-technology clusters discussed in the context of the Anglo-Saxon economies.

5.5.1. The Japanese 'Organizational Community Model'

The Japanese competence building and innovation system exhibits some of the most quintessential features of the organizational community model. The economy is characterized by a high level of cooperation and organizational integration (Lazonick and West 1998). This occurs through extensive long-term collaboration between firms in business groups and networks. Additionally, integration within large firms is particularly strong. Japanese social institutions and employment practices foster the close involvement of shop-floor workers in the development of organizational capability.

The successful state education system and large company-driven networks equip the majority of workers with a high level of skills that employers respect and so can rely on them to contribute usefully to innovation activities. The ILM system is characterized not only by long-term attachment but also by well-organized training and job rotation schemes. These practices promote continuous skills formation through learning-by-doing and systematic career progression. Hence, a strong organizational capacity to accumulate knowledge and learn incrementally. Moreover, the approach to engineering skills formation fosters strong cross-functional teams and extensive human networks in product development (Lam 1996, 1997).

Japan has historically placed a high value on the importance of developing the practical skills of their engineers in the workplace. This is due, in part, to the fact that industrial development in Japan was historically based on imported technology, and Japanese engineers have played an important role in translating theoretical knowledge into concrete operational details for shop-floor workers (Morikawa 1991). Japanese firms have always placed a strong emphasis on developing the on-site practical knowledge of their graduate engineers in order to facilitate knowledge transfer. Formal university education is less important than practical learning in the workplace. The university degree in Japan is far more general and broad-based than that in the US or Britain. Young graduate engineers normally spend their initial years in a wide range of peripheral technical tasks and gradually accumulate their knowledge and expertise through assignment to a wider range of more complex tasks. The type of knowledge transmitted tends to be judgemental, informal, and tacit.

Over the past three decades, Japanese firms have gained international competitive advantage in industries such as transport equipment, office machines, consumer electronics, electronic components for computing equipment, and telecommunication hardware. The strength of Japan in these sectors stems from the capability of firms to develop highly flexible production systems through the close integration of shop-floor skills and experience, the tight linkages between R&D, production and marketing, and a unique innovation strategy based on continual modification and upgrading of existing components and products (Womack, Jones, and Roos 1991). The Japanese organizational community approach to learning has enabled firms to thrive in 'flexible mass production' characterized by constant variation and improvement of basically standardized products. The capacity of the organization to create new knowledge through synthesis and combination of the existing knowledge has enabled firms to gain competitive advantage in relatively 'mature' technological fields characterized by rich possibilities of combinations and incremental improvements of existing components and products.

Conversely, organization-specific and path-dependent learning have constrained Japan's success in a number of leading-edge technological fields. Japan finds it harder to excel in sectors which do not exclusively rely on incremental upgrading of system components (e.g. aerospace, supercomputers), and those in which fast-paced radical innovation are crucial for success (e.g. pharmaceuticals and biotechnology). The human-network-based interaction and internal tacit knowledge transfer appear to be less effective in coordinating systems involving complex interactions among components. The insular nature of the Japanese HRD system, and the absence of an active labour market for experienced scientific and managerial staff have constrained the boundary of explorative learning of firms. They also reduce the incentives for firms and individuals to engage in risky new projects. The organizational community model of learning limits the development of highly specialized scientific expertise, and makes it difficult to adopt radically new skills and knowledge needed for radical learning. The disappointing performance of Japanese firms in such fields as software and biotechnology during the 1990s may constitute evidence of the difficulties faced by Japanese firms in entering and innovating in rapidly developing new technological fields.

5.5.2. 'Occupational Community Models': High-Technology Clusters in the US and UK

While the dominant institutions of the Anglo-Saxon economies have less capacity to foster the organization-oriented type of collective learning observed in Japanese firms, they have the potential to accommodate a more market-based and individually driven form of collective learning and to compete successfully in the highest-skill sectors. Some of the world's most innovative and prosperous high-technology clusters can be found in the US and also in the UK. California's Silicon Valley and the high-technology clusters surrounding Cambridge in the UK are two of the most famous success stories. These high-technology clusters provide good examples that illustrate the processes of knowledge creation and dynamics of innovation underpinning the occupational community model of competence building.

They also highlight the importance for the 'adhocracy' of supportive local labour markets and other external institutions typically included in analyses of national, sectoral, and regional innovation systems.

Silicon Valley has been an enormously successful and dynamic region characterized by rapid innovation and commercialization in the fast-growing technological fields. The core industries of the region include microelectronics, semiconductors, computer networking, both hardware and software, and more recently biotechnology. Firms operating in these industries undergo frequent reconfiguration and realignment in order to survive in a constantly changing environment marked by incessant innovation. The availability of a large pool of professional experts with known reputations in particular fields enables firms to quickly reconstitute their knowledge and skill base in the course of their innovative endeavours. The rapid creation of new start-up firms focusing on novel innovative projects, and the ease with which project-based firms are able to assemble and reassemble their teams of highly skilled scientists and engineers to engage in new innovative activities are central to the technological and organizational dynamism of the region. The high rate of labour mobility and extensive hiring and firing creates a permissive environment for entrepreneurial start-ups and flexible reconfiguration of project teams and knowledge sources (Saxenian 1996; Angels 2000; Bahrami and Evans 2000). Labour mobility within the context of a region plays a critical role in the generation of professional networks and facilitates the rapid transmission of evolving new knowledge—a large part of which may be tacit. Such a regionally based OLM provides a stable social context and shared industrial culture needed to ensure the efficient transfer of tacit knowledge in an inter-firm career framework. The shared context and industry-specific values within the regional community ensure that tacit knowledge will not be wasted when one changes employers, and this gives the individual a positive incentive to engage in tacit 'know-how' learning (DeFillipi and Arthur 1996). A regionally based labour market and networks of firms create a stable social structure to sustain collective learning and knowledge creation within and across firm boundaries. The creation of a wider social learning system amplifies the learning and innovative capability of the individual firms locating within the system.

The 'Cambridge phenomenon' (Segal Quince Wicksteed 2000)—a clustering of small, but successful high-tech firms around Cambridge University in the UK—has been likened to Silicon Valley. Many of the new companies in the area started as university spin-offs by Cambridge graduates and academic staff. The process has been continuing since the 1960s and has led to the area being dubbed as 'Silicon Fen'. Similar to Silicon Valley, the success of the Cambridge cluster has been helped by having a world class research university, a highly networked community, a dynamic labour market, and an entrepreneurial business culture. The area is marked by the existence of a dynamic high-tech labour market which has grown rapidly and become spatially more extensive over the years. The success of the high-tech cluster has continued to work as a 'pull' factor attracting many qualified scientists and engineers from outside to work in the area. The workforce in the area is highly skilled and is dominated by qualified scientists and engineers. The technology consultancies have played an especially important role in attracting experienced consultants and researchers from outside the area. The inflow and mobility of people have contributed to the diversity of the workforce and dynamism of the region.

Empirical studies also suggest that there is an active process of inter-firm mobility in the region, involving the movement of entrepreneurs, consultants, and researchers (Lawson et al. 1997; Segal Quince Wicksteed 2000). This takes place primarily between consultancy and clients, and between a consultancy and its spin-outs. Labour mobility and the personal and professional networks formed as a result of shared experiences in the region are important factors contributing to knowledge transfer and a growing capacity of the region for technological innovation.

It is clear from these accounts that what underlies the innovative capability of the world's most dynamic technological regions is the processes of knowledge creation and collective learning sustained by a community-based social and professional network. Labour mobility plays a critical role in the generation of these networks and facilitates the transmission of rapidly evolving knowledge—a large part of which may be tacit. There is a strong link between tacit knowledge and regional competitive advantage (Lawson and Lorenz 1999). The analysis also suggests that the processes of developing the capabilities of the individuals and organizational knowledge in the most dynamic technological sectors may be best served by an open labour market rooted in an occupational community.

Finegold (1999) argues that in turbulent, high-skill environments the responsibility for skills formation and career development shifted from the firm to the individual and regional cluster itself. This is because for the engineers and scientists, who are the key drivers of knowledge creation in the region, company-based formal training is often not the main vehicle for learning. Instead, these people enter the labour market with a high-level specialized qualification. They then continue to learn through project-based work and solving cutting-edge technical problems. Their wider personal and professional networks are another important source of learning. Inter-firm career mobility promotes learning and knowledge transfer. The willingness of the individuals to change firms, on which the collective

learning process depends, is made possible by the guarantee of job opportunities elsewhere within the region.

5.5.3. Denmark as Another Example of an 'Occupational Community Model'

Denmark represents another example of a national innovation and competence-building system that displays many of the characteristic features of the
occupational community model. And yet, the country has developed a
pattern of industrial specialization that deviates sharply from that of the
high-tech large economies. Denmark is one of the smallest OECD countries
with a population of just over 5 million. It has one of the highest levels of
GDP per capita in the world. The country is especially successful in the
production and export of low- or medium-technology goods.

The main industries include meat, fish, dairy products, wooden furniture,
and related machinery. Maskell et al. (1998) argue that the economic success
of Denmark, and also of other Nordic countries, demonstrates the possibilities for economies to generate a high level of prosperity while retaining a low-
tech industrial specialization. The main reason behind the competitive
advantage of these small countries, according to the authors, lies in the
capabilities of the social institutions to promote shared trust and interactive
learning resulting in a set of 'localized capabilities' which are tacit and difficult
to imitate for outsiders. But it is also important to note that the social and
institutional context favours a rapid and wide diffusion of advance process
technologies in the so-called low-tech sectors.

Denmark is characterized as a 'village economy' with a strong tradition for
consensus building deeply rooted in egalitarian values (Maskell et al. 1998). It
is one of the most equitable societies in the world and rich in social capital.
The business community has developed strong social networks and trade
associations enabling intense interaction and information sharing between
manufacturers and suppliers. Many Danish firms have also adopted a flexible
form of organization with a strong emphasis on cross-functional collaboration. Denmark has a well-developed state-funded vocational system resulting in a good supply of skilled workers. The flexible work system is highly
dependent on the competence and contribution of these workers. These
institutional features have enabled many small Danish manufacturers to
develop a superior ability to create and accumulate knowledge internally
and between firms through learning-by-doing and learning-by-interacting.
The success of the Danish furniture industry is a case in point (Maskell et al.
1998).

Danish firms are responsive to changes and have been able to combine technological changes with organizational innovation. Such responsive capacity is facilitated by an active labour market. It is suggested that inter-firm labour mobility in Denmark is as high, or possibly even higher than in the US but has a more limited geographical spread (Lundvall and Christensen 1999). The willingness of Danish workers to change jobs is buffered by a good social security net which reduces the costs and risks of job changes. Such social protection also contributes to the positive attitudes among the workers and trade unions to technical and organizational changes. In addition, Denmark has developed an extensive and highly regarded public system for continuous training for adults. All these institutional factors have made it possible to combine a fluid and open labour market with a high level of trust and cooperation which promote the development of learning organizations.

Although Denmark is especially successful in the relatively low- and medium-technology sectors, it also has some successful niche products in the high-technology sectors such as mobile telecommunications and also in pharmaceuticals. However, the dominant strategy has been to absorb and use technologies from abroad and the approach to innovation is incremental. This can be partly attributed to the fact that Denmark does not have a strong science base and the interaction between the private sector and universities is not well developed. Moreover, the majority of the academically trained workforce has historically opted for employment in the public sector. On the whole, the Danish system of innovation and competence building is geared towards competence-intensive low- and medium-tech sectors. It is less well developed for the large-scale science-based industries.

The Danish 'occupational community model' of competence building generates a learning pattern that is more similar to that found in Japan rather than that found in the high-technology clusters in the US or UK. The strong ability of Danish firms to learn collectively is rooted in the shared culture and village-like institutions of a small country. Such pre-existing social solidarity has shaped the formal social and economic institutions leading to a high level of cooperation and trust in the society as a whole. The whole country can be considered as a region like the industrial districts in the larger economies.

However, an important characteristic feature of village-like institutions is the exclusion of outsiders, as in the case of the corporate community in Japan. The Danish labour market is not open to immigrant workers. This is in stark contrast to the high-technology community in Silicon Valley, which builds on an extremely open and diverse labour market with a truly international character. Cohen and Fields (1999: 126) describe the foreign workforce as 'a vital transmission belt, diffusing technology and market knowledge, sometimes establishing offshore facilities that seed new districts and serve as connectors into the Valley'. The Silicon Valley labour market is local but borderless. This, arguably, is one of the region's most valuable assets and the main source of dynamism. In contrast, the localized learning capability of Danish firms is embedded in a truly local labour market with less scope for radical renewal.

5.6. CONCLUSIONS

This chapter is based on a hypothesis that we have entered a specific phase of economic development (which we refer to as 'the learning economy') where knowledge and learning have become more important than any earlier historical period. In the learning economy, individuals, firms, and even national economies will create wealth and get access to wealth in proportion to their capability to learn. This will be true regardless of their present level of development and competence. We will propose an even more far-reaching hypothesis stating that there is no alternative way to become permanently better off besides the one putting learning and knowledge creation at the centre of the strategy.

We have seen how different national systems have different pre-conditions when it comes to cope with the learning economy. The learning capability of Japanese firms is rooted in strong organizational integration and employee commitment based on stable employment relationships. Social capital is built on long-term obligational relationships within and between firms. In Denmark, the networked learning organizations are supported by a strong sense of communal trust and social solidarity that has become institutionalized in formal mechanisms for collective decision-making. In the Anglo-American economies characterized by liberal market institutions and professional individualism, the creation of regional clusters appears to be critical for promoting collective learning rooted in professional and inter-firm innovation networks.

There is a variety of approaches to promoting learning and innovation. Societies with different institutional arrangements develop different types of learning organizations and innovative competencies that appear to generate and reproduce distinctive regional or national patterns of technological specialization. The Japanese 'organizational community' model continues to orient major Japanese firms towards adopting high-quality incremental innovation strategies and sustaining competitiveness in mature technological fields. Japan may find it difficult to develop a 'societal strategic advantage' (Biggart and Orru 1997) in areas characterized by rapid and disruptive changes. The R&D globalization strategies adopted by Japanese firms in the science-based sectors appear to have limited effect in altering their established learning patterns and innovative trajectories (Lam 2003).

In contrast to Japan, the Anglo-Saxon 'occupational community' model can better accommodate a science-driven, entrepreneurial approach to innovation and perform well in sectors in which radical learning is important. A major underlying structural weakness of this model, however, is the marked segmentation between professional and production workers, and the bias of the competence-building system in favour of the interests of high-technology firms (Angles 2000). Denmark, on the other hand, has developed a specialization pattern in low- and medium-technology sectors with a focus on an incremental innovation strategy. The Danish case also suggests that an innovation-driven redeployment of competencies can be organized more collectively by public agency action and an emphasis on workforce vocational training and lifelong learning. The so-called 'new economy' configuration as observed in Silicon Valley based on deregulated labour markets and excellence in scientific personnel is not necessarily the benchmark for fostering innovation and economic growth.

It is also important to emphasize that learning is an activity going on in all parts of the economy, including so-called low-tech and traditional sectors. As a matter of fact, learning taking place in traditional and low-tech sectors may be more important for economic development than learning in a small number of insulated high-tech firms. The learning potential (technological opportunities) may differ between sectors and technologies, but in most broadly defined sectors there will be niches where the potential for learning is high. This is important in a period where knowledge policy tends to be equated with science policy and with support to science-based firms.

Finally, it should be noted that all kinds of labor have skills and a capability to learn, including what misleadingly is called 'unskilled workers'. These specifications are made in order to avoid that the learning economy hypothesis leads to a neglect of the developmental potential of parts of the economy less intensive in their use of formally acquired knowledge.

NOTES

1. Her discussion of knowledge is quite advanced and worth a much deeper analysis. Penrose defines knowledge as encompassing both information (know-what) and skills (know-how). She introduces 'learning-by-doing' as well as 'learning-by-searching'. And, finally, she insists on the fact that economists interested in industrial dynamics cannot allow themselves to neglect the systematic analysis of this 'slippery' subject.

2. Below we present four different types of organizations that differ when it comes to their basic style of knowledge management. Three of them may correspond to the three functions referred to here: Machine bureaucracy—resource allocation, J-form organization—capability based growth, Operating Adhocracy—high-speed learning.

REFERENCES

Amable, B., Barré, R., and Boyer, R. (1997). *Les systémes d'innovation a l'ére de la globalization*. Paris: Economica.

Andersen, E. S. and Lundvall, B.-Å. (1988). 'Small National Innovation Systems Facing Technological Revolutions: An Analytical Framework', in C. Freeman, and B.-Å. Lundvall, (eds.), *Small Countries Facing the Technological Revolution*. London: Pinter, pp. 1–31.

Angels, D. P. (2000). 'High-Technology Agglomeration and the Labour Market: The Case of Silicon Valley', in K. Martin (ed.), *Understanding Silicon Valley: The Anatomy of an Entrepreneurial Region*. Stanford, CA: Stanford University Press, pp. 125–89.

Aoki, M. (1988). *Information, Incentives and Bargaining in the Japanese Economy*. Cambridge: Cambridge University Press.

Bahrami, H. and Evans, S. (2000). 'Flexible Recycling and High-Technology Entrepreneurship', in K. Martin (ed.), *Understanding Silicon Valley: The Anatomy of an Entrepreneurial Region*. Stanford, CA: Stanford University Press, pp. 166–89.

Barley, S. R. (1996). 'Technicians in the Workplace: Ethnographic Evidence for Bringing Work into Organization Studies', *Administrative Science Quarterly*, 41(3): 404–41.

Biggart, N. W. and Orru, M. (1997). 'Societal Strategic Advantage: Institutional Structure and Path Dependence in the Automotive and Electronics Industries in East Asia', in A. Bugra, and B. Usdiken (eds.), *State, Market and Organizational Form*. Berlin: Walter de Gruyter.

Buechtemann, C. F. and Verdier, E. (1998). 'Education and Training Regimes: Macro-Institutional Evidence', *Revue d'economie politique*, 108(3): 291–320.

Carter, A. P. (1994). 'Production Workers, Metainvestment and the Pace of Change', Paper prepared for the meetings of the *International J.A. Schumpeter Society*, Munster, August 1994.

Cohen, S. S. and Fields, G. (1999). 'Social Capital and Capital Gains in Silicon Valley', *California Management Review*, 41(2): 108–30.

DeFillipi, R. (2002). 'Organization Models for Collaboration in the New Economy', *Human Resource Planning*, 25(4): 7–19.

DeFillipi, R. J. and Arthur, M. B. (1996). 'Boundarlyess Contexts and Careers: A Competency-Based Perspective', in M. B. Arthur and D. M. Rousseau (eds.),

The Boundaryless Career: A New Employment Principle for a New Organizational Era. New York: Oxford University Press, pp. 116–31.

Dertoutzos, M. L., Lester, R. K., and Solow, R. M. (1989). *Made in America: Regaining the Productivity Edge.* Cambridge, MA: MIT Press.

EIRMA (1993). '*Speeding up Innovation*', Conference papers for the EIRMA Helsinki conference, May.

Finegold, D. (1999). 'Creating Self-Sustaining High-Skill Ecosystems', *Oxford Review of Economic Policy*, 15(1): 60–81.

Foray, D. and Lundvall, B.-Å. (1996). 'The Knowledge-Based Economy: From the Economics of Knowledge to the Learning Economy' in D. Foray, and B.-Å. Lundvall (eds.), *Employment and Growth in the Knowledge-Based Economy.* OECD Documents, Paris.

Freeman, C. (1987). *Technology Policy and Economic Performance: Lessons from Japan.* London: Pinter.

—— (1988). 'The national system of innovation in historical perspective', *Cambridge Journal of Economics*, 19: 5–24.

Galunic, D. C. and Eisenhardt, K. M. (2001). 'Architectural Innovation and Modular Corporate Forms', *Academy of Management Journal*, 44(6): 1229–49.

Gelsing, L. (1992). 'Innovation and the Development of Industrial Networks', in B.-Å. Lundvall, (ed.), *National Systems of Innovation: Towards a Theory of Innovation and Interactive Learning.* London: Pinter.

Gjerding, A. N. (1996). 'Organisational Innovation in the Danish Private Business', *DRUID Working Paper*, no. 96–16, Department of Business Studies, Aalborg University, Aalborg.

Hedlund, G. (1994). 'A Model of Knowledge Management and the N-Form Corporation', *Strategic Management Journal*, 15: 73–90.

Jensen, E. (1992). 'Samarbejde eller konkurrence', Ph.D. thesis, Serie om industriel udvikling nr. 38, Aalalborg University Press, Aalborg.

Johnson, B. (1992). 'Institutional Learning', in B.-Å. Lundvall (ed.), *National Systems of Innovation: Towards a Theory of Innovation and Interactive Learning.* London: Pinter.

Koike, K. (1995). *The Economics of Work in Japan.* Tokyo: LTCB International Library Foundation.

Kristensen, P. H. (1996). 'On the Constitutions of Economic Actors in Denmark: Interacting Skill Containers and Project Coordinators', in R. Whitley and P. H. Kristensen (eds.), *The Changing European Firm: Limits to Convergence.* London: Routledge.

Lam, A. (1996). 'Engineers, Management and Work Organization: A Comparative Analysis of Engineers' Work Roles in British and Japanese Electronics Firms', *Journal of Management Studies*, 33(2): 183–212.

—— (1997). 'Embedded Firms, Embedded Knowledge: Problems of Collaboration and Knowledge Transfer in Global Cooperative Ventures', *Organization Studies*, 18(6): 973–96.

—— (2000a). 'Tacit Knowledge, Organisational Learning and Societal Institutions: An Integrated Framework', *Organization Studies*, 21(3): 487–513.

Lam, A. (2000*b*). 'Skills Formation in the Knowledge-Based Economy: Transformation Pressures in European High-Technology Industries', *International Industrial Relations 12th World Congress*, Tokyo.

—— (2003). 'Organizational Learning in Multinationals: R&D Networks of Japanese and US MNEs in the UK', *Journal of Management Studies*, 40(3): 674–703.

—— (2005). 'Organizational Innovation', in J. Fagerberg, D. Mowery, and R. Nelson (eds.), *Handbook of Innovation*. Oxford: Oxford University Press.

Lawson, C. and Lorenz, E. (1999). 'Collective Learning, Tacit Knowledge and Regional Innovative Capacity', *Regional Studies*, 33(4): 305–28.

—— et al. (1997). *Inter-firm Links Between Regionally Clustered High-Technology SMEs: A Comparison of Cambridge and Oxford Innovation Networks*. Working Paper, Cambridge: Cambridge University.

Lazonick, W. and West, J. (1998). 'Organization Integration and Competitive Advantage', in G. Dosi, et al. (eds.), *Technology, Organization and Competitiveness*. Oxford: Oxford University Press.

List, F. (1841). *Das Nationale System der Politischen Ökonomie*, Basel: Kyklos (translated and published under the title: *The National System of Political Economy* by Longmans, Green and Co., London 1841).

Loasby, B. (1991). *Equilibrium and Evolution*. Manchester, UK: Manchester University Press.

Lund, R. and Gjerding, A. N. (1996). 'The Flexible Company, Innovation, Work Organisation and Human Resource Management', *DRUID Working Paper* 96–17, Department of Business Studies, Aalborg University, Aalborg.

Lundvall, B.-Å. (1985). *Product Innovation and User-Producer Interaction*. Aalborg, Denmark: Aalborg University Press.

—— (1999). *The Danish System of Innovation* (in Danish). Copenhagen: Erhvervsfremmestyrelsen.

—— (ed.) (1992). *National Systems of Innovation: Towards a Theory of Innovation and Interactive Learning*. London: Pinter.

—— and Christensen, J. L. (1999). 'Extending and Deepening the Analysis of Innovation Systems: With Empirical Illustrations from the DISKO-Project', Paper for *DRUID Conference on National Innovation Systems*, Rebild.

—— and Nielsen, P. (1999). 'Competition and Transformation in the Learning Economy—Illustrated by the Danish Case', *Revue d'Economie Industrielle*, 88: 67–90.

Maskell, P. (1998). 'Learning in the Village Economy of Denmark. The Role of Institutions and Policy in Sustaining Competitiveness', in H. J. Braczyk, P. Cooke, and M. Heidenreich (eds.), *Regional Innovation Systems. The Role of Governance in a Globalized World*. London: UCL Press, pp. 190–213.

—— (1998). *Competitiveness, Localised Learning and Regional Development: Specialisation and Prosperity in Small Open Economies*. London: Routledge.

Miles, R. E., Snow, C. C., Mathews, J. A., Miles, G., and Coleman, H. J. Jr. (1997). 'Organizing in the Knowledge Age: Anticipating the Cellular Form', *Academy of Management Executive*, 11(4): 7–20.

Morikawa, H. (1991). 'The Education of Engineers in Modern Japan: An Historical Perspective', in H. Gospel (ed.), *Industrial Training and Technological Innovation*. London: Routledge.

Nelson, R. R. (1988). 'Institutions Supporting Technical Change in the United States', in Dosi et al. (eds.), *Technology and Economic Theory*. London: Pinter.

—— (ed.) (1993). *National Systems of Innovations: A Comparative Analysis*. Oxford: Oxford University Press.

Nonaka, I. and Takeuchi, H. (1995). *The Knowledge Creating Company*. Oxford: Oxford University Press.

OECD (1996a). *Science, Technology and Industry Outlook 1996*. Paris.

—— (1996b). *Transitions to Learning Economies and Societies*. Paris.

Penrose, E. (1959/1995). *The Theory of the Growth of the Firm*. Oxford: Oxford University Press.

Polanyi, M. (1962). *Personal Knowledge: Towards a Post-Critical Philosophye*. New York: Harper Torchbooks / London: Routledge and Kegan Paul.

—— (1966). *The Tacit Dimension*. New York: Anchor Day Books London: Routledge and Kegan Paul.

Porter, M. (1990). *The Competitive Advantage of Nations*. London: MacMillan.

Richardson, G. B. (1996). 'Competition, Innovation and Increasing Return', *DRUID Working Paper*, No. 10, Copenhagen Business School, Department of Industrial Economics and Strategy.

—— (1997). 'Economic Analysis, Public Policy and the Software Industry', *DRUID Working Paper*, No. 4, Copenhagen Business School, Department of Industrial Economics and Strategy.

Saxenian, A. (1996). 'Beyond Boundaries: Open Labour Markets and Learning in the Silicon Valley', in M. B. Arthur and D. M. Rousseau (eds.), *The Boundaryless Career: A New Employment Principle for the New Organisational Era*. New York: Oxford University Press.

Segal, Quince Wicksteed (2000). *The Cambridge Phenomenon Revisited*. Cambridge: SQW.

Senge, P. (1990). *The Fifth Discipline: The Art and Practice of Learning*. New York: Doubleday.

Soskice, D. (1997).'German Technology Policy, Innovation, and National Institutional Frameworks', *Industry and Innovation*, 4: 75–96.

Taddei, D. and Coriat, B. (1993). *Made in France*. Paris: le Livre de Poche.

Whitley, R. (1996). 'The Social Construction of Economic Actors: Institutions and Types of Firm in Europe and Other Market Economies', in R. Whitley (ed.), *The Changing European Firm*. London: Routledge.

Womack, J. P., Jones, D. T., and Roos, D. (1990). *The Machine that Changed the World*. New York: Rawson Associates.

6

Organizational Forms and Innovative Performance: A Comparison of the EU-15

Edward Lorenz and Antoine Valeyre

6.1. INTRODUCTION

Over the last decades European researchers have made major efforts aimed at understanding and measuring technical innovation including its diffusion and impact upon economic performance. These efforts, often supported by the European Commission programmes, have relied on the establishment of international norms for the collection of harmonized S&T measures including the Frascati Manual for R&D statistics, the Canberra Manual for human resources for science and technology (HRST), and the Oslo Manual for product and process innovation.

At present there exist no harmonized data on processes of organizational change for the EU. This lack of organizational data seriously limits our ability to compare and effectively benchmark policies for knowledge development and use and for innovative performance specifically. There is a general consensus that processes of knowledge creation in organizational settings are complex and interactive, involving multiple feedbacks between different services and functions as well as manifold interactions with customers and suppliers (Kline and Rosenberg 1985; Freeman 1987; Lundvall 1988; Nonaka and Takeuichi 1995). Moreover, it is generally accepted that while R&D and the skills of scientists and engineers with third-level training are important inputs to knowledge creation, these are not the only inputs. Improving product quality and developing new products and services also depends critically on the skills developed by employees on-the-job in the process of solving the technical and production-related problems encountered in testing, producing, and marketing new products and processes. Developing these sorts of skills in turn depends not just on the quality of formal education, but on having the right organizational structures and work environments. Work environments need to be designed to promote learning through problem solving and to effectively use these skills for innovation.

This implies that relevant indicators for knowledge development need to do more than capture R&D expenditures and the quality of the available pool of skills by measuring years of education. Indicators also need to capture how these material and human resources are used and appropriate work environments for the further development of the knowledge and skills of employees.

The main contribution of this chapter is to provide a first EU-wide mapping of organizational forms in order to better characterize the relation between work environments and organizational learning dynamics. The chapter then proceeds to explore at the national level the relation between indicators of organizational forms and indicators of technological innovation. The results show that a nation's rate and style of technological innovation is associated with the way work is organized to promote learning and problem-solving.

The chapter is structured as follows. Sections 6.2 and 6.3 describe the variables used to characterize work organization in the fifteen countries of the EU, and present the results of the factor analysis and hierarchical clustering used to construct a typology of organizational forms. Section 6.4 examines how the relative importance of the different organizational forms varies according to sector, firm size, and occupational category. The fifth section examines differences in the relative importance of organizational forms across EU nations. The sixth section considers to what extent national differences in the relative importance of organizational forms is associated with differences in measures of technological innovation and differences in the way labour markets are regulated. The concluding section considers some of the main implications of the research for European policy options.

6.2. MEASURING FORMS OF WORK ORGANIZATION IN THE EUROPEAN UNION

The research is based on the results of the third European survey on Working Conditions undertaken by the European Foundation for the Improvement of Living and Working Conditions.[1] The survey was carried out in each of the fifteen member states of the EU in March 2000. The survey questionnaire was directed to approximately 1,500 active persons in each country with the exception of Luxembourg with only 500 respondents. The total survey population is 21,703 persons, of which 17,910 are salaried employees. The survey methodology is based on a multi-stage random sampling method called 'random walk' involving face-to-face interviews undertaken at the respondent's principal residence. The analysis of forms of work organization developed here is based on the responses of the 8,081 salaried employees working in establishments with at least 10 persons in both industry and services, but excluding agriculture and fishing; public administration and social security; education; health and social work; and private domestic employees.

In order to describe the principal forms of work organization across the fifteen nations of the EU, a factor analysis and hierarchical clustering method[2] have been used on the basis of the following fifteen organizational variables:[3]

- a binary variable measuring the use of team work[4] (team);
- a binary variable measuring job rotation[5] (rot);
- two binary variables measuring autonomy in work: autonomy in the methods used (autm) and autonomy in the pace or rate at which work is carried out (autp);
- four binary variables measuring the factors or constraints which determine the pace or rate of work: 'automatic' constraints linked to the rate as which equipment is operated or a product is displaced in the production flow (caut); norm-based constraints linked to the setting of quantitative production norms (cnorm); 'hierarchical' constraints linked to the direct control which is exercised by one's immediate superiors (chier); and 'horizontal' constraints linked to way one person's work rate is dependent on the work of his or her colleagues (chor);
- a binary variable measuring repetitiveness of tasks[6] (rep);
- a binary variable measuring the perceived task monotony (mono);
- two binary variables measuring the way quality is controlled: (qn) which corresponds to the use of precise quality norms; and (qc) which corresponds to individual responsibility for the control of quality;
- a binary variable measuring the complexity of tasks (cmplx);
- and two binary variables measuring learning dynamics in work: (learn) which corresponds to whether the individual learns new things in his or her work; and (pbsolv) which corresponds to whether the work requires problem-solving activity.

6.2.1. The Main Dimensions of Work Organization

Figure 6.1 below presents graphically the first two axes or factors of the multiple correspondence analysis (MCA). The first factor, accounting for 18 per cent of the inertia or chi-squared statistic, distinguishes between taylorist and 'post-taylorist' organizational forms. Thus, on one side of the axis we find the variables measuring autonomy, learning, problem-solving and task complexity and to a lesser degree quality management, while on the other side, we find the variables measuring monotony and the various factors constraining work pace, notably those linked to the automatic speed of equipment or flow of products, and to the use of quantitative production norms.

The second axis, accounting for 15 per cent of the chi-squared statistic, is structured by two groups of variables characteristic of the lean production model: first, the use of teams and job rotation which are associated with the importance of horizontal constraints on work pace; and second, those variables measuring the use of quality management techniques which are associated with what we have called 'automatic' and 'norm-based' constraints. The third factor, which accounts for 8 per cent of the chi-squared statistic, is also structured by these two groups of variables. However, it brings into relief the distinction between, on the one hand, those organizational settings characterized by team work, job rotation, and horizontal interdependence in work, and on the other, those organizational settings where the use of quality norms and automatic and quantitative norm-based constraints on work pace are important. The second and third axes of the analysis demonstrate that the simple dichotomy between taylorist and lean organizational methods is not sufficient for capturing the organizational variety that exists across European nations.

6.3. A TYPOLOGY OF ORGANIZATIONAL FORMS

The various distinctions brought out by the MCA can for the most part be observed in the results of the hierarchical cluster analysis that has been carried out on the factor scores of all fifteen factors resulting from the MCA. The cluster analysis results in a grouping of individuals into four basic organizational forms:

- 'learning' forms of work organization;
- 'lean' forms of work organization;
- 'taylorist' forms of work organization;
- and 'simple' or 'traditional' forms of work organization

As the projection of the centre of gravity of the clusters onto the graphic representation of the first two factors of the MCA suggests (see Figure 6.1), and as Table 6.1 shows in more detail, the four clusters correspond to quite different ways of organizing work. The first cluster, referred to as the learning model, groups 39 per cent of the employees. It is characterized by the over-representation of the variables measuring autonomy and task complexity,

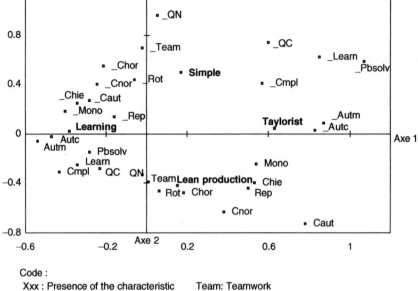

Figure 6.1. Forms of work organization

Code :
Xxx : Presence of the characteristic
_Xxx: Absence of the characteristic
Autm: Autonomy in work methods
Autc: Autonomy in work speed
Learn: Learning new things
Pbsolv: Probelms solving activity
Complx: Complex tasks
QC: Responsibility for quality control

Team: Teamwork
Rot: Job rotation
Mono: Task monotony
Rep: Task repetitiveness
Caut: Automatic constraints on work pace
Cnorm: Quantitative norm constraints on work pace
Chier: Hierarchical constraints on work pace
QN: Precise quality norms
Chor: Horizontal constraints on work pace

learning and problem-solving, and to a lesser degree by an overrepresentation of the variable measuring individual responsibility for quality management. The variables reflecting monotony, repetitiveness, and work rate constraints are underrepresented. This cluster would appear to correspond to the Swedish socio-technical model of work organization, or to what Freyssenet (1995) has referred to as 'reflexive production'. It would also appear to have much in common with what Appelbaum and Batt in their 1994 volume referred to as the 'American team production' model which combines the Swedish socio-technical principles with a contemporary emphasis on individual responsibility for quality control. A somewhat surprising result, though, is that neither teamwork nor job rotation are defining characteristics of this model of work organization, suggesting that the emphasis on the importance of these practices as a condition for promoting learning and problem-solving on the part of employees is probably exaggerated in the literature.

Table 6.1 Work organization clusters

	Learning organ- ization (%)	Lean produc- tion (%)	Taylor- ism (%)	Simple organ- ization (%)	All(%)
Autonomy fixing work methods	89.1	51.8	17.7	46.5	61.7
Autonomy setting work rate	87.5	52.2	27.3	52.7	63.6
Learning new things in work	93.9	81.7	42.0	29.7	71.4
Problem-solving activities	95.4	98.0	5.7	68.7	79.3
Complexity of tasks	79.8	64.7	23.8	19.2	56.7
Responsibility for quality control	86.4	88.7	46.7	38.9	72.6
Quality norms	78.1	94.0	81.1	36.1	74.4
Team work	64.3	84.2	70.1	33.4	64.2
Job rotation	44.0	70.5	53.2	27.5	48.9
Monotony of tasks	19.5	65.8	65.6	43.9	42.4
Repetitiveness of tasks	12.8	41.9	37.1	19.2	24.9
Horizontal constraints on work rate	43.6	80.3	66.1	27.8	53.1
Hierarchical constraints on work rate	19.6	64.4	66.5	26.7	38.9
Norm-based constraints on work rate	21.2	75.5	56.3	14.7	38.7
Automatic constraints on work rate	5.4	59.8	56.9	7.2	26.7

Note: Per cent of employees in each cluster.
Source: Third Working Condition survey. European Foundation for the Improvement of Living and Working Conditions.

The second cluster, which accounts for 28 per cent of the population, is characterized by an overrepresentation of teamwork and job rotation, the quality management variables, and the various factors constraining work pace. This cluster, like the first, displays strong learning dynamics and relies on employees' contribution to problem-solving. Yet compared to the first cluster autonomy in work is relatively low and tight quantitative production norms are used to control employee effort. One easily recognizes here the classic attributes of the 'lean' or 'high-performance work' model (Ichiniowski et al. 1997; Womack, Jones, and Roos 1990; MacDuffie and Krafcik 1992; Osterman 1994). Compared to classic forms of taylorism autonomy in work is relatively high. However, worker autonomy is bracketed by the importance of work pace constraints linked to the collective nature of the work and to the requirement of respecting strict quantitative production norms. This class has much in common with what Coutrot (1998) has described as a 'controlled' autonomy in work.

The third class, which groups 14 per cent of the employees, corresponds in most respects to a classic characterization of taylorism. The work situation is in most respects the opposite of that found in first cluster, with minimal learning dynamics, low complexity, low autonomy, and an overrepresentation of the variables measuring constraints on the pace of work. Interestingly, teams and job rotation are somewhat overrepresented in this cluster, confirming the importance of what some authors refer to as 'flexible taylorism' (Cézard, Dussert, and Gollac 1992; Boyer and Durand 1993; Linhart 1994).

The fourth cluster groups 19 per cent of the employees. It is poorly described by the work organization variables which, with the exception of monotony in work, are all underrepresented. This class presumably groups traditional or simple forms of work organization, where methods are for the most part informal and non-codified.

6.4. DIFFERENCES IN FORMS OF WORK ORGANIZATION ACCORDING TO STRUCTURAL AND OCCUPATIONAL CHARACTERISTICS

Forms of work organization vary considerably across sectors, firm sizes, and occupational category. The figures presented in Table 6.2 show that variations in the relative importance of the organizational forms across sectors are connected to differences in sectoral systems of innovation. Thus, the learning forms of organization are especially developed in such relatively knowledge-intensive service sectors, as business services and banks and insurance, where innovation typically depends on intensive knowledge exchange between producers and clients. The taylorist forms, on the other hand, are more present in such traditional manufacturing sectors as textiles, clothing and leather products, and wood and paper products, where technological standards are well established and innovation dynamics are relatively slow and incremental. The lean model of production is especially present in manufacturing sectors, such as transport equipment, electronics and electrical production, wood and paper products, and printing and publishing, where competitive performance often depends on continuously upgrading quality to meet international standards. The residual forms of work organization grouped in the fourth cluster are to be found principally in the services, notably personal services, hotels and restaurants, post and telecommunications, and wholesale and retail trade.

Table 6.3 provides evidence on variations in forms of work organization according to occupational category. The figures show that the learning forms are especially developed in occupations where work tends to be professional and individual in character and requires university education, while the lean forms are more developed in work settings characterized by teamwork and requiring regular renewal of vocational qualifications. Thus, the learning forms of work organization are especially characteristic of the work of managers, professionals, and technicians, while the lean forms are more characteristic of the work of skilled craftsmen and machine operators. The taylorist forms are

Table 6.2 Forms of work organization by sector of activity

	Learning organisation (%)	Lean production (%)	Taylorism (%)	Simple organisation (%)
Mining and quarrying	42.4	41.5	3.4	12.7
Food processing	18.4	34.9	24.6	22.1
Textiles, garments, leather products	27.2	25.9	30.2	16.8
Wood and paper products	27.6	40.7	23.9	7.8
Publishing and printing	31.1	43.8	14.1	11.0
Chemicals and plastics	34.7	34.1	21.9	9.2
Metal products and mechanical engineering	31.8	35.7	19.8	12.7
Electrical engineering and electronics	41.5	38.5	8.6	11.4
Transport equipment	28.1	38.7	23.2	10.0
Other industrial production	50.9	22.1	18.4	8.5
Electricity, gas, and water	58.5	19.4	6.2	15.8
Construction	40.9	31.4	10.6	17.1
Wholesale and retail trade	41.5	20.4	11.7	26.4
Hotels and restaurants	29.7	25.8	16.6	27.9
Land transport	26.3	24.0	10.2	39.5
Other transport	39.2	36.1	5.0	19.7
Post and telecommunications	38.1	27.1	7.7	27.1
Financial services	58.1	21.5	3.4	16.9
Business services	57.6	18.7	6.9	16.7
Personal services	39.7	18.9	7.6	33.8
Total	39,1	28,2	13,6	19,1

Note: Per cent of employees by organizational class.
Source: Third Working Condition survey. European Foundation for the Improvement of Living and Working Conditions.

most present amongst the unskilled trades as well as machine operators. Finally, the simple forms of work organization grouped in the fourth cluster are especially characteristic of the less skilled service workers and shop and market sales persons.

Establishment size constitutes a relatively unimportant factor in the use of different organizational models. As Table 6.4 shows, establishments in the 100–249 employee range are less likely to be characterized by learning forms of work organization. The lean and taylorist forms increase somewhat with establishment size, while the reverse tendency can be observed for the use of simple forms of work organization.

While the importance of the organizational forms vary according to sector, occupation and establishment size, it is important to realize that these

Table 6.3 Forms of work organization according to occupational category

	Learning organization	Lean production	Taylorism	Simple organization
Managers	69.1	24.7	0.2	6.0
Engineers and professionals	75.9	14.0	5.2	4.9
Technicians	61.0	24.6	2.4	12.0
Clerks	43.2	21.9	9.4	25.5
Service and shop and market sales persons	30.3	21.4	12.4	35.9
Craft and related trades	34.2	38.5	16.5	10.8
Machine operators and assemblers	15.7	37.7	24.3	22.3
Unskilled trades	14.8	23.9	26.7	34.5
Total	39.1	28.2	13.6	19.1

Note: Per cent of employees by organizational class.
Source: Third Working Condition survey. European Foundation for the Improvement of Living and Working Conditions.

Table 6.4 Forms of work organization according to establishment size

Establishment size (number of employees)	Learning organization	Lean production	Taylorism	Simple organization
10–49	42.7	24.6	11.2	21.5
50–99	36.4	29.0	15.2	19.5
100–249	33.8	31.5	16.0	18.6
250–499	37.9	28.4	17.6	16.1
500 and over	38.7	32.6	13.2	15.5
Total	39.1	28.2	13.6	19.1

Note: Per cent of employees by organizational class.
Source: Third Working Condition survey. European Foundation for the Improvement of Living and Working Conditions.

structural variables by no means explain all the observed variation. All four organizational forms can be observed within individual sectors and occupational categories. In the following section we show that there are important national differences in the relative use of the organizational forms independent of structural and occupational characteristics.

6.5. NATIONAL EFFECTS ON WORK ORGANIZATION

Table 6.5 shows that there are wide differences in the importance of the four forms of work organization across European nations. The learning forms of work

Table 6.5 National differences in organizational models

	Learning organization	Lean production	Taylorism	Simple organization
Belgium	38.9	25.1	13.9	22.1
Denmark	60.0	21.9	6.8	11.3
Germany	44.3	19.6	14.3	21.9
Greece	18.7	25.6	28.0	27.7
Italy	30.0	23.6	20.9	25.4
Spain	20.1	38.8	18.5	22.5
France	38.0	33.3	11.1	17.7
Ireland	24.0	37.8	20.7	17.6
Luxembourg	42.8	25.4	11.9	20.0
Netherlands	64.0	17.2	5.3	13.5
Portugal	26.1	28.1	23.0	22.8
United Kingdom	34.8	40.6	10.9	13.7
Finland	47.8	27.6	12.5	12.1
Sweden	52.6	18.5	7.1	21.7
Austria	47.5	21.5	13.1	18.0
EU-15	39.1	28.2	13.6	19.1

Note: Per cent of employees by organizational class.
Source: Third Working Condition survey. European Foundation for the Improvement of Living and Working Conditions.

organization are most widely diffused in the Netherlands, the Nordic countries, and to a lesser extent Germany and Austria. The lean model is most in evidence in the UK, Ireland, and Spain and to a lesser extent in France. The taylorist forms still have a strong foothold in the four southern nations, while simple or traditional forms of work organization are most in evidence in Greece and Italy and to a lesser extent in Germany, Sweden, Belgium, Spain, and Portugal.

The figures suggest that as EU nations have progressively moved away from more traditional or hierarchical organizational forms and have sought to increase their capacity for learning and problem-solving, they have done this in different ways. Amongst nations with relatively high per capita income levels, the UK and Ireland stand out for their intensive use of the lean forms, while the Nordic nations and to a lesser extent Germany and Austria stand out for their use of the learning forms. France and Belgium present a more balanced picture regarding the use of these two organizational forms.

The discussion in Section 6.4 has shown that the learning and lean forms tend to be associated with particular sectors and occupational categories, and this raises the question of what part of the differences shown in Table 6.5 can be accounted for by these structural variables. In order to address this question, in what follows we make use of multinomial logit regression analysis (see Table 6.6). The dependent variable is the relative likelihood of using the

Table 6.6 Multinomial regression estimates of national effects[1]

	Relative likelihood of learning over lean model	
	Without structural controls	With structural controls
Denmark	0.376*	0.464*
Germany	0.594*	0.655**
Greece	−0.755**	−0.835*
Italy	−0.199	−0.019
Spain	−1.097**	−1.119**
France	−0.308	−0.325
Ireland	−0.894*	−1.118**
Luxembourg	0.083	0.037
Netherlands	0.873**	0.854**
Portugal	−0.515*	−0.457*
UK	−0.592**	−0.888**
Finland	0.110	−0.018
Sweden	0.602**	0.565**
Austria	0.355*	0.565**
Pseudo R^2	0.030	0.151
No.	8081	8081

Notes: [1] The reference country for these estimates is Belgium.
* = significant at the 0.05 level; ** = significant at the 0.01 level.

learning forms of organization over the lean forms, and the independent variable is a categorical variable with fifteen classes corresponding to country. The reference case for the estimates is Belgium, the country whose relative use of the various organizational forms is closest to the EU average (see Table 6.5). The column 1 estimates show the relative likelihood of using the learning forms of work organization over the lean forms without structural controls. Column 2 presents the estimates of the same relative likelihood controlling for sector, establishment size, and occupational category. [7]

As the column 1 results show, the country the employee works in has a significant impact on the relative likelihood of using the learning forms over the lean forms. Compared to the Belgian case, there are five countries with a significantly higher relative use of the learning forms: Germany, Denmark, the Netherlands, Sweden, and Austria. There are five countries where the relatively higher use of the lean forms is statistically significant: the UK, Ireland, Greece, Spain, and Portugal. While the coefficients are positive in the case of Finland and Luxembourg and negative in the case France and Italy, the differences relative to the Belgium case are not significant.

When the three structural control variables are added (column 2) the pseudo R^2 increases from 3 to 15 per cent, with sector, and occupational category accounting for 39 and 58 per cent of the increase, respectively.

Regarding national effects on the relative likelihood of adopting the learning over the lean forms, the results show that the column 1 results are robust in all instances providing strong support for the importance of national effects on organizational practice.

The results confirm that among the countries with relatively high per capita income levels, the UK and Ireland are distinctive for their intensive use of the lean forms. The UK also stands out for the large absolute increase in the size of the negative coefficient once control variables are included in the regression estimate. This can most plausibly be accounted for the large size of the service sector in the UK. Relative to manufacturing, services in general tend to have a higher representation of the learning forms, and once we control for this distinctive feature of the UK's industrial structure, the tendency to adopt the lean over the learning forms in that country is even more pronounced.

6.6 THE RELATION BETWEEN ORGANIZATIONAL FORMS AND INNOVATION RATE AND STYLE

One factor that bears on organizational choice and design is the evolving nature of competition in the knowledge-based economy, which increasingly depends on the ability to mobilize employee competence in order to innovate new goods and processes. The learning and lean forms of organization, both of which draw on employees' capacity for continuous learning and problem-solving, can be expected to be more adapted to this form of competition. Although the Third European Survey of Working Conditions does not contain the data that would allow us to explore this question at the micro-level, it is possible to construct macro-level measures that provide empirical support for the proposition. Thus, Figure 6.2 shows, for the fifteen member countries, that there is a positive relation between the percentage of employees in a nation whose work is characterized either by the learning or by the lean models and a standard measure of innovative effort, R&D expenditures as a percentage of GDP (GERD).

Close inspection of the figure, however, suggests that the positive relation identified can be explained by the presence of the four southern European nations. If we restrict our attention to the Nordic and central and western European nations, which on average have much higher levels of expenditure on R&D, there is no obvious relation between the variables. This suggests that the figure is basically capturing an organizational distinction between two groups of nations with differing levels of technological capability.

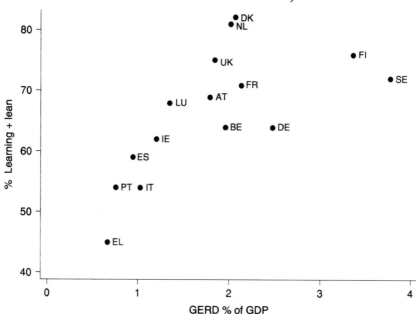

Figure 6.2. Organizational forms and R&D
Source: Third Working Conditions Survey (2000); Eurostat structural indicators (2000).

This leaves unaddressed the impact of the differences in the organizational choices of the more advanced group of nations and, in particular, the impact on innovation rate and style of the of the UK and Ireland's relatively intensive use of the lean forms. Turning first to the question of rate, Figure 6.3 shows a clear positive relation between the relative use of the learning forms of organization and a standard indicator of innovation performance, EPO patent applications per million inhabitants.

Innovation style is less easy to capture than rate. Style is often characterized in terms of the relative importance of incremental versus radical innovations. The distinction is often seen as corresponding to the degree to which innovations are competence destroying as opposed to competence enhancing. Developing empirical indicators for this distinction is problematic because survey manuals, such as the *Oslo Manual* which establishes conventions for the European Community's innovation surveys, do not propose guidelines for its measure. Here we draw on the results of the Community Innovation Surveys to develop different, though related, indicators of innovation style.

Figure 6.4 shows the relation between the relative importance of the learning forms of organization and a measure of the relative importance of

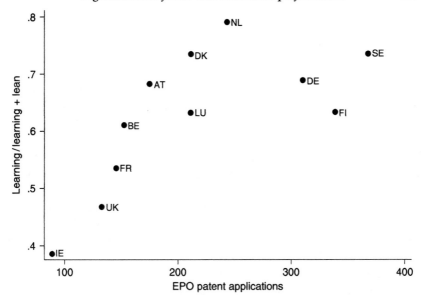

Figure 6.3. Relative importance of learning forms and patent applications
Source: Third Working Conditions Survey (2000); Eurostat structural indicators (2000).

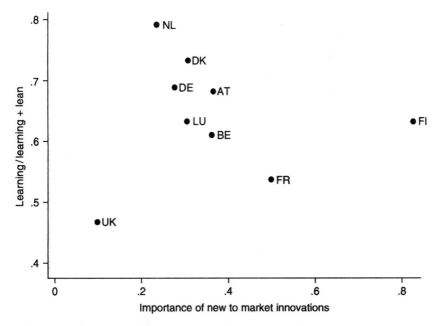

Figure 6.4. Relative importance of learning forms and new for the market innovations
Source: Third Working Conditions Survey (2000); Community Innovation Survey III.

sales of products that are new to the market as opposed to new to the firm.[8] The new to the market/new to firm distinction is not identical to the radical/ incremental distinction, since it is possible that firms will be required to make radical changes to their competence base in order to adopt a new product originally developed by another firm. Nevertheless, the new to the market/ new to the firm distinction does capture some of what the radical/incremental difference aims to represent since developing new to market innovations depends on the firm's capacity to explore new knowledge. The figure shows that the UK, the nation with the least intensive use of the learning forms, is also the nation with the lowest share of sales from new to the market product innovations.

Figure 6.5 uses results from the 1996 Second Community Innovation Survey to show the relation between the relative importance of the learning forms and expenditures on intramural R&D as a percentage of all innovation expenditures.[9] While expenditures on intramural R&D are not always required for developing new to the market innovations, one would nonetheless expect such expenditures to be positively correlated with a capacity to develop authentically new products or processes. The relation can be expected to vary across sectors, being especially pronounced in science-based sectors, as biotechnology and ICT, where R&D plays an important role in the firm's capacity to absorb the results of recent academic research. The figures show that the UK and Ireland, the most intensive users of the lean forms, rank the lowest in terms of the importance of expenditures on intramural R&D.

To the extent that Figures 6.4 and 6.5 make a plausible case for the positive relation between the use of the learning model and a capacity for exploring new knowledge and innovating, it is important to consider how features of the institutional environment may promote or inhibit the development of this organizational form. One possible explanation for the limited use of the learning forms of work organization in the UK and Ireland is that the deregulated labour market context in these nations fails to provide the necessary institutional support for establishing and sustaining this organizational form. Figure 6.6 below shows a clear distinction among nations in the relative importance of the learning model of work organization according to the degree to which the labour market is regulated, as measured by the OECD's overall index of employment protection legislation (EPL).[10]

Figure 6.7 below shows a positive correlation between the strength of a nation's vocational training system, as measured by the share of the relevant age cohort receiving vocational training, and the relative importance of the learning forms of organization.

A central argument developed by Lam and Lundvall (this volume) that may help to account for these relations concerns the institutional requirements for

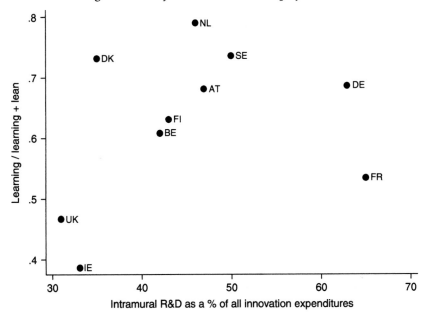

Figure 6.5. Relative importance of learning forms and intramural R&D
Source: Third Working Conditions Survey (2000); Second Community Innovation
Survey (1996).

sustaining an organization's capacity for creative problem-solving. As they observe in their discussion of the 'operating adhocracy', an organization's capacity for creative, non-standard problem-solving is based on the way its members combine professional knowledge of the sort acquired through formal vocational and third-level education with tacit knowledge derived from practical experience in adapting to new situations. Organizations with such a knowledge base are under pressure to bureaucratize because of the difficulties they face in accumulating tacit knowledge. They are especially vulnerable when it comes to individuals leaving the organization. Bureaucratization, while responding to the problem of reproducing what has been learnt in an organizational memory, tends to stifle the forms of autonomous experimentation and exploration that are integral to sustaining an organization's creative problem-solving capacity.

These considerations help to explain the fact that the UK economy overall performs so poorly in terms of new to the market innovation. The learning or operating adhocracy forms of organization tend to be found in a few isolated contexts, such as the cluster of high-technology firms around the

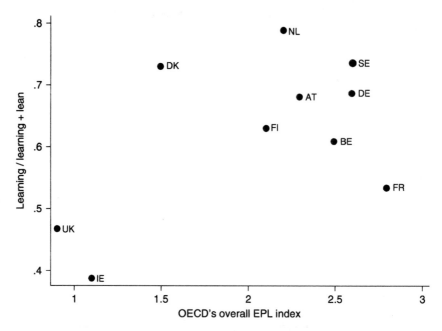

Figure 6.6. Relative importance of learning forms and employment protection
Source: Third Working Conditions Survey (2000); OECD Employment Outlook (1999).

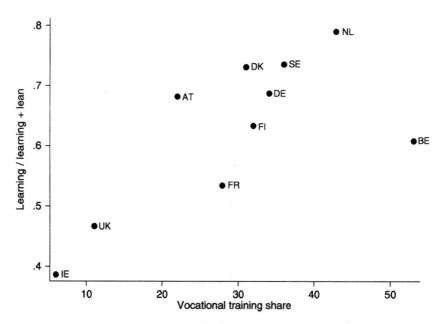

Figure 6.7. Relative forms of learning forms and vocational training
Source: Third Working Conditions Survey (2000); Unesco Statistical Yearbook (1999).

University of Cambridge, where localized networks of firms provide the necessary social capital for the efficient accumulation of tacit knowledge in an inter-firm career framework. Outside of these high-tech clusters, the UK institutional framework, with an unregulated labour market and a weak system of vocational training that is more suitable for the requirements of standard jobs than those requiring creative problem-solving, tends to support the development of bureaucratic forms of organization or possibly hybrid arrangements combining features of taylorism and the J-form (see Bessy, this volume).

6.7. CONCLUSION

We introduced this chapter by observing that the lack of harmonized organizational data at the EU level limits our ability to compare and effectively benchmark policies for knowledge development and use, and for innovative performance specifically. This limitation can be observed in such key EU benchmarking exercises as Trendchart or the 'Innovation Scoreboard' where the exclusive emphasis on standard S&T indicators such as R&D expenditures, patent applications, or the number of S&E graduates is all too apparent. We believe that this informational deficit also helps to explain why the policy instruments used to implement the Lisbon strategy have not integrated action plans or the establishment of common objectives around organizational change and innovation. Not only do such policy instruments rely crucially on harmonized data suitable for comparing the characteristics and performance of national systems, but it is also the case that in the absence of such benchmarks and comparative indicators it is hard to bring the issue to the focal attention of the EU policy community.

In this chapter, we have taken a first step towards providing an EU mapping of organizational forms. We believe that the results demonstrate the feasibility and the interest of the exercise. The results have shown that alternative models are available for achieving the combined goals of organizational learning and problem-solving, and they strongly suggest that organizational choices are not neutral relative to innovation rate and style. Our results also bear on the question of the relation between organizational change and the wider labour market and institutional setting. It is difficult to assess the frequently made claim that unconstrained competition and an absence of labour market restrictions constitute the most favourable context for introducing new forms of work organization for the simple reason that we lack a reliable mapping of the extent of diffusion of new practices across EU nations. Our results not only show that strong systems of employment protection are fully compatible with the development of advanced forms of work organization, but also suggest that nations characterized by such systems display a comparative advantage in terms of adopting organizational practices that rely on a high degree of employee autonomy and involvement at all levels of the organizational structure.

These results of course need further development. The European Survey on Working Conditions on which they are based is first and foremost a survey of working conditions, and it cannot substitute for a focused survey on organizational innovation. Adequate measures of organizational change and innovation would require complementary establishment-level data providing indicators of the way knowledge flows and sharing is organized among different services and departments and how differences in this respect relate to other aspects of corporate strategy. Moreover, our explanation for national differences should be taken as a set of tentative hypotheses consistent with the evidence rather than solid conclusions coming out of the econometric analysis. We offer them in the spirit of widening the debate and in the hope that they will stimulate further comparative research exploring the European link between organizational forms, innovative performance, and institutional context.

NOTES

1. The initial findings of the survey are presented in a European Foundation report by Merllié and Paoli (2001).
2. The factor analysis method used here is multiple correspondence analysis, which is especially suitable for the analysis of categorical variables. Unlike principal components analysis where the total variance is decomposed along the principal factors or components, in multiple correspondence analysis the total variation of the data matrix is measured by the usual chi-squared statistic for row-column independence, and it is the chi-squared statistic which is decomposed along the principal factors. It is common to refer to the percentage of the 'inertia' accounted for by a factor. Inertia is defined as the value of the chi-squared statistic of the original data matrix divided by the grand total of the number of observations. See Benzecri (1973) and Greenacre (1993: 24–31).
3. Certain of the organizational variables produced by the survey have not been included in the statistical analysis. For example, the cooperative nature of work which is measured by a question concerning whether one relies on colleagues for assistance in work has been left out of the analysis because it basically distinguishes between employees working in isolation from those that do not. The question on

whether the employee exercises autonomy in the order that his or her work is carried out has been excluded because it is highly correlated with the other questions focusing on the issue of autonomy.

4. Team work is measured by the following question: 'Does your job involve, or not, doing all or part of your work in a team?'
5. This question does not allow an assessment of the learning requirements of the job rotation involved, which vary considerably as our discussion will show.
6. The variable is coded 'yes' if the repeated task requires less than a minute to accomplish and 'no' otherwise.
7. The coefficients for Column 2 should be read in the following manner. A positive and significant coefficient for a nation, say Sweden, would imply that compared to the Belgian case, and independently of sector, occupational category, and establishment size, there is a higher relative likelihood of using the learning forms over the lean forms.
8. The figure is the percentage of all sales from new products introduced over the last three years that were new to the market.
9. The CIS2 data are used here since the relevant figures for Ireland and the UK are missing in CIS3.
10. Denmark is clearly somewhat of an outlier in terms of the relation we are proposing between employment protection and the relative importance of the lean model of work organization. A distinctive feature of the Danish institutional set-up is that while employment protection is relatively low, unemployment protection is amongst the highest in Europe. See Lundvall (2002); and Hall and Soskice (2001: 167–69).

REFERENCES

Appelbaum, E. and Batt, R. (1994). *The New American Workplace*. Ithaca, NY: ILR Press.

Benzecri, J.-P. (1973). *L'analyse des données*, 2 vols. Paris: Dunod.

Boyer, R. and Durand, J.-P. (1993). *L'après fordisme*. Paris: Syros.

Coutrot, T. (1998). *L'entreprise néolibérale, nouvelle utopie capitaliste?* Paris: La Découverte.

Cézard, M., Dussert, F., and Gollac, M. (1992). 'Taylor va au marché. Organisation du travail et informatique', *Travail et Emploi*, 54(4): 4–19.

Freeman, C. (1987). *Technology Policy and Economic Performance: Lessons from Japan*. London: Pinter Publishers.

Freyssenet, M. (1995). 'La "production réflexive": une alternative à la "production de masse" et à la "production au plus juste"?', *Sociologie du Travail*, 3(95): 365–89.

Greenacre, M. J. (1993). *Correspondence Analysis in Practice*. New York: Academic Press.

Hall, P. and Soskice, D. (2001). *Varieties of Capitalism.* Oxford: Oxford University Press.

Kline, S. J. and Rosenberg, N. (1986). 'An Overview of innovation,' in Landau, R. and Rosenberg, N. (eds.), *The Positive Sum Game.* Washington D.C.: National Academy Press.

Ichiniowski, C., Shaw, K., and Prennushi, G. (1997). 'The Effects of Human Resource Management Policies on Productivity: A Study of Steel Finishing Lines', *American Economic Review*, 87(3): 291–313.

Linhart, D. (1994). *La modernisation des entreprises.* Paris: La Découverte.

Lundvall, B.-Å. (1988). 'Innovation as an interactive process: From user-producer interaction to the National Innovation Systems,' in Dosi, G., Freeman, C., Nelson, R. R., Silverberg, G. and Soete, L. (eds.), *Technology and Economic Theory.* London: Pinter Publishers.

Lundvall, B.-Å. (2002). *Innovation, Growth and Social Cohesion: The Danish Model.* London: Elgar Publishers.

MacDuffie, J. P. and Krafcik, J. (1992). 'Interacting Technology and Human Resources for High Performance Manufacturing: Evidence from the International Auto Industry', in T. Kochan, and M. Useem, (eds.), *Transforming Organisations.* New York: Oxford University Press, pp. 209–25.

Merllié, D. and Paoli, P. (2001). *Third European Survey on Working Conditions (2000).* Luxembourg: Office for official publications of the European communities.

Nonaka, I. and Takeuchi, H. (1995). *The Knowledge Creating Company.* Oxford: Oxford University Press.

Osterman, P. (1994). 'How Common Is Workplace Transformation and Who Adopts It ?', *Industrial and Labor Relations Review*, 47(2): 173–88.

Womack, J. P., Jones, D. T. and Roos, D. (1990). *The Machine that Changed the World.* New York: Rawson Associates.

7

Learning Organizations and Industrial Relations: How the Danish Economy Learns

Peter Nielsen and Bengt-Åke Lundvall

7.1. INTRODUCTION

This chapter combines a knowledge management with an industrial relations perspective in an analysis of organizational learning in Denmark. In the first part it analyses the impact of functional flexibility on innovation. In the second part it studies what role worker participation—direct and indirect—plays in constituting learning organizations. These issues are analysed on the basis of a fresh survey that forms part of the comprehensive Danish database: *'The Innovation, Organization and Competence Panel'*.

In the management literature there is growing emphasis on organizational forms that facilitate the creation, communication, and use of knowledge; sometimes brought together under the heading: 'the learning organization'. In parallel there is a debate among industrial relations experts on employee participation in decision-making and processes of change sometimes under the heading: 'the high-performance workplace'.

The literature on learning organizations tends to emphasize the need to decentralize decisions and responsibility to a wider set of employees. This may be seen as pointing towards more *functional flexibility* and as implying empowerment and a more participatory working life. Recent labour market studies give a less rosy picture where the volume of 'precarious work' is growing and trade unions and employees see their capability to defend basic rights weakened.

The two tendencies may in principle co-evolve and result in an increasingly polarized labour market, where some employees get more influence over their own working life while others get less. But they may also be seen as working themselves out differently in different national employment and innovation systems. This chapter aims at understanding how these contradictory tendencies work themselves out in the Danish economy.

Our analysis shows that there is a strong relationship between the establishment of a functionally flexible organization and the capability to pursue innovation. More surprisingly, it also shows that while indirect forms of participation become less frequent in Danish firm, they seem to remain important in learning organizations.

7.2. THE LEARNING ECONOMY AS CONTEXT

In various contexts we have introduced an interpretation of new trends under the term 'the learning economy' (Lundvall and Johnson 1994; Lundvall 1996; Lundvall and Borras 1999; Lundvall and Nielsen 1999). The term signals that the most important change is that knowledge becomes obsolete more rapidly than before. Therefore, it is imperative for firms to engage in organizational learning and for workers to attain new competencies.

A learning economy is thus one in which the ability to attain new competencies is crucial for the performance of individuals, firms, regions, and countries. Globalization, information technology, and the deregulation of formerly protected markets lead to *more rapid transformation and change*. The rapid rate of change is reinforced by the fact that the intensified competition leads to a selection of organizations and individuals that are capable of rapid learning, thus further accelerating the rate of change.

We see the growing emphasis on internal functional flexibility and on networking as responses to the challenge of the learning economy. In a rapidly changing environment it is not efficient to operate in a hierarchical organization with many vertical layers. It takes too long to make a move if the information obtained at the lower levels should be transmitted all the way to the top and back down to the bottom of the pyramid. To enhance the capability to respond to change internal functional flexibility is combined with networking with external parties such as customers, suppliers, and knowledge institutions.

7.3. INNOVATION AND KNOWLEDGE CREATION

In this chapter we will use product innovation as an indicator of learning within the firm. This is in accordance with how other scholars analyse knowledge creation (Nonaka and Takeuchi 1995; Antonelli 1999). In new growth theory, the output of the R&D sector is viewed either as a blueprint for a new production process that is more efficient than the previous one, or as a production of new semi-manifactured goods that cannot easily be copied by competitors (Verspagen 1992: 29–30).

A striking characteristic of knowledge production resulting in innovation is the fact that knowledge, in terms of skills and competencies, is the most important input. In this sense, it recalls a 'corn economy', in which corn and labor produce corn. But it differs from such an economy in one important respect. While the corn used to produce corn disappears in the process, skills and competencies improve with use. Important characteristics of knowledge reflect that its elements are not scarce in the traditional sense: the more skills and competencies are used, the more they develop.

7.3.1. Competence as the Outcome of Knowledge Production

In economics we find various approaches to competence building and learning. One important contribution is Arrow's analysis of 'learning-by-doing' (1962), in which he demonstrated that the efficiency in producing complex systems (aeroplane frames) grows with the number of units already produced and argued that this reflected experience-based learning. Later, Rosenberg (1982) introduced 'learning-by-using' to explain why efficiency in using complex systems increased over time (the users were airline companies introducing new models). The concept of 'learning-by-interacting' points to how interaction between producers and users in innovation enhances the competence of both (Lundvall 1988; Christensen and Lundvall 2004).

In most of the contributions mentioned above, learning is regarded as the unintended outcome of processes with a different aim than learning and increasing competence. Learning is seen as a side effect of processes of production, use, marketing, or innovation. An interesting new development, which tends to make learning more instrumental, is the growing attention given to learning organizations (Senge 1990). The basic idea is that how an organization is structured will have a major effect on the learning that takes place. The appropriate institutional structures may improve knowledge production in terms of competence building based on daily activities.

The move towards learning organizations is reflected both in the firm's internal organization and in inter-firm relationships. Within firms, the accelerating rate of change makes multi-level hierarchies and strict borders between functions inefficient. It makes decentralization of responsibility to lower-level employees and formation of multi-functional teams a necessity. Inter-firm relationships with suppliers, customers, and competitors become more selective and more intense.

7.4. THE DANISH INNOVATION AND EMPLOYMENT SYSTEM

The Danish economy has some interesting features when it comes to understanding what options are open for national systems in the era of the learning economy. Denmark is among the top five countries in the world in terms of GNP per capita, and when surveyed the population appears to be highly satisfied with the society they live in—actually more so than in any other country in the world. But it is not a high-technology economy, and it is not an economy where formal science plays the most important role in processes of innovation. There are other factors behind the relative wealth of Denmark having more to do with incremental innovation, 'social capital', and participatory learning.

A predominance of small-and medium-sized firms and of an experience-based mode of innovation in Denmark is reflected in the mode of learning and in the system of HRD. Inter-firm networking is especially frequent in Denmark while the interaction with universities is less developed than abroad. Publicly organized and financed training and continuous education programmes are important in Denmark while firms' in house investment in training is more limited. Danish youth are expected to be independent and responsible. International studies show that they use little time on homework and more time on small jobs to get their own income. When finished with high school they often take a year off and work or go abroad before entering higher education. They rate weakly in international tests on skills in reading and mathematics. But they seem to be extremely well prepared for working in organizations where there is a need to delegate responsibility to the lower levels in the organization. They are used to communicating directly and freely also with authorities (teachers and employers).

The Danish labour market is characterized by high mobility between firms (as high or higher than in the US). Danish firms invest less in training their personnel than firms in other countries. On the other hand, the public sector has built a unique and quite comprehensive and costly system for continuous education. On average, Danish workers get more training time annually than workers in other countries. Firms contribute to the finance of the public training, and tripartite bodies representing labour, industry, and the public sector organize an important part of it. This division of labour between the private and the public sector reflects that there are many small firms that could not take on the responsibility on their own.

There are other features of the labour market that need to be taken into account. The substitution rate of unemployment support is higher and support is less restricted in time than other OECD countries. This is one factor behind high-participation rates, and it may also explain why workers in Denmark appear to feel more secure than colleagues in European countries with stronger legal employment protection. To a certain degree high mobility reflects that employers meet almost no legal restrictions when it comes to firing personnel. But it also reflects that workers at all skill levels are less nervous about getting lost between different jobs when looking new job opportunities.

There is one area where the Danish labour market does not work well, however. Unskilled workers and especially workers with a different ethnic background than Danish are much worse off than the rest of the labour force in terms of job opportunities and employment. Here Denmark is performing worse than most other OECD countries. The training initiatives inside firms tend to reinforce polarization. The chance for unskilled workers to get training in-house in firms is much less than for other categories of employees. The downside of the homogeneous Danish village economy (Maskell 1998) is that strangers face difficulties in being accepted by both employers and employees.

Earlier studies linking firms' innovation activities and their employment of unskilled workers indicate that the speed up of change at the firm level—the introduction of learning organizations and the introduction of new products—does *not* affect unskilled workers negatively. They show that firms that introduce new organizational practises and engage in innovation create more jobs and more stable jobs for unskilled workers. The most dramatic job losses for workers without professional training take place in firms that become exposed to stronger competition and that do not respond neither by introducing elements of the learning organization nor by introducing new products.

7.5. RESEARCH QUESTIONS

This chapter tests and finds support for the following set of hypotheses:

- the probability of successful product innovation increases when the firm has organized itself in such a way that it promotes learning;
- organizational forms promoting learning combine several of a number of internal relationships and activities and external relationships;
- internal relationships and activities include integrative organizational forms, quality management, human development efforts, and compensation systems;

– external relationships include relationships to suppliers, customers, and knowledge institutions;
– in firms going very far in the direction of promoting learning direct representation of workers is combined with indirect representation.

In the first part of the empirical analysis, we explore factors that lie behind product innovation in 2,000 Danish firms belonging to manufacturing and service industries.[1] We will demonstrate that there are important sector differences in the frequency of innovation and that big firms innovate more than small ones. Most importantly we will show that bundling a number of different characteristics having to do with a learning organization has a major positive effect on the innovation capability. The functionally flexible firms that engage in networking with customers and suppliers are more active in terms of product innovation than the firms that operate in traditional hierarchical organizations.

In the second part of the empirical analysis we explore the direct and indirect participation of workers. We find that there is a connection between the strength of the influence and at what stage of decision-making employees are engaged in the process. We also find that while the tendency is towards more direct and less indirect participation, the most advanced firms in terms of establishing learning organizations are the ones that most frequently make use of the indirect forms.

On the basis of our theoretical considerations and empirical results it is fair to conclude that incremental innovation and learning may be seen as two sides of the same coin. It is true that learning organizations are more apt when it comes to mobilize and utilize different sources of knowledge to develop new products. But it is also true that firms that engage in incremental innovation need to develop an organizational framework that can cope with new problems as they pop up during the innovation process.

7.6. DATA

The empirical analysis is based on a survey addressed in 2001 to all Danish firms in the private sector with 25 or more employees, supplemented with a stratified proportional sample of firms with 20–25 employees. The firms selected were sent 6,991 questionnaires. The survey collected information from management as well as from employee representatives by means of two separate questionnaires, implemented through two phases of collection in each of the firms selected.

In total, 2,007 usable responses from management and 473 responses from employee representatives have been collected and integrated in a cross-section data-set from this last survey. This makes the overall response rate of the survey 29 per cent, which is not very satisfactory. However, a closer response analysis broken down on industries and size show acceptable variations on response rates, and non-respondent information on some of the potential dependant variables together with comparison to other surveys do not indicate unacceptable bias.

7.7. THE FREQUENCY OF PRODUCT INNOVATION IN THE SURVEYED FIRMS

Obtaining a meaningful quantitative measure of innovation and innovative behaviour on the basis of information collected in widely different firms, belonging to industries with very different conditions, using individual developed and configured production processes and producing different products or services, is not unproblematic. The phenomenon that firms refer to may vary in relation to conditions and configurations. The fact is that we are confronted with qualitative change rather than change easily captured in quantitative terms when we ask the firms whether they, in the period of 1998–2000, have introduced new products or services on the market.

Table 7.1 shows that product innovation over a three-year period takes place in almost half the firms. It also shows that the bigger the firm, the greater the probability that it introduces a new product. There are substantial sector differences as well: firms belonging to manufacturing and business services are much more active in terms of product innovations than the average while construction firms are far below the average. Firms owned by foreign groups have the highest innovation score, firms owned by Danish groups a medium score, and single, stand-alone firms the lowest score.

7.8. THE FREQUENCY OF ORGANIZATIONAL CHANGE IN THE SURVEYED FIRMS

Table 7.2 shows a general level of organizational change slightly above 50 per cent. The larger the firm, the higher the propensity to engage in organizational

Table 7.1 Product or service innovation 1998–2000 by firm size, industry, group ownership, and production (per cent horizontal)

	P/S innovation (%)	Not P/S innovation (%)	Do not know (%)	(N)
All firms	45.4	52.4	2.2	1,974
Less than 50	36.5	60.9	2.6	1,022
50 – 99 empl.	47.3	52.0	0.7	433
100 and more	62.6	34.7	2.7	487
Manufacturing	58.1	40.8	1.1	723
Construction	21.7	75.7	2.6	309
Trade	41.4	55.6	3.1	549
Other services	31.1	67.1	1.8	164
Business serv.	58.7	37.6	3.8	213
Danish group	48.6	49.6	1.7	693
Foreign group	59.7	38.4	1.8	385
Single firm	36.6	60.7	2.7	882

Table 7.2 Organizational changes 1998–2000 by firm size, industry, group ownership, and production (per cent horizontal)

	Organizational changes (%)	No organizational change (%)	Do not know (%)	(N)
All firms	52.0	46.9	1.2	1,992
Less than 50 empl.	40.1	59.3	0.6	1,037
50–99 employees	56.6	40.9	2.5	435
100 and more	73.2	25.6	1.2	488
Manufacturing	58.8	39.7	1.5	726
Construction	33.4	65.6	1.0	311
Trade	51.0	48.1	0.9	557
Other services	43.4	54.8	1.8	166
Business services	63.0	36.6	0.5	216
Danish group	57.5	41.5	1.0	694
Foreign group	71.1	28.4	0.5	388
Single firm	39.7	58.8	1.6	895

change. Almost three-fourths of the firms with 100 employees or more have undertaken organizational changes. But even among the small firms with less than fifty employees, two-fifths have engaged in changes. Differences between the various industries are present without being particularly pronounced. Business services and manufacturing score high. Trade is at the average level while other service and construction lie below the average. Foreign-owned companies have a high proportion of organizational change and stand-alone firms have the lowest proportion.

At the next step, we study the various reasons why organizational changes were accomplished.

7.9. BUNDLING ORGANIZATIONAL CHARACTERISTICS AND ANALYSING THE IMPACT ON INNOVATION

Much empirical research has shown that when it comes to organizational performance, the 'bundling' of several dimensions is crucial. Applying just one or two of the new organizational characteristics may have a very limited impact while it is the combination of several traits that makes the difference when it comes to performance, both in relation to productivity and innovation (Lund Vinding 2000; Laursen 2001). Building on such results an additive index has been constructed applying the dimensions listed in Table 7.3:

The distribution of firms in the index of work, communication, and human development is shown in Table 7.4. We group the firms in three categories, according to how many dimensions they have adopted—in other words—how many coordination, communication, and human development features are bundled and built into the firm's organization. We thus get a group using 0 to 4 of the dimensions (low-level learning organizations), another group using 5 to 8 dimensions (medium-level learning organizations), and a third highly-developed group with 9 to 14 dimensions (advanced learning organizations).

Table 7.3 Theoretical aspects and operational dimensions in the learning organization

Theoretical aspect	Operational dimension
Integrative organization	Cross occupational working groups
	Integration of functions
	Softened demarcations
	Delegation of responsibility
	Self-directed teams
Quality management	Quality circles/groups
	Systems for collection of employee proposals
Human development	Education activities tailored to the firm
	Long-term educational planning
Compensation system	Wages based on qualifications and functions
	Wages based on results
External communication	Closer cooperation with customers
	Closer cooperation with subcontractors
	Closer cooperation with universities and techno.

Table 7.4 Index of organization, quality, human development, compensation, and external communication ($N = 2007$)

Index	Frequency	Per cent	Cumulative per cent
0	32	1.59	1.59
1	64	3.19	4.78
2	105	5.23	10.01
3	135	6.73	16.74
4	210	10.46	27.20
5	202	10.06	37.27
6	224	11.16	48.43
7	250	12.46	60.89
8	213	10.61	71.50
9	210	10.46	81.96
10	165	8.22	90.18
11	90	4.48	94.67
12	63	3.14	97.81
13	30	1.49	99.30
14	14	0.70	100.00

In Table 7.5, the results of this grouping is shown distributed according to firm size, industry, ownership, and production. We get 28 per cent in the highly-developed category, 44 per cent in the medium, and 27 per cent in the low category. The distribution is highly size-dependent. Among firms with less than 50 employees, the share of firms being most advanced is just 18 per cent while this share is 45 per cent among firms with more than 100 employees. More than 40 per cent of the firms in business services belong to the category of

Table 7.5 Learning organization development by firm size, industry, group ownership, and production (per cent horizontal)

Variables	Advanced (9–14)	Medium (5–8)	Low (0–4)	(N)
All firms	28.5	44.3	27.2	2,007
Less than 50 employees	18.1	45.9	36.0	1,048
50–99 employees	35.0	42.3	22.7	437
100 and more	45.1	43.3	11.6	490
Manufacturing	36.4	43.2	20.4	729
Construction	14.3	42.5	43.2	315
Trade	24.4	47.8	27.8	562
Other services	17.9	46.4	35.7	168
Business service	41.5	40.1	18.4	217
Danish group	30.1	44.7	25.3	701
Foreign group	40.7	43.8	15.5	388
Single firm	22.3	44.5	33.2	903

highly developed learning organizations while the same is true for 36 per cent of the firms in manufacturing. The other sectors score below the average. Firms owned by foreign concerns have a high share in the category of highly developed learning organizations. Firms owned by Danish concerns are closer to the average and single, stand-alone firms are below average.

The next analytical step is to examine how the bundling of organizational dimensions affects innovation/knowledge production in firms. In the first sections of the chapter, we interpreted product and service (P/S) innovations both as outcomes of knowledge creation and as provoking learning in the firms. The different categories of learning organization are tested in a logistic model, with P/S innovation as the dependent variable, where we control for size, industry, etc.

We find a 5.2 times higher chance of P/S innovation in the highly-developed category and even in the medium category the chance is 2.1 times higher than the low category. Among the other factors in the model, manufacturing and business services remain significant with a 2.9 times higher chance of P/S innovation and trade is significant with a 1.7 times higher chance. The effect of large size (100+) is more moderate, and the same is true for group ownership—international as well as national. In sum, the models indicate important and significant effects of sophisticated learning organizations on P/S innovation. This may be taken as support for and validation of the theoretical considerations around the concept of learning organization.

7.10. INDIRECT AND DIRECT PARTICIPATION

The leading argument motivating our analysis has been that the changing and turbulent business environment in the 1990s promoted universal organiza-

Table 7.6 Logistic regression of learning organization development categories, size, industry, ownership, and production on P/S innovation (odd ratios, estimates, and *p*-values)

Variables	Effect	Lower	Higher	Estimate	Chi-sq	*p*-value
Highly developed	5.20	3.93	6.88	0.82	132.45	<0.0001
Medium developed	2.21	1.72	2.84	0.40	38.63	<0.0001
Manufacturing	2.92	2.24	3.81	0.54	62.03	<0.0001
Trade	1.66	1.25	2.21	0.25	12.42	0.0004
Business services	2.85	1.99	4.08	0.52	32.45	<0.0001
100 and more	1.59	1.26	2.00	0.23	15.13	0.0001
Danish group	1.32	1.06	1.65	0.14	6.11	0.0134
Foreign group	1.73	1.32	2.26	0.27	15.86	<0.0001

tional solutions as institutional standards. As we have seen, Danish firms have frequently reacted and adopted the institutional standards in their internal organization. It has been shown that incorporating many of these standards as dimensions in their work organization gives firms a much higher chance of being product or service innovative. The correlation between innovative behaviour and the learning organization has been tested and confirmed.

We have stated that innovation theoretically has to do with embedded organizational competence. Embedded competence relies on the ability of employees continuously to learn and develop new knowledge as a collective resource in the organization. It is in this theoretical light we must understand the importance of employee involvement and participation in organizational change and not least in *building the learning organization.* Through the participation applied in relation to organizational change, the commitment among the employees is established. This commitment may actually be seen as a necessary precondition for continuous competence building and learning. From this follows the importance of analysing to what degree participation instruments and principles are mobilized, when changing and developing the organization of the firm.

In the literature, participation dimensions have been classified into *indirect participation,* referring to participation through local union representatives and institutions, and *direct participation,* mainly through communicative relations between management and employees. It has been argued that indirect participation forms are in decline, especially in relation to the new organizational forms. In this context, it is of interest to examine the participation dimensions applied by the firms in situations of organizational change.

Table 7.7 shows that the direct participation forms are the ones used most frequently in situations of change. In almost nine-tenths of the firms, managers use direct contacts with the individual employees. More than 80 per cent of the firms use meetings with change-affected employees and two-third use common meetings with all employees in the firm. On the theoretical borderline between direct participation and classical indirect participation, we find ad hoc project groups with management and employee representatives. Forty-seven per cent of the firms use this form. Among the classical indirect participation forms, cooperation committees score highest (30 per cent), followed by employee representative joining management meetings (18 per cent) with employee representative in the company board scoring lowest (14 per cent).

Table 7.7 shows that, in connection with organizational change, direct participation forms are more commonly used than indirect forms. It is,

Table 7.7 Instruments applied in the cooperation between management and employees in the context of organizational change (per cent horizontal)

	Yes	No	Do not know	Not relev.	(N)
Employee representatives participate in management meetings	17.6	65.9	0.9	15.6	1254
One or more project group with participants from management & employees	47.3	39.6	1.4	11.8	1251
Permanent cooperation committees	29.7	43.7	1.5	25.1	1240
Employee representative participates in firm's board	13.7	58.9	1.3	26.1	1232
Common meetings with the employees concerned	83.3	11.8	1.1	3.9	1248
Common meetings with all employees	65.0	28.2	1.5	5.2	1243
Direct ad hoc-consultation with the individual employee	89.4	7.1	1.3	2.3	1262

however, important to consider that while the direct forms may be appropriate as a sort of basic foundation, some of the indirect instruments suited for negotiations and conflict solution may become more appropriate for the firms most ambitious in terms of continuous learning and change. And obviously in such firms we should expect to find combinations of indirect and direct participation instruments. In order to test this hypothesis we have pursued a logistic regression where we use highly developed learning organization as the dependent variable and sector, size, ownership status, and the seven forms of participation as independent variables.

Table 7.8 shows that the *indirect* participation measures come out with the largest effects in relation to highly developed learning organizations. Project groups with joint participation of management and employee representatives have the strongest effect. Employees joining management meetings have the next strongest effects. Meetings with concerned employees have the next strongest effect and meetings with all employees have the third strongest effect.

The impact of participation instruments may be stronger when they are used together in consistent 'bundles'. We may expect that both indirect and direct participation instruments are used in various combinations in highly developed learning organizations. One simple way to solve this 'bundle problem' is to apply a methodology similar to the one performed in the analysis of degrees of learning organizations. Thus a similar additive index of the participation instrument has been constructed. The result is shown in Table 7.9.

Table 7.8 Logistic regression of participation instruments, size, industry, ownership, and production on highly developed learning organizations (odd ratios, estimates, and p-values)

Variables	Effect	Lower	Higher	Estimate	Chi-sq	p-value
Management meetings	2.27	1.50	3.46	0.41	14.80	0.0001
Project groups	3.31	2.40	4.56	0.60	53.19	<0.0001
Meetings all	1.73	1.22	2.46	0.27	9.54	0.0020
50–100 employees	0.65	0.43	0.97	−0.22	4.38	0.0363
Less than 50 employees	0.37	0.26	0.55	−0.49	25.78	<0.0001

Only few firms use either none or all of the participation instruments. More than half of the firms use three or four instruments. Thus, the distribution falls naturally in three categories with 3–4 instruments in the 'medium' category, 0–2 in the 'few' instruments category, and 5–7 in the 'many' instruments category.

Table 7.10 shows the results of the logistic regression. The more participation instruments applied in the firm, the higher the chance of highly developed learning organizations. As compared to the 'few instruments' benchmark, applying 5–7 participation instruments produces a chance five times as high while applying 3–4 participation instruments produces twice as high a chance for establishing a highly developed learning organization.

This indicates that, at least in Denmark, highly developed learning organizations are much more prone than other organizations to make wide use of participation instruments including indirect ones in connection with work organization change.

Table 7.9 Index of participation instruments ($N = 746$)

Index	Frequency	Per cent	Cumulative per cent
0	1	0.13	0.13
1	45	6.03	6.17
2	93	12.47	18.63
3	218	29.22	47.86
4	205	27.48	75.34
5	117	15.68	91.02
6	58	7.77	98.79
7	9	1.21	100.00

Table 7.10 Logistic regression of multiple participation instrument categories, size, industry, ownership, and production on highly developed learning organizations (odd ratios, estimates, and *p*-values)

Variables:	Effect	Lower	Higher	Estimate	Chi-sq	*p*-value
Many instrument	5.25	3.72	7.42	0.83	88.39	<0.0001
Medium instruments	1.97	1.54	2.52	0.34	29.42	<0.0001
Manufacturing	1.53	1.21	1.92	0.21	12.79	0.0003
Business services	2.41	1.74	3.34	0.44	27.92	<0.0001
Less than 50 empl.	0.45	0.36	0.56	−0.40	51.19	<0.0001
Foreign group	1.55	1.20	1.99	0.22	11.38	0.0007

7.11. CONCLUSIONS

In the management literature there is a presumption that certain organizational characteristics promote learning and competence building. Here, we have shown that the bundling of organizational characteristics having to do with respectively integrative organization, quality management, HRD, compensation systems, and external network positioning has a strong impact on knowledge creation and product innovation. The advanced learning organizations that combine several of these characteristics tend to introduce significantly more product innovations than the rest. And the effect remains strong also when we take into account differences among firms in terms of size, sector, and form of ownership.

It cannot be shown that there is a simple causality from the advanced learning organization to innovation, however. Rather, the relationship goes both ways. Firms operating in market segments where continuous incremental product innovation is a prerequisite for survival, and firms pursuing strategies of continuous product innovation will realize that they need an advanced learning organization. They will need it in order to organize the different sources of knowledge required for the innovation, and they will need it in order to cope with the unforeseen problems they will encounter as part of the innovation process.

In the literature on industrial relations, there have been different types of arguments favouring the participation of employees in decision-making either directly or indirectly through workers' representatives and trade unions. One type of arguments refers to economic democracy and empowerment of employees as positive values that should be promoted. The other type of argument refers to the presumed efficiency effects from participation. We have found it of interest to illuminate these arguments in the context of the formation of advanced learning organizations.

Our results are that direct forms of participation are almost always involved in connection with organizational change while indirect forms are used less frequently. Some degree of participation is obviously necessary in order to realize organizational change in Denmark. More interestingly, we find that the most advanced learning organizations differ from the less advanced especially when it comes to their intensive use of indirect forms of participation. At least in Denmark it may be too early to declare indirect participation and the role of trade unions to be something of the past. On the contrary, they seem to have a role to play especially in the most developed forms of learning organizations.

NOTE

1. Most of the innovations that firms report in the survey are incremental rather than radical and most of them signal something new for the firm but not something new for the national economy or the world economy. We do not see that as a weakness of the analysis, however. Especially in a small open economy of the Danish type, competitiveness and economic growth will depend on continuous upgrading of products. 'Domestic' radical innovations will take place quite seldom, and there is a high probability that they will be taken over by foreign big firms before they leave strong marks on the growth pattern of the whole economy.

REFERENCES

Antonelli, C. (1999). *The Microdynamics of Technological Change*. London: Routledge.

Arrow, K. J. (1962). 'The Economic Implications of Learning by Doing', *Review of Economic Studies*, 29(80).

Christensen, J. L. and Lundvall, B.-Å. (eds.) (2004). *Product Innovation, Interactive Learning and Economic Performance*. Amsterdam: Elsevier.

Lund, R. and Gjerding, A. N. (1996). 'The Flexible Company, Innovation, Work Organisation and Human Resource Management', *DRUID Working Paper 96–17*, Department of Business Studies, Aalborg University, Aalborg.

Lund Vinding, A. (2000). 'Absorptive capacity and innovative performance: A human capital approach,' Aalborg: Department of Business Studies, University of Aalborg.

Lundvall, B.Å. (1988). 'Innovation as an Interactive Process: from User-Producer Interaction to the National systems of innovation, in Dosi, G., Freeman, C., Nelson, R., Silverberg, G., and Soete, L. (eds.), *Technical Change and Economic Theory*. London: Pinter Publishers.

—— (1996). 'The social dimension of the learning economy', Druid Working Paper Series, Copenhagen.

—— and Borras, S. (1998). *The Globalising Learning Economy: Implications for Innovation Policy*, Bruxelles, DG XII-TSER, the European Commission.

—— and Johnson, B. (1994). 'The Learning Economy', *Journal of Industry Studies*, 1(2): 23–42.

—— and Nielsen, P. (1999). 'Competition and Transformation in the Learning Economy—Illustrated by the Danish Case', *Revue d'Economie Industrielle*, 88: 67–90.

Maskell, P. (1998). 'Learning in the Village Economy of Denmark. The Role of Institutions and Policy in Sustaining Competitiveness', in H. J. Braczyk, P. Cooke, and M. Heidenreich (eds.), *Regional Innovation Systems. The Role of Governance in a Globalized World*. London: UCL Press, pp. 190–213.

Nonaka, I. and Takeuchi, H. (1995). *The Knowledge Creating Company*. Oxford: Oxford University Press.

Rosenberg, N. (1982). *Inside the Black Box: Technology and Economics*. Cambridge: Cambridge University Press.

Senge, P. (1990). *The Fifth Discipline: The Art and Practice of Learning*. New York: Doubleday.

Verspagen, B. (1992). 'Uneven growth between interdependent economies: An evolutionary view on technology gaps, trade and growth,' Maastricht: Universitaire Pers Maastricht.

8

Organizational Structure and the Diffusion of New Forms of Corporate Governance in Europe

Andrew Tylecote

8.1. INTRODUCTION

Corporate governance—broadly understood as the relationships and mechanisms of control over firms—is in flux, throughout Europe. There is strong dissatisfaction both with traditional insider-dominated corporate governance modes as practised on the Continent, and their opposite, the arm's-length variety typical in the UK (and somewhat less typical in the US).[1] It seems appropriate in such a situation to be as much prescriptive as descriptive or predictive: to ask what changes in corporate governance and associated changes in modes of learning will work, together. That is what I seek to do in this chapter.

We have to begin by identifying the key changes that are taking place, which may be driving the diffusion of new forms of corporate governance, and modes of learning, or otherwise interacting with them. In this section, I discuss the two most salient ones. In the next section, I discuss how changes in organizational structure (more in prospect than achieved) create a new context (and target) for organizational learning. Section 8.3 offers the promised prescription. Section 8.4 concludes by asking to what extent my recipe goes with the grain of the systems of a number of European countries.

8.2. GLOBALIZATION OF PRODUCTION AND INNOVATION

As is well known, this is propelled by reductions in tariffs, and costs of transport and communication. A major incentive for a firm to disperse its operations across frontiers is large differences in costs—notably labour costs—between countries. Thus, the rapid integration of the ex-Soviet bloc economies into the world economy, with their well-educated labour forces (relative to their wage levels), is providing a strong incentive for globalization; and within Europe there is what might be called a regional form of globalization through the re-integration of the Central European economies (the Czech Republic, Hungary, Poland, Slovakia, and Slovenia) and the Baltic ones (Estonia, Latvia, and Lithuania) into the European economy in general and the EU in particular.

Such globalization poses a severe challenge to the main alternative form(s) of corporate governance to the Anglo-American shareholder model—the various versions of stakeholder capitalism (German, Japanese, Dutch, and Scandinavian) which reach beyond shareholders to give employees and other firms an acknowledged stake in the enterprise. These are based on specific national laws, institutions, and understandings, and are accordingly very difficult to operate on a multinational scale (see Richard Whitley's chapter in this volume). Moreover, the process of globalization tends to involve the sacrifice of existing (usually domestic) employees in favour of cheaper ones further afield. Domestic suppliers are also sacrificed, though the more important ones tend to accompany the globalizing firm, and set up new branch plants alongside its own—at the expense likewise of their domestic employees. This implies the primacy of the interests of shareholders over employees and suppliers. One could argue that (given the strength of competitive pressures) the only way to save some employees (and perhaps suppliers) is to sacrifice others; but how does one decide which go and which stay, and where does the process stop?

It makes decision-making much easier for managers in such a situation if they steer by the simple compass of shareholder interest. It is striking that the main stakeholder economies are now on the edge of some extremely steep labour cost gradients—Germany is next to Poland and the Czech Republic, with labour costs perhaps a fifth of German levels, and the Nordic countries are in a similar position vis-à-vis the Baltic economies. (Likewise Japan is very close to the coast of China, where labour is no more than a tenth of the Japanese cost.) Jobs are accordingly being exported from Germany to its eastern neighbours (as from Japan to China) at a rapid rate.[2] Small and medium firms may maintain their cohesion in such circumstances—being relatively specialized by product and process, they may be at, or quickly move to, technological 'high ground' suitable to be located in the most high-wage, high-technology economy; or else they are likely to go under altogether. A large firm is by contrast much more likely to see salvation—or higher profits—in a relocation of large parts of its operations in the lower-wage neighbour.

8.2.1. The Rapid Diffusion of the New ICT Techno-Economic Paradigm

It is now generally accepted that the world economy in general, and the most advanced economies in particular, is being profoundly affected by the diffusion of what Freeman and Perez long ago called the ICT techno-economic paradigm (Perez 1983; Freeman and Perez 1988; Tylecote 1992; Freeman and Louca 2001). This is the latest of a sequence of five such technological revolutions—massive technological discontinuities—since the Industrial Revolution began with the first of them in the 1780s (Tylecote 1992, ch. 2; Perez 2002). Arguably it is the greatest of them all, since there is no sector anywhere that is not being transformed by it, or liable soon to be—unlike 'Fordism',[3] its predecessor, whose requirement for rather large scale was restrictive.

The new paradigm's implications for both corporate governance and modes of learning are far-reaching. We focus first on the implications for corporate governance. To begin with the most obvious, it is clear that improvements in communications within ICT are helping to drive globalization, and thus, as we have seen above, to undermine stakeholder models of governance. The new paradigm is also changing relationships among firms, and the boundaries between them. For example, as Sturgeon (2002) has shown, most of the main computer firms—Compaq, Hewlett-Packard, Apple, IBM—no longer manufacture: they contract this out to specialist manufacturers like Flextronics. One reason that this is thinkable for them is that the advances of CAD-CAM make the output of the development and design process fully codifiable and thus highly communicable between firms. It is a great advantage for a firm to be ready to reconfigure itself radically to take advantage of such changes. A firm that is partly controlled by those who would be 'reconfigured' out of a job, will naturally be less inclined to do this than one in which a small group of top managers takes decisions and is accountable only to shareholders.

This is an example of a general proposition which can be put about the relative merits of different corporate governance systems with respect to innovation: to the extent that radical reconfiguration is a key requirement, shareholder capitalism generally has an advantage over stakeholder capitalism (Tylecote and Conesa 1999; Tylecote and Visintin 2002; Ramirez and Tylecote 2004). Again, suppliers as well as employees are affected. Thus, once the received wisdom was 'lean manufacturing' (including just-in-time production methods), which required close relationships with long-standing suppliers and customers. This fitted very well with stakeholder governance models like the Japanese (and to a lesser extent the German model) in which such relationships were strengthened by shareholdings—reciprocal between big firms, and one-way between big firms and their smaller suppliers. Now as fashionable (in the higher-technology areas) is 'agile manufacturing' in which partners can be quickly changed. Significantly, lean manufacturing originated in Japan, agile manufacturing in the US (Kidd 1994).

Another general proposition which is supported by Sturgeon's findings for computer manufacturing is that knowledge, as with ICT it becomes digitalized, is thus becoming increasingly codifiable. On inspection this proposition is highly arguable. Clearly any given body of knowledge can only move in one direction—towards codification—as the control of machines and machine tools did, with CAD-CAM. However, it appears highly plausible that as fast as existing knowledge is codified, new tacit knowledge is developed; or faster; so that the proportion of tacit knowledge in the total does not change much, and may in principle move in either direction. Which way it moves is not simply determined by technological change, for what is codifiable is not necessarily codified: there is a choice, and it is a choice which is highly sensitive to the type of corporate governance. One can, for example, expect that knowledge which Japanese firms were well content to keep tacit, would be strenuously codified by their US counterparts, because of the different relationship between the firm and its workforce. According to the 'historic compromise' reached within large Japanese firms around 1950, the permanent employees belong to the firm, and indeed it belongs to them. Knowledge in their heads in any form is the firm's knowledge, and if it is tacit so much the better, since it is the harder to steal. For the US firm the position is quite different. Tacit knowledge held by an employee can go anywhere, as the employee can go anywhere, and it is impossible for the firm to assert ownership over it. If all the employees with a particular body of tacit knowledge leave, then not only may rivals gain it, but the firm has lost it. If it is codified, then at least it will not be lost when the employee leaves, and in codified form the firm can assert ownership over it, through patent or copyright.

We can therefore predict that the shareholder capitalist firm will be more inclined to codify than the stakeholder capitalist one. Further, an economic system pervaded by shareholder capitalism will have a stronger interest in the legal protection of intellectual property—principally through patenting. Equally, globalized firms will have a stronger interest in codification, and the protection of intellectual property, than those whose operations and knowledge transfers are restricted to one locality or country. This applies to any globalized chain of production, whether the links in the chain belong to one MNC or are owned by different, domestic firms: indeed in the latter case the 'lead' firm may be particularly reluctant to transfer knowledge to its foreign partners if it does not have reliable IPR. It is thus hardly surprising that it was the US—leader in shareholder capitalism, globalization, and indeed the commercialization of knowledge—which took the lead, around 1980, in the reinforcement and extension of IPR. Given its global power and influence it was able to move this process on from a domestic to an international one (Macdonald 1990).[4]

The proposition that shareholder capitalist firms and systems support codification and the protection of codified knowledge, connects with another of the general propositions in Tylecote and Conesa (1999) and Tylecote and Visintin (2002): the relative merits of 'shareholder' and 'stakeholder' corporate governance systems in fostering innovation depend largely on the relative feasibility of two alternative strategies for appropriating the returns to innovation. The first is 'shareholder primacy': to define the costs and benefits of innovation as restricted to shareholders, except in so far as they are managed contractually. Only the shareholders (through the cash flow and profits of the firm) are expected to bear the costs of the innovation; only they, in the same way, are expected to benefit. The second is 'stakeholder inclusion': to accept that various stakeholders—notably employees, customers, and suppliers— will benefit from and contribute to innovation, and to try to manage these spillovers within a set of trusting relationships. The reinforcement and extension of IPR increases the feasibility of the shareholder primacy strategy, and is then another factor tipping the balance in favour of Anglo-American, shareholder capitalism.

We now turn to the implications of ICT for modes of learning. The diffusion of ICT brings with it entirely generic elements in the process of technological change and organizational learning. Improvement in processes is no longer so much a matter of proceeding along a trajectory specific to the sector, as a struggle to incorporate ICT-based modes of manufacturing (or service provision), design/development, and coordination—with the goal of becoming a full 'e-business'. The generic nature of these changes is apparent from the key role now being played by IT consultants and software providers. Thus, major firms have been induced to contract out much of their IT function (Miozzo and Grimshaw 2003) to specialist IT consulting firms: specialists in IT, but in no way specialists in one sector (though they may have sector-specific knowledge). Again, such contracting out is an important reconfiguration, and to the extent that it is advantageous, it gives advantage to 'shareholder' governance—though on the other hand it does at the same time require a close and trusting relationship with the provider. Clearly the key internal player in ICT-driven change is the IT department, and the most important form of human capital is the IT professional; though perhaps as important, though much less visible, is the specialist in another area who is thoroughly at home with ICT and able to interact productively with the IT professional (see below).

These developments disrupt established patterns of skill formation within both the main stakeholder systems—the industry-based German system, in which domestic rivals cooperate to train, to confer, and to accept common qualifications, and the firm-based Japanese system, in which young entrants with a broad general education are given training which is intended to be as far as possible specific to the needs of the firm, in which they are expected to spend all or most of their careers. The German system is designed to prevent poaching and internalize human capital externalities—now it can no longer do this for the most important category of employee. The same is true for the Japanese system—indeed it is more disrupted, because now firms need to encourage 'mid career entry' of IT employees by offering them much higher pay than their lack of seniority within the firm would imply. As Richard Whitley points out in his chapter for this volume, the legal systems of stakeholder capitalist countries generally include provisions to make movement of key employees among firms more difficult, and thus protect internal or cooperative systems of skill formation. However, these restrictions generally relate to firms in the same sector; if someone with cross-sectoral expertise such as that in ICT is likely to be, moves into another sector, the restrictions do not apply.[5]

8.3. THE NEW CONTEXT FOR LEARNING: CHANGES IN ORGANIZATIONAL STRUCTURE AND THEIR IMPLICATIONS

We can identify four structural changes in organizations which the ICT revolution makes possible in principle—one of them vertical, the other three horizontal. Let us take the first three together, for they are all clichés of e-business, important though they are, and difficult though they all are to realize:

1. Much flatter organizations, in which much information can flow quickly and easily between bottom and top without mediation by a complex hierarchy of middle management. (It must be stressed that middle managers do many things that ICT systems could not do as well: organizational capabilities and memories may be lost through overenthusiastic 'delayering' (McGreevy 2000). Nonetheless these can be conserved and augmented without having as many middle managers or having them operating in the same way.)
2. Much closer and quicker connections among functions, such as sales, production, development and design, purchasing; while each of them

sheds much routine employment, brains and paper-pushing being replaced by bytes.

3. Much closer and quicker connections with the firm's suppliers and customers. This allows much more to be bought-in rather than made or done in-house, and thus facilitates globalization: a simple component may be outsourced to China, say, while back-office jobs move to India. Some of the employment that is lost upstream in this way, can be won back by expanding what is provided to industrial customers. Thus, GE's aero-engine division no longer defines its product as engines, but as propulsion services: it seeks to take responsibility for maintaining and repairing engines for its customers as well as making them. (ICT systems are key here, since they can be used to keep the supplier informed in real time about stocks of components, and even linked to machines in such a way that a fault diagnosis travels instantly to 'base'. Indeed instructions for repair may travel instantly back—as with Alsthom's trains operated by Virgin in the UK (Davies 2004.) As Davies shows, some firms have already moved to the ultimate stage of being (upstream) pure systems integrators, not manufacturing anything, while downstream they take over many responsibilities for the operation of the systems they have integrated.

Let us briefly examine the implications of our three clichés for the connection between corporate governance and national modes of learning. If they are to be put into practice, rather radical reconfiguration will be required, and this suggests that they may be more effectively pushed through by shareholder capitalism. On the other hand, each of them makes heavy demands on the employees who remain—demands not only on their competence but on their trustworthiness. Thus shop-floor or front-line employees have fewer supervisors, and must thus take more responsibility for their actions—which may indeed include direct contact with customers or suppliers, where that previously passed through Sales or Purchasing. Competence (if not too rapidly redefined) and trustworthiness may be more characteristic of stakeholder capitalism. Likewise the connections with the suppliers and customers need to be underpinned by trust and an understanding of their situation and requirements; again, this is stakeholder stuff.

Where competence and trust are lacking, the firm will be deterred from such exploitation of ICT's potential. Instead, the emphasis may be on the scope for tightening control and cutting the lower echelons of the workforce. Tightening control and shedding staff is indeed what a generation of managers in shareholder capitalist countries and firms has seen as the main benefit of ICT: the arrival of the Internet and its intranet/EDI precursors led them to extend the area over which the control could be tightened, and to look for their staff-shedding to outsourcing as well as to simple replacement by hardware and software. Stakeholder capitalist firms (to judge by studies in Germany) have been naturally less inclined to go in this direction—or rather, in all these directions. They have often preferred to add ICT skills to their shop-floor workers' existing portfolio of skills than to dispense with them. On the other hand ICT systems like ERP are an excellent way of tightening control, and it is hardly an accident that the leader in the field, SAP, is a German firm which must have benefited heavily from working with German lead customers.

We must then distinguish emphatically between the potential of ICT and e-business for the productive reconfiguration of firms, and the way it is likely to be exploited within any given corporate governance system. A cliché is merely a statement that everyone agrees with—it need not be one that is widely followed in practice.

Our third horizontal transformation is, however, not even a cliché:

4. The new paradigm makes possible much closer and quicker connections between different divisions (by product or geography) within the firm.

This is now becoming, belatedly, a key issue. The division, subdivision, and sub-subdivision of firms into profit centres have been one of the most important trends in Anglo-American capitalism over the last thirty years. If a unit within an organization can be defined as a profit centre, its performance can be measured in financial terms. Targets and budgets can be set, and the treatment— and remuneration—of those in charge can be determined by performance relative to them. They can be given more autonomy in operational matters, on the assumption that the financial control systems provide suitable constraints and motivations. And any difficulties in getting interfunctional coordination—between say R&D, production, and marketing— will be diminished by the smaller size of the unit within which it is to take place.

The more a firm is subdivided in such a way, the more it is necessary, but the more it is difficult, for knowledge to pass between profit centres. The everyday operations of the firm are little affected: the problem lies mostly with organizational learning. Suppose a motor vehicle firm has three plants, which are profit centres: two car assembly plants, and the engine plant. The engine plant supplies both the others, and therefore has regular contact with them, which may be made somewhat more tense by the fact that the profits of all are affected by the transfer price of the engines. Nonetheless this *vertical* relationship is likely to be close—as it might indeed be if an outside firm supplied the engines. What is problematic is the *horizontal* relationship between the two car plants. Their normal operations probably require little or no contact, but their capabilities are likely to have much in common, and they need therefore to be regularly 'exchanging notes'. However, the control structure to which they are subjected gives them no incentive to do so—quite the contrary, since their relationship is likely to be rivalrous. The one with the higher profit will probably be praised and left in peace; the poorer performer will attract adverse attention from top management.

It is an old complaint against Anglo-American capitalism that its structures, going right to the top, discourage constructive relationships among profit centres. In *Core Competence of the Corporation*, Prahalad and Hamel (1990) described the Strategic Business Unit approach as having such an effect, and as being normal, though not universal, among large US and British firms.[6] My own research on corporate governance and innovation in British firms has found a consistent pattern of complaints among middle managers that the financial controls and pressures to which they were subjected had discouraged them not only from making appropriate investments but also from maintaining suitably close relationships with other profit centres, and with other firms. I have called this distortion *sectionalism* (Demirag, Tylecote, and Morris 1994).[7] There is nothing peculiarly British about this cause and effect relationship: anecdotal evidence from Mercedes Benz indicates that when Jurgen Schrempp (as Daimler Chrysler chief executive) in the late 1990s sharply increased the emphasis on divisional financial performance within Daimler Benz, it had precisely the same effect.

It may well be possible to avoid sectionalism without rolling back the trend of divisionalization into profit centres. The devil is in the rigidity and inbuilt short-termism of conventional financial controls, above all the annual budget. There is now a strong school among academic management accountants (Hope and Fraser 2003) arguing that it is necessary to go Beyond Budgeting (the name of the school) to a more long-term and flexible system of financial controls and performance targets, precisely so as to lift the short-termist and sectionalist pressures the budget induces. The Beyond Budgeting control systems continue to monitor the performance of profit centres, but by doing so longer term they remove or reduce the inhibition of cooperation, because the pay-offs to it are longer term. If A helps B, B will no doubt help A— but not tomorrow.[8] While the main academic thrust of Beyond Budgeting appears to be in Britain—we know the enemy best—the examples of creative change in the right direction appear to be mostly in Scandinavia, notably Borealis (Denmark) and Svenska Handelsbanken (Sweden). The difficulty for a typical British shareholder-capitalist firm in going Beyond Budgeting is that the conventional budget fits rather neatly with the arm's length relationship between institutional shareholders and management. The former effectively say to the latter, 'don't bemuse us with too much information, focus on telling us what profits and dividends we can expect (preferably steadily rising ones) and then make sure you deliver them next year'. Beyond Budgeting goes much more with the grain of a corporate governance style in which the shareholder has a long-term commitment.

There is another way of categorizing the changes which ICT and above all the Internet make possible: by the extent to which they involve the initiative of middle-and lower-level employees. Connections between functions, and between suppliers and customers, may be routinized and tightly controlled by rules, and alternatively they may be directly determined by senior management, as with a major joint project. They may, on the other hand, be initiated and carried on by more junior employees, if they have, or exercise, enough discretion. So they may have contacts among divisions, and indeed this is particularly likely since those at either end will more often have worked together. Even among firms, the flow of useful information has been shown by von Hippel (1987) and Assimakopoulos and Macdonald (2001) to be largely on an informal basis, relying on personal relationships within which favours are done and returned. The Internet, as academics know from personal experience, allows such networks to be operated (if not built up) with less cost in time and effort. At the same time the growing complexity of technology, and markets, makes it necessary for a firm to have more such networks. Junior employees will resist even the monitoring by senior management of such learning links, still more their control over them. If they broadly share the objectives, or at least the interests, of their firm, they will exercise their discretion in such learning links in the interests of the firm. It is only through alignment of objectives and perceived interests that such anarchic learning can realize its great potential.

8.4. A PRESCRIPTION FOR 'HYBRID' CORPORATE GOVERNANCE, WITH IMPLICATIONS FOR MODES OF LEARNING

We have seen that the typical, or stereotypical, Anglo-American 'shareholder capitalist' firm is better able than the typical northern European 'stakeholder capitalist' firm to cope with the opportunities and threats of globalization. However, both types appear to be thoroughly ill-equipped to exploit the potential of the new ICT 'paradigm'. In this section I sketch a hybrid form of corporate governance which offers much better prospects.

It seems reasonable, by this stage, to take it as given that shareholders will rule. But who will the shareholders *be*, in the larger firms? In the slower-changing sectors major suppliers or customers may sensibly have substantial stakes, and so, even more, may families. For the rest, banks, and government at some level, may cling on here and there, but their day is gone. The new institutional shareholders—pension funds and mutual funds, and the (less new) insurance companies— are rapidly growing in size of total assets, and it is generally accepted that pension funds should be allowed to invest a substantial proportion of their assets in equities, as of course the US and UK pension funds have long done. So they will dominate the equity landscape.

So far, so Anglo-American. Yet we have seen that stereotypical Anglo-American arm's-length relationships do not work.[9] There, is, however, an alternative to the stereotype. Major 'new institutional' shareholders can *engage* with management. They may do so as major shareholders have traditionally done, through 'their' non-executive directors on the board. They can however also do so very effectively without a non-executive and without compromising their freedom to trade by becoming privy to the firm's secrets. This has been demonstrated by the Capital Group's relationship with Astra-Zeneca (Ramirez and Tylecote 2004). Such a position, somewhere between 'arm's-length' and 'insider', allows a shareholder decently to hold stakes in more than one firm in the sector, and thus more effectively to build *industry-specific expertise*, which it can use to guide management. The more high-tech (and thus fast-changing) a sector is, the more valuable are shareholders with industry-specific expertise (Tylecote and Conesa 1999).

Both engagement and the building of industry-specific expertise cost money. That can only be justified by the holding of substantial stakes in each firm with which the investor engages, or (in total) in each sector in which it builds industry-specific expertise. To simplify slightly, that gives two plausible postures, the choice between them depending on the size of firm.

• In a big firm, an adequately large stake in absolute terms can be built with a relatively small proportionate holding—a holding small enough for the stake to be liquid. The investor is then free to 'exit' if 'voice' does not give satisfactory results. Influence can be secured even with a stake of (say) 5 per cent if other shareholdings are dispersed, as is typical in the UK and increasingly the case on the Continent of Europe. Moreover, a shareholder coalition can be put together, either with other major investors who have also engaged and come to the same view, or with a number of smaller investors who simply respect the engaged investor's reputation and are accordingly willing to support its position. (There have been some recent examples of the latter type of coalition around the UK investor Hermes, when it bought into underperforming firms with the intention of forcing changes in management and strategy (Steele 2005).)

- In a small firm (by stock market standards) an adequate stake means a large fraction of the firm's shares. That means liquidity must be sacrificed. Exit is therefore obstructed, if not entirely impossible, and so voice must be made to work. The simplest way to achieve that is to get a non-executive seat on the board. (If that makes the investor an insider, restricting its freedom to trade, so what? It has lost that freedom anyway, in practice.) New institutional investors already engage in this way through *private equity*: the purchase of large blocks of shares in unlisted companies (including those created by management buyouts). The findings of British Venture Capital Association surveys (and our own interviews) indicate that, even in the traditionally arm's-length British system, the private equity firms display the requisite engagement and (where necessary) industry-specific expertise.[10]

We can label these two investor postures as Outsider Engagement with Liquidity and Insider Engagement without Liquidity. So far, British investors have not regarded either of these postures as permanent ones: the engagement is, so to say, episodic. The Hermes' style of buying into underperforming firms gives the prospect of a substantial one-off capital gain once other investors conclude that a turnaround has been achieved (or is on the way). Private equity investments are made with a view to a subsequent stock market flotation (or sale of the firm), within a period of perhaps five years. However, the larger and more diverse American system has investors which engage long-term—like Capital Group in the AstraZeneca example above, and Warren Buffett's insurance company Berkshire Hathaway. There is no reason why episodic engagement should not evolve into permanent engagement. It is a question of the availability of funds and the attractiveness of alternative disengaged postures. So-called actively managed investment portfolios have performed poorly in recent years—worse than passively managed index-tracking portfolios, net of management fees (Tylecote and Ramirez 2005). Permanent engagement may soon be recognized as the 'only game in town' capable of offering supernormal investment returns. That point would come sooner if there were tax disincentives to the fast share turnover (or 'churn') typical of active management.

There is, or there should be, another category of shareholder which can naturally be expected to engage with management and possess industry-specific expertise: employees. We have to distinguish two possibilities here. Employees may hold shares (or share options) purely as individuals. It is then not very likely that they will play any role in corporate governance, except perhaps by their decisions if the firm is faced with a hostile takeover bid.

(If they only have share options they have no role even then.) What individual shares and/or share options can do, as Blasi, Kruse, and Bernstein (2003) have persuasively argued, is to increase the employee's commitment to the firm, which delivers most of the key advantages of the stakeholder firm as discussed above. If employees have a collective holding, as with ESOPs in the US, they can also wield power. Such power is unlikely to be wielded with the same conservative bias as codetermination, since the employee as shareholder cares about profits. It is difficult to see much difference between the engaged new institutional shareholder and the shareholding employee in the objectives they would prefer for the firm, except in the more mature industries where the preservation of jobs might be preferred by the employee at the cost of some reduction in profit. Even this, if it increases the employees' commitment to the firm, might be seen as a long-term profit-maximizing path.

It is the emphasis on long-term profit which is likely to distinguish both employees and engaged institutional shareholders from the disengaged kind—as argued for institutions by Ramirez and Tylecote (2004). One route to long-term profit is, as we have seen in the last section, radical restructuring to exploit the possibilities of ICT. In most firms it is unlikely that senior managers will fully appreciate either the possibilities or the route by which they may be best exploited: in the midst of a technological revolution they are, to put it brutally, just too old. A friend of the author served recently as a non-executive director of a listed British firm. Having much expertise in e-business, he had been invited onto the board by the senior management because they thought he might give useful advice on their moves in an e-business direction. They meant, advice *to them*. He found it more useful to talk to middle managers who had some understanding of what he was talking about. Predictably, the senior management found this behaviour subversive, and the overintrusive non-executive was soon asked to leave the board. He had to go, of course, because the non-executives on a British board serve at the pleasure of top management, not of the (disengaged) shareholders. In the dispensation that I have in mind, such a non-executive director could have been brought onto, or at least kept on, the board by engaged institutional shareholders and/or employees.

8.5. GOING WITH THE GRAIN? DIFFERENT ROUTES FROM HERE TO THERE

The argument of Section 8.3 was that it was mainly to new institutional shareholders, plus employees, that we must look for the changes advocated in corporate governance, and (through them) to the corresponding changes in modes of learning. This would be particularly the case in larger firms and in more high-technology industries. (The smaller the firm, and the lower-tech the sector, the better-suited to family control.) As the example of Britain demonstrates, however, it is not enough for the new institutional shareholders to be dominant shareholders: they have to change their behaviour from their traditional disengagement. In tracking the movement in each country from here to there, then, we might ask four questions:

1. What is the level and rate of increase of new institutional shareholding in that country?
2. What is the level and rate of increase of equity holdings by that country's new institutions?
3. What is the level of employee shareholding in that country?
4. How far does the culture and tradition of the country predispose to shareholder engagement and employee participation in control?

On the three first quantitative questions, I cannot offer acceptable comparative data here, but will instead paint some broad-brush pictures of the six countries covered by our project, the UK, Germany, France, Sweden, Italy, and the Netherlands.

A key difference is that three of them—the UK, Sweden, and the Netherlands—have well-established funded pension systems; the other three do not. The UK leads, with Sweden, in level of new institutional shareholdings within its industry—mostly UK-owned, but with a strong US-owned element, and an even stronger US role in the management of them.[11] It also leads in the development of the total equity holdings of the new institutions. The Netherlands has new institutions of similar age and size, but its pension funds are much more constrained in the proportion of equity they can hold; this constraint has been somewhat relaxed recently. All three countries are thus *quantitatively* in a position to develop systems of control by engaged new institutional shareholders at an early stage. The other three countries are clearly not in such a position. One of them, however—France—is in an exceptional position: a massive programme of privatization beginning in 1986 put a huge number of shares onto the open market, and (for want of French pension funds) they ended up mainly in the hands of foreign, mostly the US and UK, institutions (Reberioux 2002). New institutional shareholding in French industry is thus important, indeed dominant in many of the privatized firms. The privatized firms also have substantial employee shareholdings: which appears to put France rather improbably in the lead in this dimension, for no European country has gone far to follow the American lead.

On shareholder engagement and employee participation, we look at the countries one by one. The UK has no substantial tradition of either (Tylecote and Ramirez 2005). We have seen that shareholders are generally thoroughly disengaged, leaving management to operate on the market for corporate control as best it can. What can be said for the UK is that there is no entrenched *old* way of engaging or participating: the ground is clear for the new way, and there is enough evidence of success in that—by private equity and venture capital in unlisted firms, and by the few firms which have experimented with employee shareholding or coownership (John Lewis, Scott Bader)—to suggest that it will work very well once the reluctant asset managers have exhausted the alternatives.

The Netherlands also has a tradition of shareholder disengagement but with a different outcome, because while UK company law is unusually severe in exposing management to the rigours of the market for corporate control, Dutch law has been exceptionally lax: it has allowed various schemes for the defence of management from takeover bids as from shareholder intrusion (Maassen 2000). For the larger firms management's self-control has had to be shared with employees. All this is now in question and under attack. The great Dutch advantage is the very strong 'polder' tradition of interest reconciliation among different groups: a tradition which management carried on, protected from shareholder pressure. In this context, stereotypical Anglo-American capitalism is deeply unattractive. The modification of it proposed here would appear to fit much better with Dutch culture.

Swedish culture has a great deal in common with Dutch. Consensus is much to be valued, and to be achieved by talking things through. There is, on the other hand, a very strong tradition of shareholder engagement. This was over many years undermined by another Swedish tradition, egalitarianism, expressed in a highly progressive tax system (Henreksson and Jacobsson 2005). A number of families once played an important role, but faded in the face of the relentless demands of the Swedish tax system. The founding families of IKEA and Tetrapak held on by taking refuge abroad—not an ideal location for engagement. The vacuum was filled by two investment vehicles, Investor and Industrivaerden, controlled by the Wallenberg family and the Handelsbank respectively. The bigger of the two, Investor, controlled most of the giants of Swedish industry for decades—arguably an excessive range for one organization. The Wallenbergs' control of Investor was through family foundations which were relatively, but not perfectly, protected from the tax system. Over time this control became increasingly precarious, with a more and more inadequate capital base; it was only Sweden's dual class share system which made it possible at all. By the end of the 1990s the old engaged shareholders were effectively played out. By then, ironically, the egalitarian tax system had been thoroughly remodelled. There was no longer anything to keep entrepreneurs and their families from exercising control indefinitely—and the dual class share system would help them do so. But for the time being the big battalions of shareholders were Swedish and foreign (mostly US) new institutions. The biggest were the pension funds. This was unfortunate, given that the fact that they had been set up by Social Democratic governments which had intended them to carry out a sort of nationalization-by-stealth. Disengagement was for them a way of disavowing such an intention. It will therefore take time for them to move from thesis to anti-thesis to a final synthesis of engagement for profit. As for employees, Swedish law gives them at least one non-executive director and significant influence. There is thus an established *old way* of employee participation. There is at the same time a strong desire for employee belonging: in Sweden as in the Netherlands participation goes very much with the grain. One last Swedish characteristic is worth mentioning here: though reaching a consensus for change takes time, the process is also thorough, and often rather uniform across the country. Consequently, when Sweden moves, it really moves.

In France there is an important tradition of engaged family shareholding in big firms (e.g. Michelin, PSA, Dassault), but as Rébérioux (2002) emphasizes, the kingpin of French corporate governance is the Président Directeur Générale (PDG) an august title only limply rendered by 'chief executive'. The French cultural predisposition for individualism combined with strong hierarchy gives the PDG an exceptional degree of independence, and an exceptional inclination to resist outsider engagement. Until there are well-established domestic new institutional shareholders—not yet in sight—this resistance is not likely to be overcome. French PDGs appear to be much more comfortable, rather ironically, with stereotypical Anglo-American capitalism, whose demands for rising profits and share prices have been made their own by an extremely generous (self-) allocation of stock options. They would be even less comfortable with engagement from below. A series of laws in support of employee participation has constrained the PDG's power, but the participation tends to be confrontational rather than consensual. Accordingly, the road from here to there seems long.

Germany, on the other hand, has an entrenched custom of shareholder engagement backed by non-executive directorships. The engagement is by family shareholders even in many of the largest firms (e.g. BMW), by banks,[12] and by other firms in Germany; in a few firms, like VW, also by the state. Old-style engagement, old-style engagers. New domestic institutional shareholders are conspicuous by their weakness—although many of the largest firms have listed abroad and acquired large numbers of foreign new institutional shareholders. Likewise Germany has the most highly developed and entrenched form of old-style employee participation (Reberioux 2002). Codetermination gives employees half the (supervisory) board seats in Germany; works councils are also strong. Although new-style engagement seems perfectly consistent with German culture, there is a great deal of baggage which needs to be dumped before it can be reached.

Prospects in Italy seem least promising of all. As in Germany, there is entrenched old-style engagement, by families above all. As Pagano and Trento (2002) argue, the importance of families has even increased in the last decade. It is revealing and appropriate that the Prime Minister himself is an entrepreneur, the most successful one in the country. As in Germany, again, the new institutions are conspicuous by their weakness. As in France, on the other hand, there is strong hierarchy, and while in the large firms employees are far from meekly obedient, their participation is confrontational rather than consensual. A further obstacle to reform is that the typical Italian firm is small- or medium-sized, a natural for family control and for relatively informal relationships with employees. Failing a huge wave of mergers, there simply is and will be no large enough core of large firms in which a large pool of new institutional capital can quickly develop, and in which the practices of outsider and employee engagement can be developed.

8.6. CONCLUSIONS

I have argued above that we can see 'the diffusion of new [Anglo-Saxon] forms of corporate governance' across Europe as partly responding to developments which themselves call into question 'traditional systems of labour market regulation and in particular established systems of employment protection'. Thus, German employers' associations are rapidly losing control of wages in large firms and small—ahead of changes in corporate governance, which in Germany are rather slow. It is difficult to see large (and therefore, almost inevitably multinational) firms making traditional stakeholder forms of governance really work in the new situation; in that sense one must say that for large, even medium German firms faced by the need to globalize, the codetermination element in corporate governance is dead or dying already. For most of them some softened version of the 'Anglo-Saxon forms' of labour market regulation and employment protection seems to be the only option. Smaller firms which can remain national—perhaps by simply giving up the low-technology activities which are more cheaply carried out elsewhere—are less directly affected. However, if large firms in their sector desert the 'German model' the sectoral cohesion on which they have depended is lost. It may be necessary for them to move towards a relatively flexible form of stakeholder capitalism, with the emphasis on 'employee inclusion' through stock options and/or profit-based bonuses, and on the 'low-patenting strategy' sketched.

This is not to say that the organization of training and skill certification will rapidly become a matter internal to the firm. Existing practices for existing definitions of skills will probably survive a long time, given inertia on all sides. The clear exception, as we have noted above, is IT skills, where sectoral provision is inappropriate anyway. In any case, as we can see from Section 8.2 above, what is now key for exploiting the possibilities of the new techno-economic paradigm is the ability and determination of top management to reconfigure the organization, and the ability of the rest to operate appropriately within the reconfigured structure. Conventionally defined skills may be necessary for this, but they are a long way from being sufficient. The German emphasis on formal qualifications and on detailed job descriptions is likely to be a problem here.

The French economy was highly successful in increasing productivity during the 'trente dorées' of 1950–80, and as of 2002, had by some measures higher labour productivity per hour than Germany or the US (and 25 per cent higher than the UK) (*The Economist*, 2004). In many ways this seems to have involved a rather faithful replication of American Fordism: as Maurice, Sellier, and Silvestre (1986) showed twenty years ago, French industry like American favours 'strong staff, weak line' against the 'strong line, lean staff' system of Germany and Japan in which each level of production workers, up to and including production directors, has relatively high levels of skill and responsibility. Among the 'strong staff' functions in France, the engineering department, responsible above all for process improvement, has pride of place. In a comparative survey of relative pay levels in 1992, it was only in France, out of ten European countries surveyed, that the engineering director was paid more than the production director (Tylecote 1996a: 141). Relatively unconstrained by finance (at least in large firms) the engineering department in French firms was able to lead the progressive re-equipment of production, within what may be called the Fordist trajectory.

As in the US, French corporate governance focuses on an all-powerful chief executive (unlike the UK model in which there is a non-executive chairman who can exercise some restraint). Indeed the low trust and high power distance of French national and corporate culture lead the French autocrat to take more responsibility than his American counterpart, who will be more comfortable with dissent and devolution of power. A number of recent studies (e.g. Jeffers and Plihon 2001) have shown how far, with privatization, the French corporate governance system has moved in the US direction—as far as anywhere in Europe. A large proportion of large firms have shifted, since 1986, partially or wholly from state ownership to private ownership, and the private shareholders are principally American and British institutions such as dominate the US and UK finance and corporate governance systems. It has been well argued (Reberioux 2002) that the greater willingness of these institutions to invest in French than in German firms is due precisely to the greater scope for them (and others) to push the French system in the American direction. It is, after all, simple enough, when the chief executive is God's representative on earth—not boxed in as a German CEO is by obligations to other earthlings—to make him or her subject to a different God—outside shareholders rather than the government. Nothing much needs change on earth, except the demands that God's representative transmits. These now put new emphasis on short-term profit, which must rather inhibit the engineering director.

What is much worse is that the French system, new or old, has now to cope not with following an established Fordist trajectory but coping with a paradigm shift. The same 1992 survey that showed the engineering director above the production director in France, showed the IT director at the bottom of the list. This has no doubt now changed. What does not appear to have changed is the relatively low level of responsibility of direct production workers, entrenched partly by low trust and high power distance. While the strong German line can in principle, with time, get a good enough understanding of ICT to respond reasonably well to the challenges of e-business, what hope is there for the weak French line (or the British)? The French reflex will be to rely on a strong staff function, in this case the IT department. But the universal experience is that new IT systems can only be successfully introduced if those who design and implement them fully understand: (*a*) the operations of the firm and (*b*) its IT legacy—the systems already in place. IT is now far too important to be left to the IT specialists. The French adaptation to e-business appears to be very slow; the rate of increase in productivity per hour between 1995 and 2002 was slower than in the US, Germany, or even Britain (*The Economist* 2004).[13]

NOTES

1. For an eloquent statement of the latter see Monks and Sykes 2002.
2. The macroeconomic data are consistent with the view that Germany and Japan are being particularly affected by this 'gradient': both have suffered rising unemployment over the last five and ten years, and both show respectable rises in labour productivity over the same period, as one would expect if the more labour-intensive operations were being moved abroad. Thus, according to *The Economist's*

figures (*The Economist* 2004) German growth in productivity per hour kept pace with American over the 1995–2002 period, in spite of the massive investment in US industry during the period, while Britain and (still more) France lagged behind. The recent Japanese recovery does not belie the continuing shift of labour-intensive operations to China—it simply indicates that the strength of the Chinese boom has generated many more new high-tech jobs in Japan.

3. I use 'Fordism' in Perez's relatively restricted sense to refer to the techno-economic paradigm, as opposed to the broader sense of the French regulationists, who include all kinds of institutional features.

4. As it is clearly in US economic interests, it can be seen as an expression of US hegemony. As such, there is every reason to be sceptical of the alleged benefits, as Macdonald very much is (and see also Chang 2002 for the problems posed by it for developing countries). On the other hand, if there are to be globalized chains of production, in which the location of each operation is determined by comparative advantage, they must be held together by the communication of codified information, including information on product and process technology, as Sturgeon (2002) shows. This will not *be* communicated unless it enjoys strong legal protection. (I owe this point to Peter Gammeltoft.)

5. I understand that there is a German law preventing employees moving to a rival firm within twelve months, and an Italian rule putting similar restrictions on setting up one's own firms. These would be laws meant to bolster the stakeholder coalition/tacit knowledge system, now obstructive of desirable movement among firms.

6. The alternative they favour seems to involve a rather strong and large HQ such as is typical in the Japanese firms they praise. This, like enthusiasm for things Japanese in general, seems a little dated.

7. The main UK exception is the pharmaceutical industry, where structures are different—far less divisionalized—and outcomes much better (Tylecote and Ramirez 2005).

8. A recent study of UK firms' relationships with suppliers and industrial customers (Cantista and Tylecote 2003) finds that listed firms (the typical UK shareholder capitalist form) were significantly less inclined to develop close relationships than were firms controlled by families or subsidiaries of foreign MNCs based in stakeholder-capitalist countries.

9. For further argument to this effect see Ramirez and Tylecote (2004) and Tylecote and Ramirez (2005).

10. Venture capital in the strict (American) sense is a subset of private equity, invested in genuinely new firms with prospects of high growth—most typically in high-tech sectors.

11. Thus, for example, the largest of the UK asset management houses, Mercury Asset Management, was recently acquired by (the American) Merrill Lynch.

12. The banks' engagement has weakened steadily over the last thirty years (Edwards and Fischer 1994).

13. What then of the Americans, who are generally agreed to be leading in the adaptation to e-business and have the fastest rate of productivity increase over the period since 1995? The US is institutionally diverse and creative, and it has been grappling with these challenges longer than any other country. Nonetheless, as Henwood (2003) argues, one must regard these statistics with grave suspicion. The US advantage seems confined to retailing and the IT-producing industries, and there the numerator and/or the denominator seem to be mis-measured.

REFERENCES

Assimakopoulos, D. and Macdonald, S. (2001). 'A Dual Approach to Understanding Information Networks', *International Journal of Technology Management*, 12(1–2), 96–112.

Blasi, J., Kruse, D., and Bernstein, A. (2003). *In the Company of Owners: The Truth About Stock Options, And Why Every Employee Should Have Them*. New York: Basic Books.

Cantista, I. and Tylecote, A. (2003). 'Innovation, Corporate Governance, and Supplier-Customer Relationships: A Study From the Speciality Chemicals and Electrical Equipment Industries', Sheffield University Management School Working Paper No. 2003.15.

Chang, H.-J. (2002). *Kicking Away The Ladder: Development Strategy in Historical Perspective*. London: Anthem.

Davies, A. (2004). 'Moving Base into High-Value Integrated Solutions: A Value Stream Approach', *Industrial and Corporate Change*, 13(5): 727–56.

Demirag, I., Tylecote, A., and Morris, B. (1994). 'Accounting for Financial and Managerial Causes of Short Term Pressures in British Corporations', *Journal of Business Finance and Accounting*, 21(8): 1195–213.

The Economist (2004). 'The Missing Guest at Gordon's Party: Why Productivity Growth has Slowed in Britain While Rising in America'. *The Economist*, 24 January: 28.

Edwards, J. and Fischer, K. (1994). *Banks, Finance and Investment in Germany*. Cambridge: Cambridge University Press.

Freeman, C. and Louçã, F. (2001). *As Time Goes By: From the Industrial Revolution to the Information Revolution*. Oxford: Oxford University Press.

—— and Perez, C. (1988). 'Structural Crises of Adjustment: Business Cycles and Investment Behaviour', in G. Dosi, C. Freeman, R. Nelson, G. Silverberg, and L. Soete (eds.), *Technical Change and Economic Theory*. London: Pinter, pp. 38–66.

Henwood, D. (2003). *After the New Economy*. New York: New Press.

Henrekson, M. and Jakobsson, U. (2005). 'The Swedish Model of Corporate Ownership and Control in Transition', in H. Huizinga and L. Jonung (eds.), The Internationalisation of Asset Ownership in Europe. Cambridge: Cambridge University Press, pp. 207–46.

Hope, J. and Fraser, R. (2003). *Beyond Budgeting*. Cambridge, MA: Harvard Business School Press.

Jeffers, E. and Plihon, D. (2001). 'Investisseurs institutionelles et gouvernance des entreprises', *Revne d'Économie Financière*, No 63, pp. 137–52.

Kidd, P. T. (1994). *Agile Manufacturing: Forging new Frontiers*. Reading, MA: Addison-Wesley.

McGreevy, M. (2000). 'The Changing Nature of Work', *Industrial and Commercial Training*, 34(5): 191–5.

Maassen, G. F. (2000). *An International Comparison of Corporate Governance Models*, 2nd edn. Amsterdam: Spencer Stuart.

Macdonald, S. (1990). *Technology and the Tyranny of Export Controls*. London: Macmillan.

Maurice, M., Sellier, F., and Silvestre, J. J. (1986). *The Social Foundations of Industrial Power*. Cambridge, UK: Cambridge University Press.

Miozzo, M. and Grimshaw, D. (2003). 'The Other Side of IT Outsourcing: The New Boundaries and Coordination of the Large Innovating Firm', CRIC Working Paper.

Monks, R. and Sykes, A. (2002). *Capitalism Without Owners Will Fail: A Policy-Maker's Guide to Reform*. London and New York: Centre for the Study of Financial Innovation.

Pagano, U. and Trento, S. (2002). *Continuity and Change in Italian Corporate Governance: The Institutional Stability of One Variety of Capitalism*. University of Siena Department of Economics Working Paper No. 365.

Perez C. (1983). 'Structural Change and Assimilation of New Technologies in the Economic and Social Systems', *Futures*, 15(5): 357–75.

—— (2002). *Financial Capital and Technological Revolutions*. Cheltenham, UK: Edward Elgar.

Prahalad, C. K. and Hamel, G. (1990). 'The Core Competence of the Corporation', *Harvard Business Review*, 68(3): 79–91.

Ramirez, P. and Tylecote, A. (2004). 'Hybrid Corporate Governance and Its Effects on Innovation: A Case Study of AstraZeneca', *Technology Analysis and Strategic Management*, 16(1).

Rébérioux, A. (2002). 'European Style of Corporate Governance at the Crossroads', Journal of Common Market Studies, 40, 111–34.

Steele, M. (2005). 'Time for Investors to Come in From the Cold'. FT Mastering Corporate Governance, *Financial Times*, 20 May: 6–7.

Sturgeon, T. (2002). 'Modular Production Networks: A New American Model of Industrial Organization', *Industrial and Corporate Change*, 11(3): 451–96.

Tylecote, A. (1992). *The Long Wave in the World Economy*. London and New York: Routledge.

—— (1996a). 'Managerial Objectives and Technological Collaboration: The Role of National Variations in Cultures and Structure', in R. Coombs, A. Richards, P. P. Saviotti, and V. Walsh (eds.), *Technological Collaboration: the Dynamics of Cooperation in Industrial Innovation*. Cheltenham UK: Edward Elgar, pp. 34–53.

Tylecote, A. (1996*b*). 'Cultural Differences Affecting Technological Innovation in Western Europe', *European Journal of Work and Occupational Psychology*, 5(1): 137–47.

—— and Conesa, E. (1999). 'Corporate Governance, Innovation Systems and Industrial Performance', *Industry and Innovation*, 6(1): 25–50.

—— and Ramirez, P. (2005). 'UK Corporate Governance and Innovation'. Sheffield University Management School Working Paper No. 2005.08.

—— and Visintin, E. (2002). 'Financial and Corporate Governance Systems and Technological Change: The Incompleteness of Fit of The UK and Italy', *Revista de Economia Politica e Industriale*, 114: 81–108.

Von Hippel, E. (1987). 'Cooperation Between Rivals: Informal Know-How Trading', *Research Policy*, 16: 291–302.

Part III

Education Systems
and Science–Industry Links

9

Science–Technology–Industry Links and the 'European Paradox': Some Notes on the Dynamics of Scientific and Technological Research in Europe

Giovanni Dosi, Patrick Llerena, and Mauro Sylos Labini

9.1. INTRODUCTION

We originally began this work simply meaning to address what is known as the 'European Paradox'. Such a paradox—which sounds quite similar to an earlier 'UK paradox', fashionable around thirty years ago—refers to the conjecture that EU countries play a leading global role in terms of top-level scientific output, but lag behind in the ability of converting this strength into wealth-generating innovations. However, we soon realized, first, that the paradox mostly appears just in the flourishing business of reporting to and by the European Commission itself rather than in the data. Second, both the identification of the purported paradox, and the many proposed recipes suited to eliminate it, happen to be loaded with several, often questionable, assumptions regarding the relationship between scientific and technological knowledge, and between both of them and the search and production activities of business enterprises.

Hence we decided to move a couple of steps backward and start by making explicit where we stand in the long-lasting controversy on the nature and properties of scientific and technological knowledge and on the institutions supporting its generation (Section 9.2). The proposed framework, we suggest, fits quite well with a series of robust 'stylized facts', notwithstanding the multiple criticisms recently undergone by the institutional setup which grew in the West over more than a century ago and fully developed after the Second World War (Sections 9.3 and 9.4). Having spelled out the interpretative tools, we turn to the evidence supporting the existence of a 'European paradox' (or a lack of it) (Section 9.5) and discuss the European comparative performance in terms of scientific output, proxies for technological innovation, and actual production and export in those lines of business which draw more directly on scientific advances. Indeed, one does not find much of a paradox. Certainly one observes significant differences across scientific and technological fields, but the notion of an overall 'European excellence' finds little support. At the same time one does find ample evidence of a widespread European corporate weakness, notwithstanding major success stories.

The interpretation bears also far-reaching normative implications (Sections 9.6 and 9.7). If we are right, much less emphasis should be put on various types of 'networking', 'interactions with the local environment', 'attention to user need'—current obsessions of European policymakers— and much more on policy measures aimed to both strengthen 'frontier' research and, at the opposite end, strengthen European corporate actors.

9.2. SCIENCE AND TECHNOLOGY: SOME INTERPRETATIVE YARDSTICKS

One of us has written extensively elsewhere on the subject (Dosi 1982, 1988; Dosi, Marengo, and Fagiolo 2004). Here, it suffices to sketch out what one could call the Stanford-Yale-Sussex (SYS) synthesis, sure to displease almost everyone, as a shorthand for the confluence between works on the economics of information (including Nelson 1959; Arrow 1962; David 1993, 2004) and works focusing on the specific features of technological knowledge (including Nelson 1959; Freeman 1982, 1994; Nelson and Winter 1982; Freeman and Soete 1997; Rosenberg, 1976, 1982; Winter 1982, 1987; Pavitt 1987, 1999; and also Dosi 1982, 1988). In such a synthesis, first, one fully acknowledges some common features of information and knowledge—in general, and with reference to scientific and technological knowledge, in particular. Moreover, second, one distinguishes the specific features of technological knowledge and the ways it is generated and exploited in contemporary economies.

As to the former point, both information and knowledge share the following properties:

− Some general features of public goods: (*a*) non-rival access (i.e. the fact that one holds an idea does not constrain others from holding it too); (*b*) low marginal cost of reproduction and distribution, which in principle makes it difficult to exclude others from having access to newly generated information (except for legal devices such as copyrights and patents), as compared to high fixed costs of original production [The latter point applies primarily to information, *stricto sensu*].

– A fundamental uncertainty concerning the mapping between whatever one expects from search activities and their outcomes.

– (Relatedly) serendipity in the ultimate economic and social impact of search itself (Nelson 2004*a*).

– Quite often, very long lags between original discoveries and 'useful' applications.

However, scientific and even more so technological knowledge share, to a different extent, some degrees of tacitness. This applies to the pre-existing knowledge leading to any discovery and also to the knowledge required to interpret and apply whatever codified information is generated. As Pavitt (2001) puts it with regards to technological knowledge:

most technology is specific, complex ... cumulative in its development ... 'Specificity' applies in two senses: It is specific to firms where most technological activity is carried out, and it is specific to products and processes, since most of the expenditures is not on research, but on development and production engineering, after which knowledge is also accumulated through experience in production and use on what has come to be known as 'learning by doing' and 'learning by using'. (Pavitt 1987: 9)

Moreover,

the combination of activities reflects the essentially pragmatic nature of most technological knowledge. Although a useful input, theory is rarely sufficiently robust to predict the performance of a technological artefact under operating conditions and with a high enough degree of certainty, to eliminate costly and time consuming construction and testing of prototype and pilot plant. (Pavitt 1987: 9)

A distinct issue regards the relations between scientific knowledge, technological innovation, and their economic exploitation. In this respect, note that the SYS synthesis is far from claiming any linear relation going from the former to the latter. On the contrary, many contributors to the SYS view have been in the forefront in arguing that the relationships go both ways (see Freeman 1982, 1994; Rosenberg 1982; Kline and Rosenberg 1986; Pavitt 1999 among others).

In particular, one has shown that, first, technological innovations have sometimes preceded science in that practical inventions came about before the scientific understanding of why they worked (the engine is a good case for the point).

Second, it is quite common that scientific advances have been made possible by technological ones especially in the fields of instruments (e.g. think of the importance of the microscope).

Third, one typically observes complementarity between science and technology, which however 'varies considerably amongst sectors of application, in terms of the direct usefulness of academic research results, and of the relative importance attached to such results and to training' (Pavitt 1987: 7).

Having said that, it is also the case that since the Industrial Revolution, the relative contribution of science to technology has been increasing and its impact has become more and more pervasive, while the rates of innovation have often been shaped by the strength of the science base from which they draw (Nelson 1993; Mowery and Nelson 1999). In turn, 'this science base largely is the product of publicly funded research and the knowledge produced by that research is largely open and available for potential innovations to use. That is, the market part of the Capitalist Engine [of technological progress] rests on a publicly supported scientific commons' (Nelson 2004a: 455).

Together, the fundamental vision underlying and supporting such a view of publicly supported Open Science throughout a good part of the twentieth century entailed: (*a*) a sociology of the scientists community largely relying on self-governance and peer evaluation, (*b*) a shared culture of scientists emphasizing the importance of motivational factors other than economic ones, and (*c*) an ethos of disclosure of search results driven by 'winner takes all' precedence rules.[1]

So far, so good. However, both the factual implications of the SYS synthesis and the normative implications of the Open Science institutional arrangements have been recently under attack from different quarters.

9.3. THE OPEN SCIENCE SYSTEM UNDER THREAT

It is worth to start asking the question why the institutional setup governing the generation of scientific knowledge and the relations between science, technology, and industry has been put into question despite the fact that it has worked remarkably well through most of the twentieth century. (More detailed analyses from different angles, which we largely share, can be found in David 1997, Pavitt 2001, and Nelson 2004a.) In that, note that the challenges to the 'Open Science' institutions often have come confusingly folded together with plenty of remarks regarding the two-way interactions between science and technology, offering the misleading impression that lack of smooth flows between science and its applications would bear any direct consequence in terms of the publicity of scientific results themselves.

Here are, telegraphically, what we consider major drivers and by-products of the critique of the Open Science system.

First, as Pavitt (2001) succinctly puts it, the consensus to the institutional arrangement supporting publicly funded open basic science, *in primis* in the US, has been a sort of 'social pact' catalysed by the 'fear of communism and cancer'. Nowadays, half of the reasons have disappeared, substituted by 'terrorism', which, however, can hardly play the same role. Indeed, in Guantánamo times it is difficult to imagine 'universalist' missions linking scientific research and political objectives akin to those of the anti-communist era.

Second, the critique of the 'linear model', the one, to repeat, naively suggesting unidirectional 'trickle down' flows from science to technology to profit-driven production activities, has gone far too far. It has done so with the help of plenty of economists who did finally take on board some of the 'economics of information' findings (cf. above all the pioneering works of Nelson 1959 and Arrow 1962) while totally neglecting at the same time the differences between sheer information and technological knowledge, mentioned earlier. The result has been a widespread notion of 'plasticity' of both scientific and technological search to economic incentives. Sure, if information bears public good features, then 'market failure' problems are bound to arise. But whenever the incentive structure can be fixed—this story goes—then knowledge production should properly respond to incentives much alike the production of steel or automobiles. Together the fundamental specificities stemming from the very nature of the scientific and technological problem-solving activities disappear. 'Incentives' can fix anything, from the cure to cancer to the proof of the last Fermat theorem, as easy as one can elicit a variation in any ordinary production. (On the contrary view which we largely share, cf. Nelson 2003; see also a critical review of parts of the discussion on technology and problem-solving in Dosi, Marengo, and Fagiolo 2004).

If one lets this dangerous stuff get into the hands of religious believers, one indeed gets an explosive mixture. An archetypical case is Kealy (1996)—properly reviewed by David (1997)—disciple of the economist inspired zeitgeist on the 'magic of market place'—as Ronald Reagan used to say—and of the miracles of property rights. David (1997) warns us about how a 'market ideology' in conducive times may easily become a 'scholarly' reference for all those who are just eager to believe it, irrespectively of the soundness of the underlying evidence. And indeed our times seem particularly favourable to the spread of such ideologies.

Another point of attack against Open Science has been the extension of the Property Right System to the institutions generating scientific knowledge (*in primis*, universities) and the expansion of the domain of patentability.

Regarding the former, the Bayh-Dole Act (1980) in the US is considered a landmark, allowing (indeed encouraging) universities to take out patents on their (publicly funded) research results. Similar legislation is nowadays common throughout the world.

Concerning the domains of patentability, one has seen a progressive extension of what is patentable, which has now come to include living entities, genes, algorithms, data banks, and even 'business models'. These institutional changes have been implicitly or explicitly supported by the idea that more property rights are generally better in that they cure the 'market failure' associated with the public nature characteristics of scientific knowledge (as if it were a problem). An outcome has been that

important areas of science are now much more under the sway of market mechanisms than used to be the case. And in particular, in some important fields of science important bodies of scientific understanding and technique now are private property rather than part of the commons. (Nelson 2004a: 462)

The last challenge to the Open Science System—and to a significant extent also to the SYS synthesis—has come from quite distinct quarters, which could come under the heading of the 'social constructivism/deconstructivism' perspective. The current is made of multiple streams which however share some similar notion of 'plasticity' of science and technology, this time under the pressure of social forces and 'political negotiation'.

There is little doubt on the importance of the social shaping of technology, as MacKenzie and Wajcman (1985) put it (see also Rip et al. 1995). However, important controversies concern (*a*) the bounds which the nature of specific technical problems and of specific bodies of knowledge put upon the reach of 'battling competing interests and more or less effective campaigns to capture the hearts and minds of (different constituencies)' (Nelson 2004b: 514) and (*b*) the degrees of 'social determinism' driving technological and scientific change. And indeed many versions of social constructivism depart a long way from the SYS synthesis, pushing it to a caricature. Sometimes one has the impression that with good bargaining skills even gravitation and thermodynamics laws may be renegotiated with nature!

Finally, on the institutional side it is suggested that the modes of organization of scientific and technological search—centred on universities, corporate laboratories, relatively structured disciplinary fields, peer review of the outcomes of scientific search, etc.—has been progressively replaced by what Gibbons et al. (1994) call 'Mode 2 of knowledge production'. In brief, as summarized by Martin (2003),

such a mode involves 'multi-or trans-disciplinary research carried out in a growing variety of institutions and with a blurring of the boundaries between the traditional sectors (university, industry, and so on ...) and also between science and society ... [and] knowledge is increasingly being produced in the context of application [...]

with societal needs having a direct influence from the early stage and with relatively explicit social accountability for the funding received by the government. (Martin 2003: 1213)

9.4. SOME PERSISTENT 'STYLIZED FACTS'

The empirical grounds for such a statement are of course crucial for the entire 'revisionist' story to hold.

Consider the following pieces of evidence partly drawn from Pavitt (2001) and Pavitt (2003).

1. Contrary to the claim that scientific and technological knowledge can be increasingly reduced to sheer 'information', the distinction between the two continues to be highly relevant. A good deal of knowledge is and is likely to continue to be rather 'sticky', organization and people embodied and often also spatially clustered. Related to this is the persistence of widespread agglomeration phenomena driven by top level research (see Jaffe, Trajitenberg, and Henderson 1993 among many others and Breschi and Lissoni 2001 for a critical review).

2. Useful academic research is good academic research. 'Systematic evidence from the US shows that the academic research that corporate practitioners find most useful is publicly funded, performed in research universities, published in prestigious referred journals' (Pavitt 2001: 90), and frequently cited by academic themselves (on these points see Narin, Hamilton, and Olivastro 1997 and Hicks et al. 2000).

3. Government funding of basic research is responsible, especially in the US, for most major scientific advances, including in the fields of information sciences and biosciences (Pavitt 2001 and the references cited therein).

4. The proportion of university research that is business financed is very low everywhere (typically less than 10 per cent) and lower in the US than in Europe (see Table 9.7 and the discussion below).

5. The expansion of US university patenting has resulted in a rapid decline of the patent quality and value (Henderson, Jaffe, and Trajitenberg 1998).

6. Increases in licensing income in leading US universities are concentrated in biotech and software, and have preceded the Bayh-Dole Act. Moreover, income flows from licensing are quite small as compared to the overall university budget: in most cases they are unable to cover even the administrative costs of the 'technology transfer office' in charge of them!

At the same time still anecdotal evidence begins to hint at the ways the new appropriation regimes for public research tend to corrupt the ethos of researchers and twist their research agendas and in the US even:

[s]ome of the nations largest and most technology intensive firms are beginning to worry aloud that increased industrial support for research is disrupting, distorting, and damaging the underlying educational and research missions of the university, retarding advances in basic science that underlie these firms long-term future. (Florida 1999) (On many of the foregoing points see also Nelson 2004*a*.)

7. Interestingly, only very rarely a critique of the Open Science System and public funding of basic research has come from corporate users, except for peripheral countries and peripheral entrepreneurs—such as the Italian ones—hoping to transform universities in sorts of free training subsidiaries. On the contrary, notably, 'in the UK, where critical rhetoric is among the strongest, it comes mainly from government sources. In the US, companies like IBM have complained recently about the potentially armful effects on future competitiveness of reduction in public support to academic research in the physical sciences' (Pavitt 1999: 90). At the same time, there is an increasing perception, also among business firms that 'too much appropriability' hurts also firms themselves. In fact, as noted by Florida (1999):

[l]arge firms are most upset that even though they fund research up front, universities and their lawyers are forcing them into unfavourable negotiations over intellectual property when something of value emerges. Angered executives at a number of companies are taking the position that they will not fund research at universities that are too aggressive on intellectual property issues.... One corporate vice president for industrial R&D recently summed up the sentiment of large companies, saying, 'The university takes this money, then guts the relationship'. [But also] [s]maller companies are concerned about the time delays in getting research results, which occur because of protracted negotiations by university technology transfer offices or attorneys over intellectual property rights. The deliberations slow the process of getting new technology to highly competitive markets, where success rests on commercializing innovations and products as soon as possible.

More generally, both upstream researchers and downstream product developers begin to perceive what Heller and Eisenberg (1998) have called the anticommons tragedy: the excessive fragmentation of intellectual property rights among too many owners can slow down research activities and product development because all owners can block each other.

With this general background in mind, broadly supporting the SYS interpretation and the continuing effectiveness of Open Science institutional arrangements, let us turn to the comparative assessment of the mechanisms of generation and economic exploitation of scientific and technological know-ledge in the EU.

9.5. IN SEARCH OF THE PURPORTED 'EUROPEAN PARADOX'

The central point of the 'paradox' is the claim that the EU scientific perform-ance is 'excellent' compared with its principal competitors, while Europe's major weakness lies in its difficulty in transforming the results of research into innovations and competitive advantages.

One of the first official documents that popularized the 'paradox' was the Green Paper on Innovation (EC 1995). The two pieces of evidence provided therein in support of it, and thereafter too often taken for granted, were first, the (slightly) higher number of EU publications per euro spent in non-business enterprise R&D (non-BERD) and second, the lower number of granted patents per euro spent in BERD vis-à-vis the US and Japan. Those phenomena, as important as they can be, do not shed much light on the substance of the 'paradox' and, as a matter of fact, even the European Commission seems to admit in its Third Report on Science and Technology Indicators (EC 2003) that the 'paradox is vanishing'.[2]

What does indeed the overall evidence tell us? In what follows, we illustrate some of the strengths and weaknesses of European Science and Technology (S&T) system, arguing that the paradox is nowhere to be seen.

First, let us briefly consider the claim on 'scientific excellence'.

9.5.1. The Pieces of Evidence and Myths on the European Scientific Leadership

A central part of the paradox regards the width, depth, and originality of European science. Discerning whether the data support the claims of a purported European leadership[3] is not a trivial task. Bibliometric analysis offers important insights, but also presents drawback and biases. To begin with, the main source of data, the Thomson ISI data-set, is itself a business activity of the Thomson Corporation responding to economic incentives. For example, the decision on whether to include a given journal is focused more on libraries (which have to decide which journal is worth buying) than on scientific reasons as such.[4] Second, comparing citations across disciplines is likely to be misleading, given different citation intensities (e.g. papers in medical research are much more cited than mathematical ones). Nevertheless, bearing in mind such limitations, measuring the Scientific Impact of Nations continues to be a revealing exercise. And indeed, as we show below, the picture that emerges from data on publications and citations is far from pinpointing a European leadership in science.

Advocates of the paradox notion have emphasized that, during the second half of the nineties, Europe has overtaken the US in the total number of published research papers. However, the latter indicator needs to be adjusted by a scaling factor due to sheer size: otherwise one could claim that the Italian science base is better than the Swiss one, given the higher total number of papers published! The first column of Table 9.1 shows that, despite a slight catching up, if one adjusts for population, European claimed leadership in publication disappears.[5]

Moreover, in science, together with the numbers of publications, at least equally important, are the originality and the impact of scientific output upon the relevant research communities. Two among the most used proxies of such an impact are articles' citations[6] and the shares in the top 1 per cent most cited publications.

As shown in the second and the third column of Table 9.1, the US is well ahead with respect to both indicators. In particular, controlling for population, the outstanding EU output is still less than half than the US one.

Similar results are obtained from another measure of research performance based on individuals' citations in distinct scientific fields. King (2004: 315) reports that considering fourteen scientific fields:

Of the top 1,222 scientists [...] 815, or 66%, are from the United States and only 251 from the sum of the United Kingdom (100), Germany (62), France (29), Switzerland (26), Sweden (17) and Italy (17).

Table 9.1 EU shares of Publications and Citations

Aggregate						
	Publications		Citations		Top 1% cited publications	
Years	1993–7	1997–2001	1993–7	1997–2001	1993–7	1997–2001
EU-15 (US=100)	94	106	70	79	50	59
Adjusted for population						
EU-15 (US = 100)	67	81	50	59	35	44

Notes: Our calculations based on numbers reported by King (2004) and obtained from the Thomson ISI data-set.

Analogously, a recent Royal Society report, shows that the overwhelming majority of the most highly cited authors in ten disciplines have US affiliations (Royal Society 2004: 17; Figure 9.1).

In line with the above is the evidence concerning Nobel Prize winners displayed in Figure 9.2. After the Second World War, the gap between US and the EU has been growing at an impressive rate.

Of course, despite the variety of ways of categorizing scientific disciplines, there is a high interdisciplinary variation in the revealed quality of European research. Following EC (2003: 287), consider eleven subfields (Agriculture and Food, Clinical Medicine and Health, Physics and Astronomy, Basic Life Science, Chemistry, Mathematics and Statistics, Biology, Earth and Environment, Computer, Biomedicine and Pharmacology, and Engineering) and compare a composite index which takes into account the number of publications, number of citations, and relative citation impact score. Then, one finds that NAFTA (US plus Canada and Mexico) compared to EU-15, performs better in clinical medicine, biomedicine, and does especially well in chemistry and the basic life sciences. Using a different and more aggregate classification and comparing citations shares, King (2004) also finds US superiority in life and medical sciences, while Europe performs slightly better in physical sciences and engineering (see Figure 9.3). Incidentally, a few important distinctive patterns within the EU also emerge: for example, France

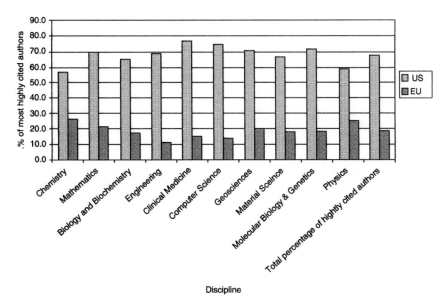

Figure 9.1. Most cited authors

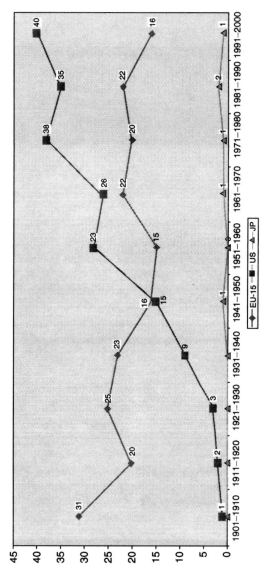

Figure 9.2. Number of Nobel prizes in chemistry, physics, medicine, or physiology by ten-year periods, EU-15, US, JP

Source. EC (2004).

is strong in maths, while Germany and the UK do relatively well in physical and life science respectively (King 2004).

Figure 9.4 focuses on the citation patterns in one of the knowledge drivers of the ICT revolution, namely computer sciences. Regrettably, the EU performance is on average rather disappointing.

The general message from bibliometric data is therefore far from suggesting any generalized European leadership. On the contrary, one observes a structural lag in top-level science vis-à-vis the US, together with some average catching up and a few sectoral outliers in physical sciences and engineering and few single institutional outliers (such as Cambridge also in computer science and several other disciplines: but outliers are precisely outliers).

The first fact on which the paradox conjecture should be based is simply not there. Rather, a major EU challenge regards how to catch up with the US in scientific excellence.

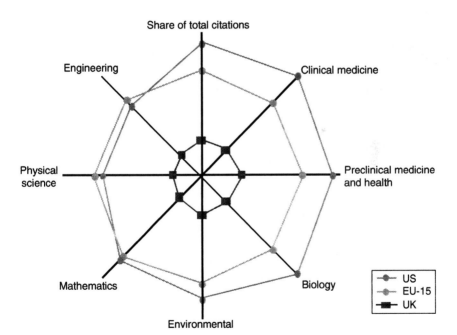

Figure 9.3. Strengths in different disciplines

Notes: Plot shows research footprints based on the shares of citations. The distance from the origin is citation share. See King (2004) for sources (ISI Thompson) and details.

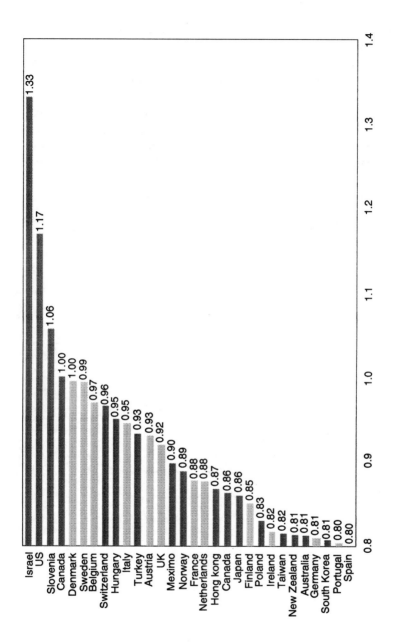

Figure 9.4. Citation impact in computer sciences (1993–9)

Source: DG Research, EC (2003).

Data: ISI.

9.5.2. Poorer Technological Performances: R&D Inputs and Innovative Outputs of the EU

In order to explore in detail the European performance in technology and innovation, one also needs to match European investments in science and technology (i.e. inputs typically proxied by education and R&D expenditures) with outputs (typically proxied by patents).

First, as shown in Figure 9.5, at aggregate levels the EU-15 underinvests in R&D with respect to both US and Japan and, notwithstanding wide variation within EU itself (as showed by Figure 9.6), the gap is not shrinking.

Second, the usual claim concerning the higher share of government funded R&D in the EU as compared to the US is simply groundless.[7] On the contrary if one compares the shares of government-financed R&D on GDP (Figure 9.7), EU is still lagging behind.

Third, the gap is much wider in business enterprise R&D (BERD) expenditures (see Figure 9.8). Again, despite diverse countries patterns, there is no sign of catching up (Figure 9.9).

Fourth, important factors in explaining the above asymmetries are the wide and persistent differences in the efforts devoted to knowledge production and absorption across industrial sectors. Table 9.2 shows that, if one measures the latter with R&D sectoral intensities, industries differ a lot. This in turn is partly due to intersectoral differences in technological opportunities and partly to the way the latter are tapped—which in some industries involves formal R&D activities and in others more informal processes of learning-by-doing, learning-by-using, and learning-by-interacting with suppliers and customers.[8] It happens that Europe is largely penalized by a composition effect, in that it is relatively strong in technologies (such as mechanical engineering) wherein a good deal of search is not recorded under the 'R&D' heading. Moreover, even pairwise sectoral comparisons with the US sometimes reveal a European gap. So, for instance, US R&D investments are well above European ones in 'Offce, Accounting, and Computing Machinery', 'Electrical Machinery', and 'Instruments' industries, while similar levels are observed in 'Motor Vehicle' and 'Non-Electrical Machinery'.

Finally, note that research investments by the leading firms in a selected number of sectors suggest that the EU gap is prominent precisely in those activities which are the core of the current 'technological revolution', namely ICT and Pharmaceuticals (see Figure 9.10 and EC 2003: 143 for details).

Consistently with the above evidence, one observes also a lower ratio of 'knowledge workers' in the total workforce in Europe as compared with the US (cf. Table 9.3 depicting the percentage of tertiary level graduates on the population and researchers on the labour force).[9]

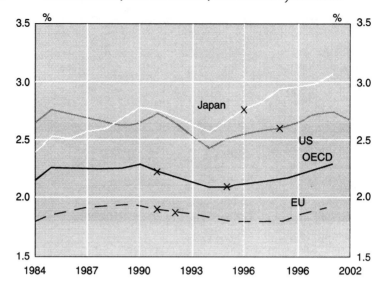

Figure 9.5. R&D intensity (per cent) in the EU-15, US, and Japan
Source: OECD (2004*a*).

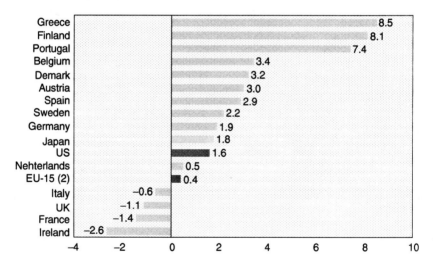

Figure 9.6. Average annual real growth (per cent) of R&D expenditure

Source: DG Research.

Data: OECD - MSTI database (STI, EAS Division) with DG Research provisional estimates.

Notes: (1) JP: 1996–2000; FN, UK, US, EU-15: 1995–2000; DE, ES, AT: 1995–2001; IT: 1997–99; FR: 1997–2000; all other countries: 1995–99. (2) LU data are not included in EU-15 average.

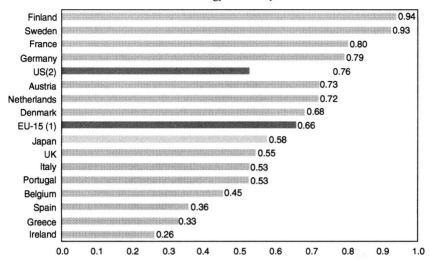

Figure 9.7. Government financed R&D as a per cent of GDP, 1999

Source: DG Research.

Data: OECD; DG Research.

Notes: (1) L data are not included in EU-15 average. (2) US: excludes most or all capital expenditure.

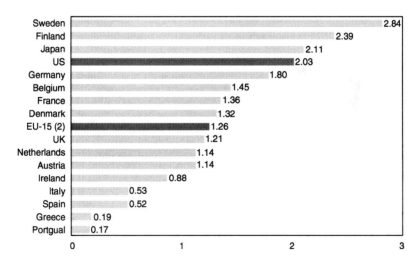

Figure 9.8. Business enterprise expenditure (BERD) on R&D as a per cent of GDP, 2000 or latest available year

Source: DG Research.

Data: Eurostat OECD.

Notes: (1) A: 1998; DK, EL, IRL, NL, PT, SE: 1999; DE, ES, IT: 2001. (2) EU-15 calculated by DG Research; LU not included.

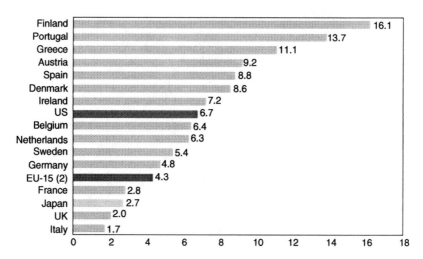

Figure 9.9. BERD—average annual growth since 1995

Source: DG Research.

Data: Eurostat / OECD.

Notes: (1) AT: 1993–98; DK, EL IRL, NL, PT, SE: 1995–1999; BE, FIN, UK, US, EU: 1995–2000; DE, ES, IT: 1995–2001; JP: 1996–2000; F: 1997–2000. (2) EU-15 calculated by DG Research; LU not included.

Complementary to proxies for the intensities of innovative search efforts and for the skills of workforce involved, patent-based indicators are generally used to shed light on the technological output of nations. Needless to say, institutional differences, distinct corporate appropriability strategies, and different propensity to patent across sectors may bias the international comparisons. Moreover, these indicators are generally constructed on the basis of patent applications issued by national patent offces having an 'home advantage' bias. However, the OECD has developed 'patent families' (i.e. patent filed in different countries to protect the same invention) that try to mitigate this latter bias and generally capture patents of relatively high economic value.[10] In Table 9.4 we report EU25 and US shares in 'triadic' patent families (i.e. inventions filed with the EPO, the Japanese Patent Office (JPO), and the USPTO). Shares are relatively stable with a slight European decline.

Again, EU performance varies significantly in distinct technology fields. The upper part of Table 9.5 depicts the shares of US and EU patents filed at the EPO in five main fields. It shows that, having as benchmark the All Fields column, EU has relative strengths in Processes and Mechanics and, conversely, major weaknesses in Electricity/Electronics, Instruments, and Chemistry. At a more disaggregated level, the lower part of the same table, which focuses on

Table 9.2 R&D intensities across industries: BERD as per cent of value added

	BE	DK	DE	SP	FR	IT	AT	FN	SE	UK	EU-7	US	JP
Tot. manufacturing	6.4	5.7	7.5	2.1	7	2.2	4.6	8.3	11.3	5.4	5.7	7.8	8.4
Food, bev. & tob.	1.6	1.4	0.6	0.5	1.0	0.4	na	2.8	1.0	1.2	0.8	na	1.9
Tex. apparel & leather	2.0	0.8	2.1	0.6	0.9	0.1	na	2.2	1.2	0.4	0.7	0.6	2.1
Paper & print	0.9	na	0.3	0.4	0.3	0.1	0.5	1.3	na	na	0.4	na	na
Pharmaceutical	25	40	na	10.1	27.6	na	15.1	na	46.5	48	na	23.3	19.0
Nonelectrical mach.	6.6	6.6	5.8	2.9	4.6	1.4	4.4	9	11.1	4.8	4.6	4.7	5.7
Comp. & office mach.	12.3	18	17	7.5	13.3	7	3.7	na	39.5	3.5	14.1	22	na
Electrical mach.	7.6	8	3.4	3.3	7.7	na	5.7	na	18.2	7.8	4.5	12	17.6
Electronic mach.	32.7	13.5	39.6	19.1	34.1	na	28.5	28.1	38.6	12.1	32.7	na	23.6
Instruments	11.3	15.3	11.9	3.7	16.9	2.2	6.8	22.5	18.5	7.3	11.5	32.6	23.8
Motor vehicles	4.0	na	18.3	2.6	13.1	10.4	10.1	3.6	28.9	9.2	14.3	16	13.2
Aerospace	6.5	na	na	25	40.1	na	na	na	na	24.3	na	30.9	0.6

Notes: EU-7: Belgium, Denmark, Germany, Spain, France, Italy, and Finland. Electrical machinery does not include data for Italy and Finland. Electrical equipment does not include data for Italy. Paper and printing and aerospace do not include data for Denmark.
Source: DG Research (EC 2003).

six selected subfields whose technological dynamism has been particularly high, suggests that in Information Technologies, Pharmaceutical, and Biotech the US is well ahead, while Europe has comparable shares of patents in Telecommunication and does particularly well in Materials, especially due to the Germany score.

To sum up, R&D expenditures and patent-based indicators pinpoint a European lag in terms of both lower search investments and lower innovative output. This is largely the effect of the weaknesses in technological fields that are considered as the engine of the contemporary 'knowledge economy'. On the other hand, data show a few points of strength in more traditional technologies related to mechanical technologies and new materials.

9.5.3. Structural Weaknesses of European Corporations and Science–Industry Interaction

The third angle to explore the paradox conjecture concerns the limits and weaknesses that European business enterprises display in innovating and competing in the world economy. The evidence, in our view, suggests that a

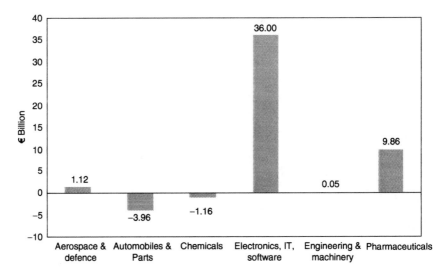

Figure 9.10. R&D investment gap between US and EU-15 by sector

Source: DG Research.
Data: R&D Scoreboard (2001); DTI Future & Innovation Unit and Company Reporting Ltd.

fundamental factor underlying the worsening performance of European firms is their lower commitments to research and international patenting and, in several sectors, their relatively weak participation to the core international oligopolies, quite apart from any imagined weaknesses in the industry–university links.

Table 9.3 Shares of university graduates and knowledge workers

	Share of the population aged 25–64 with tertiary-level graduates	Researchers per 1,000 of total employment
EU-15	23	5.8
US	38	8.6

Source: The numbers relarive to researchers refer to 1999 (OECD 2004a). The numbers relative to tertiary education refer to 2001 (OECD 2003).

Table 9.4 Shares in 'triadic' patent families

	1994	1996	1998	2000
EU25	34	32	33	32
US	35	37	35	35

Source: OECD (2004a).

Table 9.5 Shares of patents filed with EPO for different fields

Electricity		Instruments	Chemistry	Processes	Mechanics	All fields
EU-15	36.3	36.5	37.5	50	54.1	42.6
US	35.2	39.7	39.9	27.1	22.1	33.1
	Telecom	IT	Semi conductor	Pharma	Biotech	Materials
EU-15	37.9	26.9	29.2	35.7	28.3	55.1
US	35.7	49.3	36.2	43.5	51.3	19

Source: EC (2003).

Let us focus in particular on those industries where the consequences of European lags in science and technological innovation are likely to be more severe.

Figure 9.11 shows the production shares in several ICT sectors. If the overall rankings of EU-15, US, and Japan have remained more or less stable, variations in individual shares show that EU has lost the lead even in the telecommunications industry, where in the 1990s it had a big advantage. Europe has also declined relative to the US in office equipment. On the other hand, in radio communications and radar equipment the US has somewhat lessened its lead relative to Europe (in turn, this has probably been the outcome of the formation of few European companies especially in the military sector with sizes and capabilities at least comparable with the American counterpart).

A less straightforward, but still rather dismal, picture comes from the data measuring performance in trade in major high-tech sectors. Table 9.6 depicts export market shares of large EU countries[11] and the US in 1996, 1999, and 2002. While in aerospace US has lost some ground and EU has grown, the opposite has happened in Instruments (interestingly the European gains in aerospace, mainly due to Airbus has implied a more even distribution of exports between France, the UK, and Germany with a relative loss of France itself). In the remaining sectors shares are relatively stable with the exception of Germany's losses in pharmaceutical.

Combining different sources, the last OECD Information Technology Outlook (OECD 2004*b*) explores the performance of the top 250 ICT firms and the top 10 ones in four subsectors (communication equipment and systems, electronics and components, IT equipment and systems, and IT services, software, and telecommunications). It turns out that 139 of the top 250 firms (56 per cent) are based in the US and only 33 (13 per cent) in the EU, confirming an overall weak EU amongst the world industrial leaders, notwithstanding subsectoral exceptions. So, six EU firms appear in the top 10 of

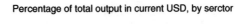

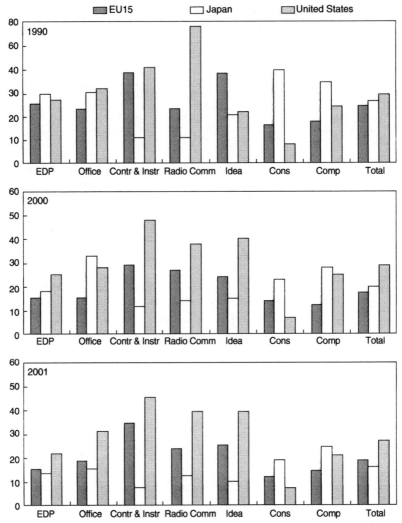

Figure 9.11. Share of world ICT production—percentage of total output in current USD

telecommunication services firms, three in the top 10 of communications equipment and systems firms, two in the top 10 of electronics and components firms, and only one in the top 10 of software ones.

Finally, there are no European firms among the ten larger firms in IT equipment and systems.

Table 9.6 Trade in high-tech industries: export market shares (percentages)

	1996	1999	2002
Aerospace			
France	16.71	14.26	13.55
Germany	10.71	12.67	13.73
Italy	2.70	2.38	2.95
UK	12.87	11.85	17.09
US	41.02	43.60	36.37
Japan	1.39	1.76	1.35
Electronic			
France	5.18	5.43	4.77
Germany	7.84	7.34	8.75
Italy	2.42	1.83	1.92
UK	7.72	6.72	8.52
US	19.24	23.69	20.95
Japan	25.33	18.76	17.64
Office machinery and computers			
France	5.68	4.85	3.65
Germany	6.98	6.84	8.09
Italy	2.80	1.64	1.27
UK	10.83	10.29	8.59
US	22.96	27.07	20.22
Japan	20.29	15.69	13.08
Pharmaceutical			
France	9.89	10.55	9.60
Germany	14.84	15.13	10.84
Italy	6.17	5.73	5.68
UK	11.42	9.98	9.17
US	10.63	11.98	10.52
Japan	3.53	3.03	2.28
Instruments			
France	5.64	5.15	5.35
Germany	15.05	14.11	14.55
Italy	4.17	3.34	3.44
UK	7.42	6.85	6.60
US	22.87	25.84	25.33
Japan	16.74	14.90	13.54

Notes: Our calculations are based on OECD (2004*a*). ISIC revision 3: Aerospace industry (353); Electronic industry ISIC (32); Office machinery and computer industry (30); Pharmaceutical industry (2,423); Medical, precision and optical instruments, watches and clocks (instruments) industry (33).

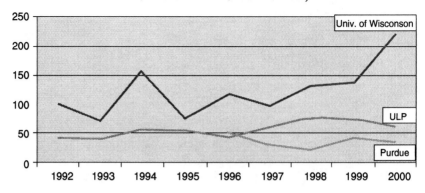

Figure 9.12. Number of patent applications by Univ. of Wisconsin at Madison, Purdue Univ., and ULP
Source: Llerena (2004).

These data support indeed the conjecture that, quite independently of the 'bridges' between scientific research and industrial applications, potential corporate recipients are smaller, weaker, and less receptive than transatlantic counterparts.

This is well highlighted also by those revealing cases where science is world top class, all the 'transfer mechanisms' are in place but hardly any European firm is there to benefit. A striking example of this is computer science at Cambridge, England: an excellent scientific output is most exploited by non-European firms (from Fujitsu to Microsoft and many others).

Note that the presumed feeble links between science and industry should be one of the most important aspects of the paradox conjecture. Surprisingly, the evidence here is simply non-existent. Curiously the Third Report does not address the issue explicitly, but just discusses the 'science content' of EU technology, which is a rather distinct issue (EC 2003: 422). Concerning the latter, the number of citations to scientific journal articles in patents that cite science is indeed higher in the US, but the hypothesis that this reflects the EU weaknesses in Science–Industry interaction is a questionable one. Rather, it might primarily reveal the different composition of European technological output, with patterns of specialization which tend to be less 'science based'.

The few indicators available which may be considered more direct measures of the interaction between business and higher education pinpoint to conclusions opposite to the conventional wisdom. As Table 9.7 shows the share of private investment in higher education R&D, while low everywhere, is marginally higher in EU than in the US and much higher than Japan. Similar results are obtained if one considers the private sector's annual investment in the public research sector (i.e. the sum of higher education and government R&D) and King (2004: 314) reports that in the last years a few EU countries experienced larger growth.

Another often-cited evidence concerning the paradox conjecture is the low-revealed technological productivity of European University and research centres, usually measured by patent propensity. However, a few case studies have shown that the technology outputs of European public research laboratories are higher than usually believed if one considers relevant institutional differences. For instance, once we take into account the whole number of patents filed by European researchers and not just those that are directly owned by the research institutions where they are employed, the inter-Atlantic differences across comparable institutions are not so big (Figure 9.12).[12]

9.6. FROM THE WRONG DIAGNOSIS TO MISGUIDED POLICIES

To sum up, certainly the European picture is variegated with respect to the generation of both scientific knowledge and technological innovation. However, no overall 'European paradox' with a leading science but weak 'downstream' links is there to be seen. On the contrary it seems to us that significant weaknesses reside precisely at the two extremes with, first, a European system of scientific research lagging behind the US in several areas and, second, a relatively weak European industry. The latter, we have argued, is characterized on average by comparatively lower presence in the sectors based on new technological paradigms—such as ICT and biotechnologies—a lower propensity to innovate and a relatively weak participation to the international oligopolies in many activities. In turn, such a picture as we argue below, calls for strong science policies and industrial policies. However, this is almost the opposite of what have happened. The belief into a purported paradox together with the emphasis on 'usefulness' of research has led to a package of policies where EU support to basic research is basically non-existent.

Research proposals are expected to identify possible practical as well as scientific benefits; higher priority is being given to user involvement (including partial funding), universities are being invited to extract more revenue from licensing their intellectual properly, and substantial public funds have been spent on 'foresight' exercises designed to create exchange and consensus around future opportunities of applications. (Pavitt 2001: 768)

The 'Frame Programmes' have all being conceived with such a philosophy, which in the most recent one is pushed to the extreme with the 'Networks of

Table 9.7 Shares of higher education expenditure on R&D (HERD) financed by industry, 1999

Country	%
Germany	11.3
Spain	7.7
France	3.4
Ireland	6.6
Italy	4.8
Netherlands	5.1
Finland	4.7
Sweden	3.9
UK	7.2
EU-15	6.8
US	6.3
Japan	2.3

Notes: Austria 1993, Ireland 1998, US 2000. EU-15 calculated by DG research, Luxembourg not included.
Source: EC (2003).

Excellence': not only they do not support research, but they explicitly prohibit the use of EU money for that purpose!

Similarly, with regards to industrial R&D, the focus on 'pre-competitive' research has meant the emergence of a sort of limbo wherein firms—often in combination with academics—try to tap community money in areas that are marginal enough to not justify the investment of their own funds. Moreover, the networking frenzy has gone hand in hand with the growth in number and power of research bureaucrats (both at European and National level) whose main competence is precisely in 'networking', 'steering', writing lengthy reports, and demanding researchers to do the same. Here again the extreme is in social sciences. A bit like the old Soviet Union where even papers in mathematics had to begin with 'according to the clever intuition of comrade Breznev...', in many areas one has to begin each research proposal by arguing that what follows is crucial in order to foster fashionable keywords such as 'cohesion', 'enlargement', 'citizenship', etc. even if in fact the real scientific interest goes to, say, the econometrics of panel data or the transmissions mechanisms of monetary shocks. And with all this goes yet another type of corruption of the ethos of the researchers who have to develop the skills of camouflage and peddling.

If our diagnosis is correct, this state of affairs is bad for the research, wasteful for society, and also bad for business.

9.7. A CONCLUSION WITH SOME MODEST PROPOSALS WHICH MIGHT HELP BOTH SCIENCE AND BUSINESS

Some general implications of the analysis are the following.

First, increase support to high-quality basic science, through agile institutions, much alike the American National Science Foundation (NSF), relying on world class peer review and also physically located far away from Brussels—as May (2004) suggests! In this direction the constitution of a European Science Council is a welcome development.[13]

Second, fully acknowledge the difference within the higher education system between: (*a*) research-cum-graduate teaching universities, (*b*) undergraduate teaching universities and liberal art college, and, (*c*) technical colleges.

The well-placed emphasis of the role of the first type of institutions comes often under the heading of 'Humbold model' as pioneered by Germany more than a century ago. However, nowadays the practice is most American, while Europe (especially Continental Europe) often offers in most universities a confused bland of the functions which is neither good for research nor for mass level training.

Third, push back the boundaries between public open research and appropriable research.

One often forgets that appropriability is socially justified only in so far it is an incentive to innovation itself. As we have argued above, appropriation of the output of public research does not perform that role. Of course this applies primarily to basic research while the picture is much more blurred for practically oriented disciplines such as engineering and a lot of pragmatism is required. However, we would stand by the general point that too much of an emphasis on appropriability and IPR is likely to exert a pernicious influence on both the rates and directions of search. Moreover, as we suggested above, it might also represent a significant hindrance to business-led innovation.

Our lag in the institutional changes leading to a much more property-based system of research as compared to the US for once might play in our favour in that it might be easier for us to stop and reverse the tendency (for a thorough discussion of the forgoing appropriability related points, see Nelson 2004*a*).

Fourth, build ambitious, technological daring missions justifiable for their intrinsic social and political value.

As Pavitt (2001) reminds us, 'Scandinavian countries and Switzerland are able to mobilize considerable resources for high quality basic research without the massive defence and health expenditures of the world's only superpower'

(p. 276). Hence, he suggests, also the larger European countries and the European Union itself, have more to learn from them than from the US.

Granted that, however, one should not rule out the importance of large-scale far-reaching European programmes with ambitious and technologically challenging objectives in the fields of, for example, energy conservation, health care, environmental protection (and perhaps also the European rearmament, although there is not much agreement on it even among the authors of this work!).

Fifth, rediscover the use of industrial policies as a device to foster a stronger, more innovative, European industry.

We are fully aware that nowadays 'industrial policy' is a bad word, which cannot be mentioned in a respectable company without being accused of supporting Jurassic era 'national-champions', distorting competition, fostering production patterns which go against 'revealed' comparative advantages, etc. We are tempted to answer 'why not'?! Certainly the period—until the late Seventies/early Eighties—characterized by discretionary intervention of policymakers on the very structure of various industries has been characterized not only by many failures but also several successes. For instance, the European strength in telecommunications, the presence in semiconductors, the growing competitiveness in aircraft, etc. are also the outcomes of the policy measures of the 'interventionist' era. Today, even within the constraints of the new trade arrangements, much more, we think, can be done in order to strengthen the European presence in the most promising technological paradigms, were it not for a self-inflicted market worship (yet another commodity largely exported by the US, but consumed there quite parsimoniously and pragmatically!).

We are well aware that these modest proposals might be accused of conservatism. However, for once we do not mind at all be in the camp of those who try to defend and strengthen a system producing top level publicly funded Open Science—too often under threat by both the 'property right' colonization and the 'practical usefulness' advocates—, and together a pragmatic view of the role that public policies might have in fostering the growth of corporate actors able to efficiently tap an ever-growing pool of innovative opportunities.

NOTES

1. On those points following the classic statements in Bush (1945), Polanyi (1962), and Merton (1973), see the more recent appraisals in Dasgupta and David (1994), David (2004), Nelson (2004a), and the conflicting views in Geuna, Salter, and Stainmuller (2003).

2. One of the documents published by the Commission that presents the results has a revealing title: 'From the "European Paradox" to declining competitiveness'.
3. A view, again forcefully endorsed by most of the EU Commission: so, the chapter of the Third Report devoted to measure the European performance in knowledge production is titled 'Scientific output and impact: Europe's leading role in world science'(EC 2003).
4. Eugene Garfield, founder and stockholder of the ISI, suggests indeed to use the Impact Factor based on ISI citations mainly to evaluate journals themselves, but not individuals or single works (Garfield 1996). Straightforward unweighted citations may yield less of a bias.
5. Certainly normalization by population is a very rough proxy, which also averages across very different entities, ranging from Sweden, Germany, and the UK all the way to Italy, Greece, and Portugal (just sticking to EU-15). However, it is also the US average over Massachusetts and California but also Mississippi and Idaho.
6. Typically they are very skewed: only a few publications are highly cited, while the overwhelming majority of articles receives zero citations.
7. The misunderstanding is usually based being on the use of the share of publicly funded R&D on total R&D expenditures, which does not carry much economic sense. The meaningful figures regard normalizations with the economic size of the economy.
8. Within an enormous literature, on these points see Dosi (1988), Klevorick et al. (1995), Nelson (1993), Lundvall (1992), and Malerba (2004).
9. This data should be taken however with some care, given the uneven state of secondary education across different countries.
10. See Dernis, Guellec, and van Pottelsberghe (2001) for details.
11. Data on EU total would have required to exclude trade within EU countries
12. Azagra-Caro, Carayol, and Llerena (2005), Balconi, Breschi, and Lissioni (2002), Llerena (2004), Meyer (2003), Saragossi and van Pottelsberghe (2003), Wallmark (1997) for more details on national and European pieces of evidence.
13. See also the arguments recently put forward by a communication of the European Commission, which appears to hint at a promising break with respect to previous policies (EC 2004).

REFERENCES

Arrow, K. J. (1962). 'Economics of Welfare and the Allocation of Resources for Invention', in R. Nelson (ed.), *The Rate and Direction of Inventive Activity*. Princeton, NJ: Princeton University Press.

Azagra-Caro, J., Carayol, N., and Llerena, P. (2005). 'Patent Production at a European Research University: Exploratory Evidence at the Laboratory Level', *Journal of Technology Transfer*, forthcoming.

Balconi, M., Breschi, S., and Lissoni, F. (2002). 'Networks of Inventors and Location of University Research: An Exploration of Italian Data', Conference 'Rethinking Science Policy', SPRU, Brighton, 21–3 March.

Breschi, S. and Lissoni, F. (2001). 'Knowledge Spillovers and Local Innovation Systems: A Critical Survey', *Industrial and Corporate Change*, 10(4): 975–1005.

Bush, V. (1945). *Science: The Endless Frontier.* Washington, DC: Government Printing Office.

Dasgupta, P. and David, P. A. (1994). 'Toward a New Economics of Science', *Policy Research*, 23: 487–521.

David, P. A. (1993). 'Knowledge, Property and the System Dynamics of Technological Change', in Proceedings of the World Bank Annual Conference on Development Economics: 1992. Washington, D.C., pp. 215–48.

—— (1997a). 'Knowledge, Property and the System Dynamics of Technological Change', in L. Summers, and S. Shah (eds.), *Proceeding of the World Bank Conference on Development Economics*, pp. 215–48.

—— (1997b). 'From Market Magic to Calypso Science Policy. A Review of Terence Kealey's The Economic Laws of Scientific Research', *Research Policy*, 26: 229–55.

—— (2004). 'Understanding the Emergence of Open Science Institutions: Functionalist Economics in Historical Context', *Industrial and Corporate Change*, 13(3): 571–89.

Dernis, H., Guellec, D., and van Pottelsberghe, B. (2001). 'Using Patent Counts for Cross Country Comparisons of Technology Output', STI Review No. 27, Paris: OECD.

Dosi, G. (1982). 'Technological Paradigms and Technological Trajectories: A Suggested Interpretation', *Research Policy*, 11: 147–62.

—— (1982). 'Sources, Procedures and Microeconomic Effects of Innovation', *Journal of Economic Literature*, 26: 1120–71.

—— Marengo, L., and Fagiolo, G. (2004). 'Learning in Evolutionary Environments', forthcoming, in K. Dopfer (ed.), *Principles of Evolutionary Economics.* Cambridge: Cambridge University Press.

European Commission (1995). Green Paper on Innovation.

—— (2003). Third European Report on Science & Technology Indicators. Directorate General for Research.

—— (2004). 'Europe and Basic Research'. Communication from the Commission, November.

Florida, R. (1999). 'The Role of the University: Leveraging Talent, Not Technology', *Issues in Science and Technology.*

Freeman, C. (1982). *The Economics of Industrial Innovation.* London: Francis Pinter.

—— (1994). 'The Economics of Technical Change: A Critical Survey', *Cambridge Journal of Economics*, 18: 150.

—— and Soete, L. (1997). *The Economics of Industrial Innovation*, 3rd edn. Cambridge, MA: MIT Press.

Garfield, E. (1996). 'How Can Impact Factors be Improved?', *British Medical Journal*, 313: 411–3.

Geuna, A., Salter, A., and Stainmuller, W. E. (2003). *Science and Innovation: Rethinking the Rationale for Funding and Governance*. Cheltenham UK: Edward Elgar.

Gibbons, M., Limoges, C., Nowotny, H., Schwartzman, S., Scott, P., and Trow M. (1994). *The New Production of Knowledge: The Dynamics of Science and Research in Contemporary Societies*. London: Sage.

Heller, M. and Eisenberg, R. (1998). 'Can Patents Deter Innovation? The Anticommons in Biomedical Research', *Science*, 280: 698–701.

Henderson, R., Jaffe, A. B., and Trajitenberg, M. (1998). 'Universities as a Source of Commercial Technology: A Detailed Analysis of University Patenting, 19651988', *Review of Economics and Statistics*, 80(1): 119–27.

Hicks, D., Breitzman, A., Hamilton, Sr, K., and Narin, F. (2000). 'Research Excellence and Patented Innovation', *Science and Public Policy*, 27: 310–20.

Jaffe, A. B., Trajitenberg, M., and Henderson, R. (1993). 'Geographical Location of Knowledge Spillovers as Evidenced by Patent Citations', *Quarterly Journal of Economics*, 108(3): 577–98.

Kealey, T. (1996). *The Economic Laws of Scientific Research*. New York: St. Martins Press.

King, D. A. (2004). 'The Scientific Impact of Nations', *Nature*, 430: 311–16.

Klevorick, A. K., Levin, R. C., Nelson, R. R., and Winter, S. G. (1995). 'On the Sources and Significance of Interindustry Differencies in Technological Opportunities', *Research Policy*, 24(2): 185–205.

Kline, S. J. and Rosenberg, N. (1986). 'An Overview of Innovation', in S. J. Kline, and N. Rosenberg, (eds.), *The Positive Sum Strategy: Harnessing Technology for Economic Growth*. Washington, DC: National Academy Press.

Llerena, P. (2004). 'Recherche et innovation: une comparaison internationale', *Cahier Francais*, 123.

Lundvall, B. A. (1992). *National Systems of Innovation: Towards a Theory of Innovaton and Interactive Learning*. London: Pinter.

MacKenzie, D. and Wajcman, J. (1985). *The Social Shaping of Technology*. Buckingham, UK: Open University Press.

Malerba, F. (2004). *Sectoral Systems of Innovation*. Cambridge: Cambridge University Press.

Marimon, R. (2004). 'Report Evaluation of the Effectiveness of the New Instruments of Framework Programme VI'.

Martin, B. R. (2003). 'The Changing Social Contract for Science and the Evolution of the University', in Geuna et al. (2003).

May, R. M. (2004). 'Raising Europe's Game', *Nature*, 430: 831–2.

Merton, R. K. (1973). *The Sociology of Science: Theoretical and Empirical Investigations*. Chicago, IL: University of Chicago Press.

Meyer, M. (2003). 'Do Patents Reflect the Inventive Output of University Research?'. Mimeo, KU Leuven: Finnish Institute for Enterprise Management, Helsinki.

Mowery, D. and Nelson, R. (1999). *Sources of Industrial Leadership*. Cambridge: Cambridge University Press.

Narin, F., Hamilton, K., and Olivastro, D. (1997). 'The Increasing Linkage between U.S. Technology and Public Science', *Research Policy*, 26: 317–30.

Nelson, R. R. (1959). 'The Simple Economics of Basic Scientific Research', *Journal of Political Economy*, 67(2): 297–306.

—— (1993). *National Systems of Innovation*. Oxford: Oxford University Press.

—— (2003). 'On the Uneven Evolution of Human Know-How', *Research Policy*, 32(6): 909–22.

—— (2004*a*). 'The Market Economy, and the Scientific Commons', *Research Policy*, 33(3): 455–71.

—— (2004*b*). 'Perspectives on Technological Evolution', forthcoming, in K. Dopfer (ed.), *Principles of Evolutionary Economics*. Cambridge: Cambridge University Press.

—— and Winter, S. G. (1982). *An Evolutionary Theory of Economic Change*. Cambridge: the Belknap Press of Harvard University.

—— (2004*b*). OECD Information Technology Outlook. Organization for Economic Cooperation and Development.

Pavitt, K. (1987). 'The Objectives of Technology Policy', *Science and Public Policy*, 14: 182–8.

—— (1999). *Technology, Management and Systems of Innovation*. Northampton, UK: Edward Elgar Press.

—— (2001). 'Public Policies to Support Basic Research: What Can the Rest of the World Learn from US Theory and Practice? (And What they Should not Learn)', *Industrial and Corporate Change*, 10(3): 761–79.

—— (2003). 'Commentaries', in Geuna et al. (2003).

—— (1962). 'The Republic of Science', *Minerva*, 1: 54–74.

Rip, A., Misa, T. J., and Schot, J. (1995). *Managing Technology in Society*. London and New York: Pinter Press.

Rosenberg, N. (1976). *Perspectives on Technology*. Cambridge: Cambridge University Press.

—— (1982). *Inside the Black Box: Technology and Economics*. Cambridge: Cambridge University Press.

Royal Society (2004). 'The Future Funding of the European Science Base', Background Working Paper V2.0.

Saragossi, S. and van Pottelsberghe de la Potterie (2003). 'What Patent Data Reveal About Universities: The Belgium Case', *Journal of Technology Transfer*, 18: 47–51.

Winter, S. G. (1982). 'An Essay on the Theory of Production', in Hymans S. H. (ed.), *Economics and the World Around It*. Ann Arbor, MI: University of Michigan Press.

—— (1987). 'Knowledge and Competences as Strategic Assets', in D. Teece (ed.), *The Competitive Challenge*. Cambridge, MA: Ballinger.

10

European Universities Under the Pressure of Globalization

Patrick Cohendet, Chantale Mailhot,
and Véronique Schaeffer

10.1. INTRODUCTION

The debate on the role of the university in the modern society is a growing one among policymakers, scientists as well as industrialists (Etzkowitz and Leydesdorff 2000: 109). This debate reflects a general concern with the profound changes in the mode of production of knowledge and in the organization of science that are seen as characterizing the knowledge-based economy. A polyphony of academic voices from various fields and disciplines (including sociology of innovation, social anthropology of learning, evolutionary economics, economic history, economic geography, cognitive psychology, and competence- or resource-based approaches to enterprise strategy) have proposed a diversity of models (Triple Helix, Mode 2, sociology of networks, etc.) aiming at throwing light on public policy and academic strategy (Rip 2002: 125). Though diverse, these models generally affirm that the mode of production of knowledge is becoming fundamentally interactive, and that the new role of the university should not be considered in isolation from other diverse sources of production and transmission of knowledge.

The debate on the role of universities is particularly active in Europe at the very moment that the EU has set the goal of making Europe the leading region of the world in terms of creation, exchange, and use of knowledge. For the EU, the focus on the knowledge-based economy naturally implies a renewed interest in universities as the traditional core locus of production, diffusion, and emission of knowledge. The quality of Europe's universities has always been considered to be one of its main assets, despite well-recognized differences in the systems of high education and research between European countries. Achieving greater coherence within such diversity is certainly an objective which may offer potential advantage for the EU. Nonetheless, the existing diversity should not a priori be considered a handicap. Gaining benefits from diversity is precisely one of the main features of the knowledge-based economy.

The search for greater effectiveness and coherence for the higher education and research system in the EU is often marked by a preoccupation with strengthening interactions with industry and the commercialization of scientific output. Furthermore, the pressure of globalization implies that universities, as with other organizations, are being pressed to adapt to the 'best practices' in the world. In this perspective the US research and higher education system is clearly pinpointed as the 'best model' to follow. Some specific features of the US system such as high tuition fees in the education system or the Bayh-Dole Act in the domain of appropriation of research results by universities are considered by many policymakers as measures that should be taken up quickly in Europe. For a growing number of voices, the accelerated commercialization of science is seen as the main tendency to be pursued by European Universities, especially at a moment when public funding is becoming scarce. A quick and arguably naive interpretation of these issues would be that they logically call for a single clear solution for EU policy towards its universities: increasing private sector financing in all domains of research and higher education in substitution of public financing, with a blind fascination for the US model.

Much in common with Dosi, Llerena, and Labini (this volume), our view is that such a policy would not only be disastrous for European universities, but that it also rests on a misinterpretation of the real nature of the US model. In our view, it is imperative that governments continue to devote a proportion of their resources to the funding of basic research.

While the links between economic development and the production of knowledge have clearly changed and these changes demand new policies and responses from universities, it is nonetheless the case that these changes need to be analysed and put in perspective. All too often evidence of an intensification of the relations between science and economy are simply transformed into normative prescriptions. The interactive models of knowledge production that have been developed to replace the linear model are all too often used to justify initiatives for public–private cooperation regulated by the market without a serious discussion of the desired orientation of research and without an adequate treatment of the question of the incentives.

The plan of the chapter is as follows. In the first part, we briefly recall the main features of the traditional model of production of knowledge and the justifications given for public financing of research. In the second section we discuss in detail the consequences of the development of the knowledge-based economy on the model of production of knowledge. In the third section we investigate the consequences of the pressures of globalization for the financing of universities. In the fourth section we critically discuss these consequences. Finally, in the concluding section we propose a resource allocation mechanism designed to drive and to enhance the effectiveness and coherence of the high education and research system in the EU.

10.2. THE TRADITIONAL MODEL OF PRODUCTION OF KNOWLEDGE

The traditional vision of knowledge production is characterized by two simple dichotomies. On the one hand, the distinction between science and technology which is logically deduced from the linear model of innovation implies a division of labour between fundamental research and applied research. While the role of the former is to increase (through publications of scientific articles, conferences, seminars) the stock of knowledge of society, the role of the latter is to transform the stock of knowledge and the technological results obtained (through patents, licences, copyrights, etc.) into useful applications.

On the other hand, the separation between public and private research is related to the fact that science, as a pure public good, is considered to be non-exclusive and non-rival and thus subject to problems of underinvestment by the private sector. From this Arrow (1962) deduced that basic research should be left completely 'open' and public, whereas appropriable applied research should be protected by strong property rights devised to discourage any free riding in the private sector. The distinction between public/open and private/appropriable justified the following 'contract' between the state, science, and industry: 'Government promises to fund the basic science that peer reviewers find most worthy of support, and scientists promise that the research will be performed well and honestly and will provide a steady stream of discoveries that can be translated into new products, medicines, or weapons' (Vavakova 1998: 210).

More recently, the rationale for public support of basic research has been questioned on a number of grounds:

• The partially tacit nature of knowledge including scientific knowledge implies that Arrow's characterization of knowledge as a pure public good is in need of qualification. 'Know-how' and competences do not easily lend themselves to codification and transfer in the form of 'information' (Cohendet and Joly 2000; Lundvall 2002).

- The increasing number of public labororatories that have fallen into private hands goes contrary to the thesis of underinvestment in basic research by the private sector (Callon 1994: 6).
- In the knowledge-based economy, which underlines the interactive nature of the process of production of knowledge, the idea of the university as the sole institution that assures the production of knowledge should give way to a new vision based on continuous interactions between economic agents including firms in the process of knowledge production.

If the principal arguments which served to justify the public financing of research no longer hold, it remains the case that most theoretical contributions neither specify what the new mode of financing for universities is, nor do they identify what the new rules and incentives mechanisms for researchers are. Abandoning the assumptions which underlie the linear model of knowledge production entails the risk that the central lesson for European universities is simply that private funding should progressively substitute for public financing. While we find this entirely unsatisfactory, we nonetheless would not want to argue in favour of the traditional status of science without acknowledging the significant changes that are taking place in the modes of production of knowledge.

In the following section we consider some of the implications that have been drawn due to the emergence of a new mode of knowledge production, notably the idea that universities should be involved in the commercialization of research as well as the production and transmission of knowledge. Again, the question of the necessary conditions for the adoption of such a mission in relation to the university's research and educational missions has, for the most part, been skirted over.

10.3. THE CONSEQUENCES OF THE DEVELOPMENT OF THE KNOWLEDGE-BASED ECONOMY: THE INTERACTIVE VISION OF THE PROCESS OF THE PRODUCTION OF KNOWLEDGE

There is a large consensus among scholars that we are witnessing a radical and irreversible transformation in the way that science is carried out (Cozzens 1990; Ziman 1994). Science's activities and products are clearly linked in new ways to the social and economic domain. The activities of creation, diffusion, and usage of knowledge in the economy have an increased importance and the scientific and technical systems are more collective: 'knowledge becomes an activity that is whole and openly multidimensional that must contribute simultaneously to the creation of certified knowledge, collective goods, competitive advantages, professional competencies but also to a culture of decisions shared by the greatest number' (Callon et al. 1995: 12).

A few main models serve to describe these tendencies, notably the model of Mode 2 knowledge production by Gibbons et al. (1994), and Etzkowitz and Leydesdorff's Triple Helix model (2000). Each of these models describes non-linear dynamics, interaction, and circularity processes between institutions and between local and global dynamics. They are frequently quoted and used to justify the elaboration of new science policies. They account for and promote the fusion between science and society's interests, and the hybrid-ization of the institutional systems that sustain science and innovation.

Mode 2 knowledge production (Gibbons et al. 1994; Nowotny, Scott, and Gibbons 2001) is probably the most discussed model characterizing the transformation of science. The Triple Helix overlay (Leydesdorff and Etzkowitz 1998; Etzkowitz 1999; Etzkowitz and Leydesdorff 2000) is not fundamentally different from the Mode 1–Mode 2 model, but is more specific regarding different social and historical contexts. The Triple Helix model portrays university–industry–government relations and the variety of insti-tutional arrangements and policy models that these relations comprise. Gib-bons et al.'s Mode 2 of knowledge production and Etzkowitz and Leydesdorff's Triple Helix, both stress the role the university can now play in economic development. Although both models aim at describing and analysing the new hybrid forms of knowledge production, they also are normative in that they explicitly welcome the new institutional arrangements, where the accent is on porosity, hybridity, and the fusion of different stakeholder interests (Wouters et al. 2002), and the move towards the marketing of science by the universities (Etzkowitz et al. 2000).

Even if Europe is composed of many different systems having their specifi-cities (some aspects of this diversity is captured in this volume by Verdier and by Nohara and Lanciano), governmental policies in EU countries are based to varying degrees on these collective innovation models in which neither the State nor academic institutions nor innovating firms have a dominant place (Callon et al. 1994; Gibbons et al. 1994; Gulbrandsen and Etzkowitz 1999). These models account for, reinforce, and legitimize the emergence of hybrid organizations that lie within the network of heterogeneous organizations: universities, public laboratories, private consultants, etc. (Wouters et al. 2002). They translate into measures[1] of direct or indirect financial incentives to strategic alliances between firms, or to university spin-offs, for example.

Public policies concerning research aim at formalizing and focusing the links between science and the rest of the economy. Thus, a series of empirical observations are transformed into normative prescriptions without any critical analysis. It is important to recognize the normative dimension of these models, which tend to implicitly assume that the new institutional and hybrid arrangements between science, government, and industry are necessarily a valuable and 'good' response to new innovation challenges. A similar normative view is implicitly expressed as regards the progressive privatization of science.

10.3.1. Interaction with Global Social Objectives: The 'Utilitarian Vision of University'

Today, at the international level, there would appear to a growing tendency to hold up the US as a model for designing policies for coordinating research and scientific activity in the interests of achieving significant national objectives. The US model was initiated during the Second World War and was promoted in the 1960s at the peak of the cold war in order to justify the financing of the space programmes. It also took shape in the 1980s at a moment when the dominant preoccupation guiding science policy was the lack of competitiveness of American industry, strongly challenged by German and Japanese industry.

Innovation policies in the US are founded on strong interactions between public research and industry, in particular as regards small high technology companies. Two mechanisms have been established to allow the US to capitalize on the innovation potential of its universities, notably by facilitating the creation of spin-off firms: the Bayh-Dole Act and the programme of 'small business innovation research' (SBIR). At the same time, as is also starting to be the case in Europe, there was a process of externalizing research undertaken by large American companies towards the universities.

The legislation supporting the commercialization of research in establishments of higher learning, such as the Bayh-Dole Act, has been used as a model for several countries, including Finland, Austria, Japan, Korea, and France (Gingras and Gemme 2003: 57). For example, French legislators cited the US model in framing the 1999 'Loi sur l'innovation', which modified the civil servant status of French researchers by giving them the right to launch start-ups and to increase the revenues gained from their private research activities. In the UK, public financing of R&D became dependent on demonstrating the direct contribution of the research to the economy. Various measures were put in place in the UK in order to support the marketing of research results, including the possibility for universities to apply for patents, the creation of Liaison Offices of Science and Industry, the creation of business incubators, and taking into account patents in the career advancement of researchers (Etzkowitz et al. 2000).

EU framework programmes have clearly been designed to strategically manage the development of research and technology at the European level in the spirit of interactive models. The basic instruments of European support take the form of research projects targeted on strategic actions and topics which support the construction of a European research and innovation space. Pavitt (2000) observed that most of the other EU initiatives for universities have supported the creation of networks rather than the performance of research itself.

The Fifth Framework Program stressed the need to solve problems and achieve concrete socio-economic results as fast as possible. The clear intent was to identify the problem from the start, taking into account the advice of the final users, and to find scientific solutions. This fifth programme attributed a special place to industrial research and appointed a number of influential industrial advisors (Nowotny, Scott, and Gibbons 2001).

The objective of the Sixth Framework Program is in part to focus European research and development investments in the fields likely to generate, in the medium term, profits for the economy and society at the European level. Within this framework, a set of instruments is put in place. The traditional instruments have become secondary, and the main financial effort is now deployed through new instruments:

– Networks of excellence, which aim at supporting the emergence of poles of excellence in given fields of research;
– Integrated projects, where the objective is to support European competitiveness or to meet essential needs for society, through the creation of knowledge within the framework of projects associating complementary actors;
– The joint setting of national programmes.

The most significant share of finance concentrates on the thematic priorities, but in parallel a more limited, but not insignificant, support is attributed to anticipating scientific and technical opportunities by supporting research which is transversal or external to these priorities.

10.3.2. Interactions with Industry

Hybrid arrangements aiming to promote closer relations between university and industry in the EU have multiplied in the last twenty years. Governments are involved in the development of research partnerships and promote various forms of collaboration between industry and academia. These partnerships are celebrated as 'learning alliances' and new 'communities of innovation', well suited to the innovation demands of a globalized, marketplace

(Carayannis, Alexander, and Ioannidis 2000). Shortages of scientific personnel in industry and revenues in universities partly account for the multiplication of these partnerships. More fundamentally, both public research and technological innovation have undergone major transformations that have opened the way for increasing collaboration between university and industry (Gibbons et al. 1998; Etzkowitz et al. 1998).

In contrast to the linear model between basic and applied research, scientific research, and technological innovation are merged into a combined process of collective production of knowledge by both industrial and academia actors. For basic research laboratories, the increasing interaction with industry implies that research themes are more and more influenced by applications. Knowledge and scientific theories are supposed to be partly dependent on the context in which they are produced. The scientific themes are not only constructed from the accumulated expertise of researchers, but also from strategies adopted by the laboratories for securing access to resources. Researchers increasingly have incentives to exploit the opportunities offered by industry to complement their private funding: by doing so, they participate in the economic competitiveness of firms, and contribute to reinforce the co-evolution of research and industry. This tendency varies from one discipline to the other, but it can be shown that in certain areas such as biotechnologies, the development of 'strategic' basic research strongly supported by private funds is an evergrowing phenomenon.[2]

10.3.3. The Transformation of Universities and the Pressure of Globalization

Today, universities experience important internal and external pressures from globalization: changes in the nature of governmental support, increase in financial support from companies, proliferation of institutional networks, emergence of new sites, production processes and flow of knowledge as well as the need to define, integrate, and develop the internationalization of scientific research (Caraça 2002: 32).

A first series of pressures comes from governments of the principal OECD countries (OECD 1999). Various governments have tried to develop an entrepreneurial culture amongst universities, which leads to the emergence of the multiplication of start-ups and an increasing number of interdisciplinary research centres aimed at promoting the exploitation of public research while being capable of responding to the increase in interdisciplinary research subjects that companies as well as scientific parks are interested in (Conceiçao and Heitor 1998; Rip 2002: 126).

In recent OECD reports, the connections drawn between the knowledge-based economy, innovation policies, and the role of universities in the system of creation, distribution, and use of knowledge leads to practices of partnership and entrepreneurship being presented as exemplary practices, since they allow universities to adjust to changes and they contribute to governments reaching their objectives. A 1999 report[3] stresses the need for universities to act with more flexibility in order to 'prospect the research market' and 'promote the economic value of their competencies' in a way that allows universities' entrepreneurs, with their teams of researchers-entrepreneurs to be in a position to ensure their competitiveness with global firms 'making their market in matter of research in the area where competencies are at their best value'.

According to Etzkowitz et al. (2000), in many countries, under pressure from major scientific and technical policies, a model of the entrepreneurial university emerges, despite resistance, criticisms, institutional problems, and the questions of governance that this evolution brings.

A second series of pressures weighing on universities are internal to institutions. By multiplying their applied research activities, by getting preoccupied (Feller 1990) with the commercialization of research, by accepting the idea that it is possible to make money (Faulkner and Senker 1995) with research, and by multiplying universities' research centres and organizing them in a different way than on a disciplinary basis, universities have favoured partnership with companies and have had to adopt, in part, the firm's model.[4]

Universities have adopted three groups of complementary strategies (Hamdouch and Depret 2001: 146). They have multiplied, especially in the US, industrial promotion agreements which associate public and private sector researchers. They have adopted active policies concerning patents and licensing arrangements. They have rapidly developed academic 'swarms'. From this point of view, entrepreneurial universities emerge in part from pressures internal to the universities.

These changes, affecting university institutions today (change of mission, budget crisis, re-evaluation of structures, etc.), raise a number of questions. Some wonder what future role universities will be able to play in countries determined to improve their economic performance in a global and highly technological environment (Rosenberg 2002). Others wonder if universities will be able to metamorphose again. After having taken on a mission of research in addition to that of education in the nineteenth century, in accordance to the needs of mass education (Caraça 2002), will they be able to reconcile new, apparently opposing objectives? Finally, from the moment where companies also come to be qualified as learning organizations (Nonaka and Takeuchi 1995), can universities still be seen as the factory of knowledge

(Conceiçao and Heitor 2001)? Given the diversification of its activities (research, teaching, and 'ties with society'), must it then structure itself like a company?

As Caraça (2002) observes, 'Several alternatives are possible: the refoundation of the university may proceed according to the principles of a "factory of knowledge", or submit to the rules of interdisciplinarity, evolving from a university to a "multi-university". It may continue to be a real school or survive just by redefining itself as a "no walls" virtual school. These are, at the moment, open questions.'

10.4. A CRITICAL ANALYSIS OF THE CONSEQUENCES OF THE EU POLICIES BASED ON THE NEW INTERACTIVE MODEL OF KNOWLEDGE PRODUCTION

10.4.1. Discussion of the Models

Several important critiques have been made of the Mode II production of knowledge model on which EU policies seem to rely. It has been argued, in particular, that Mode 1 never actually existed and was only a construct to justify autonomy for science after the Second World War. Conversely, it can be argued that Mode 2 is not new and was in fact the dominant mode of scientific knowledge production before the academic institutionalization of science in the nineteenth century (Pestre 1997; Weingart 1997; Shinn 1999; Etzkowitz and Leydesdorff 2000). Shinn (1999) in particular shows that there never was a single mode that could fully describe the functioning of science and innovation at one period, and that several modes of knowledge production always coexisted.

Pavitt (2000) observed that, 'critics point out that Mode 2 research has existed for a long time, and is a complement to publicly funded and validated research, rather than a substitute for it'. To concentrate on Mode 2 would lead to 'cut-price research motels' to the neglect of fundamental research.

One of the major supports for the strengthening of the system of science came from Dasgupta and David (1994). For them, the incentive schemes and norms associated with the institutional settings are the main explanation for the reasons why codified forms are preferred by some agents (researchers who have incentives to publish articles, theorems, treaties, etc.) while tacit forms are preferred by others (engineers working in private firms).[5] They consider that the specific features of the scientific domain must be preserved for reasons of economic efficiency.[6] They advocate maintaining two clear distinct systems of incentives, one governing 'open' science (and requiring massive public intervention), and the other governing the market side of the economy.

While we are in agreement with their conclusions in terms of public support for research, their demonstration skips over the problem of the interactive nature of the process of production of knowledge, or at least the coexistence of several modes of knowledge production.

The sociology of science and technology has also showed that scientists who claimed to work according Mode 1 of knowledge production were nevertheless always integrated into networks described by Mode 2 (Callon 1994; Pestre 1997). These results do not necessarily lead to the conclusion that research should only be guided by the market mechanism but rather point to the pertinence of governmental support.

Reflecting on the limits of the argument that scientific knowledge can be reduced to information—an argument that classically justified public support of research—Lundvall (2000: 2–3) observes that it proves on the contrary, 'that the public research system has functions beyond supplying the private sector with new knowledge. This type of insight, implying that not all knowledge can be easily copied, does not weaken the argument for public support of research'. Similarly, Callon (1994: 12–13) argues that, 'the main result of scientific activity is not to produce information but to reconfigure heterogeneous networks (hybrid collectives)'. On his account this justifies the public financing of science since, 'In a regime of perfectly privatizable science, science would be privatized so rapidly and so brutally that it would become a captive of the techno-economics networks. And there would be a double movement towards irreversibilization and convergence'. He even states, 'Science is a public good, which must be preserved at all costs because it is a source of variety' (p. 19).

10.4.2. A Critical Analysis of the EU Policies Orientation

Europe has given priority to a series of measures that: (*a*) favour the setting up of 'intermediaries' between universities and industry to stimulate the interactive process of production of knowledge; (*b*) reinforce 'centres of excellence' in some specific domains of knowledge; and (*c*) encourage the imitation of some 'tricks' elaborated by the US system, such as the Bayh-Dole Act.

In the following section, we investigate the main strategic directions of the EU in terms of research and higher education:

1. *The importance of 'intermediaries':* The role of intermediaries is effective and important in the process of production of knowledge. However it does not solve the conflict of incentives. It just creates a 'grey zone' between the

functioning of the market mechanism and open science, which requires heavy support from the state.

2. *The centres of excellence:* Europe has given priority to the reinforcement of 'poles of excellence'. Such a priority is certainly a useful one to compete against the advances of the US research system. However, here again, such a policy must rely on strong public financing of basic science. If not, not only will talented scientists in Europe who do not work in these domains be tempted to leave Europe but also those scientists in the fields of excellence who need to develop interactions with other fields of research, or develop new disciplines, or do multidisciplinary approaches will be tempted to find these creative conditions elsewhere. Only a strong financing of basic research could contribute to the building of a creative milieu in Europe. A creative milieu supposes that any good idea coming from any discipline could find a way to be developed.

3. *The pressures to imitate some of the US 'tricks':* The adoption of partial devices elaborated in the US and considered as best practices, such as the Bayh-Dole Act, is a risky one. First, it is risky because such policies remain an object of debate in the US. Second, it is risky because these policies convey the wrong idea that public authorities can simply let private forces substitute progressively for declining public funding. Geuna (1997) has studied the respective financing of British universities by government and firms in the period 1989–93. The analysis developed offers some evidence to support the hypothesis that policies oriented towards a decrease in state financing of university research may be disappointing in two senses: First, industrial funding is not likely to be large enough to replace major cuts in public support. Second, the universities hit hardest by budget cuts are pushed to do routine contract research for industry, which neither leads to higher publication rates (and spillovers), nor provides a basis for long-term fundamental innovations.

The American experience inspired a model which seems to be regarded as universal in spite of the existence of many historical and sociological studies which point to its limits or contradictions (Milot 2003). In particular, practices of university entrepreneurship and of partnership are presented as exemplary practices. However, this view is typically supported by the examination of specific cases, which are always the same cases of success. As Trépanier and Ippersiel (2003: 77) observe, the focus is on, 'developed industrial and university systems where the involved players have financial, scientific and technical resources that determine a very specific type of relations: presence of hi-tech firms, industrial demand for knowledge at the state of the art, availability of high-tech scientific equipment in universities . . .'.

Lundvall (2002: 10–11) also notes that if it is true that there are certain groups in universities that can supply interesting results to industry, this is not the case for the majority of researchers. After all, a small fraction of university researchers and departments interact with a small fraction of industry. 'This implies, of course, that it would be dubious to design the organisation and regulatory frameworks of the universities exclusively with reference to the quite exceptional tendencies in the research fields of biotechnology and life sciences.'

Increased interactions with industry also mean that research themes will be more and more dependent on the strategies of firms, in particular in the perspectives of the strategic re-organizations of firms along their 'core-competencies', which can be interpreted as specific bodies of competitive knowledge accumulated, controlled, and managed by firms. The risk is that this will render the knowledge base more fragile, because its development is mainly driven by short-term considerations. Also, it has to be emphasized that the knowledge bases of particular firms are highly localized. Firms tend to have one or a few technologies which they understand well and which form the basis of their competitive position. The highly specific character of this knowledge is not simply technical, it is also social, concerning the way in which technical processes can be integrated with skills, production routines, use of equipment, explicit or tacit training, management systems, etc. These potential biases in the accumulation of knowledge lead to a possible fragmentation of scientific knowledge.

If the experience of certain American universities and the Bayh-Dole Act is often quoted to justify the adoption of similar measures and initiatives in countries seeking to support innovation, some research shows that it is not so much the legislation which is responsible for the changes in the universities but rather the general increase of research costs and the drop of public support towards university research. The universities, even without Bayh-Dole, would undoubtedly have started up commercial activities in areas such as biotechnology or data processing, given their potential for application and new sources of income (Gingras and Gemme 2003: 57).

At the same time, Lundvall recalls:

historically, the university has had room for slow and in-depth learning, and has been a place where one can keep a long-term perspective, and reflect critically both on theory and reality. One problematic aspect with current developments is that these traditional functions are undermined. Growing specialisation, combined with a demand for faster speed and a demand for permanent and intense interaction with many external partners, does not leave much time for critical reflection. (Lundvall 2002: 6)

This implies that universities must reconcile with their traditional functions of generating new learning and developing new generations of scientists and engineers, with a new role of cooperating with industry to favour the transfer of knowledge and technology. Thus, public laboratories and universities which increasingly collaborate with industrial partners not only for financial reasons but also to appropriate innovation, 'must combine these functions with their basic role in generic research and education' (Milot 2003: 69).

10.5. THE DIFFICULT ELABORATION OF A NEW MODEL OF PRODUCTION OF KNOWLEDGE THAT INTEGRATES THE INTERACTIVE PROCESS VISION AND A NEW MODE OF ALLOCATION OF RESOURCES TO UNIVERSITIES

If there is a convergence on the interactive nature of the process of production of knowledge, there is not a clear vision on what should be the incentive system for researchers in the interactive process of production of knowledge. Should we maintain an open system of science, and if so how can we reconcile an open system of incentives based on peer review and reputation with a market-oriented system of incentives? If not, does the model of the entrepreneurial university necessarily have to be followed?

The pressure of empirical and political changes has to be taken into account. Science, and thus researchers, must strengthen their interaction with the rest of society and EU programmes have worked in this sense by establishing networks. But in our view these networks must firstly rely on high quality academic research. That means that a space for long-term critical research must be preserved. As Lundvall (2002: 7) observes, 'We should therefore consider how we might introduce institutional solutions that could re-establish some of the *advantages* that were attached to the "Ivory Tower"'.

The different models characterizing the interactive nature of the production of knowledge do not pay sufficient attention to the incentives schemes of the researchers and to the related sources of funding that flow into the system of production of knowledge, as if these constraints no longer are real with the generalization of the new mode of production of knowledge. The increasing production of knowledge by private entities raises the problem of the role of public institutions of knowledge production (public laboratories, public centres of research, etc.). Market forces are penetrating the 'Republic of

Science' to such an extent, that many voices are now calling for measures designed to protect the specific traits of the research system (see Dosi, Llerena, and Labini this volume).

Our hypothesis is that the compromise, if there should be one, is clearly a sequential one. The Republic of Science should be governed first by the classical incentives of open science of being the first to publish. This mechanism inherently implies a mechanism of construction of reputation. Then, a second mechanism based on market incentives could function. In other words, we consider that the interactive nature of the process of production of knowledge calls for a compromise between the incentives of open science and the incentives of the market, within the domain of Republic of Science itself.

The interactive model suggests that market forces and mechanisms could complement the open mechanism, but under the condition that the market mechanism functions *once* the open mechanism has been effective. This perspective clearly implies the need for strong public financial support of universities in order to maintain the viability of the open system. But it allows for the possibility of the functioning of a second mechanism *within* the sphere of open science, at least for those researchers who have gained sufficient academic reputation and intend to be more involved with private ventures (the public effort should be strong enough to guarantee a stimulating career to those researchers who are not interested in private interactions).

For Lundvall (2002: 7) there is a need for 'institutional differentiation' between and within institutions concerned with the production and diffusion of knowledge. He believes that, 'differentiation could mean flexibility in the use of time for the individual researcher, over the career, where there are periods of slow, in depth, research as well as periods of education and periods of intense interaction with external users of research'.

Of course, there are drawbacks in the development of a sequential mode of incentives. This vision may give place to much emphasis on individual incentives much in accordance with the Mertonian model of scientific activity, where the individual trajectory of the researcher and his or her capacity to accumulate a stock of credibility is the main driver of the academic domain. This leads for instance to the well-known 'Matthews effect', 'as public funding of scientific research is related to previous accomplishments, the system may give disproportionate recognition to scientists who attained early discoveries' (Diamond 1996).

However, even if the sequential mode could be viewed as a second best solution, we consider that the sequence cannot go the other way without significant risk of irreversible damages to the process of production of knowledge and more specifically to universities. Let market forces play first or substitute progressively for the domain of open science, and one runs the risk that some fundamental knowledge will stay hidden and that society will lose the preservation of diversity as well as the possibility to invest in long-term options. Society will face the risks of an 'anticommons' tragedy, with the reduction of the body of common scientific knowledge and the reduction of technological variety.

The success of the US model is due to a large extent to the adoption of the sequential combination of the incentive mechanisms with open science first, followed by the market incentive system. Pavitt (2000) advocates for similar policies in Europe, which would require a drastic change in the present orientations of science and technology policies in the EU.

However, if we consider that the US model has been successful, this does not mean that we take the US model in its entirety as the reference model for European universities. It has severe drawbacks. For example, the quality of the top-ranked universities in the US hides the poor quality of many regional universities. Measures, such as the Bayh-Dole Act, have been criticized by some scholars as providing benefits to only a handful of universities throughout the country and for being very costly without generating rewards for most of the universities (Mowery and Sampat 2005). A more equitable distribution of funding to diverse regions and institutions would counteract these sort of drawbacks.

Callon (1994) coming out of a sociology of science perspective also reaches the conclusion that the incentive system in science should rely on the following principles: (*a*) a principle of free association, which means that no collective should be ostracized a priori; (*b*) a principle of freedom of extension, which means that a collective must have the means—essentially financial means—to extend itself; and (*c*) a principle of fighting against irreversibility and convergence.

The idea of the EU establishing an agency to complement national agencies in funding academic research is interesting. Pavitt (2000: 455) suggests that such an agency could, 'identify and support exciting multi-disciplinary programmes of research and related training in promising fields, rather forecast or demonstrate specific applications'.

Again it is important to stress that the success of measures taken by the EU supposes a strong initial financing of basic research. Given this, Europe could deploy successfully its strategy of intermediary entities, poles of excellence, networking of regional universities, etc. Our view is that the series of measures adopted by the EU will benefit European countries to the degree they are based on the principle of strong initial public support of basic research in line with the sequential mode of incentives. If this is not the case, then the risk is more than high that the best researchers in Europe will leave for other places to do research.

10.6. CONCLUSION

Changes in the mode of production of knowledge have generated a number of analyses and reflections concerning the new role which universities should play. This research has led to interesting conclusions around the idea that the mode of production is becoming interactive and that the role of the university must change in accordance with this new reality. These perspectives are often used to support policies which aim at creating partnerships and hybrid arrangements. While these analyses are interesting, and Europe will indeed have to raise the question of coordination between the various national systems and of the valourization of this variety, we think it is essential to first raise the issue of new incentives mechanisms for researchers and new modes of financing of universities adapted to the knowledge-based economy. For the moment, the tendency in Europe is to adopt certain prominent characteristics of the American model, character- istics which appear to correspond well to the new requirements the inter- active mode of knowledge production, namely an acceleration of the marketing of science and an increase in the private financing of research and education.

We believe that such policies would be disastrous for European universities and European research. European policies towards universities must be built and adapted to Europe's specificities and not simply based on charac- terizations of the American model, which is the current trend. These policies must also take into account the diversity existing inside Europe, because this diversity is also a source of strength in a knowledge-based economy. We have argued in favour of a strong system of public financial support for the universities so as to maintain the viability of the 'open system' of science. Only under these conditions can rich interactions occur between universities and other diverse sources of production and transmission of knowledge. Of course, institutionalizing the sequential system of incentives would have to take into account the existing diversity between the different Euro- pean countries.

At the empirical level, taking into account the changes in the modes of production of knowledge, the question of the reconciliation of an open system of incentive based on peer review and reputation with a market- oriented system of incentive cannot be dismissed. We have proposed a sequential system combining these different types of incentives, within the domain of republic of science itself. At the research level, a converging vision on what could be the incentive system for researchers in the interactive process of production of knowledge would have to be produced, a vision on which a clear policy framework could be built.

NOTES

1. For example, the Bayh-Dole Act in the US, the Foundations in Sweden, etc.
2. Lundvall (2002: 6) looks at how different types of research are prioritized in the learning economy. He shows that, 'international statistics of research expenditure indicate that the private sector increasingly pursues research that will give immediate pay-offs, rather than basic and strategic research with a long horizon'.
3. *The Management of Science Systems* (OECD/STI Paris) 1999.
4. Etzkowitz (2003) gives the example of research groups that are, from universities standpoint, 'quasi-firms', with directors spending their time at managing students and post-doctoral students instead of doing research.
5. As expressed by David and Foray (1995), 'The critical factor governing the distribution and the utilization of new findings are those regarding the rules structures and behavioural norms about information disclosure that dominate in the particular social organizations within which the new knowledge is found or improved.'
6. One of the associated risks is that in a period of budgetary cross-cutting, governments will focus their attention on the larger and politically more visible items of the basic science budget, namely the large-scale research facilities. For them, such a decision will be damaging the whole system of research, and the competitiveness of industry.

REFERENCES

Arrow, K. J. (1962). 'Economic Welfare and the Allocation of Resources for Invention', in Nelson, R. (ed.), *The Rate and Direction of Inventive Activity: Economic and Social Factors*. Princeton: Princeton University Press: 609–625.

Callon, M. (1994). 'Is Science a Public Good?', *Science, Technology and Human Values*, 19(4): 395–424.

—— et al. (1999). *Réseau et coordination*. Paris: Economica.

—— (1995). *Gestion stratégique de la recherche et de la technologie. L'évaluation des programme*. Paris: Economica.

Caraça, J. (2002). 'Introductory Note: Should Universities Be Concerned with Teaching or with Learning?', in P. Conceiçao et al. (eds.), *Knowledge for Inclusive Development*. Westport, CT: Quorum Books.

Carayannis, E. G., Alexander, J., and Ioannidis, A. (2000).'Leveraging Knowledge, Learning, and Innovation in Forming Strategic Government–university–industry R and D Partnerships in the US, Germany and France', *Technovation*, 20(9): 477–88.

Cohendet, P. and Joly, P. B. (2000). 'The Production of Technological Knowledge', in Archibugi, D. and Lundvall, B. A. (eds), *The New Economics and Globalization*. Oxford: Oxford University Press.

Cozzens S. E. (1990). *The Research System in Transition*. Boston: Kluwer Academic Publishers.

Conceiçao, P. and Heitor, M. (1998) 'On the Role of the University in the Knowledge Economy', *Science and Public Policy*, 26(1): 37–51.

—— —— (2001). 'Universities in the Learning Economy: Balancing Institutional Integrity with Organizational Diversity', in D. Archibugi and B. A. Lundvall (eds.), *The Globalizing Learning Economy*. Oxford: Oxford University Press.

Cozzens, S. et al. (1990). *The Research System in Transition*. Dordrecht: Kluwer.

Dasgupta, P. and David, P. A. (1994). 'Toward a New Economics of Science', *Research Policy*, 23(5): 487–521.

David, P. A. and Foray, D. (1995). 'Accessing and Expanding the Science and Technology Knowledge Base', *STI Review*. 16. Paris: OCDE, pp. 13–68.

Diamond, A. M. (1996). 'The Economics of Science', *Knowledge and Policy*, 9: 6–49.

Etzkowitz, H., Healey, P. and Webster A. (1998). *Capitalizing Knowledge: New Intersections of Industry and Academia*. New York: State University of New York Press.

Etzkowitz, H. (1999). 'Bridging the Gap: The Evolution of Industry-University Links in the United States', in L. Branscomb and F. Kodama (eds.), *Industrializing Knowledge: University-Industry Linkages in Japan and the United States*. Cambridge, MA: MIT Press.

—— (2003). 'Research Groups as Quasi-Firms: The Invention of the Entrepreneurial University', *Research Policy*, 32: 109–21.

—— and Leydesdorff, L. (2000). 'The Dynamics of Innovation: From National Systems and "Mode 2" to a Triple Helix of University-Industry-Government Relations', *Research Policy*, 29(2): 109–24.

—— et al. (2000). 'The Future of the University and the University of the Future: Evolution of Ivory Tower to Entrepreneurial Paradigm', *Research Policy*, 29(2): 313–30.

Faulkner, W. and Senker, J. (1995). *Knowledge Frontiers*. Oxford: Oxford University Press.

Feller, I. (1990). 'University as Engines of Economic Development: They Think They Can', *Research Policy*, 19: 335–48.

Geuna, A. (1997). 'Allocation of Funds and Research Output : The Case of UK Universities", *Revue d'Economie Industrielle*, 79: 143–62.

Gibbons, M. et al. (1994). *The New Production of Knowledge. The Dynamics of Science and Research in Contemporary Societies.* London: Sage.

Gingras, Y. and Gemme, B. (2003). 'La commercialisation de la recherche'. *Actes de la recherche en sciences sociales*, 148.

Gulbrandsen, M. and Etzkowitz, H. (1999). 'Convergence between Europe and America: The Transition from Industrial to Innovation Policy', *Journal of Technology Transfer*, 24: 223–33.

Hamdouch, A., Depret, M. H. (2001). *La nouvelle économie industrielle de la pharmacie.* Paris: Elsevier.

Leydesdorff, L. and Etzkowitz, H. (eds.) (1998). *Triple Helix Issue of Science and Public Policy*, 25(6): 358–415.

Lundvall, B.-Å. (2002). 'The University in the Learning Economy'. Presentation on the Future role of Universities. BETA, Strasbourg.

Milot, P. (2003). 'La reconfiguration des universités selon l'OCDE. Économie du savoir et politique de l'innovation', *Actes de la recherche en sciences sociales*, 148: 70.

Mowrey, D. and Sampat, B. (2005). 'Universities in National Innovation Systems', in J. Fagerberg D. Mowrey, and R. Nelson (eds.), *The Oxford Handbook of Innovation.* Oxford: Oxford University Press.

Nowotny, H., Scott, P., and Gibbons, M. (2001). *Repenser la science.* Paris: Éditions Berlin.

OECD. (1999). *The Management of Science Systems.* Paris: OECD.

—— (2000). 'Why European Union Funding of Academic Research should be Increased: A Radical Proposal', *Science and Public Policy*, 27(6): 455–60(6).

Prestre, D. (1997). 'La production des savoirs entre académies et marché: une relecture historique du livre "The New Production of Knowledge"', *Revue d'Économie Industrielle*, 79: 163–74.

Rip, A. (2002). 'Regional Innovation Systems and the Advent of Strategic Science', *Journal of Technology Transfer*, 27: 123–31.

Rosenberg, N. (2002). 'Knowledge and Innovation for Economic Development: Should Universities Be Economic Institutions?', in P. Conceiçao et al. (eds.), *Knowledge for Inclusive Development.* Westport, CT: Quorum Books.

Shinn, T. (1999). 'Change or Mutation? Reflections on the Foundations of Contemporary Science', *Social Science information*, 38/1: 149–76.

Trépanier, M. and Ippersiel, M.-P. (2003). 'Hiérarchie de la crédibilité et autonomie de la recherche. L'impensé des analyses des relations universités-entreprises', *Actes de la recherche en sciences sociales*, 148: 77.

Vavakova, B. (1998). 'The New Social Contract Between Governments, Universities and Society: Has the Old One Failed?', *Minerva*, 36: 209–28.

Weingart, P. (1997). 'From Finalization to Mode 2: Old Wine in New Bottles?', *Social Science Information*, 34/4: 591–613.

Wouters, P., Elzingo, A. and Annimeike, N. (2002). 'Contentious Science—Discussing the Politics of Science', EASST Review, 21(34).

Ziman, J. M. (1994). *Prometheus bound: Science in a dynamic steady State*. Cambridge: Cambridge University Press.

11

Learning Industry Against Knowledge Economy? Lessons from the French Case

Eric Verdier

11.1. INTRODUCTION

France frequently resists classification in international comparisons aimed at bringing out the features of developed economies. To paraphrase Stanley Hoffmann, it is the 'agony' of the researcher embarking on international comparisons. Thus, in terms of social welfare analysis, it long escaped Esping-Andersen's famous system—which led that author to prepare a special preface for the French edition of his book (1999). Similarly, in terms of institutionalist economics, it was so out of place in the New Political Economy's distinction between 'LMEs' and 'CMEs' (Hall and Soskice 2001) that it gave rise to a specific thesis intended to meet this analytical challenge (Hancké 2002).

We take this second approach as our point of departure because it is directly related to the subject of this book. The theoretical approach developed in Hall and Soskice's (2001) work on 'varieties of capitalism' opposes LMEs (predominantly Anglo-American) to CMEs. In the former, companies coordinate their activities mainly by relying on hierarchies and competitive devices in the context of the markets; educational systems give priority to general qualifications; and innovation dynamics tend to be radical rather than incremental. In the latter, companies are more likely to rely on non-market relations to coordinate their efforts with other players and build their main competences and they call upon vocational training systems which are specific to one industry or company. They tend to excel in generating incremental innovations (Germany and Japan in particular). Integrating France into this analytical scheme has led to a refinement of the original typology in so far as a distinction is now made between 'coordination at industry level' (Northern Europe), 'coordination at group level' (Japan), and 'coordination by public elite networks' (France).[1]

The objective here is not to produce an additional typology. Rather, we propose to examine France's international position in order to bring out the role of the higher education and research systems in the 'societal' dynamics of innovation.

The French situation is stimulating for analysis in two respects. First, higher education has undergone remarkable expansion since the early 1980s, and especially during the 1985–95 period. A determined public policy aimed to eliminate a considerable lag with respect to the other industrialized countries, and this was widely supported by the choices of young people and their families, as well as intermediary actors such as the regional councils, which were given broader powers in this area.

Second, following this apparently favourable period, a number of official reports emphasized the lack of efficiency of the higher education and research system. The research sector drew the most criticism (see the Guillaume report 1998) but the educational dimension was not exempt from harsh diagnoses (see the Attali report 1998). These reports gave rise to significant reforms: the 1999 law on innovation which was intended to forge new relations between higher education and industry; and the 2003 alignment of higher-education diplomas to the consecutive bachelors–masters–doctorate (B–M–D) system in accordance with the Bologna declaration of the European ministers of higher education and research.

In recent years, many criticisms have focused on the organizational features of the French education and research system and notably the two 'great divides' that characterize it: that between universities and major public research bodies such as the National Centre for Scientific Research (CNRS); and that between highly selective 'Grandes Ecoles' where students are closely supervised and the universities which are open to anyone holding a *baccalauréat* from the secondary system but which have limited means (expenditures per student are 40 per cent below the OECD average). We come back to these features which are obviously important. But the following paradox requires further consideration; the societal inadequacies of the higher education system have become patent at the same time as it has undergone exceptional development. This paradox is all the more interesting to examine because the changes have not simply been quantitative. In terms of university education, which generally receives the sharpest criticisms, we may cite the increasing vocational orientation of the curricula, and in terms of public research, which is often disparaged for its Byzantine administration, the increased recourse to contractual relations between universities and research bodies on the one hand, and between public laboratories and industry on the other. Such criticisms have called into question the effectiveness and political legitimacy of the higher education system, giving rise to demands for radical reforms.[2]

In what follows, we argue that the structural difficulties of the French higher education and research system are symptomatic of the 'societal' exhaustion or inadequacy of the two forms of industrial and institutional specialization which have dominated France's system of non-market coordination: *design-based flexible mass production*; and *high-tech complex engineering goods* (Hancké 2001). The first, which is relatively recent, results from the adjustments of the 1980s, while the second belongs to the classic lineage of an economy marked by the central role of the State. In both cases, education, training, and research play a key structuring role. We argue that it is not enough to expand and make more professional higher education and training; policies must also contribute to positioning the economy on favourable, lasting areas of industrial specializations. From this standpoint, it is not certain that the French model is sufficiently coherent.

11.2. OUTSTANDING DEVELOPMENT OF HIGHER EDUCATION: STRONG INCREASE OF EDUCATION LEVELS AND 'VOCATIONALIZATION'

In the context of this chapter, it is more pertinent to focus on the higher training programmes which are most aligned with research and (potentially) innovation activities inside industries. In less than fifteen years, French higher education has undergone a spectacular development which in certain respects is unequalled among major OECD countries.

11.2.1 Rapid Rise in Education Levels Among the Younger Generations (1985–95)

The number of students rose from 1,181,000 in 1980–1 to 2,169,000 in 1995–6 followed by stagnation or a slight decrease. Since the mid-1990s, over 40 per cent of those exiting the educational system (all levels combined) have been higher education graduates, while the proportion was barely 20 per cent at the beginning of the 1980s.

This is not the place to go into the basis for the rise of mass higher education in France, which was a complex result of voluntarist public policies and incentives arising from a macroeconomic context which made holding a higher level diploma an important advantage on the labour market (for an overview see Buechtemann and Verdier 1998). Table 11.1, taken from Vincens

Table 11.1 Generational structure by diploma[1]

Type of diploma	Germany	United Kingdom	France	Italy
		Born in 1950		
1a	8	24	18	31
1b	14	—	18	—
2	2	12	7	34
3	53	38	30	5
4	—	4	10	20
5	21	22	17	10
		Born in 1970		
Type of diploma	Germany	United Kingdom	France*	Italy
1a	8	11	17	6
1b	9	—	1	—
2	3	23	4	41
3	58	31	30	7
4	—	9	16	39
5	20	26	32	7

Notes: Vincens and Steedman (2000).

[1] Table 11.1 compares the generations born in 1950 and 1970 through the use of a simplified classification system proposed by Hilary Steedman. The categories are as follows:

■1a. No diploma: in the UK; 'no qualifications'; in France, 'sans diplôme'; in Italy, 'primary school certificate or no diploma (not distinguished in data)'; in Germany, 'no diploma and no response'; in Spain, 'sense estudis'.

■1b. Compulsory schooling completed and primary school certificate: in France, 'certificat d'études primaires', in Spain, 'primaries'; in Germany, 'Hauptschule'.

■2. First-level secondary school certificate: in the UK, 'O levels', CSE and GSCE; in France, BEPC; in Germany, 'Realschule'; in Italy, 'scuola media' graduates; in Spain, 'Bachillerato elemental', EGB higher cycle.

■3. Vocational training certificate: in the UK, 'others', including Trade Apprenticeship, City and Guilds, ONC/OND, NVQ 2/3; in France, CAP/BEP; in Germany, apprenticeships, BFS; in Italy, 'scuola professionale' graduates; in Spain, FP.

■4. Second cycle secondary certificate (general, technical, or vocational) giving access to higher studies: in the UK, 'A Levels', in Germany, 'Abitur' and 'Fachhochschulreife; in France, 'baccalauréats'; in Italy, 'Maturita', 'Magisterio' and 'Scuola Technica' diplomas; in Spain, Bachillerato Superior, BUP, COU.

■5. Higher education: in the UK, 'degrees', HNC/HND, teaching and nursing diplomas; in France, 'licences' and above, Bac+2 diplomas; in Germany, university diplomas, Meister and Techniciens; in Italy, university diplomas; in Spain, short and full university diplomas.

(2001), offers a good inter-generational and comparative perspective on the scope of the ongoing societal transformations which are introducing the human resource bases for a 'knowledge society'. The figures point to the relatively rapid increase in the importance of higher level education in France.

11.2.2. Sharp Increase in Flows from Technical Colleges, Engineering Schools, and University Science Programmes

Table 11.2 shows that the university's share of the total number of students declines during the period 1960–2002 in favour of the vocationally oriented training programmes within short-course higher education (two years after the *baccalauréat*): the polytechnics (Instituts Universitaires de Technologie [IUT], which are attached to the universities but enjoy considerable autonomy) and the Higher Technicien Sections (Sections de Techniciens Supérieurs [STS], which are special college departments introduced in the high schools).[3]

In addition, within the growing numbers of university students, the vocational courses show a much greater increase than the general academic courses: on average, the proportion of students in the former rose from 29 per cent of the total in 1996 to 36 per cent in 2002.[4] It must be emphasized that the training content—notably for the BTS and DUT[5]—is determined not unilaterally by the school administration but is subject to dialogue and negotiation with the occupational branches concerned, even if the role of the social partners is not as decisive as in Germany (Möbus and Verdier 2000).

As Table 11.3 shows, it is quite significant that during the most favourable period for the development of higher education (1984–95), the growth of the second and third cycles in the sciences was much more rapid than it was in the humanities and social sciences and economics as a whole, notwithstanding the fact that the latter were considerably less expensive and selective in terms of admission policies. The same is true, moreover, for the most selective programmes of all, namely the Grandes Ecoles. The number of engineering

Table 11.2 Numbers of higher-education students and distribution by type of training body (in percentage)

Education and training providers	1960	1970	1980	1990	1995	2001	2003
University	69	75	68	65	64	60	59.7
IUT	—	2	4	4	5	5	5
STS	3	3	6	12	10	12	10.8
CPGE[1]	7	4	4	4	4	3	3.2
Other institutions	21	16	18	15	17	20	21.3
Total %	100	100	100	100	100	100	100
Total numbers (in 1,000s)	309.7	850.6	1174.9	1717.1	2140.9	2159.0	2256

Note: [1]Preparatory classes for 'Grandes Ecoles'.

Sources: Ministry of Education, Statistics for 2003 (MEN-DEP).

school graduates more than doubled (+150 per cent from 1984 to 1996) at a pace which was slightly greater and above all more regular than that of the business schools. The increase in the number of industrial vocational diplomas (BTS-DUT) was more limited, but it must be stressed that the expansion of this programme occurred earlier than that of full higher education (see Table 11.1).

There was thus a distinct orientation of the different higher-education mechanisms towards the areas of science and technology. In a country marked by the considerable structural weight of the humanities and social sciences, this trend is worth emphasizing.[6] In 1996, for example, the flow of graduates from the second and third cycle science programmes represented nearly 30 per cent of the total number of graduates, as compared to 38 per cent in law and economics and 34 per cent in humanities and social sciences.

The success of these training programmes on the labour market clearly declined during the first half of the 1990s (as was the case for higher education graduates in general), given the double bind of slackening recruitment and a sharp rise in the number of graduates in the programmes concerned. Among the university programmes, it should be noted that the sciences held up better in terms of job level, as reflected in the proportion of managers with these qualifications. Graduates of the Grandes Ecoles continued to enjoy an especially favourable position on the labour market in spite of the doubling of their numbers in eight years. However, they were not the only ones

Table 11.3 Exits by specialization and diploma

	1988	1992	1996	96/88
Universities				
2nd + 3rd cycle sciences	9,424	17,768	34,260	264%
2nd + 3rd cycle law-economics	17,324	22,089	45,381	162%
2nd + 3rd cycle humanities/social sciences	14,729	22,458	40,296	174%
2nd + 3rd cycle total	41,477	62,315	119,937	189%
Grandes Ecoles				
Business schools	5,416	6,790	6,906	28%
Engineering schools	8,807	11,543	17,843	103%
Higher vocational education				
Vocational industry (DUT-BTS)	15,196	16,896	23,561	55%
Vocational services (DUT-BTS)	26,047	35,105	46,817	80%
Vocational total (DUT-BTS)	41,243	52,001	70,378	71%

Source: MEN-DPD, processing Céreq.

in this situation. Nearly 70 per cent of those with a DESS in a science field (professional diploma at bac+5 level) became engineers less than four years after they left university. This was also the case for half the graduates of professional university institutes [*instituts universitaires professionnalisés*] (bac+4).[7]

New reasons for concern about the future have emerged, however, stemming from a certain loss of interest in university science programmes among science *baccalauréat* holders since 1995. This trend is such that certain universities are trying to introduce reforms in order to stem the decline in the number of students enrolled in these studies (Péan 2001: 3).

Notwithstanding the evidence of a declining interest on the part of recent high school graduates for science studies, the attractiveness of vocationally oriented curricula shows no signs of wavering. By way of evidence we note:

1. The proven success of the DESS (professional masters) relative to the DEA (academic masters). Nearly 800 new DESS programmes were set up in three years (1999–2001), generating 15,000 additional places (between 1991 and 1999, the number of graduates annually increased from 14,000 to 29,000). This trend has been so pronounced that there is now a real risk of 'Balkanizing' training programmes and thus compromising the effectiveness of the labour market 'signals'. In the context of the B–M–D reform, an attempt at rationalization is underway through reorganization by subject matter.
2. The rapid growth of the vocational *licence* (the French equivalent of the bachelors) introduced from 1999, in spite of the reluctance of industrialists to recognize qualifications corresponding to three years of training after the *baccalauréat* (Maillard and Veneau 2003). In 2002–3, this diploma showed a 68 per cent increase, involving a total of 9,000 students in nearly 350 vocational *licence* programmes.

The overall equilibrium of the French educational system has thus been profoundly transformed, to the point where the extremely academic orientation of traditional instruction has now been sharply 'hybridized' with a highly vocational-oriented perspective. Indeed, certain observers consider that the French system is now too sharply focused on the production of qualifications specific to a given activity or occupation at the expense of high-level general education. And it is true that enrolment rates at the highest educational levels (excluding short non-tertiary programmes) lag considerably behind the countries of Northern Europe which are most committed to building a 'knowledge society'. In 2001, the figures were 37 per cent in France, 67 per cent in Sweden, and 71 per cent in Denmark.

11.3. THE CONTRIBUTION OF EDUCATION AND TRAINING TO NEW FORMS OF COMPANY ORGANIZATION AND GOVERNANCE: TOWARDS A NEW 'COORDINATED ECONOMY'

Here we focus on how education, training, and the socialization of the actors interacted with two dimensions of the new forms of company regulation that emerged from the mid-1980s. The first has to do with generating innovative changes in the area of training that favour new forms of company organization. The second concerns corporate governance and the companies' ability to make use of banking and public resources to their advantage.

11.3.1. Professionalization of Higher Education and Organizational Changes

The general rise in training and qualification levels did not come about simply as a result of transformations within education and training. In terms of economic strategy, a clear objective was to increase the competitiveness of the French economy as a whole and more particularly industry and the large corporations. The 'professionalization' of higher education thus took place in the context of a policy of competitive restructuring of industry in 1984, and it is not by chance that this date coincides with the beginning of a sharp expansion in education and the growing vocational orientation of curricula. The in-depth restructuring of the companies, notably the largest among them including the former 'national champions', aimed at restoring company profitability through improving non-cost competitiveness. The availability of a young labour force which was better trained and more readily operational was accompanied by human resources policies which, beyond the search for external flexibility, had two major interrelated features:

- First, the privileged hiring of recent graduates, notably those with higher technician or polytechnic diplomas (BTS and DUT) at the expense of the promotion of those with the least qualifications (Béret 1992);
- And second, a restructuring of productive organization, partly based on these new career profiles (Campinos-Dubernet 1995).

Large French companies, as we know, were model examples of Fordist organization (see Salais and Storper 1997). As a result, they were confronted with the need to undertake major structural changes in their work organization. Comparative studies of France and Germany (Maurice, Sellier, and

Silvestre 1986) and France and Japan (Maurice et al. 1988) have brought out the distinctive features of the French firm: extended organizational hierarchy, compartmentalization of functions, extremely low training level of workers, including skilled workers. All of these features translate into a lack of organizational flexibility to adapt to the requirements of shortened production series, improved quality, and so on.

Two potential paths thus emerged. Either the qualifications of existing personnel had to be upgraded or the labour force had to be renewed through massive recourse to early retirement and accelerated automation. The adoption of the latter path tended to reinforce the development of qualifications and functions peripheral to manufacturing per se: quality control, production management, maintenance of new facilities, logistics, and so on. The new BTS and even DUT diplomas provided the necessary competences, sometimes at a relatively low cost given the extent of the downgrading imposed on young recruits. In spite of the difficulties of integrating graduates who were in fact waiting for higher quality jobs, the companies were thus able to carry out a considerable consolidation of managerial functions, in both the industrial and service sectors. This reorganization resulted in a double segmentation of the workforce characterized by:

(1) highly pronounced intergenerational inequalities in levels of education and vocational training. The half of the labour force holding no diploma at the beginning of the 1980s was sidelined as quickly as possible through early retirement. After 1995, 40 per cent of the young people entering the labour market were recent higher education graduates.[8]
(2) a clear-cut hierarchy of functions and a marked split between operating personnel with few qualifications and often precarious work situations (see Beaud and Pialoux 1993) and the young technical personnel in the peripheral functions with permanent positions.

By relying on a functional reorganization made possible by the availability of middle-level (BTS-DUT) and higher-level (engineering and business schools, university masters-DESS) qualifications, French companies in a number of sectors (automobile manufacture, electrical construction, intermediate goods, the iron and steel industry, but also banking and insurance) made a forced march towards repositioning themselves in higher-quality end of product markets.

Through their ability to exploit both economies of scale and market niches, the major French companies were progressively able to compete with the emblematic firms of the CMEs (Amable and Hancké 2001). In much the same vein, a recent report by the French Council for Economic Analysis (Aghion and Cohen 2004) argues that higher education *à la française* has been effective in supporting the development of a strategy of imitation based on incremental innovations but is not organized to support economic development on the 'technology frontier'.

11.3.2. Changing Direction in the Education System's Selection of Elites

The reorganization of the structure of qualifications is inseparable from another institutional transformation. One of the major features of the present period has been the reorientation of the system of elites from the public to private sector. A number of studies have pointed to the role of the upper branches of the French civil service coming from the elite engineering schools and the civil service college (ENA) in conducting a State-led economic policy based on their control of the larger enterprises which were nationalized in 1945 and 1981 (Suleiman 1995). Hancké (2001) shows quite clearly how the centre of gravity of this system of coordination was reoriented towards private enterprise during the 1990s. This occurred in three phases: the privatizations beginning in 1986; the break-up during the first half of the 1990s of the 'hard core' of institutional (i.e. public) shareholders which had been put in place in order to avoid takeovers by foreign capital; and finally, the massive entry of the pension funds, for the most part American, into the capital of the large firms of France's CAC-40 index (an average of 40 per cent).

In fact, the members of these elite networks enjoyed a privileged position within the three 'worlds' of finance, major industrial concerns, and State administrations. This meant that they were able to mobilize resources in the interests of a management structure which was autonomous both with regard to the State (something new) and with regard to the greatly weakened union organizations (less recent). Considerable public resources—employment incentives to speed up productive restructuring, new human resources produced by the school system, and aid from the newly created regional governments for industrial and technological development—bolstered the reorganizations carried out by this newly autonomous management.

What remains to be seen, however, is whether the growing weight of the financial markets and pension funds is not going to favour market-led rather than firm-led adjustments. The evolution of corporate governance (see Goyer 2001) probably makes France the most likely of all the CMEs to swing towards adjustments of the liberal market economy kind (see Amable and Petit 2002). Outside of the public sector, the trade unions and employee representatives in general are not in a position to oppose such changes which contrast to the prevailing situations in most of the other CMEs. In any case, this transition will not be lacking in fits and starts, as demonstrated by the State's periodic return to centre stage in the area of company restructuring, to the great displeasure of Brussels.[9]

The construction of a new enterprise management structure is thus weakened by two factors: the ability, in the medium term, to reconcile economies of scale and industrial niches within a work organization which remains hierarchical; and the protection of corporate management from the stock market.

11.4. EXHAUSTION OR RESILIENCE OF THE INSTITUTIONAL MECHANISMS FOR PRODUCING 'COMPLEX HI-TECH ENGINEERING GOODS'?

The higher education and research system has played a determinant role in supporting a mission-oriented innovation model. It has backed up the latter's industrial successes but has also compensated for certain of its failures (e.g. computer science).

11.4.1. The Limits of a Mission-Oriented Innovation Model and its 'Colbertist' Version in France

The term 'mission' refers to technological fields which are of strategic value to the State (Ergas 1992). The main features of this model are the centralization of decision-making processes, the definition of objectives within government programmes, the large number of firms involved, and the creation of a special public agency endowed with discretionary powers to coordinate operations. The relations between science and innovation are explicitly set out and correspond to what is generally known as the 'Colbertist' model (see Laredo and Mustar 2001). This set of arrangement sets the relations between science and innovation under the aegis of a 'higher' socio-economic entity, since scientific policy and national policy are taken to have a common objective.

The organization is based on the 'large-scale technological programme' model, in which a public agency, a higher education and research institution, and a leading industrial group (and/or several other privileged operateurs) participate, supported by a series of sub-contractors. It operates on the basis of a classical hierarchical pyramid, the prototype for which originated in the military industrial field. The objectives of the programme, the actors who participate in it, the operations to be launched and their timing are all strictly defined a priori. This highly industrial, managerial approach with a voluntarist, modernizing bias is largely coordinated by leading corps and the elite Grandes Ecoles for engineers and by applied research centres under governmental control to which ministerial policy is directly transmitted.

Certain authors have referred to this as a 'top-down' innovation model, 'suitable for dealing with the complex technological products encountered in large public infrastructures'.[10] This kind of organizational framework has turned out to be a particularly useful one for manufacturing high technology products sold on public markets (aeronautics, space, military, nuclear, telecommunications, etc.).

11.4.1.1. A Typical Case: Success in the Telecom Industry

Aspects of this framework are particular to France. There is a historic 'telecommunications circle' in France which established strong linkages between science and industry by bringing together the different players including the Ministry of Telecommunications, France Telecom (the French telephone company, recently privatized), the Centre National des Etudes en Télécommunications (National Centre for Telecommunications Research, CNET) and the three national telecommunications schools. The schools have some 2,000 engineering students as well as 400 doctoral candidates and 400 research professors distributed across a hundred laboratories. With their strong potential for combining training and research, these schools constitute a crossroad of scientific production and the dissemination of results and the success of the telecommunications industry is not unrelated to this institutional infrastructure. The historic 'telecommunications circle' has been disrupted, however, by the recent deregulation and partial privatization of France Telecom.

11.4.1.2. Information Technology: Failure in Hardware Manufacturing, Success in Services

At the various stages in the development of the IT industry, French hardware manufacturers were largely incapable, despite spurts of inventiveness, not only of translating technological advances into industrial products but even of understanding the new opportunities these advances offered.

Nevertheless, French providers of IT services have had considerable success both on the domestic and wider European markets. The argument advanced here is that a very active education policy, particularly at the higher education level, has produced a supply of valuable competences. It has to be acknowledged, though, that the hardware industry also had these same resources at its disposal. However, the software firms were able to exploit the competitive advantage of proximity between clients and suppliers, whereas Bull was scarcely in a position to do so. Moreover, the software firms did not have to overcome the same barriers to entry as hardware manufacturers.

The sector is highly dependent upon the quality of its human resources, as is the case with the majority of services based on high-level technical knowledge. French computer engineering services firms cream off a significant share of newly qualified engineers from the Grandes Ecoles. The mutual attraction established between these firms and the 'best engineers' is certainly one of the strengths of the French IT services sector. Besides, the French higher education system has been able to increase its supply of computer engineers without compromising the quality of its training. The entire French economy has thus benefited from the production of increasingly well-trained IT professionals. As a result, mobilizing societal resources produced by the education system has produced some very positive effects. For example, certain French software firms excel in scientific calculation or the production of state-of-the-art software because of their proximity to the aerospace and nuclear industries.

While French companies in the computer services sector have managed to defend their domestic market and capture positions of strength on the international consulting market, they have not been able to do the same in the area of standardized software development. This is an activity which arguably demands a high level of risk-taking for technological breakthroughs (radical innovation) of the sort typically generated by small-size start-ups which are 'guided by "high-powered" market incentives' (Casper, Lehrer, and Soskice 1999).

11.4.2. Inability to Develop a Diffusion-Oriented Innovation Model: A Failure of the Higher Education System

The reasons for this failure are multiple. Some bear no direct relationship with higher education per se, such as the shortage of venture capital or the extreme scarcity of business angels, the excessive polarization of public funding for research in mission-oriented sectors, the inefficiency of aid schemes for the SMEs, and the lack of incentives for researchers to develop their knowledge in the private sector (for a critical analysis see Branciard and Verdier 2003).

We focus here on those factors more explicitly connected to the higher education system in order to explain the difficulty public policies have encountered in encouraging the emergence of a diffusion-oriented innovation model.[11] These overlap once again with the conclusions of the Aghion-Cohen report (2004), intended to explain the difficulty of 'French-style' public institutions and organizations to promote entry into a system producing radical innovations through competitiveness at the 'technology frontier' and not simply through a strategy of incremental innovation.

11.4.2.1. Ph.D. Theses: Increased Numbers and Uncertainty

Training through research, although recognized in all the industrialized countries, 'still has to acquire its letters of nobility in France' (Cohen and Le Déaut 1999). This expression, close to that of 'academic nobility' dear to Pierre Bourdieu, is a good indication of the distance that remains to be covered in facts and mindset alike.

Between 1992 and 1997, the overall number of theses completed rose by 29 per cent, with particularly sharp increases in the social sciences (+45 per cent) and large disparities among physical and life sciences: stagnation in chemistry (+1 per cent); a slight increase in fundamental biology (+9 per cent); a veritable explosion in 'applied biology/ecology' (+67 per cent); and a considerable increase in engineering (+31 per cent); and in physics (+30 per cent) (see OST 2000).[12]

The growth of doctoral studies stems not only from the overall expansion of higher education but also from public intervention which has done its best to increase the possibilities for thesis funding, job openings in the academic arena, and the bonus for dissertation and research supervision (Cohen and Le Déaut 1999). The rates of funding through grants (private and public, excluding salaried doctoral students) are high in the 'hard' sciences, ranging from 72.8 per cent in applied biology or ecology to 89.5 per cent in physics, with an average of 63.2 per cent, as compared to 24.6 per cent in the social sciences.

Overall, the examination of labour market entry conditions for Ph.D.s shows that 'the path of training through research does not [yet] seem to be totally recognised in France' (Bourdon 1999). The majority of Ph.D.s still enter the public sector (62 per cent in 2004) and primarily in public research and higher education (47 per cent). Furthermore, 'among youth from the 1994 cohort holding an in-company research post in March 1997, only 8.7 per cent held purely academic Ph.D.s. Fully 63.7 per cent held an engineering school diploma, 23.6 per cent a lesser university diploma, and 3.7 per cent an engineering Ph.D.' (see Beltramo, Paul, and Perret 1999). In the business world, the societal image of the engineer trained in a specialized school still dominates recruitment to the R&D function (see Lanciano and Nohara, this volume). In the large companies, the title of engineer opens possibilities for internal mobility towards other functions which are less accessible to purely academic Ph.D.s. This encourages a model of innovation based on a, 'high degree of human circulation and hybridisation of knowledge between research activities and the other functions' (Béret 2000) which favours incremental innovation.

Along with the ever-present weight of the Grandes Ecoles–university divide, these features show the limits of political voluntarism in the area, as the authors of the parliamentary mission on research priorities implicitly recognize: 'The research sector, for reasons of French company culture, recruits less than 20 percent of the PhDs trained in our universities.... It is clear that concrete proposals for increasing the recruitment of PhDs in the private sector are indispensable, (Cohen and Le Déaut 1999).

Structural difficulties in channelling Ph.D.s, and all those having advanced graduate studies, towards the companies help to explain why the number of researchers per inhabitant is relatively low in France. If this ratio is comparable to that found in Germany and the UK, it is considerably lower than that in the US and Japan despite a sharp increase during the 1980s (from 3.6 per thousand in 1981 to 6 per thousand in 1998). But above all—and this is our main point—it must be stressed that the relative presence of in-company researchers in France is the lowest of all the industrialized countries with the exception of Spain and Italy.

11.4.2.2. The Ambiguity of Post-Docs: Job Queue or Career Path?

Post-docs have been enjoying a rapid increase. Among those awarded a Ph.D. in 2001, 31 per cent held post-doctoral fellowships after the defence of their theses, against 21.7 per cent in 1996, with the proportion varying between 9 per cent for those in social sciences to more than 47 per cent in biology, medicine, and health (Giret 2005). The double bind of the drop in the number of academic jobs offered to Ph.D.s between 1993 and 1997 and the sharp increase in the number of theses completed, 'has amplified the gap between the number of Ph.D.s and the number of researcher or lecturer posts. This has created the phenomenon of the job queue; many candidates who are unsuccessful in recruitment examinations for getting a job in the public sector decide to do a post-doc while waiting to reapply the next year with a more solid CV' (Cohen and Le Déaut 1999). The fact that this segment of the labour market is 'societally' dominated by young engineers coming from the Grandes Ecoles makes reorientation towards the private sector all the more uncertain (Lanciano and Nohara, this volume).

This situation makes the stabilization of another, more research-orientated model for the labour market entry of Ph.D.s even more crucial: the start-ups, as incarnated in the SMEs, which allocate relatively more money to basic research (Béret 2000). Characterized by more intensive external mobility, as well as by a greater representation of Ph.D.s and those holding foreign diplomas, these small-scale companies constitute a domain of innovation which, though just beginning to emerge, is of strategic importance for the future. Certain complementary resources in initial or continuing training might well bolster the creation of these new all too rare enterprises at this stage.

11.4.2.3. A (Diminishing?) Lag in Entrepreneurship Training

Business start-ups do not depend solely on the quality of the knowledge produced by fundamental research. It is also necessary to have access to the relevant competences in order to respond to customers and face up to competitors in new markets which often remain to be invented. However, 'if the French educational system produces large cohorts of science graduates, it does not sufficiently push the young talents towards entrepreneurial careers, in accordance with a scale of values forged by a history which, in this century, has reserved an exceptional role for State entrepreneurship' (OECD 1999: 135).

This approach is reflected in the overall diagnosis of French higher education, which is said to, 'train employees more than it cultivates entrepreneurial talents' (Guillaume 1998), as demonstrated by the limited opportunities for training in entrepreneurship or SME management. Nonetheless, since 1995 there has been a clear trend towards the creation of such training programmes (15 in 1995, 155 in late 1998, plus 75 in the planning stage). This is, 'making entrepreneurship a recognised academic discipline, as in the United States' (Stéphane Marion, professor at the Ecole de Management in Lyons, cited by Reverchon 1999). Such an effort brings into play the forms of regulation and organization of higher-education structures which, in France, do not easily recognize new disciplines, especially when they come from the business world. Indeed, the difficulties of organizing public action in favour of innovation manifest themselves most clearly in relation to SMEs.

11.4.2.4. Organizational Complexity, Undersized Higher Education Institutions

The Balkanization of higher education in France is even more extreme than is the case for research. In addition to the 81 public universities with a population of 1,300,000 young people (excluding the polytechnics) there is a constellation of 238 engineering schools and 230 business schools which receive some 142,000 students by selection (Attali 1998). The Attali Report speaks of 'Gulliver tied up in knots' to characterize the higher education system. An often inefficient 'government of the universities' is caught between a ministerial supervision, which is much more extensive than the autonomy (partially formal) accorded the university presidents, and the feudalism of the training and research units, heirs of the old schools, which resist participation in any global policy for the institution. This is especially true because behind the national standardization of university rules and diplomas, 'an implicit hierarchy of universities has emerged. ... Their size and their means vary considerably from one university to another' (Cohen and Le Déhaut 1999). And in the name of the excellence of their training profiles, a number of the Grandes Ecoles jealously exercise their individual prerogatives, which only accentuates the Balkanization of the system, while it is far from certain that in the future these schools will have the necessary critical mass, notably in the area of research. The system as a whole is difficult to comprehend and is resistant to reform.

In this context, the evaluation of the universities by the present National Evaluation Committee clearly constitutes an advance in relation to a past characterized by the absence of any institutional mechanism for assessing higher education establishments. However, 'it is neither fast enough nor transparent enough. In general, it is not followed by any budget decision or reform. For the time being, it succeeds only in helping the universities to prepare for their own internal monitoring' (Attali 1998).

More generally, the evaluation of programmes, procedures, and institutions does not seem to be as reliable as the stakes would demand. It is supposed to lead to the elaboration of recommendations for the heads of the programmes or institutions, as well as the authorities requesting it. In fact, it must be recognized that the main concern is not to destabilize the 'scientific government' in place (Attali 1998: 19). It is not at all clear that such a structure is capable of facing up to the pressures of global competition in the field of research and education, which is all the more formidable given the spread of long distance education via the Internet.

11.4.3. The Development of Local Cooperative Relationships Between Industry and Research: An Opportunity for Local Resiliency?

Another paradox of the French situation has to do with the fact that the resources most important for going beyond the 'technology frontier' have emerged in part as the unanticipated result of major technology programmes of the past. ICTs and now nanotechnologies provide convincing examples.

The system of cooperation between industry and research in the French IT industry continues to be modelled in large part on a past policy of the French state for promoting large-scale scientific programmes (see Nohara and Verdier 2001).[13] As the case of the Plan-Calcul illustrates at the end of the 1960s, major scientific and industrial programmes have been implemented by public establishments with a large degree of financial autonomy. Centralization of technological innovation has gone hand in hand with a preoccupation with national and regional development, which has led the State to intervene by making financial contributions to regional economic development and installing scientific and technical infrastructures.

As far as the IT industry is concerned, the Plan-Calcul and the various national programmes designed to boost the electronics industry have contributed to the development of certain regional technological centres, in part through the choices made in the location of public sector research establishments (CNRS, INRIA, etc.), in part through the expansion of the engineering schools and to some degree through the establishment of research facilities by public and private companies with high scientific potential (CEA, the atomic agency, CNET—in telecommunications, etc.).

Apart from the Greater Paris region (Ile-de-France), which accounts for fully half of the national R&D capacity, there are four other dynamic regional centres for electronic technologies with a high IT component.

By far the most important centre outside Paris is the Grenoble region. Often dubbed the French 'Silicon Valley', this area occupies first place in the European league table for microelectronic research. In particular, the semiconductor industry benefits from synergies based on a close link between research and production. This region accounts for 10 per cent of national expenditure on R&D in electronics. The region has a strong university tradition, which acts as a catalyst for cooperation between public sector research establishments and engineering schools and companies, including both large groups (Bull, Hewlett-Packard, Thomson, Cap-Gemini, etc.) and small- and medium-sized firms. The latter produce hard disc reading heads, are engaged in optoelectronics, produce software packages for structural calculation, and develop software validation tools (case of an INRIA spin-off). With the support of national and regional public agencies and bodies, this district is now becoming a major player in nanotechnologies: the main private stakeholders are FMN, European players like ST Microelectronics, or American ones like Motorola.

The second centre is constituted around Motorola and IT firms linked to the aerospace/space industry in the Toulouse region. This concentration was explicitly created through national policies in aerospace, space sciences, and electronics, namely the decentralization of the CNES (National Centre for

Space Research), the location of Airbus-Industrie, and the arrival of Motorola within the framework of the Plan-Calcul. This productive infrastructure is fed by flows of engineers trained by engineering schools such as the Ecole Nationale Supérieure de l'Aéronautique as well as scientific universities. The third centre, in the Brittany region, is organized around digital telecommunications technology (IT, telecommunications, and networks). The fourth centre, Sophia-Antipolis in the Nice region, was one of the first prototypes of the now-familiar science park (Longhi 1999).

In this kind of institutional configuration, the State is no longer acting on its own behalf in pursuit of 'royal' objectives determined from above, but rather, permits local actors to move towards the realization of a common good (Salais 1998).

According to this model, the future site of the coproduction of knowledge lies at the intersection between three interacting institutional spheres, the university and the research organizations, industry, and the public authorities.

This attempt to create bridges between academic research structures and industry by integrating the knowledge-generating infrastructures into the innovation-producing systems might lead to the existence of three-part networks reflecting the involvement of these three kinds of institutional spheres, and to the emergence of hybrid organizations at the interfaces between the three (Etzkowitz and Leydersdorf 2000). The aim of the bridging schemes is to create an environment propitious to innovation including spin-offs originating from the universities and to produce research sites at which to launch economically stimulating multiple initiatives based on scientific knowledge, strategic alliances between firms of various sizes working at various technological levels, public research laboratoires, and groups of university research workers. In encouraging the implantation of R&D structures bridging the traditional frontiers between institutions (the public–private sector, academic or applied research, etc.) and founding scientific and industrial parks at the local level, these public interventions subscribe to the organized accumulation of knowledge and the creation of innovative skills at the micro, meso, and macroeconomic levels combined.

11.5. CONCLUSION

In the context of the 'knowledge economy' paradigm, the paradoxes and tensions observed in the evolution of the French higher education and research system are instructive for an appreciation of the impact and limits of public policies in this area. As we have seen, the rapid increase in enrolment rates during the 1988–98 period was accompanied by a very clear 'vocationalization' of curricula. This was particularly true in higher education, which made a significant effort to develop a system of higher technological education recognized and appreciated by industry. These educational resources were mobilized for an in-depth productive reorganization, notably in the large industrial concerns but also in the financial sector. This reorganization was carried out by the elites traditionally coming from the Grandes Ecoles, especially those producing the upper-level branches of the civil service. What distinguishes this phase of the restructuring, as Hancké (2002) has clearly shown, is the managerial elite's growing autonomy in relation to the State. This has ensured the return of France's major firms to industrial competitiveness and high profitability. Nonetheless, such an 'economy coordinated by an elite network' seems fragile in so far as it is challenged by the firms of other coordinated economies which can rely on compromises reached with labour.

These questions are all the more vital in face of serious doubts about the ability of vast technological programmes to renew a capacity for innovation on the 'technology frontier'. This was achieved in the past through a mission-oriented innovation policy centred on hi-tech goods and largely realized within the framework of State markets. As the telecommunications example shows, this model relied heavily on the excellence of the elite engineering schools and specialized public research centres. This institutional configuration, however, does not respond as efficiently to the demands of the 'diffusion-oriented' model.

From this standpoint, the French experience, in spite of the considerable expansion of its higher education system, reveals an inadequacy and a tension. Entrepreneurship training, notably in order to develop knowledge and create hi-tech start-ups, seems largely inadequate; training through research is not really recognized in the private sector, which is reluctant to hire Ph.D.s to man R&D teams if the Ph.D. thesis is not combined with an engineering diploma from a Grande Ecole. In addition, masters level vocational training programmes tend to attract the best university students and thus to divert them from training through research. As a result, the base of knowledge and competences produced by the higher education and research system seems much too narrow for a diffusion-oriented innovation model. If the recruitment pool for the top levels of higher education at the highest levels is not considerably broadened, the tension between a policy of vocational-oriented training and one valuing career paths based on training through research will only be reinforced. In some way, this might give rise to a tension between the 'learning industry' *à la française*, an unquestionable success of the vocationalization of studies as attested by the emergence of a new form of coordinated economy, and the 'knowledge economy' which is struggling to achieve social legitimacy.

One irony of this history, however, is the emergence of highly dynamic technology parks which are spin-offs of the heyday of the great technological programmes and notably of one of the most flagrant industrial failures, the Plan-Calcul which was intended to stimulate a national computer industry. The new forms of public policy likely to support the growth of these technology parks and promote the creation of others remain to be invented.[14]

NOTES

1. These distinctions recall the typologies of the French Regulation School (Boyer 2002), which identifies four forms of capitalism which are 'dominant financial market, meso-corporate, social-democratic, and State-driven'.
2. See Postel-Vinay (2002) who, in the area of research, advocates adoption of the American model pure and simple.
3. These two structures train technicians within a two-year programme. Diploma-holders may then enter working life or opt to continue their studies in another programme (university, sometimes engineering school).
4. It should be pointed out, however, that the internal regulation of the university system gives strong impetus in this direction. Thus, the Higher Education Division, which has been negotiating four-year contracts with the universities since the mid-1980s to develop the overall map of the programmes offered, encourages them to develop vocationally-oriented training.
5. The Brevet de technician supérieur (BTS) and the Diplôme universitaire de technologie (DUT) are two-year post-*baccalauréat* higher technician training programmes for industry.
6. In 1998, the social sciences accounted for 60 per cent of the total number of students.
7. For further details, see Martinelli and Molinari (2000).
8. In terms of early retirement, France has the lowest rate of labour-force participation for the 55–60 age group among all OECD countries.
9. It was indeed under the aegis of a government defending liberal economic policies that the State intervened in 2003–4 to maintain the autonomy of the French management of major groups: the Aventis–Sanofi merger in favour of a French board of directors, the defence of GEC-Alstom against the risks of industrial break-up and takeover by German competitors, and so on.
10. R. Barré and P. Papon, 'La compétitivité technologique de la France', in Guillaume, Henri 1998, *Rapport de mission sur la technologie et l'innovation*, submitted to the Ministry for National Education, Research and Technology, the Ministry of

Economy, Finance and Industry, and the Secretary of State for Industry, Paris, 216–27, 1998.

11. Such a policy is characterized by its decentralized nature. The role of public bodies is limited and the accent is placed on the association of cooperative forms of research and institutions promoting the systematic dissemination of scientific knowledge and technology. Innovations emerge locally on the basis of researcher–entrepreneur initiatives supported by multiple partnerships.

12. In 2002, 17 per cent of Ph.D. theses were completed in social sciences, 14 per cent in engineering, 10 per cent in mathematics, 10 per cent in chemistry, 5 per cent in fundamental biology, and 5 per cent in applied biology/ecology.

13. The following paragraphs are based on Nohara and Verdier (2001).

14. See the recent 'Beffa report' (2005) based on the main conclusions of a commission led by the Chairman of MNF Saint Gobain, calling for support to develop 60 projects for competitive clusters, after a selection process.

REFERENCES

Aghion, Ph. and Cohen, E. (2003). *Education et Croissance*, Conseil d'Analyse Economique, La Documentation Française, Paris.

Amable, B. and Hancké, R. (2001). 'Innovation and Industrial Renewal in France in Comparative Perspective,' *Industry and Innovation*, 8(2): 113–35.

—— and Petit P. (2002). 'La diversité des systèmes sociaux d'innovation et d eproduction dans les années 1990', in R. Solow (ed.), *Institution et Innovation, de la recherhe aux systèmes sociaux d'innovation.* Paris: Albin Michel.

Attali, J. (1998). *Pour un modèle européen d'enseignement supérieur*, rapport au Ministre de l'éducation nationale, de la recherche et de la technologie, miméo.

Barré, R. and Papon, P. (1998). 'La compétitivité technologique de la France,' in H. Guillaume 1998, *Rapport de mission sur la technologie et l'innovation*, submitted to the Ministry for National Education, Research and Technology, the Ministry of Economy, Finance and Industry and the Secretary of State for Industry, Paris.

Beaud, M. and Pialoux, M. (1999). *Retour sur la condition ouvrière, Enquête aux usines Peugeot de Sochaux-Montbéliard.* Paris: Fayard.

Beffa, J.-L. (2005). 'Pour une nouvell politique industrielle', Paris: La documentation française (Collection des rapports officiels).

Beltramo, J.-P., Paul, J.-J., and Perret, C. (1999). 'Le recrutement des chercheurs et l'organisation des activités scientifiques dans l'industrie', *Journée AFSE*, Nice-Sophia Antipolis.

Béret, P. (1992). 'Salaires et marchés internes'. *Economie Appliquée*, 45/2: 5–22.

—— (2000). *Les transformations de l'espace de qualification des chercheurs des entreprises*, rapport pour le Commissariat général du plan, LEST, Aix en Provence.

Bourdon, J. (1999). 'Formation et normes d'emploi dans le secteur de la reproduction des connaissances avancées: convergence ou divergences'. *Séminaire 'Enseignement supérieur et recherche' de l'IDEP*, miméo, CNRS-IREDU, Dijon.

Boyer, R. (2002). 'Varieties of Capitalism et Théorie de la Régulation', *L'Année de la Régulation*. Paris: Presses de Sciences Po, pp. 125–194.

Branciard, A. and Verdier, E. (2003). 'La réforme de la politique scientifique française face à la mondialisation: l'émergence incertaine d'un nouveau référentiel d'action publique', *Politiques et Management Public*, 21(2): 61–81.

Buechtemann, Ch. and Verdier, E. (1998). 'Education and Training Regimes: Macro-Institutional Evidence', *Revue d'économie politique*, 108(3): 291–320.

Campinos-Dubernet, M. (1995). 'Le baccalauréat professionnel: une innovation?', *Formation Emploi*, 49: 3–30.

Casper, S., Lehrer, M., and Soskice, D. (1999). 'Can High-Technology Industries Prosper in Germany? Institutional Frameworks and the Evolution of the German Software and Biotechnoly Industries', *Industry and Innovation*, 6(1): 5–25.

Cohen, P. and Le, Déaut, J.-Y. (1999). *Priorités à la recherche. 60 propositions pour la synergie entre recherche et enseignement supérieur, la mobilité et les échanges, l'évaluation et l'autonomie des jeunes*, Special Report Submitted to the French Prime Minister.

Ergas, H. (1992). '*A Future for Mission-Oriented Industrial Policies? A Critical Review of Developments in Europe*'. Paris: OECD.

Esping-Andersen, G. (1998). *Les Trois mondes de l'Etat-providence: essai sur le capitalisme moderne*. Paris: Presses Universitaires de France.

Etzkowitz, H. and Leydesdorff, L. (2000). 'The Dynamics of Innovation: From National Systems and "Mode 2" to a Triple Helix of University-Industry-Government Relations', *Research Policy*, 29: 109–23.

Giret, J.-F. (2005). 'De la thèse à l'emploi: les débuts professionnels des jeunes titulaires d'un doctorat', *BREF*, 215.

Goyer, M. (2001). 'Corporate Governance and the Innovation System in France. The development of Firms' Capabilities and Strategies', *Industry and Innovation*, 8(2): 135–58.

Guillaume, H. (1998). *Rapport de mission sur la technologie et l'innovation*, submitted to the French Ministry of National Education, Research and Technology, the Ministry of Economy, Finance and Industry and the Secretary of State for Industry, Paris.

Hall, P. and Soskice, D. (eds.) (2001). *Varieties of Capitalism, the Institutional Foundations of Comparative Advantage*. Oxford: Oxford University Press.

Hancké, R. (2001). 'Revisiting the French Model: Coordination and Restructuring in the French Industry', in P. Hall and D. Soskice (eds.), *Varieties of Capitalism, the Institutional Foundations of Comparative Advantage*. Oxford: Oxford University Press.

—— (2002). *Large Firms and Institutional Change: Industrial Renewal and Economic Restructuring in France*. Oxford: Oxford University Press.

Larédo, Ph. and Mustar, Ph. (2001). 'French Research and Innovation Policy: Two Decades of Transformation', in Ph. Larédo and Ph. Mustar (eds.), *Research and Innovation Policies in the New Global Economy: An International Comparative Analysis*. Cheltenham UK: Edward Elgar.

Longhi, C. (1999). 'Networks, Collective Learning and Technology Development in Innovative Technology Regions: The Case of Sophia Antipolis', *Regional Studies*, 33(4): 333–42.

Maillard, D. and Veneau, P. (2003). 'La licence professionnelle: une nouvelle acceptation de la professionnalisation au sein de l'université?', in G. Felouzis (ed.), *Les mutations actuelles de l'Université*. Paris: PUF.

Martinelli, D. and Molinari, (2000). *L'insertion professionnelle en 1999 des diplômés de l'enseignement supérieur*. Coll. Documents, n° 150, Céreq, Marseille.

Maurice, M., Sellier, F., and Silvestre, J.-J. (1986). *The social foundations of industrial power. A comparison of France and Germany*. Cambridge, MA.: MIT Press.

——— Mannari, H., Takeoka, Y. and Inoki, T. (1988). 'Des entreprises françaises et japonaises face à la mécatronique, acteurs et organisation de la dynamique industrielle'. mimeo LEST, Aix en Provence.

Möbus, M. and Verdier, E. (2000). Diplômes professionnels et coordination de la formation et de l'emploi: l'élaboration d'un signal en France et d'une règle en Allemagne', *Economie Publique*, 201–30.

Nohara, H. and Verdier, E. (2001). 'Sources of Resilience in the Computer and Software Industries in France', *Industry and Innovation*, 8(2): 201–20.

OECD (1999). France, *Etudes économiques*, Paris: OECD.

OST (2000). *Science et Technologie, indicateurs 2000*, rapport de l'Observatoire des Sciences et Techniques, sous la direction de Barré, Rémi. Paris: *Economica*.

Péan, S. (2001). 'Les bacheliers et leur accès immédiat dans l'enseignement supérieur à la rentrée 1999', *Note d'information* 01.15, mars, Ministère de l'Education Nationale, Paris.

Postel-Vinay, O. (2002). *Le grand gâchis: splendeur et misère de la Science française*. Paris: Eyrolles.

Reverchon, A. (1999). 'Les formations à l'entrepreunariat'. Supplément Economie Emploi, *Le Monde* du 18 mai.

Salais, R. (1998). 'Action publique et conventions: état des lieux', in J. Commaille and B. Jobert (eds.), *Les métamorphoses de la régulation politique*. Paris: Librairie generale de droit et de jurisprudence.

Storper, M. and Salais, R. (1997). *Worlds of Production: The Action Frameworks of the Economy*. Cambridge, MA: Harvard University Press.

Suleiman, E. (1995). *Les ressorts cachés de la réussite française*. Paris: Le Seuil.

Vincens, J. (2001). 'Dynamique de l'éducation et systèmes éducatifs', *Revue européenne de formation professionnelle*, Thessaloniki, CEDEFOP.

——— and Steedman, H. (2000). 'Dynamique des systèmes éducatifs et qualification des générations'. Report for the EDEX Project (Educational Expansion and Labour Market) TSER No. SOCE–CT–98–2039, European Commission.

12

Science–Industry Links and the Labour Markets for Ph.D.s

Caroline Lanciano-Morandat and Hiroatsu Nohara

12.1. INTRODUCTION

In order to flow between academia and industry, knowledge and competences must take on a tangible form: scientific articles, data, patents, technical objects, computer programs, trainees, engineers, post-docs, etc. Although it is the task of the scientific community to formalize or codify knowledge (David and Foray 1995), some knowledge remains tacit: a part of the new knowledge generated remains embodied in human actors in the form of competences. Since knowledge is fundamentally 'sticky' (von Hippel 1988) and tacit knowledge is context-dependent, it cannot easily be separated from the contexts or individuals that generated it. Even if we accept Callon's argument (Callon 1991) that technical objects are also actors that serve as a medium for human capacities and play a part in constructing networks, we would argue that a particular status should be attributed to human actors such as researchers, post-docs, professors, experts, and so on. These human actors play a central role in the structuring of the hybrid 'space' that is emerging at the interface between academia and industry. As occupational categories, they are constructed through the interdependent relationships between, on the one hand, forms of socialization forged within the higher education and research system (HERS) and, on the other, modes of organizational behaviour structured by firms' R&D and HRM practices. The principles governing the functioning of institutions and the linkage between the HERS and firms, which are often unique to a region or country, are embodied in these human actors. At the same time, these communities of actors draw on the cognitive resources at their disposal and on the principles governing their professional *modus operandi* in order to help specify this hybrid space and construct specializations in various technological fields.

In view of the importance of human actors in the circulation of knowledge, the formation and mobility of the competences embodied in workers becomes a crucial factor in any analysis of technology transfer. For this reason, we will attempt to introduce the notion of 'intermediate labour market' with a view to capturing the new modes of coordination between universities and firms, particularly by analysing the movements of individuals (or graduates). This intermediate labour market can be seen as one of the 'bridging institutions' that function as intermediaries in the transfer of knowledge and competences between the academic and industrial spaces. It goes without saying that this mobility, embedded as it is in a set of societal contexts, has to be captured across the entire set of institutions that contribute to the production and circulation of knowledge (Eyraud, Marsden, Silvestre 1990). By adopting such an approach, we will be able to reveal societal specificities in the generation of scientific knowledge.

12.2. THE EMERGENCE OF NEW TYPES OF COORDINATION BETWEEN SCIENCE AND TECHNOLOGY

12.2.1. Hybridization of the Academic and Industrial Spaces

As technology and science converge to produce interactive innovation in accordance with the chain-link model (Kline and Rosenberg 1986), industry and academia intersect and begin to merge with each other. The scientific labour market,[1] hitherto divided into the 'republic of the scientists' and the 'kingdom of the technologists', cannot remain unaffected by such a trend. Although these two spaces still have their own aims and principles governing the utilization and evaluation of results, their convergence gives rise, nevertheless, to hybrid forms of rules and coordinating practices. It seems to us that at least three new types of labour market segments can be identified, all of them produced by the hybridization of two spaces or domains. They give rise in turn to new modes of functioning, involving new forms of mobility or new actors at the interface between academia and industry (see Figure 12.1).

Restrictions, relative to growing needs, on the resources available not only to universities and research organizations but also to firms, combined with an increasingly short innovation cycle, have led to changes in their innovation strategies. They are all now seeking to establish partnerships in order to pool resources, minimize risk or increase synergies. Thus, collaborative relations between research units and firms are proliferating and taking on forms that are increasingly contractual, long-term, and productive for both parties.

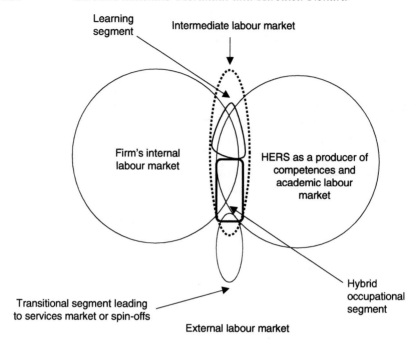

Figure 12.1. The new scientific labour market: An intermediate labour market between academia and industry

Such collaboration may take the form of a framework 'research agreement' laying down the conditions for a series of contracts between the two parties over a stipulated period, a research consortium, a joint laboratory, or even jointly funded doctoral programmes, in which the students are jointly supervised by the firm and the research institution to which they are affiliated. These links give rise to networks through which not only knowledge but also, and above all, scientists themselves (private and public sector researchers or research-active university teaching staff) circulate on a temporary or permanent basis (Laredo and Muster 2001). This increasingly dense two-way traffic constitutes a segment that we denote by the term 'hybrid occupational'. It is in this *first segment* that the greatest share (in both quantitative and qualitative terms) of hybrid careers straddling the academic and industrial domains is to be found.

Similarly, the formation of competences is increasingly taking place on a collaborative basis. As a result, a growing share of scientists is being jointly produced by the HERS and firms, which is creating what might be called a *learning segment*. There are two typical scenarios in this second segment. In the first, doctoral students contribute to their institution's output in exchange for grants. In view of their numbers, they constitute a pool of skilled labour that is essential to the scientific output of HERS research units. In the second, increasingly frequent scenario, students are enrolled in programmes whose content is common to firms and HERS research units; examples include the CIFRE programme in France and the CASE scheme in the UK. Doctoral students are selected and jointly funded on the basis of criteria negotiated between the academic and industrial partners and their academic progress and/or work in industry are jointly monitored and evaluated. Increasingly, they are guaranteed subsequent employment in the organization in which they have completed their education.

The *third segment*, which we describe as 'transitional' between the academic and industrial spaces, is characterized either by the creation of 'new services', such as consultancy services, which contribute to the innovation process and straddle the academic and commercial worlds, or by spin-offs set up by researchers or universities. Postdoctoral contracts proliferate in this segment. Located half-way between 'training' and precarious scientific employment, such contracts give firms access to a highly skilled workforce, a veritable repository of new knowledge and know-how, without having to commit themselves to a period of employment greater than one-and-a-half years. They also enable research institutes to employ new Ph.D.s to work on projects, while they wait for a permanent position or to implement technology transfer projects aimed at industry. Sometimes, the same individual may hold a succession of post-doc positions, particularly in high-tech areas such as biotechnology. Nevertheless, this holding of a succession of post-doc positions, which is caused by the 'queuing' phenomenon, often makes it more difficult for the individuals concerned to obtain a permanent academic position (Mangematin and Mandran 1999).

Thus the scientific labour market is evolving from a form in which there was a clear distinction between academic and industrial careers towards increasingly less 'pure' and increasingly more 'mixed' or hybrid forms (Paradeise 1988).

12.3. THE EMERGENCE OF THE 'INTERMEDIATE LABOUR MARKET'

The existence of these various, mutually interacting segments is leading to the construction of a new type of labour market in which the networks through which scientists circulate new career paths, such as those offered by academic spin-offs, are disrupting the previously well-established mobility system. We use the term intermediate labour market to denote this new market because it is the product of different dynamics jostling up against each other in a new hybrid space, and at its core lies the threefold relationship between industrial, academic, and public actors that is familiar from 'triple helix' theory (Ezkovitz and Leydesdorf 2000).

In our definition, the intermediate labour market denotes a set of coordinating mechanisms by means of which two (or more) partners are able to procure the human resources, competences, or expertise required to generate new ideas or realize innovations. This notion goes beyond the general definition of the labour market as a system for allocating labour through the price mechanism. It is a notion in which the principles governing markets and those governing organizations interpenetrate, reflecting a process of hybridization between what economists customarily describe as the 'external market', in which adjustments are effected through both the price mechanism and the free movement of individuals, and the 'internal market', whose rules (embodied in incentive systems) guide the construction of career paths over time (Doeringer and Piore 1971). This hybrid space is essentially structured around the use of mobility networks, which give tangible form to the compromises that emerge from 'bilateral governance'[2]—in the sense of the term ascribed to it by Williamson (1985). Within this space, and despite differences arising out of frequently contradictory institutional objectives, the strategies of universities and those of firms, together with the individual choices made by students and researchers, come up against each other in order to determine common interests.

12.4. THE LABOUR MARKET FOR PH.D.s IN INTERNATIONAL PERSPECTIVE

Drawing on the results of the SESI European research project,[3] we will make an initial attempt to compare the conditions under which science Ph.D.s are produced and integrated into the labour market in five countries (US, France, Great Britain, Japan, and Germany).[4]

It is true that this category of actors is only one of the elements around which the intermediate labour market is structured. However, quite apart from the fact that they account for the highest share of the annual flows of scientists and therefore of the circulation of knowledge, their training and integration into the labour market brings into play a whole set of public and private institutions in the sphere of science and innovation (Buechtemann and Verdier 1998).

Thus our aim here is to highlight a certain type of socialization the actors undergo in a given sectoral and/or national context by using the mode of production and deployment of Ph.D.s in science and engineering as our analytical tool. In other words, although the hybridization of the academic and industrial spaces is taking place everywhere, it takes different forms depending on the characteristics of the sectoral and/or national space whose pre-existing institutional arrangements exert a strong influence over the actors, in this case Ph.D.s and doctoral students, being socialized within it. In this sense, our analysis falls completely within the institutional framework of the NSI approach (Lundvall 1992, 1997; Nelson 1992; Edquist 1997). However, drawing on the lessons to be derived from Societal Analysis (Maurice, Sellier, and Silvestre 1982), we stress the importance of incorporating into the institutional analysis the notion of actors who, despite being socialized by the system, are also capable, as they go through their own learning processes, of acting on it and amending or modifying it.

We will begin by presenting some quantitative data on the production of Ph.D.s. We will then return to a more qualitative analysis, focusing on some of the aspects that structure the process whereby Ph.D.s are socialized.

12.4.1. Annual Flows of Ph.D.s in Natural Sciences and Engineering

We will briefly examine the state of the production of new Ph.D.s in the five countries. Table 12.1 summarizes the flows of Ph.D.s in 1997 and their evolution between the end of the 1980s and 1997 in all five countries.

Of the countries under consideration, the three European countries are, in relative terms, the largest producers of Ph.D.s. France heads the league table,

Table 12.1 Doctoral degrees in natural sciences and engineering, 1997

	UK	Germany	France	Japan	US
A) labour force (1,000 persons)	28,552	39, 455	26,404	67,110	133,943
B) Ph.D. S and E	6,315 (100)	9,499 (100)	7,333 (100)	5,769 (100)	19,309 (100)
Of which Ph.D. sciences	3,589 (57)	5,964 (63)	4,494 (61)	1,315 (23)	10,290 (53)
Of which Ph.D. engineering	2,726 (43)	3,535 (37)	2,939 (39)	4,454 (77)	9,019 (47)
A/B (ratio 0.000)	0.22	0.24	0.28	0.09	0.14
Ratio of progression (1989/1997)	1.28	1. 08[1]	1.74	1.70	1.28

Source: Calculated from NSF Science & Engineering indicators 1999.
Note: [1] For Germany, the ratio is for 1990 to 1997.

in terms of density, with 7,300 new Ph.D.s per year, closely followed by Germany (9,500) and the UK (6,300). The US is in a paradoxical situation: throughout the 1990s, it was the unchallenged leader in scientific output and technological innovation and yet the standard human capital indicators (R&D density in terms of personnel or Ph.D.s) for that period seem to be relatively mediocre. Nevertheless, in absolute terms, those indicators do record massive inflows into the scientific labour market of 19,000 new Ph.D.s. It should be noted, nevertheless, that in the US, one-third of doctorates in natural sciences and more than 40 per cent in engineering are submitted by foreign students, which shows that the international reputation of American research universities exerts considerable power abroad. If these foreign students are excluded, the ratio of Ph.D.s to the economically active population of the US drops to the level found in Japan, which lags avery long way behind the others in this respect. Moreover, like the US, Japan has a very pronounced bias towards engineering Ph.D.s, to the detriment of those in basic science. The European countries, in contrast, particularly France and Germany, where the public research institutions have a significant influence, produce more doctorates in natural sciences (Amable, Barre, and Boyer 1997).

Examination of the evolution over the 1990s reveals two trends. The first is the increasing level of the highest degree obtained by university graduates in the various scientific and technological disciplines, and in particular the rise in the number of Ph.D.s. Thus the production of Ph.D.s has risen in absolute terms in all the countries. However, the rate of increase varies from country to country: virtual stagnation in Germany, moderate growth in the US and the UK, and sustained growth in France and Japan. The second is the more or less pronounced slowdown (except in Japan) in the flows of new entrants into science and engineering faculties, despite the general trend towards widening access to higher education. Thus as early as the mid-1990s, Germany and the US were already experiencing a slight decline in the flows of new doctoral students. France and the UK have experienced the same phenomenon more recently, which does not bode well for the number of Ph.D.s produced in future. Germany is a particularly interesting case, since the country has already seen a drop in the absolute numbers of students enrolled in departments of electrical engineering, chemistry, biology, pharmacy, etc. This phenomenon, which can also be observed to varying extents in France and the UK, seems to be linked to two factors. The first is the economic boom of the late 1990s based on the new technologies, which absorbed many postgraduate students, and the other is the declining attractiveness of academic careers because of the saturation of the academic labour market.

12.5. ANALYSIS OF THE NATIONAL MODES OF PRODUCTION AND DEPLOYMENT OF PH.D.S

From our analytical perspective, the function of Ph.D.s—and of doctoral students—is threefold: they are the resources used to produce the scientific output of the teams within which they operate, the pool from which the next generation of scientists will be drawn, and the primary vector for the transfer of knowledge between academia and industry.[5] As a collective entity, they implement these three different functions, although individually they are often devoted to one function, according to their strategic choice. This category of young scientists as a whole is thus produced by and constitutes an institutional nexus which emerges at the frontiers between academia, industry, and public authorities. They reveal the quality of the intermediate space and at the same time contribute to forge this space.

In other words, we presume here that doctoral training investment and mobility are not merely the result of individual rational choice, as supposed often in the neoclassical literature. On the contrary, our basic assumption is that there exists the intermediate level of organizations between the macro public policy frameworks/regulatory institutions and the micro decisions at the individual level. Our analysis is precisely to focus on the organizational and institutional tensions created often by contradictory dynamics between policy objectives, goals of organizations (labs, universities, firms, etc.), and individual choices.

The production of Ph.D.s brings into play a multiplicity of institutions at various national or local levels and mobilizes the various resources available to them. The interaction between them requires the actors involved to adopt a variety of different behaviours based on a diversity of animating principles. Thus in order to reveal the various societal modes of the construction of new scientific knowledge and competences, we need simultaneously to analyse the socialization of the actors and the various institutional configurations. To this end, we will continue by analysing some of the essential elements that structure this process, such as the funding system, the nature of the contract between doctoral students and their supervising institutions (implicit contract, according to Stephan 1996), the rules governing the academic community, training-job transition, career paths, etc. (see Table A.12.1 in Annex).

12.5.1. The Funding of Doctoral Programmes

The US has the most highly systematized Ph.D. programmes, although they are decentralized and differ from university to university. The power of the graduate schools run by the research universities, which are characterized by their autonomy, the competitive environment in which they operate and, above all, their concentration (there are about fifty research universities of international standing), gives this model the status of an international reference point. The American system produces slightly fewer than 20,000 new Ph.D.s in science and engineering each year. Its scale makes it possible to rationalize academic programmes, manage research funds, tap the various sources of funding, and create the conditions for the efficient production of scientific output and Ph.D.s based on economies of scale. As far as funding is concerned, many students receive assistance from research funds gathered outside the university system but managed directly by the universities (and the individual research teams). These funds are used to establish assistant teaching or research posts. On the other hand, relatively little use is made of national or federal core funding. In other words, the quality—and the reputation—of individual research teams and universities depends to a large extent on their ability to tap the various sources of funding (federal, military, and private) that make it possible to put the 'best' doctoral students to work on promising topics. Thus reputation plays an essential part in effecting the match between financial resources and 'talent'.

Japan is one of the countries that produces the fewest scientific doctorates per year, whether measured in absolute or relative terms. This reflects the low status of basic science in that country and the low level of state investment in it. Weighed down by their oligarchic mode of governance based on the 'chair' system, which gives professors considerable independence, the universities have lacked the flexibility to set about transforming their doctoral programmes. Since the late 1990s, the state has been trying, nevertheless, to establish the so-called 'daigakuin daikagu', modelled on the American graduate schools, with a view to increasing the number of Ph.D.s produced and creating 10,000 postdoctoral positions in order to expand job opportunities within the university system (Kodama and Florida 1999). With a few exception, however, the major source of funding for doctoral students remains interest-free loans[6] from some specific associations.

In Europe, doctoral programmes are much less systematized than in the US and still reflect the various national institutional heritages (Clark 1993). Nevertheless, the three European countries under consideration here did initiate reforms during the 1990s, albeit in their own different ways.

The system in *France* is characterized by the fragmentation of university research teams and the dichotomy between the universities, on the one hand, and the elite Grandes Ecoles, on the other. In recent years, however, doctoral programmes have been reformed in order rapidly to increase the number of Ph.D.s produced. The universities have tended to set up research schools in order to take advantage of economies of scale. The Grandes Ecoles have also expanded the part they play in the production of Ph.D.s by strengthening their 'engineer-Ph.D.' programmes. Funding for doctoral students is based to a large extent on the various grants awarded by government ministries, and in particular MENRT (Ministère de l'Education Nationale et de la Recherche). Thus 85 to 95 per cent of doctoral students in science and engineering, depending on the discipline, are funded by one or other of these grant-awarding bodies (MENRT 2000). The distribution of these grants among the various research units seems to remain relatively stable, at least in the medium term. Similarly, the grants awarded by organizations such as the DGA (General Directorate for Armaments), the CEA (Nuclear Energy Centre), the CES (Space Studies Centre), France Télécom, and so on go mainly to a certain number of laboratories with whom they have established good working relations. In contrast to the US, the funding of doctoral students is relatively unconnected to direct academic competition; the system of grant allocation tends rather to be administrative in nature (MENRT-type awards) or to be based on long-term partnerships.

Although the Humboldt model, in which teaching and research is seen as an indivisible whole, has been the basis for the effectiveness of *German* universities, little distinction is made between doctoral research and other advanced training programmes, and the production of Ph.D.s is relatively non-systematic. In other words, the selection process, courses, and pedagogic content are not highly structured as they are in the American system. In consequence, the career paths for students embarking on a doctorate are not very well signposted, particularly since the length of time they take to complete their theses remains highly variable. In this respect, the reform of doctoral training is under way.

Three quarters of doctoral students are employed as junior staff in universities, although their conditions of employment (full-time/part-time, length of contract, and so on) seem to differ considerably from one field to the next. These posts are funded partly from local (*Länder*) and national (federal) government grants provided for in annual budgets and partly from the public or private research funds that selectively finance projects on which doctoral students can apply for assistantships. Especially in this latter case, they are dependent on the reputation of the professor/Ph.D. supervisor, who often manages scientific projects involving both the university and research institutes, on the one hand, and the university and industry, on the other. As a result, many doctoral students are from the outset members of research teams in which their personal work forms part of the team's collective programme.

In the *UK*, as in Germany, Ph.D. students can take a number of different routes. Entry conditions for those who have completed the three-year undergraduate degree, the length of time taken and the way in which the doctorate is obtained differ from discipline to discipline, even though efforts are being made to formalize programmes and the final assessment. As far as funding is concerned, the research councils distribute the major share of grants on the basis of individual academic merit, with other public organizations, notably the universities themselves, accounting for most of the remainder. Thus 75 per cent of full-time Ph.D. students have their tuition fees[7] paid by public bodies. Half of them receive money from the research councils and a quarter from the universities, government ministries, or local authorities; firms seem to make only a very limited financial contribution to the production of Ph.D.s (funding a mere 337 students out of a total of 5,180) (SET Statistics 2000). On the other hand, more than half of all part-time doctoral students are self-funding because of their restricted access to government grants (23 per cent) or funding from business and industry (15 per cent). However, the general trend in the funding of doctoral students is towards a gradual withdrawal by the state, which is forcing the universities and the research councils to diversify their sources of finance. An increasingly large share of doctoral students is being co-funded by industry and the universities within the framework of programmes such as CASE[8] and PTP.

12.5.2. Institutional Forms of University Systems and the Characteristics of Doctoral Students

Doctoral students in the US constitute a very heterogeneous population, reflecting the great diversity within the university system itself. The freedom each university has to fix its own rules or procedures for awarding Ph.D.s, combined with the relatively large numbers of students who interrupt and then return to their studies, means that the socio-demographic characteristics of doctoral students are fairly disparate. The absence of any centralized (federal) certification for doctoral programmes also has the effect of making the quality of the degrees awarded less than transparent. Furthermore, the number of foreign doctoral students and post-docs, which varies from discipline to discipline (34 per cent in natural sciences, 49 per cent in engineering, according to the NSF), is still very high as we have already seen. The large number of foreign students is proof of the attraction exerted by certain American research universities; at the same time, they constitute a pool of skilled labour on which the scientific labour market, particularly that for post-docs, can draw.

For slightly different reasons, the UK also has fairly diversified populations of doctoral students. Since specialization begins at a very early age, from 16 onwards, and the total time spent in higher education can be relatively short (six years may be sufficient to reach Ph.D. level), some students obtain their doctorates at a young age, around 25. On the other hand, a significant share of doctoral students, working part-time for their Ph.D.s, take a very different path through the education system, in terms of both time spent in the system and scientific background or motivation. In the 1995 academic year, there were 5,180 new entrants to full-time doctoral programmes in science and engineering, compared with 1,883 students registering to study part-time; thus a quarter of new entrants in that year were part-timers. This category of students, many of whom have previously worked or are continuing to work while studying, accounts for a not insignificant part of the total doctoral student population in the UK. Moreover, as in the US, foreign students account for a significant share of the new doctorates awarded (30–50 per cent). This diversity, combined with that of the universities themselves, makes quality standards a little difficult to assess.

On the other hand, the Ph.D. populations in the other three countries are relatively homogeneous, although this homogeneity is not of the same kind. In *Germany,* many students embark on a higher education course in a technical or scientific subject on completion of an apprenticeship begun after obtaining the Abitur at age 19.[9] Even though they may subsequently leave higher education at various levels, the professional experience acquired during the two to three-year apprenticeship serves as a sort of common basis for creating a professional identity that facilitates cooperation among technicians, engineers, and researches. Graduates tend to obtain their degrees late because of the relatively long time taken to complete the bachelor's and master's programmes, which have no real cut-off point. For example, the average age at which a university student becomes a graduate engineer is 29, and 31 for students in the *Fachhochschulen.* Consequently, those who prolong their studies beyond the graduate engineer level in order to obtain a Ph.D. are delaying still further their entry into the labour market. Doctoral students tend to complete their doctorates between the age of 31 and 35, which seems late compared with the French average of 29. Even though the funding arrangements mean that their academic careers are slightly different, the Ph.D. population retains a certain homogeneity, which is further reinforced by the fact that Germany attracts significantly fewer foreign students (8 per cent).

France and *Japan,* on the other hand, are characterized by the relative coherence of their doctoral student populations: virtually all Ph.D. students in these countries study full-time, apart from those Japanese employees who submit theses based on their work and some of the foreign students in France. In both of these countries, students' progression through the system follows a relatively linear path from high-school graduation to Ph.D. The procedure for completing theses is standardized and takes a relatively short time, with students often completing before age 30. This normative procedure creates a certain coherence among each cohort of doctoral students, although in France, of course, there is the duality between universities and Grandes Ecoles, while in Japan the university hierarchy tends to divide the Ph.D. student population. Foreign students account for around 20 per cent of doctoral students in both countries.

12.5.3. The Training-Career Transition in Academia

Obtaining a Ph.D. has traditionally been regarded as preparation for an academic career, either in universities or in publicly funded research institutions, where the careers of teaching and research staff are governed by strict rules: recruitment based on academic publications record, peer evaluation, tenure or employment guarantees, and so on. The tenure system often emerges as a major issue in academic careers, particularly in the English-speaking world, since it serves both as an incentive mechanism for those starting their careers and as the boundary marker beyond which job stability in the internal market allows academics to specialize and extend their knowledge without the threat of academic obsolescence or dismissal. This canonical model of the academic labour market seems to be largely a fiction, however, if only because, in reality, it functions very differently in different societal contexts.[10] In order to fully understand its diversity, we will need to consider two mechanisms: the first concerns the internal workings of universities, while the second relates to the nature of the implicit contract between doctoral students and their supervisors, who fix the rules governing the balance to be struck between students' contribution to collective research and the development of individual careers. The first influences the rules or practices governing recruitment, while the second tends to shape the strategies Ph.D. students adopt in respect of their own career aims.

(a) In the US, the academic labour market is characterized, first, by extensive segmentation between two types of universities, teaching universities and research universities (public research institutions), with teaching and research staff being managed in accordance with the different missions of the two types of institutions.[11] Second, it is characterized by the tenure system, which offers young academics an incentive to produce knowledge, particularly in the second category of university, among which there is intense competition. This dual competition at the individual and collective (inter-establishment) level is based on the '(academic) reputation system', which functions as a sort of stock market quotation in a quasi-commercial marketplace and is the basis for the hierarchy that characterizes the American university system. Unlike France or Germany, 'where the discourse is egalitarian and where the universities are all supposed to be of comparable quality and to award degrees of the same value' (Brisset-Sillon 1997), universities in the US are systematically ranked, which has the effect of making hierarchical and segmenting the academic labour market. The main differentiating factor in this hierarchy is research: the best institutions are those that have a high level of academic/scientific output and manage both to tap the available financial resources to the fullest extent possible and to attract the best talents. The careers of teaching and research staff tend to espouse the same principle of competition based on reputation.

In accordance with this same principle, the contract between doctoral students and their supervisors seems to be based on a reciprocal commitment to a relatively explicit form of exchange. Ph.D. students, while working on their theses, undertake to contribute to the production of new knowledge within the group research directed by their supervisors or professors, while the latter agree to provide them with an academic environment as conducive as possible to the production of interesting findings and, above all, articles for publication in the leading academic journals, which in turn guarantees their academic future. However, this mutual commitment is limited in both time and space, since a Ph.D. thesis is only one staging post on the route to academia, access to which remains highly uncertain. The allocation of research funds, including assistantships, is extremely competitive; the process of obtaining tenure is both lengthy and selective and mobility between projects or research teams is the rule. It is important for young academics, therefore, to adopt a strategic approach to constructing their academic reputation by accumulating positive signals as they work with various research teams, collaborate with various professors, and help to run a variety of different projects. Each commitment to these various contracts is intended to create a positive dynamic.

Currently, slightly fewer than two-thirds of Ph.D.s are employed in university or academic positions three years after obtaining their doctorates, while only one-quarter are employed in firms (NSF 1998). Thus Ph.D. students in the US are being prepared mainly for careers in the 'academic space', and particularly in the university system. Nevertheless, the vast majority of new Ph.D.s find themselves accepting temporary posts and thereby joining the queue for tenured or tenure-track positions (Cosepup 2000). This selectivity, which has become more intense in recent years, makes the situation of young academics precarious to some extent, which reduces the attractiveness of academic careers and tends to restrict enrolment on Ph.D. programmes, at least in some subject areas.

(b) The situation in the UK is not dissimilar to that in the US. Here, the higher education system comprises a total of 113 university institutions and has been unified since 1992. Nevertheless, these institutions can be divided into two distinct categories, the 'old' or pre-1992 universities and the 'new' or post-1992 universities, which grew out of the former polytechnics. Universities in the first category, which forms the basis of the British system, provide courses at all levels, with teaching and research being closely linked. It includes the ancient universities as well as technological universities and the so-called 'redbricks', founded in major cities such as Manchester and Leeds in the late nineteenth and early twentieth centuries. The post-1992 universities concentrate more on undergraduate teaching. They have a significant number of part-time students and students on sandwich courses. Although current policy in Britain is aimed at creating a homogeneous system by increasing the number of crossover points between the two categories, the academic labour market is highly segmented between the new universities, which concentrate mainly on teaching, and the traditional universities, in which most research is conducted. Although they are less autonomous than American universities, the most prestigious British universities enjoy a not-insignificant degree of freedom, far more in any event than their French and German counterparts, in matters of recruitment, promotion, and incentives for teaching staff. The allocation of public research funds on the basis of the Research Assessment Exercise increases competition between universities, which in turn influences academics' career paths, as it does in the US. Furthermore, although the tenure system was formally abolished in the late 1980s, the goal of most young academics is to obtain a permanent lectureship, which offers far greater job security than that enjoyed by contract research staff, the vast majority of whom are employed on fixed-term contracts. The contract researcher category, which accounts for almost 30 per cent of faculty staff and provides support for university research activities (Bryson 1999), acts as a sort of 'airlock' in which young academics destined for lectureships are sorted out from the rest, who are likely to seek work in the private sector.

The implicit contract between doctoral students and their supervisors, which is based on a mutual commitment, is intended here, as elsewhere, to ensure that the work students do for their theses also adds to the research teams' output and reputation, with benefits for both parties. Doctoral students appear to enjoy greater room for manoeuvre here in constructing their individual strategies, since most of them receive grants to support their studies. In this sense, British Ph.D. students are able to adjust their level of involvement in their teams' research in accordance with the likelihood of their obtaining a position in the academic community. Nevertheless, those seeking such a position have to go through a lengthy selection process, which forces them to take part in a sort of protracted knock-out tournament. By way of illustration, a survey carried out by the Welcome Trust, a private research foundation, shows that, after completing their theses, 80 per cent of young Ph.D.s in the biological sciences find their first jobs on fixed-term contracts in academia; however, only 60 per cent remain after three years and this figure falls further to 47 per cent beyond the four-year mark.

In the other two European countries, the higher education system is managed by centralized supervisory bodies whose management procedures are more or less bureaucratic. The market mode of coordination based on reputation or 'share price' is replaced here by an administrative mode. While it is true that certain establishments are more 'recognized' than others, the inter-institutional competition and hierarchies are not as explicit or as transparent as in the US or the UK.[12] Thus the doctorates awarded in these countries, regulated and controlled as they are, reflect a certain quality standard.

(c) In *Germany*, the academic labour market is organized by the supervisory authorities, which operate on two different levels: 'the federal government lays down a general framework of rules and procedures governing the university system, a framework within which the individual Länder or states are able to develop a certain number of options. The Länder are also very active in negotiating professors' salaries, since they are requested by the universities to find the necessary funds' (Musselin 1994). Although university teaching staff in Germany are civil servants, as they are in France, they do not generally obtain a permanent position until the age of about 40, when they are appointed to a professorship following completion of their *Habilitation*, a second doctorate that confers entitlement to teach in a university. Moreover, the system attaches a certain number of supplementary conditions to the recruitment procedure: candidates already in post cannot be promoted unless they change institutions; once selected, they may negotiate additional payments and working conditions with the university, in particular research budgets (including assistantships). Compared with the conditions in the French market, young assistant staff have to be mobile in order to obtain a permanent position and also have to go through a lengthy apprenticeship and selection process under a professor's authority that lasts until the age of about 40. The status of professor is the central pivot around which the German university and research systems are organized. Indeed, unlike in France, where university staff and public sector researchers have separate career paths, it is the university career path leading to the status of professor that is the obligatory route for all academics and allows them subsequently to be considered for positions of responsibility in extra-university research institutions funded by the state or industry, such as the Max-Planck-Institute, the Helmholtz Centres, the Fraunhofer Gesellschaft, etc.

It is through these public or semi-public research organizations that German industry receives a steady flow of professors, doctoral students, and post-docs as part of a process of cross-fertilization that reflects the close cooperation between science and industry.

In view of the importance of the status of professor, the implicit contract is based more on the individual relations between professors and Ph.D. students, or even on a master–pupil relationship along the lines of the classic Humboldt model in which they come together around a common research object. This type of personalized relationship, based less on the value of the student's immediate performance, tends to restrict the scope for young academics to adopt individual strategies. As a result, they seem to be more dependent on the relational networks established by their professors in order to gain a toehold on the various professional career paths. This is particularly true of those who embark on academic careers.

(d) In *France*, the higher education and research system is an archetypal example of a system controlled by the central state, even though the state is currently seeking to reduce its financial commitment and give establishments greater autonomy under local management. It is further characterized, over and above the university/Grande Ecole duality,[13] by a clear distinction between the universities and public research establishments, which each have their own separate missions, namely teaching and research respectively. This distinction has served to create two separate professions: researchers and lecturers. Thus the academic labour market is divided into separate segments between which there is little mobility. Nevertheless, the same rules govern the service of all academics, whether teaching staff or full-time researchers, since virtually all of them are civil servants. In France, therefore, the rules governing the service of university staff and researchers are laid down by the state. The distribution of posts is managed by the central administration within each system. The management of individuals—recruitment and promotion— is the responsibility of the relevant corporate body. University teaching staff and researchers become civil servants on obtaining their first permanent lecturing position (*maître de conference*) or research post (*chargé de recherché*). Having gained tenure around the age of 30, university teaching staff and researchers enjoy job security, behave as 'insiders' in the internal market and display a propensity to shut themselves off from its economic environment.

As far as the nature of the contract governing relations between doctoral students and their supervisors is concerned, there is a not-insignificant element of personal commitment, as in Germany. In France, however, these relations are shaped more by the institutional aspect of the contract that links Ph.D. students to their laboratories or research units. Indeed, since the conditions under which they complete their theses, particularly the allocation of grants or the industrial contracts under which support is provided, depend to a very large extent on the laboratory to which they are affiliated, they feel themselves more involved in the workings of their institutions. This tendency is further reinforced by the fact that the competitive procedures by which young academics are recruited to teaching or research posts frequently go beyond the selection of individuals to become competitions between individual laboratories. Individual strategies certainly exist, but they have to be implemented, in the form of co-option, within a space shaped by the constraints imposed by wider institutional strategies.

(e) In *Japan*, the academic labour market is characterized by the coexistence of the private sector (private universities) and the public sector (national universities and public research bodies). In this latter sector, young academics gain tenure at a relatively early age, as in France. Even though each institution has the freedom to determine its own procedures and criteria for selection and promotion, they are all governed by the national scales. This system has the effect of rigidifying the management of teaching and research careers by destroying incentive mechanisms. A recent reform created 10,000 fixed-term post-doc positions funded entirely by the state with the aim of introducing greater flexibility into the organization of public or university-based research. Private universities enjoy greater room for manoeuvre in career management, at least in theory, although in fact the employment system closely resembles that in the public sector. This rigidity in the academic labour market is further reinforced by the 'chair' system which, as in Germany, tends to freeze the boundaries between disciplines or subdisciplines. Moreover, it gives every professor, whether in the public or private sector, considerable freedom when it comes to the choice of courses, programmes, and appointments. The importance accorded to the status of professor places doctoral students and young Ph.D.s in a position of both academic and professional allegiance, which creates a sort of master–pupil relationship. The implicit contract is replaced by this type of highly personalized relationship, which reflects a wider system of mutual expectations.

12.5.4. The Recruitment of Ph.D.s in the Private Sector

Labour market transactions are characterized by uncertainty caused by informational asymmetries. One of the ways in which this uncertainty can be reduced is to evaluate individuals and their competences on the basis of the signals they transmit in the form of qualifications, experience, areas of specialization, research topics, institutional affiliation, etc. (Spence 1973).

These signals include, on the one hand, more or less objectified elements, such as degrees and publications record, which constitute a form of certification of competence and quality and, on the other, subjective elements, interpreted by the actors, which provide the basis for reputations. Thus 'certification' and 'reputation' are two major modes of coordination around which the encounter between supply and demand in the labour market is organized (Nohara 2004). Nevertheless, these modes of coordination become increasingly less satisfactory as subject curricula evolve ever quicker and the boundaries between disciplines become blurred in certain areas of academic and scientific specialization (Lam 2000). Nor do they any longer provide an absolutely sound basis for matching supply to demand in certain R&D activities. As a result, an alternative mode of adjustment is emerging at the interface between the academic and industrial spaces; networks make it possible not only to identify, contact, and sift the talents that best match specific needs but also, and above all, to co-produce them through university–industry collaboration. The recruitment of Ph.D.s depends to a fairly large extent on these types of mechanisms. However, these mechanisms, which are intended to reduce uncertainty or to bring the two spaces closer together, are deployed within a set of national institutional arrangements. In consequence, they are regulated differently and have meanings that differ considerably from country to country, particularly as far as the recruitment of Ph.D.s is concerned.

(a) In the US, the university system can be said to have integrated itself into its economic environment by adopting the principles that animate the business world, that is the provision of commercial services in the marketplace. Thus American universities position themselves in the same competitive arena as firms in order to satisfy their funding requirements. This inter-institutional competition and the provision, on a commercial footing, of various services based on the academic and scientific knowledge at their disposal have helped to legitimate the notion of the 'entrepreneurial university'—a symbol of institutional innovation that dates back to the founding of the Massachusetts Institute of Technology. This type of strategic behaviour, duly legitimated and consistent with the American university ethic, enables universities to trade in patents or to establish, on a large scale, high-tech companies as spin-offs from their research activities. It is this general context that shapes the use and flows of doctoral students and Ph.D.s.

According to an NSF survey (S&E Indicators 2000, NSF), slightly fewer than two-thirds of Ph.D.s are employed in academic jobs three years after obtaining their doctorates, while one-quarter are employed in business and industry. Apart from the scale of the academic market, this survey reveals two phenomena.

First, the Ph.D. recruitment rate in industry shows an upward trend over time, although it fluctuates with the business cycle and, even more so, from subject to subject. The share of Ph.D.s in engineering entering industry is greater than that of Ph.D.s in science: 57 per cent of those with doctorates in engineering were working in the private sector in 1997, compared with 40 per cent for computer science and 20 per cent for the life sciences.

Second, the share of young scientists in intermediate positions at the intersection between academia and industry is growing fairly rapidly. This increase, due largely to the establishment of post-doc positions, reflects a strengthening of the competitive selection mechanism governing entry to the academic market and the increasingly precarious nature of their situation as a result of being employed on a succession of short-term contracts (Cosepup 2000). This phenomenon is most apparent in the life sciences, one of the areas in which American science excels. For example, 60 per cent of new Ph.D.s in this area find themselves in such intermediate positions, and they account for half of all post-docs (5,600 out of 10,700) in the US. In areas such as this, young high-level scientists employed on extremely flexible contracts alternate between research programmes, temporary posts in industry and academia, or even the start-ups established by university teaching staff while they wait to settle down in permanent positions.[14] Individual mobility of this kind is mediated essentially through reputation, established by formatting knowledge in the form of academic publications, or through socio-professional networks. Fluidity of this kind creates a labour market that is often embedded in a local academic community (Palo Alto, Biotech-Bay in California, Boston, etc.) gravitating around a core of university institutions and academic spin-offs that functions as an 'intermediate space' in which scientific knowledge is disseminated (Saxenian 1994). Combined with the influx of foreign post-docs seeking to familiarize themselves with the latest developments in biotechnology, it also influences the trend towards the externalization of R&D activities by pharmaceutical companies and the constitution of an international space within which certain hybrid actors move, transcending the long-established national and professional boundaries of the university, the industrial researcher, or the entrepreneur.

(b) In the UK, there is a tradition of autonomous universities able to manage, at local level, their own relations with the political and administrative authorities as well as with firms. The universities' ability to take advantage of their autonomy in order to establish and sustain local links explains the existence of clusters of innovative companies around certain universities, most notably Oxford and Cambridge. At the same time, the free-market policies of successive governments and its corollary—the reduction of public funding for teaching and research—have further encouraged universities to develop their activities in this area.

Against this background, an increasingly high share of doctoral students is being supported by joint industry/university programmes, such as the CASE and PTP programmes (see note 8). A comparative study of France and Great Britain (Mason, Beltramo, and Paul 2000) also found that doctoral students in Great Britain seem to be significantly more involved than their French counterparts in industrial projects, particularly in SMEs in the electronics and biotechnology industries. Apart from the fact that many multinationals have established laboratories in the vicinity of certain universities, which in itself creates a strong demand for scientists, British firms are more likely to recruit Ph.D.s to work in their R&D departments than French firms, which display a marked preference for 'engineers' trained in the Grandes Ecoles. Consequently, a good number of doctoral students look to industry for employment once they have completed their theses. According to the OST, one-third of the doctoral students funded by the Research Councils find jobs in the private sector on completion of their Ph.D.s. Whereas it is becoming increasingly difficult to find stable employment in academia, because of cuts in university funding, the increase in contract research and the drastic reduction in publicly funded research laboratories, industry is seeking to co-produce and reclaim a certain proportion of Ph.D.s by forging strategic partnerships with universities. Similarly, a certain degree of disintegration in the publicly funded research sector and the presence of a significant pool of contract research staff in the universities have helped to create a specific category of hybrid actors made up of professionals and academics who have become self-employed in order to provide services to firms or to act as sources of high-level skills that can be called on for specific scientific/industrial projects. The presence of this category of actors makes the British R&D system extremely flexible.

In order to regulate the links between the HERS and firms, the two continental European countries make less use of 'market intermediation' than the US, where scientific reputation can be as financially profitable in academia as it is in industry, or the UK, where the porous boundaries between the public and private spheres have created an enormous area of great flexibility. In their different ways, Germany and France have each structured a space in which industry/academia collaboration takes place, the nature of which influences the ways in which Ph.D.s enter the labour market.

(c) In Germany, close links between academic research and industry have existed for a long time, both in large firms and in SMEs. There are many research centres jointly funded by the state and firms in which university and private sector researchers work together with a view to developing products up to the pre-competitive stage (the Fraunhofer Gesellschaft, for example). In addition to the long-established practice of firms providing periods of training in the workplace for university students, German industry frequently calls on university professors and doctoral students in a process of 'cross-fertilization' that is regarded as the key to its success, particularly in the chemical and pharmaceutical industries. Moreover, these links seem to be forged at local level, since the universities and research institutes, most of which are administered by the *Länder*, are deconcentrated, which encourages the diffusion of academic research within the local industrial fabric.

These close links between industry and academia based on local networks are constructed around a professoriate whose individual members enjoy considerable personal autonomy in managing science–industry relations (Granovetter 1983). This has a direct influence on the integration of German doctoral students into the labour market. Thus Ph.D. students and post-docs are very often involved in the collaborative projects that university professors manage on behalf of firms. Industrial contracts, and the funds they bring in, are an integral part of Ph.D. programmes. Professors are in effect part of the corporate management hierarchy and are responsible for supervising young researchers in both the industrial and academic aspects of their work. Furthermore, post-docs are sometimes strongly encouraged by their professors or other academic associates to launch spin-offs on the basis of their joint research. This type of 'patronage' seems to reduce the probability of young Ph.D.s finding themselves in precarious employment situations in the early stages of their careers.

From a statistical point of view, Enders (2001) shows that one year after obtaining their doctorates, only 60 per cent of Ph.D.s in biology and mathematics stay in the public sector, mainly in the universities. On the other hand, 60 per cent of Ph.D.s in electronic engineering and almost one-third in biology are employed in the private sector. Thus the career paths of German Ph.D.s seem to be more diversified than elsewhere.

Whatever the discipline, German Ph.D.s seem to be much less reluctant than their counterparts in other countries to seek careers in industry.[15] One reason for this is the 'cognitive proximity' between the academic and industrial worlds. Another reason is the high status of researchers in industry which opens up very good promotion prospects.

(d) Despite a higher education and research system that is characterized both by state centralism and by a certain degree of inwardness—except in the prestigious engineering schools (*Grande École d'ingénieurs*), which have always maintained close links with industry—France has developed forms of collaboration between academia and industry that have sometimes proved to be very efficient. Governments have frequently initiated sectoral action programmes (such as the Plan Calcul, which was meant to ensure French strategic independence in computers, Plan Télécom, etc.) and, adopting a mission-orientated approach to policy, have also provided the impetus for large-scale technological programmes. In doing so, they looked to numerous scientific and technological research organizations for support, as well as to the large national firms, both private and publicly owned, that were the leaders in their sectors. These latter were involved in the large-scale technological programmes more as 'purchasers' than as the initiators of scientific collaboration. Thus technological diffusion was conceived in a centralized, top-down way, with companies being little involved in defining objectives. However, this organizational structure, which prevailed until the early 1990s, has begun to change, with greater decentralization helping to break down the boundaries between the public and private spheres. Thus the French system is evolving in two directions. On the one hand, reduced centralism is giving technological support programmes a more regional character and is leading to the development of local networks involving universities, research laboratories, and SMEs. On the other hand, there is increasing financial autonomy within the HERS and the financial flows from firms to academia are increasing.

That said, relations between the HERS and French companies are still deeply influenced by the weight of the past in that they remain highly formalized and structured. Thus some large companies continue to maintain long-standing, privileged relations with certain public laboratories or universities; these relations may take the form of jointly operated laboratories, so-called 'economic interest groupings', or partnerships, or research agreements. These forms of links involve mutual, long-term commitment, exclusive 'one-to-one' relations, and formalized transactions.

It is within this framework of science–industry relations that Ph.D.s in France are deployed and integrated into the labour market. According to one study (Cereq 1999), slightly fewer than two-thirds of them are employed in the public sector (higher education and public research institutions) three years after obtaining their doctorates, while one-third are employed in the private sector. Thus the academic labour market, which operates in accordance with the rules laid down for the civil service, remains the main source of employment for Ph.D.s (Martinelli 2001). The differentiation between public and private career paths emerges at a fairly early stage, therefore, with each 'space' creating its own relatively impervious segment within the ILM. This differentiation is even present at the time when funds are allocated to prospective Ph.D. students.[16] Those in receipt of public funding tend to seek employment in the academic labour market, while those supported by industry or the CIFRE programme are very likely to seek employment in industry, possibly even in the companies that have been funding their studies.[17]

In this latter case, both the allocation of industrial contracts (or grants) and the labour market integration of those being supported in this way depend on the networks that university or other public research laboratories have established with certain companies (Perret 2000). It is the recurrent nature of these relations that encourages the establishment of these networks between the partners. Doctoral students play a central role in maintaining these networks, since they become integrated into them by virtue of the reputation of the institution to which they are affiliated and at the same time function as a key link in their reproduction.

The use of doctoral students in university–industry collaboration in France is further characterized by two considerations of an economic nature. For both partners, it is one of the least costly and least risky ways of organizing such collaboration; a Ph.D. thesis that takes three to four years on an average to complete can serve as an exploratory study of emerging areas or topics. This type of technological wager gives firms a certain degree of flexibility; they can decide whether to internalize the co-produced knowledge or competences depending on the potential revealed by the doctoral students' findings.

(e) In Japan, only a small minority of young Ph.D.s find employment in the private sector; the vast majority enter the academic labour market. Considered to be inflexible when it comes to the selection of research topics, Ph.D.s are not held in high regard by Japanese companies, which prefer young scientists with master' degrees requiring six years of higher education for their R&D function. As in Germany, it is the professors and the networks they have established that play the pivotal role in matching demand from firms to the supply of new graduates, including Ph.D.s.

Despite the lack of opportunities for young scientists in industry, it should be noted that an increasing number of engineers making their careers in the private sector are submitting their theses to universities after acquiring a certain amount of professional experience (Lanciano-Morandat and Nohara 2001). Half of the 3,000 theses submitted annually in engineering fall into this category. This would suggest that a new category of 'researcher/Ph.D.' might be emerging within firms, one that is clearly distinct from the R&D engineer category. With a greater affinity with the academic space, this category might provide the first 'hybrid' actors capable of transcending the boundaries between academia and industry.

12.6. CONCLUSION

The hybridization of science and technology is creating a new intermediation space between academia and industry. The creation of this new space has been accompanied by the emergence of new structures, such as academic start-ups, university incubators, technology licensing offices (TLOs), research consortiums, etc., whose purpose is to facilitate the interactive circulation of knowledge between the academic and industrial spaces (Ezhovitz et al. 2000). The emergence of the 'intermediate' labour market as a mechanism for the co-production and transfer of competences is an important element of this general phenomenon.

In all the countries investigated, this hybridization gives rise to a dual trend that is sometimes contradictory, sometimes complementary. On the one hand, there is undeniably a trend towards convergence between countries. The scientific world is 'globalized', and indeed has been for a long time, since the system of competition and scientific reputation is now being built up in the international arena, at least at the top level. Consequently, all the outputs of scientific activity (articles, patents, Ph.D.s, etc.) tend to be evaluated relative to a few 'universal' criteria of excellence. This in turn sets in motion similar trends in all countries. Thus systems for producing new Ph.D. programmes are converging markedly towards the American graduate school model—or at least towards various interpretations of that system—which is, as it were, acquiring universal legitimacy. Similarly, the increase in scientific projects involving international teams (research consortiums, joint publication of articles, etc.) is having the effect of standardizing research practices and researchers' professional rules. Finally, the globalization of multinationals' R&D functions serves to reinforce this trend further by standardizing HRM norms for researchers beyond national boundaries.

On the other hand, while this form of competition based on global reputation is leading to the emergence of centres of excellence, many of them in America, and at the same time causing scientists and students to migrate towards them, it is not completely eliminating the specificities of the national institutions involved in the production of scientific output.

In fact, more detailed observation shows that this convergence towards the American model, whether assumed or desired, has met with a variety of responses in the different national contexts. As our analysis suggests, the market for Ph.D.s functions in different ways depending on the particular institutional arrangements associated with the various industrial sectors and disciplines or with national policies on the higher education and research system. Higher education and research institutions, which in all the countries are the heirs to a considerable national heritage, are in fact shaping the basic architecture on which the arrangements, rules, and practices governing university–industry relations are based. In this sense, the intermediate labour market and the innovation space are 'social constructs' that are deeply embedded in an overall societal context[18] (Maurice, Sellier, and Silvestre 1986).

Thus the coordination mechanisms, such as signalling, reputation, networks, etc. that regulate the labour market for scientists have to be interpreted in the light of this societal context. Regulatory mechanisms may bear the same designations, but their significance often differs, depending on the space in which they function.

This is true of the notion of 'network', which plays an essential role in the intermediate labour market. Far from being homogeneous or polymorphic, it has a multiplicity of meanings and a variety of functions depending on whether it is part of a local community context in California, German, or Japanese context characterized by personalized relations based on the status of professor or in a French context in which relations between the various entities are quasi-institutionalized (see Table A.12.1). Although the networks in which scientific knowledge and competences are produced transcend, in theory, the various boundaries and are transnational in nature, they are also fragmented or differentiated by the construction of human and social realities, in particular societal reality (Granovetter 1985; Lanciano et al. 1998).

Over and above this general conclusion, which bears out some of the arguments advanced by the national innovation system schools (Lundvall 1992; Edquist 1997) and the varieties of capitalism approach (Hall and Soskice 2001), particularly in terms of institutional advantages, two policy implications can be briefly outlined.

– The policy of establishing a limited number of centres of scientific excellence along the lines of the American university model, which has been pursued almost everywhere for some time, creates certain tensions in western European countries and in Japan. It tends to produce a Matthews effect (a self-reinforcing mechanism in a situation of informational asymmetry), which encourages the emergence of a small group of renowned establishments and a separation between research universities and training universities, with the latter concentrating almost exclusively on teaching at the expense of research. Apart from the fact that segmentation of this kind between research and teaching is not desirable from the point of view of educational effectiveness, there is a risk that this trend will not only reduce the diversity of research, in terms of both form (applied, basic, etc.) and approach (theoretical, normative, experimental, etc.), but also restrict the range of possible research topics. Moreover, it strengthens the position of standard theories as the dominant academic and scientific paradigms and often leads to the homogenization of Ph.D. quality norms. This competitive model particularly disadvantages many regional universities of average size that meet specific local needs. Consequently, science and higher education policy, whether national or European, should take greater account of the need for variety in research and use public research funds to support a certain degree of institutional diversity, which remains the best way of guaranteeing creativity in the long term.

– The training-job transition of new Ph.D. recipients is becoming increasingly difficult and uncertain everywhere, because there is a structural shortage of the academic jobs for which they are primarily being trained. As the use of postdoctoral research positions is increasing and being extended, precariousness among young researchers is increasing well beyond any 'reasonable' limit. A certain degree of precariousness at the beginning of academic careers—associated with the well-known phenomenon of the labour queue—seems to be inherent in the nature of scientific and academic research, in that time is needed for the selection process in a situation of uncertain quality. As we have seen, this precariousness was traditionally managed through the relationships between actors and organizations in the networks that operate in the intermediate space. Nevertheless, the rapid development of the systematic use of post-doc positions, which are regarded in part as a source of cheap labour, is tending to unbalance or even disrupt the intermediate labour market. The public authorities have an important role to play in bringing this market segment back under control through the use of various regulatory or incentive mechanisms. Without intervention, which should certainly be adapted to each country's circumstances, the pool of young researchers may well dry up, either through depletion or because young people are discouraged from entering academia. In the long term, this would undermine the very basis of knowledge production upon which the new 'knowledge economy' rests.

NOTES

1. The notion of a labour market for scientists used in this chapter is defined as 'a labour market for individuals engaged in research activities, whether they be public or private, basic or developmental and whether the activities in question may properly be deemed to be those of a researcher or those of a scientific assistant contributing to the actual realisation of research activities' (d'Iribarne 1987).

2. We are in fact dealing here with 'trilateral governance' if we include the state as an actor intervening in science or higher education policy. This last actor, whose activity varies in intensity from country to country, has the capacity to structure the intermediate labour market by various means, including grants, research funding, management of university posts, and so on.

3. Our investigation is based on the empirical results of a comparative study, funded by the European Commission during 1998–2001, of the relations between firms' innovation systems and higher education and research systems (SESI) in five European countries and the US. See in detail, http://www.univ-aix. fr/lest/sesiweb/

4. From a different point of view, B. Clark had made a significant comparative study on the research training system at the graduate school level with the same five countries (Clark 1993).

5. The doctorate study implies a multifunctional mechanism and corresponds, in a traditional sense, to the 'apprenticeship system'. The students are, first of all, to acquire knowledge of the latest scientific advances. In return, they contribute to the collective scientific output by specializing in a specific area within their team. Second, it serves to produce the next generation of lecturers and researchers whose task it will be to provide leadership in the scientific research of the future; this equates of course to the reproduction of the academic community. Finally, the flows of doctoral students and Ph.D.s between the HERS and firms are the means by which the new knowledge produced in academic research institutes is diffused beyond the boundaries of academia.

6. Generally the reimbursement is however exempted for those who get the job in the academic position.

7. In most cases, the grant covers both tuition fees and student's living expenses for three years.

8. Like the CIFRE programme in France, the aim of the CASE scheme is to place Ph.D. students whose work will be supervised jointly by academia and industry. This programme is largely funded by the research councils. CASE funding was originally restricted to the universities, but in 1994 the rules were modified to include business and industry. As a result, the research councils can now award grants directly to selected firms on the basis of Ph.D. proposals submitted (Office of Science and Technology 1997).

9. This applies to 82% of new students entering the Fachhochschulen (polytechnics) and to 55% in the universities.

10. Moreover, as we will see later, academia does not have a monopoly in the Ph.D. market, since industry absorbs a significant share of Ph.D.s, albeit one that varies from country to country.

11. This is a very simplified typology of the 3,600 such institutions in the US, which can be further distinguished by their nature (public or private), by the length and level of courses offered and by reputation. The classification drawn up by the Carnegie Foundation in fact has ten categories.

12. Except, of course, for the distinction between universities and Grandes Ecoles in France.

13. The French case is somewhat exceptional, since universities in France are not the centres of excellence that they are in other countries. They are regarded as the 'second choice' relative to the elitist Grandes Ecoles and also as less productive in terms of research output than the public research institutions (Nohara 2001).
14. However, this fluidity on the part of candidates does have its downsides; there is a risk that talent will be exhausted and academic careers made to seem less attractive.
15. And also, in a negative sense, because the trajectories of young academics are lengthy, tortuous, and dependent on their professors until they themselves obtain a tenured position.
16. In addition, there are the engineers graduating from the Grandes Ecoles with Ph.D.s who have a dual competence as researchers and engineers that enables them to operate within both the academic and industrial spaces. In itself, the status of researcher has no legitimacy in French industry, unlike in Germany. However, it is the status of graduate engineer that really marks out the elite and opens up prospects of promotion through the management hierarchy.
17. In the case of the CIFRE programme, in which participants are jointly funded by industry and the state, 78% of new Ph.D.s enter the private sector, with 54% remaining with the partner companies (ABG Formation 2001).
18. This general construction process can obviously take different forms depending on whether it takes place at the sectoral, local, or supranational level (Grossetti 1995 and Gadille, D'Iribarne, and Lanciano 1998). Further studies will highlight the variety of forms at sectoral and local level.

REFERENCES

Amable, B, Barré, R., and Boyer, R. (1997). *Les systèmes d'innovation à l'ère de la globalisation*, Paris: Economica.

Brisset-Sillon, C. (1997). *Universités Publiques dux Etats-Unis:une autonamie sous tutelle*. Paris: Dharmattan.

Bryson, C. (1999). 'Ontract Research: The Failure to Address the Real Issues', *Higher Education Review*, l31(2).

Buechtemann, C. and Verdier, E. (1998). 'Education and Training Regimes; Macro-Institutional Evidence', *Revue d'économie politique*, 108(3).

Callon, M. (1991). 'Réseaux technico-économiques et flexibilité', in R. Boyer (ed.), *Figures de l'irréversibilité*. Paris: Editions de l'EHESS.

Cereq (1999). *De la compétence universitaire à la qualification professionnelle: l'insertion des docteurs*. Document Synthèse Céreq N°144, Marseille.

Clark, B. (1993). *The Research Foundations of Graduate Education: Germany, Britain, France, United States and Japan*. Berkeley, CA: University of California Press.

COSEPUP (2000). *Enhancing the Postdoctoral Experience for Scientists and Engineers*. Washington, DC: National Academies Press.

David, P. and Foray, D. (1995). 'Accessing and Expanding the Science and Technology Knowledge Base', STI Review, 16: 13–68.

d'Iribarne, A. (1987). 'Programme de recherche interdisciplinaire sur le marché de l'emploi des scientifiques en France'. PIRTTEM.

Doeringer, P. B. and Piore, M. (1971). *Internal Labor Markets and Manpower Analysis.* Lexington, MA: DC Health.

Enders, J. (2001). 'Serving Many Masters: The Ph.D. on the Labour Market', Paper prepared for the CHER conference, September 2–4, Dijon, France.

Edquist, Ch. (1997). *Systems of Innovation, Technologies, Institutions and Orgaanisations.* London, Washington, DC: Pinter.

Eyraud, F., Marsden, D., and Silvestre, J. J. (1990). 'Occupational and Internal Labour Market in Great Britain and in France', *International Labour Review,* 129(4): 501–17.

Ezkovitz, H. and Leydesdorff, L. (2000). 'The Dynamics of Innovation: From National Systems and "Mode 2" to a Triple Helix of University–Industry–Government Relations', *Research Policy,* 29(2): 109–24.

—— Webster, A., Gebhardt, C., and Terra, C. (2000). 'The Future of the University and University of the Future: Evolution of Ivory Tower to Entrepreneurial Paradigm', *Research Policy,* 29(2).

Gadille, M., D'Iribarne, A., and Lanciano-Morandat, C. (1998). 'The French Science and Technical System Between Societal Constructions and Sectoral Specificities', Communication for the 14ème seminar of EGOS, Mastrich University, 9–11 July.

Granovetter, M. (1983). 'The Strength of Weak Ties', *American Journal of Sociology,* 87: 1360–80.

—— (1985). 'Economic Action and Social Structure: The Problem of Embeddedness', *American Journal of Sociology,* 91(3): 481–510.

Grossetti, M. (1995). *Science, Industrie et territoire.* Presses Universitaires du Mirail.

Hall, P. and Soskice, D. (2001). *Varieties of Capitalism: The Institutional Foundations of Comparative Advantage.* Oxford: Oxford University Press.

Kline, S. J. and Rosenberg, N. (1986). 'An Overview of Innovation', in R. Landay and N. Rosenberg (eds.), *The Positive Sum Strategy.* Academy of Engineering Press.

Kodama, F. and Florida, R. (eds.) (1999). *University–Industry Linkages in Japan and the United States.* Cambridge, MA and London: MIT Press.

Lam, A. (2000). 'Skill Formation in the Knowledge-Based Economy: Transformation Pressures in European High-Technology Industries', IIRA 12th World Congress, Tokyo.

Lanciano, C., Maurice, M., Nohara, H., and Silvestre, J. J. (eds.) (1998). *Les acteurs de l'innovation et l'entreprise, France-Europe-Japon.* Paris: L'Harmattan.

—— and Nohara, H. (2001). 'A Comparative Study of R&D Staff in France and Japan', Communication to the European Socio-Economic Research to the Benchmarking of RTD Policies, European commission DGXII, 15–16 March.

Lundvall, A. (1992). *National System of Innovation. Toward a Theory of Innovation Interactive Learning.* London: Pinter.

Lundvall, A. (1997). 'The Globalising Learning Economy: Implication for Innovation Policy', Repport to the European Commission, DGXII, TSER programme.

Mangematin, V. and Mandran, N. (1999). 'Ph.D. Job Market: Professional Trajectories and Incentives During the Ph.D.', *Research Policy*, 29: 741–56.

Martinelli, D. (2001). 'Labour Market Entry and Mobility of Young French Ph.D.s', *Science and Innovation*. Paris: OECD.

Mason, G., Beltramo, J. P., and Paul, J. J. (2000). 'Knowledge Infrastructure, Technical Problem-Solving and Industrial Performance: Electronics in Britain and France', Paper prepared for DRUID, University of Aalborg.

Maurice, M., Sellier, F., and Silvestre, J. J. (1982). *Politiques d'Education et Organisation Industrielle en France et en Allemagne. Essai d'Analyse Sociétale*. Paris: Presses Universitaires de France.

—— —— —— (1986). *The Social Foundations of Industrial Power: A Comparison of France and Germany*. Cambridge, MA: MIT Press.

Musselin, C. (1990). 'Les marchés universitaires, comme économie de la qualité'. *Revue française de sociologie*.

Laredo, P. and Mustar, P. (2001). 'Innovation and Research Policy in France (1980–2000) or the Disappearance of the Colbertist State', *Research Policy*, 32(4): 621–38.

Nohara, H. (2001). 'Joint Production of Competences Between Academia and Industry as a Bridging Institution in Emergence', Rapport SESI.

—— (2006). 'An International Comparison of Labour Markets for Engineers and Scientists: Strategic Behaviours and Collective Capacity for Innovation', Rapport PIEP, London School of Economics.

National Science Foundation (1997, 1998, 1999). *Science and Engineering Indicators*. Washington, DC.

Nelson, R. (ed.) (1993). *National Systems of Innovation: A Comparative Study*. Oxford: Oxford University Press.

Paradeise, C. (1988). 'Acteurs et institutions. La dynamique des marchés du travail'. *Sociologie du travail*. 1: 79–105.

Perret, C. (2000). 'L'accès aux emplois en entreprise des docteurs scientifiques'. thèse du doctorat, Université de Bourgogne et IREDU.

Saxenian, A. (1994). *Regional Advantage: Competition and Cooperation in Silicon Valley and Route 128*. Cambridge, MA: Harvard University Press.

Spence, M. (1973). 'Job Market Signalling', *Quarterly Journal of Economics*, 87: 355–74.

Stephan, P. (1996). 'The Economics of Science', *Journal of Economic Literature*, 34: 1196–1235.

Von Hippel, E. (1990). *The Sources of Innovation*. New York: Oxford University Press.

Williamson, O. E. (1985). *The Economic Institutions of Capitalism: Firms, Markets, Relational Contracting*. New York: Free Press.

APPENDIX

Table A.12.1 Typology of Ph.D. student socialization models

Country	US	Japan	France	Germany	UK
Funding of doctoral programmes	Multiple (grants, fellowship, job), but importance of direct employment cost in the form of research contracts (research or teaching assistants: 65–75 %): (Source: NSF)	Mainly bank loan without interest, few grants and fellowship	National grant MNRT (30–50%) + research contracts: In total 75–95% of Ph.D. are financially assisted (Source: MNERT)	Federal research/teaching contracts or research grant (70–90% as junior university staff—full- or part-time) + diverse fellowship	Grants from research councils or publics funds (75 % of full-time students); attribution based on individual merit, auto-financing for 20% of full-time and 50% of part-time students
Characteristics of doctoral student	Heterogeneous population; lot of foreign students (40–60%) (Source: SEI-NSF Appendix Table 2-33)	Young Ph.D. or lot of thesis on works presented by salaried engineers (50% in engineering), less foreign students (20%)	Young Ph.D. (30-year olds) + less foreign students (20–25 %)	Students graduate later (33-year old in engineering, 31.5 in science); less foreign students (8–15% in 1996)	Heterogeneous population: very young Ph.D., part-timers and more foreign students (30–50%) (Source SEI-NSF Appendix Table 2-33)
Implicit contract between student and director	Contract based on individual scientific merit	Personalized contract (master –disciple relationship)	Institutional contract (laboratory – candidate)	Personalized contract (master –disciple relationship)	Contract based on individual scientific merit
Ph.D. training-career transition	Dual orientation (75% in universities or IRP and 25% in industry, three years after the graduation)	Dominant academic orientation = more than 80%	Dual (academia/industry) orientation (50–70% academia against 20–30% industry, three years	Diversified orientation (30–60% public sector [HE+IRP]) against 30–60% in industry, one year after)	Dual orientation (welcome foundation survey; 80% for first job and 60% three years after in academia); case granted students for industry

(Continued)

Table A.12.1 (*Continued*)

Country	US	Japan	France	Germany	UK
	and progressive transfer towards industry	after); Cifre granted students 75% in industry			
Academic labour market	Tenure effects, competitive selection of scientists + precarious situation and mobility of young Ph.D.; labour market segmentation training/ research universities	Early occupational stabilization of young Ph.D.; internal promotion; segmentation univ./ private lab public and private	Early occupational stabilization of young Ph.D. (civil servant status); internal promotion; segmentation public and private research	Division between professors with habilitation and non-full term assistants, long selection process + precarious situation of young scientists	Tenure effects in spite of its formal suppression; precarious situation and long selection process of young scientists; segmentation polytech-univ./ traditional univ.
Ph.D. status in industry	Average, but combined status of professor/entrepreneur highly esteemed	Weak and hardly distinctive from other educational titles	Relatively non-distinctive, competed by title of graduated engineer 'ingénieur diplôme'	High status of Ph.D., possibility of career promotion	Average, status of scientific expert esteemed
Career path	Inter-establishment mobility in academia and transversal mobility between academia and industry are high (Career mix)	Weak mobility (industrial/academic careers in separation)	Weak mobility (industrial/academic careers in separation)	Relatively high mobility in the first part of career (diversified careers)	Relatively high mobility in the first part of career (diversified careers)
Type of model	Reputation-based competition model (quasi-market model)	Relational (professorial) model	Institutional hierarchy model	Professorial centred model	Professional model

13

Competence Certification and the Reform of Vocational Education: A Comparison of the UK, France, and Germany

Christian Bessy

13.1. INTRODUCTION

Lifelong learning is one of the main objectives towards which European education and training policy has been orientated since the early 1980s. Among the different means used to reach this objective, the EU encourages the development of new systems of competence certification in order to change education and training systems according to the 'principle of equivalence' of the different routes to 'qualification' throughout a person's life. This leads to a conception of a system of competence certification that is based on a single nomenclature of certification levels in which the certification is defined by common criteria (or results) and independently of particular training programme or methods.

Such a conception of certification is justified by the fact that it favours competence flexibility and transferability. In this way, individuals can carry their competencies with them when they find a new job. Moreover, this conception opens access to superior levels to all by defining individual training itineraries. In this perspective, we can talk about an 'intrinsic logic' of certification to indicate that the notion of competence is based on the idea of the transferability of individual potential and in different work contexts. This intrinsic logic of certification can be opposed to an 'institutional logic' in which competence certification cannot be detached from the institutional context, that is, from a social construction of the certification process based on shared values and common practices.[1]

In this chapter we propose to analyse the issues raised by the reform of education and training systems based on an intrinsic logic of certification in comparison with reforms more inspired by an institutional logic. We start with the British government's creation of the NVQ system in the mid-1980s, which is a systematic attempt to introduce a system of national certification of occupational competencies. This system has inspired various projects to reform certification systems, particularly the European Commission's White Paper on Education and Training (1995). Therefore, it can help us to have a better understanding of the factors that inspired European policy as well as its limits, given the less than convincing results from introducing the NVQ system in relation to the initial objectives. In particular, such a system of competence certification points to the difficulty of defining standards for training and competency that are recognized by all the actors within an industry.

In the following section we analyse the origins and development of the British NVQ experience in its institutional context (see Box 13.1). The system, initially set up in 1986, was modified in the early 1990s with the introduction of government funding for the training of young people. From then on the number of certificates delivered increased rapidly, almost doubling between 1992 and 2000. The first part of this article presents the NVQ system and its relation to the traditional British apprenticeship system. We highlight its main characteristics, especially the functioning of the labour market it pre-supposes, and associated forms of recognition for competencies. We point out coordination problems around the definition of common standards for competency evaluation which serve as a benchmark for NVQs. Next, we consider how this apparatus fits into the overall reform of the British educa-tion and training system, aimed primarily at creating a quasi-market for training.

In the second part, we present the experiences of two other European countries in which the reform of the education and training system follows a more institutional logic of certification: France and Germany. In the French case, the new system was introduced in a context where, compared to the UK, vocational training is more developed and the 'degree/diploma' is more recognized by employers. While the reforms did not result in a complete restructuring of the French education and training system, the new forms of certification do constitute a real alternative to the traditional degree/diploma. The content of the new vocational 'certificates' and its recognition is a matter of collective bargaining involving workers' unions and employers' organiza-tions.

Germany's 'dual' system of vocational training offers a good point of comparison because it relies on a strong system of collective regulation of all aspects of the employment relationship within an industry. Training programmes and competencies are defined according to occupations (*Beruf*) without any reference to a single nomenclature of certification levels, as is the case in France and the UK. On the other hand, this dual training system is changing in order to cope with new challenges, in particular rapid technical changes and new forms of work organization.

In conclusion, we present the main results of our comparative analyses and question the orientation of the European education and training policy. We point out the limits of an intrinsic logic of competence certification for favouring innovation and constructing functionally flexible labour markets.

13.2. NVQS AS A NEW QUALIFICATION SYSTEM

The creation of NVQs was part of a reform to the British education and training system intended to improve the competencies of the labour force by redefining relations between training and employment, and by a systematic revival of initial and continuous occupational training which, in the past, was seldom recognized by British employers (Buechtemann and Verdier 1998). Although we do not explore the factors accounting for the collapse of the traditional British apprenticeship system,[2] we nonetheless take it as a basis for comparison in order to bring out the particular conception of occupational skills developed in the NVQ system and, more generally, the particular model of training and of the job market that the NVQ system presupposes. This comparison also shows NVQs to constitute a new model of work evaluation designed to become a general benchmark for qualifications in the labour market. After presenting the model, we analyse the tensions generated by the introduction of NVQs and their use by firms.

13.2.1. The NVQ Model: A General Benchmark for Qualifications

The aim of the NVQ system (see Box 13.1) was to define standards for education and training by specifying the results to achieve in the performance of certain types of jobs. It introduced a new occupational education and training model to replace former systems. Instead of designing training programmes to meet the needs of the labour market, leading industry bodies composed of representative employers set out to codify occupational competencies by describing what efficient work meant in specific occupational areas. It is on the basis of these occupational competencies that training programmes were supposed to be defined (Jessup 1990).

The idea was to formulate analytical criteria that were general enough to be applicable to all types of training. Training courses could thus be divided up

---

Box 13.1. The NVQ system

The system was created in 1986. Reforms in the 1990s resulted in a steep increase in the number of certificates delivered. Below, we present the general architecture of the system as it existed in 1999 (NCVQ 1999).

Accreditation of NVQs is the responsibility of the National Council for Vocational Qualifications (NCVQ), a government body that manages the entire NVQ system and defines levels of training for the country as a whole, to be achieved in a certain number of years. It has Awarding Bodies, which define standards of competency for particular occupations, in liaison with 'Lead Boards', composed of employer organizations for each occupational area. Over one hundred Awarding Bodies function in liaison with 170 Lead Boards. The Awarding Bodies are also responsible for accrediting the organizations that award qualifications on the basis of quality assurance procedures (Norm ISO 9000), including firms that volunteer to do so. Employees can thus have their occupational skills recognized directly at their workplace.

The general architecture of the system is based on the classification of all NVQs in terms of eleven occupational areas and five levels of competency. The aim is to facilitate the transferability of competencies within and between occupational areas, and to define possibilities for advancement from one level to the next. These levels of competency are defined in relation to various dimensions of work at that level, including complexity, predictability, autonomy, supervision, and responsibility. For example, Level 1 defines the competency required to accomplish routine or predictable work activities, while at the other end of the scale Level 5 groups together activities requiring a range of fundamental skills and complex techniques across a wide and often unpredictable variety of contexts. Level 3 corresponds to work activities which are predictable and serve as a sound basis for advancement, that is, skilled labour.

In the 1992 reform of the NVQ system, the NCVQ introduced General National Vocational Qualifications (GNVQs), designed for young people in the 16–19 age group who are in training. It established equivalences with National Education qualifications. GNVQs serve as a basis for professional life or for further studies. They were defined in terms of fourteen occupational areas and three competency levels. Key competencies were added later. In 1997, The Qualifications and Curriculum Authority (QCA) replaced the NCVQ.

---

into modules corresponding to units of certification. These criteria make the evaluation of each element of competency composing an NVQ possible in concrete terms. It can thus be assumed that each element of competency can be standardized within a particular area of work. For example, performance criteria associated with the element of competency around the task of 'Identify and find documents in an existing filing system' are:

- the specific documents are rapidly located, extracted, and transmitted to the required person or place;
- delays in delivery of the files and/or documents are reported and reasons for the delays are explained politely;
- all movements of files and documents are correctly and legibly recorded and updated (Wolf 1994).

This analytical conception of competencies is based on a codification of human actions peculiar to cognitive psychology, the language and methods of which were used to define competency frameworks. This atomistic view, coherent with a tayloristic form of work organization (Marsden 1998), contrasts with a more synthetic conception of competencies that highlights the tacit dimension of knowledge which can be shared within occupational communities.

In the NVQ system, units of certification are acquired during a period of training which is not predetermined, may be long, and may take place in several firms. This modular conception contrasts with the one underlying the traditional apprenticeship system which did not, in principle, allow partial validation of the vocational qualification or a distinction between different levels (Marsden 1998). In the apprenticeship system, the organization of work in firms depended heavily on constraints imposed by the content of training, while in the new system the quest for flexibility orients training along the lines of a functional approach to work. All forms of training are considered comparable, whether they have been delivered by the firm itself (on-the-job (OTJ) training) or by an outside concern.

For the designers of this system, one of the advantages is to take the first step towards the acquisition of recognized qualifications by people without any occupational qualifications (in the traditional sense) and thus to promote the transfer of capabilities that are not necessarily characteristic of a particular organization of labour. It thus should facilitate inter-firm mobility and limit the risks of exclusion inherent in existing occupational fields that are too restrictive. It can also serve to update competency frameworks in the event of technological change, although this has the disadvantage of limiting the lifespan of certificates.

The system architecture and the hierarchy it introduced between different levels of competency (see Box 13.1) clearly reveal the underlying conception of competency. This conception relates to the notion of capability considered as a matrix generating a particular performance, like academic training which follows on from the general to the particular. In this framework, training is intended not only to transmit (certifiable) competencies but also to facilitate occupational transferability through motivation via diverse incentive mechanisms, since capabilities can be applied in a multitude of tasks and contexts.

This type of design tends to establish a single scale for measuring competencies or, at least, a general benchmark for qualifications which is supposed to be more relevant than the traditional system of classification because it is closely linked to the requirements of the job market. As Marsden (1998) mentions, competencies are treated as 'quantitatively' different and are graded hierarchically according to different levels of NVQs, whereas in the old system of apprenticeship the work of various occupations and of skilled and semi-skilled workers was 'qualitatively' different.

In this new system, the conception of the job market corresponds to the supply and demand of occupational skills defined very generally, that is to say, hardly related to a specific occupational context. It is assumed that the basic elements of skills can be recombined to suit the needs of a particular job. Due to the processes of standardization and certification, competencies are detached from the occupational communities and collective context in which they are acquired, thus creating the conditions for greater fluidity of the job market and enhanced flexibility in firms' work organization.

The extreme case of a conception of competencies detached from any occupational context is when the criteria for validation of skills do not involve a recognized network of evaluating bodies. The criteria are then based on batteries of tests administered from a distance (via Internet, for example) by an accredited organization (e.g. tests on a foreign language, on accounting techniques, on use of software). What is then tested are competencies common to a vast range of occupational situations, right down to the classic aptitude test.[3] This type of conception is based on the idea that competency can be isolated from the situations in which it is mobilized. It is in this sense that we can talk of a 'substantial' approach to competency, in which individuals carry their competency with them, as opposed to an approach that tries to contextualize evaluations to fit the specific nature of the environment (Eymard-Duvernay and Marchal 1997). In this latter approach, the judgement is more local since the evaluation can be renegotiated in different contexts. In this perspective, the tension between 'capabilities' and 'practical knowledge' analysed below is a clear illustration of the more general tension between these two approaches to competency.

By taking into account all the above characteristics we can posit that the NVQ model is a new system of worker qualification aimed at restructuring the systems of training and, more broadly, occupational guidance and recruitment. It is diametrically opposed to the system of qualifications related to traditional apprenticeship in practice in the job market (See Table 13.1).

Table 13.1 Synthetic comparison between NVQ system and traditional apprenticeship

Qualification systems characteristics	NVQs	Traditional apprenticeship
Origins	Government's creation	Vocational
Goals	National standards for education and training	Collective management of the working force in a specific labour market
Bargaining	No bargaining	Collective bargaining
Notion of competency	Analytical approach defining explicit criteria of performance; individual capability considered as a matrix of particular performance	Synthetic approach taking into account the tacit dimension of knowledge; practical knowledge
The nature of training	Promote vocational mobility; competencies must be deployed in a multitude of tasks and contexts	Skills acquisition and knowledge transfer
Mode of certification	Modular approach	Partial validation not allowed
Duration of certificates	Limited	Not limited
Organization of work within the firm	Flexibility and functional approach to work	Determined by training constraints
Labour market	Vocational skills supply and demand defined very generally; greater fluidity	Narrow vocational skills; craft market with entry barriers

13.2.2. Tension Caused by the Establishment of NVQs

With the establishment of NVQs, tensions arose between this analytical and modular approach to competence and conceptions of occupational competence based on accrediting practical knowledge acquired through experience. In order to understand these tensions, it is interesting to look at the origins of the NVQ system and its evolution. Initially this system was based on a competency evaluation method developed in the US, in which a set of target objectives are specified. The key assumption in this method is that objectives can be clearly defined so that evaluators, the people they evaluate, and outside persons have a thorough understanding of what is being evaluated. It thus assumes the definition of generally agreed performance criteria that can be used to simplify the evaluation process.

Yet Wolf (1994) has clearly shown the limits of this assumption. This author highlights the difficulties inherent in this type of assessment since evaluators rely on their expertise in order to take into account the variability of contexts framing the evaluated competency. They proceed on the basis of a complex, internalized, and synthetic model, not a basic set of descriptors drawn from a series of performance indicators. According to Wolf, the quest for definitions and clarity has spawned an increasingly complex methodology. It was first necessary to create the notion of 'field specification' in order to describe the limits in which performance must be executed to qualify the person as competent. Prescriptions for evaluation were then added to make evaluation conditions more transparent. Later, problems of interpretation made it necessary to stipulate basic knowledge and comprehension. In fact, the Awarding Bodies are equipped with methods to verify the possession of capabilities underlying the execution of tasks, and not only the efficient performance of the tasks themselves.

The latter point clearly highlights the fact that the difficulties inherent in the evaluation of competencies lead to an emphasis being placed on general capabilities, when in fact this system was designed to give particular importance to the certification of occupational skills, in the sense of practical knowledge learned on the job. The idea was to enable employees with no degree or diploma to have access to a qualification. It was also to enable firms to identify sources of expertise, with a view to more efficient human resource management (HRM) entailing tighter control over work situations.

The subsequent introduction of 'key competencies' relate to general capabilities (ability to communicate, deal with hazards, adapt, do numeric calculations, etc.) was an obvious continuation of an approach aimed essentially at the transferability of competencies and thus potentially in conflict with the firm's specific operational goals. This is even clearer when it comes to giving employees the possibility of extending their training through the acquisition of 'basic knowledge'. Steedman and Hawkins (1994) cite an example in the building industry where many employers refused to include the acquisition of mathematical knowledge in the definition of training standards associated with an NVQ. It seems that such resistance characterizes employers who do not wish to invest in training either because they manage very short-term manpower or because they fear poaching. It may also be that employers consider that the acquisition of vocational skills is best left to informal training on the shop floor.

While these additional measures attest to the intention to ensure that competency can be applied in very different contexts or in related occupational situations, and that candidates can continue their training, they also show the difficulty of defining competencies in the absence of an occupational community sharing the same knowledge and rules of interpretation, as in traditional occupational or craft systems. Only the existence of common expertise makes it possible to stop the endless spiral of specifications, especially when intuitive knowledge is concerned (Dreyfus and Dreyfus 1986). By broadening areas of mobility, the goal of transferability is likely to increase the cost of processes of definition and certification of competencies, or else to promote a 'substantial' approach to competency by giving considerable weight to recognition for very general capabilities. In this case, it would entail the risk of excluding even more people from training when they are seen to have little potential.

Observations in firms, in the framework of the 'Modern Apprenticeship' programme at the end of which participants obtain a Level 3 NVQ, clearly illustrate the tensions described above. Here we draw essentially on a study by Gospel (1998) who investigated three sectors: mechanical construction, building, and computer technology. He shows that the success of the programme depends on employers' incorporation of training into their general human resources strategies. This is most often the case in large companies with the internal capacities to dispense training and to support the development of young people. The definition of a competency framework is part of their training and career-management policy and is articulated to their occupational qualifications grid. Gospel nevertheless highlights two limits: first, the risk of deadweights due to grants for training; and second, the fact that firms which provide training may be tempted to award the certification to candidates who do not meet the standard, because the grant is contingent on the number of persons trained. As Gospel shows, the quality of NVQs can vary even within the same sector, especially when key competencies are concerned. This can reduce their recognition by other firms. We see here the tension between the specific interests of the firm and the general interest.

Gospel also shows that the programme's success depends on the tradition of each sector as regards apprenticeship (except in the case of computer technology), and on the existence of coordination between firms and training institutes. Both conditions have been met in the mechanical construction industry[4] but not entirely in the building industry. The coordination deficit in the latter sector is huge because firms tend to rely on the outside market to recruit and dismiss workers, or else use subcontractors. The result is an insufficient number of firms with in-house resources to organize training. Hence, in certain situations this programme can be presented as a revival of traditional apprenticeship which allows a good compromise between recognition for occupational skills and the need for transferability of competencies. It appears that there is a balance between different forms of evaluation of competencies. Reference to NVQ candidates' capabilities is made contextually, on the basis of expertise shared by the actors. In this configuration, the NVQ system's goal of occupational insertion is achieved, without any major risk of exclusion of candidates with weak academic results.

Table 13.2 Number of NVQ certificates awarded since 1989

Year Cumulative total	March 2001 3.2 MM	Sept. 92 288 440		Sept. 94 713 481		Sept. 96 1 333 435		Sept. 98 2 223 186		Sept. 99 2 651 478	
Distribution by level	%		%		%		%		%		%
Level 1	18.0	93 926	32.6	196 496	27.5	309 166	23.2	456 373	20.5	516 255	19.5
Level 2	60.0	154 206	53.5	415 501	58.2	793 331	59.5	1 323413	59.5	1 576426	59.5
Level 3	19.0	25 041	8.7	66 391	9.3	178 867	13.4	369 499	16.6	470 570	17.8
Level 4	2.9	15 149	5.3	33 772	4.7	48 790	3.7	68 365	3.1	81 833	3.1
Level 5	0.1	118	0.0	1321	0.2	3281	0.2	5 536	0.2	6 394	0.2

Source: NCVQ.

These different characteristics probably explain the development of Level 3 NVQs since the launching of this programme in 1995. Their share in the total number of certificates awarded rose from 9.3 per cent in 1994 to 19 per cent in 2001 (source: NCVQ). Despite this trend, 80 per cent of the certificates awarded concern the lowest levels of competency, corresponding to the most standard jobs with little prospect of innovation. Moreover, far more traditional certifications are awarded than NVQs.

On the one hand, these results show the tendency of the NVQ system to support tayloristic patterns of work organization rather than high performance work systems (team working and delegating decisions to ordinary workers). On the other hand, it is likely that firms which introduce practices of competence recognition, practices which are to some extent equivalent to those existing in the NVQ system, do so more to individualize the employment relationship and to increase the flexibility of work organization than to certify the competencies of employees. This reflects the externalities issue and concerns over a loss of skilled labour to competitors due to the lack of an appropriate institutional framework.

13.2.3. Restructuring the Training System and Individualization of Competencies

To clearly understand the significance of the NVQ system and its consequences for how certain competencies are evaluated, we also need to take into account other elements of the reform, especially the extension of the NVQ system to initial education and training from 1992, and the use of this system in the constitution of a quasi-training market. This extension was part of the turnaround in government policy in favour of young people and their entry into employment (Lindley 1996). This leads to the set up of new training programmes directly linked to the acquisition of an NVQ, including the 'Youth Training' programme and, since 1995, the 'Youth Credits' system in which a credit is granted to jobless school-leavers. This credit is used for training within a firm or an accredited entity with a warranted placement for two years. For developing training programme at the end of which participants obtain at least a level 3 NVQ, different apprenticeship formula have been designed within the 'Modern Apprenticeship' programme (those aged 16–17 and 18–19). The cost of training is shared among the enterprise, the apprentice, and the government, which contributes to reducing externality problems inherent to the certification of vocational competencies.

All of these programmes can explain the increase in the number of NVQ certificates awarded since 1992 (see Table 13.2). These new policy orientations have tended to transform unemployment among the youth into a problem of education and training, that is, of investment in human capital. All school-leavers in Britain have a 'National Record of Achievements' setting out their results (school examinations, qualifications, basic skills, etc.) and career history. This 'competency portfolio' (recommended by the European Community) is used more and more in schools and by vocational guidance and recruitment agencies as a tool to plan educational and career choices (Coraldyn 1996). It is an evaluation tool suited to the individualization of training that is not necessarily attached to a work context.

The introduction of General National Vocational Qualifications (GNVQs) (see Box 13.1) also contributed to the individualization of training. This procedure provides a standard for the certification of occupational competencies acquired during initial education and training. The idea is not only to encourage occupational training at secondary school, traditionally reserved for general studies, but also to group together and reorganize existing titles granted for occupational training. In this way horizontal equivalence can be introduced between GNVQs, NVQs, and general education degrees/diplomas in order to ensure equivalence in the status of different types of qualification (or certification).

Note that this goal of equivalence led to a transposition of the NVQ system onto initial education and training. But the notion of competency used in formulating NVQs seem to be ill-suited to initial education and training (Coraldyn 1996). Originally, recognition for competencies was designed essentially for continuous adult education and training, as part of the management of careers and mobility. This required different models to those of initial education and training: other access criteria, other forms of organization, and other approaches to certification in order to identify and collectively recognize competencies that could be transferred from one situation to another. NVQs were moreover designed to be taught and evaluated in the workplace. In these circumstances, competency is the result of a long learning process that starts at school and continues throughout the person's working life.

This approach to competency, based on certification of occupational skills, poses problems when applied to initial education and training for young people. First, it poses pedagogical problems such as the definition of what basic knowledge is. Second, and more relevant to our study, it challenges the mechanisms of socialization of young people and of the progressive constitution of their occupational identity.

But this transposition was to be expected in so far as the standardization and certification procedures of the NVQ system contained the seeds of reference to general capabilities transcending precise professional contexts. Capabilities are considered as a matrix generating particular performance. Likewise, the enhanced role of key competencies in obtaining NVQs and GNVQs tends to rigidify the distinction between general and technical knowledge. Authors such as Steedman and Hawkins (1994) suggest that this insistence on general capabilities is a way of improving the basic general education of young people and of consolidating the fundamental knowledge necessary for further training. Without wishing to enter into the debate on this issue, it is nonetheless important to point to the risk this engenders of reproducing selection procedures at play in the school system, and thus of excluding the very same young people that were supposed to be rehabilitated.

This quest for equivalence must be related to competition between the actors in training. Reorientation of the NVQ system followed transformations to the system of education and occupational training[5] related to the creation of Training Enterprise Councils (TECs) in 1989. These replaced the former tripartite and regulatory Industrial Training Boards (ITB) that had gradually disappeared during the 1980s. The main function of TECs is to manage public sector business-oriented training programmes for young people and the jobless (respectively, Youth Training and Employment Training). The evaluation of these programmes is based on the training standards defined by the NVQ system. The standardization of service providers' performance was designed to reduce incompleteness of contracts, signed between TECs and different training providers who compete, and to increase the advantages of relying on the market (vs. allocation of funds according to administrative rules) while nevertheless safeguarding the national interest. This was the British government's intention with the NVQ reform in 1992. Obtaining an NVQ after a period of training is a guarantee of good allocation of public funds for that training. But the granting of public funds in relation to quantifiable performance objectives runs counter to the obligation to safeguard equal opportunities in access to training. This obligation has progressively changed the way of granting in order to reduce risks of exclusion of the most underprivileged categories (West, Pennell, and Edge 1998). More generally, competitive mechanisms are difficult to set up on markets characterized by the scarcity of agents and by options limited by outside factors (e.g. transport costs). Although they are, under certain conditions, favourable to innovation, they generate numerous dysfunctions and are factors of inequality. Ryan (1995), for example, shows that inequalities have grown in the UK faster than any other industrialized country. As regards occupational training, no specific national objectives exist for the underprivileged.

The above developments describe the different reorientations of the NVQ system, initially designed by the British government to encourage mobility by providing for certification of competencies acquired by workers through experience or training. We have shown that these reorientations, especially the introduction of competition into all branches of training and education, can increase risks of exclusion of the most disadvantaged groups. But these risks of exclusion are not related only to risks of creaming off, due to the existence of a system of funding reproducing the selection methods in practice in the school system. By opting for evaluation of potential, this type of certification system tends to de-contextualize the evaluation of competencies, which are detached from a precise occupational context, and to valorize the most general capabilities, so that competencies are seen as belonging to isolated individuals. This logic of individualization of competency is reinforced by public policies that consider young people and the unemployed as individual subjects who enter into contracts with 'producers' of training to improve their 'human capital'.

13.3. REFORMS INSPIRED BY A MORE INSTITUTIONAL LOGIC

Reform of the education and training systems in France and Germany were more inspired by an institutional logic of certification. We begin with the case of France which shared the feature of the UK reforms of basing them on the construction of a single nomenclature of certification levels. Next, we present the German system that has evolved while maintaining the reference to occupations in the definition of training curricula and competence certification.

13.3.1 A Comparison with France

In France, the correspondence that exists between job and training classifications is linked to an institutional set-up where the state certifies and guarantees 'training titles'. The introduction of the new system of competence certification tends to reinforce the correspondence, but within a more decentralized regulation of the education and training system.

13.3.1.1. *Correspondence Between Levels of Training and Employment*

In general, France differs from the UK in that occupational training carries relatively more weight within a general training and education system which is more unified and hierarchical (Buechtemann and Verdier 1998). There is a close correspondence between the levels of classification in education and training and those in employment, especially in sectors where diplomas are taken into account in France in classification grids resulting from industrial collective bargaining.

   In turn, the notion of 'qualification', in so far as it pertains to the formation of a social judgement of an individual's occupational qualities, has a rather different meaning in France. In the UK, the notion of qualification is linked to the diploma an individual holds, whereas in France it is associated to a classification grid applied collectively at the industry level. The French system can be seen as corresponding to a bureaucratic model of an ILM, in which the qualification level is based on the features of the work post occupied by the employee (Marsden 1999).

   Work by Jobert and Tallard (1995) shows that although reference to diplomas and titles, certified by the French state, is clearly present in classification grids, their role in the structuring of occupational hierarchies, the guarantees they give those who have them, and their links with continuing education and training vary widely. It depends on the sector. The reference to diplomas is particularly present in the classification grids, called 'classifying criteria grids' (opposed to the traditional 'Parodi grids'), in which diplomas are a way to assess the 'level of knowledge', one of the most often used criteria for job classifying (the other criteria are 'technical dimension, 'autonomy', and 'liability').

   More generally, the correspondence (or the 'equivalence relation') between degrees/diplomas and jobs constitutes the basis of the 'the training levels nomenclature' established by the French 'Commissariat du Plan' in the beginning of the 1960s for anticipating training needs and so solving 'qualified' manpower shortages. Work by J. Affichard (1983) shows admirably how the domain of application of this nomenclature has been extended beyond its initial use as a statistical tool. In particular, this nomenclature allows the state to provide guarantees for 'training titles' whose value on the market is less certain than that of the national degree/diploma.[6]

At the beginning of the 1990s, faced with rising unemployment among the youth, the French government introduced a set of procedures designed to improve the insertion of people in difficulty into the job market, via occupational training and new modes of certification of occupational skills or access to degrees/diplomas.

Whereas traditionally, certification was considered in terms of a diploma at the end of a training course, different forms of validation of competencies gained either through experience or training were established (Merle 1997). While the French state defended the idea of different routes through which a diploma could be obtained,[7] the 'social partners' (unions and employers) focused rather on the introduction of new forms of certification controlled by professional bodies. In one respect, the different forms of validating experience-based competencies support the role of the diploma/degree quite simply by diversifying the ways in which it can be obtained. But the aim was also to reduce their importance through the definition of alternative paths to certification.

In the UK, in the absence of industrywide agreements and given the weak involvement of the state in the certification of vocational competencies, NVQs do not have the same implications. There is nevertheless some convergence of the two training systems. The British NVQ system aims to establish the narrowest possible correspondence between levels of training and those of employment, via the analytical definition of required competencies, and to promote the continuation of studies by building bridges between occupational training and general education.

In this way it corresponds to some extent to the present French system. The French system, however, increasingly takes into account the 'needs' of firms (diversification and 'professionalization' of branches, creation of degrees/diplomas in cooperation with industry, etc.) and is becoming more and more decentralized through the growing weight of the regions and of consular bodies in the regulation of the training–employment link.[8] This tends to challenge the unified nature of the French system, guaranteed until now by strong state intervention and the importance of nationally recognized degrees/diplomas. A clear illustration of the withdrawal of the French state is the recent creation (law of January 2002) of a National Directory of Vocational Qualifications (*Répertoire National des Certifications Profession-nelles*) to replace the certification list drawn up by the Technical Certification Commission (*Commission Technique d'Homologation*), aimed at unifying all occupational certifications in a single frame (according to levels of training in National Education). The latter Commission was replaced by a National

Vocational Certification Commission (*Commission Nationale de la Certification Professionnelle*). This new directory of vocational certifications includes not only diplomas but also industry-specific certifications. One issue raised was the fact that new 'certificates' would be introduced and recognized in the system without any probationary period to identify the nature of the jobs to which they might afford access. Even more innovatively, it specified the competencies to be targeted and not only the training programme and terms of access.

13.3.1.2. Alternatives to the Degree/Diploma

The French experience regarding certification of occupational competencies as an alternative to the traditional national degree/diploma is a clear illustration of the decentralization of the regulation of education and training.[9] In the 1990s, Occupational Qualification Certificates (*Certificats de Qualification Professionnelle*—CQPs) were introduced first in metallurgy and subsequently in other sectors. These certificates for young people in apprenticeship and for employees were situated in the framework of training plans and were initially part of 'qualification agreements' (*Contrats de qualification*).[10] This certification system can be compared to the NVQ system in so far as it has the same rationale regarding training and an analytical definition of competencies.

The construction of CQPs was nevertheless a matter of collective bargaining involving the unions and not only employers' organizations (Jobert and Tallard 1997). This difference compared to the UK NVQ system is related to the fact that, in France, certification of competencies affords access to a higher qualification (Charreau et al. 1998). Thus the CQP is more closely linked than the degree/diploma to the issue of classification of jobs within an industry, even if access to the qualification is not entirely automatic. Apart from the embryonic state of the certification procedure, this may explain the low number of certificates granted (about 20,000 during the period 1987–2000),[11] in comparison with the NVQ system.

This, in turn, illuminates a major difference with of the British system, the dynamic of which is structured to a large degree by the reorganization of the training system and the attempt to impose a single certification procedure for all occupational competencies. The competency frameworks underlying each NVQ can be used to implement policies for training and internal mobility within firms, but when it comes to recruitment, little recognition is given to this certification.

Apart from this key difference, the sectors which most often use this new certification procedure are those which, as in the British case, participate in the government programme to renew training methods, based on strong ties between training organizations and industry. In 1999, the CQPs granted by the metallurgical sector accounted for close to 50 per cent of all CQPs granted by industry. Likewise, over 50 per cent of the firms concerned had over 500 employees. An analysis of the construction of CQPs in these sectors shows that the same tension exists between different ways of defining and evaluating competencies.[12]

Certification procedures based on the evaluation of practical knowledge are resulting in a proliferation of certificates defined in a highly decentralized way. These certification procedures are used by firms to solve problems of recruitment for very specific jobs. They are complementary to the degree/diploma in so far as they complete the training of young school-leavers with low qualifications, or qualifications considered too general by employers. They help to enhance the employee's qualification in her/his firm or in other firms in the same industry. This is particularly true in the metallurgical sector.

By contrast, in the plastics industry standardization and certification are more centralized. Criteria of access to training and current methods used to evaluate occupational skills are similar to the criteria and methods applied in the initial education and training system. The number of certificates is lower but their scope of validity is generally far broader because these certificates are more focused on the transferability of competencies. In this context, the CQP, intended mainly for persons in employment,[13] in a sense replaces preparations for a diploma or degree. Firms take advantage of government funds and more flexibility in the definition of the training content and structure.

It is in this respect that the CQP corresponds most closely to the rationale of the NVQ system which, as we have shown, involves risks of exclusion from training of employees with the lowest academic performance.

13.3.2. Comparison with Germany

Germany represents the case in which competence certification is the most inspired by an occupational and institutional logic. Its dual training system is linked to the construction of 'professional labour markets' which are strongly regulated by the rules issued from collective bargaining at the level of each industry and each region (*Länder*). Vocational competencies are certified during the period of dual training and the worker can progress within the vocational channel, thanks to their experience and their participation to training programmes for adults. The certificates (or credentials) are not detached from the training itineraries. That leads to a long-term involvement of the workers within the occupation and to the possibility of inter-firm mobility. Concerning continuous training, the content of programmes and the credentials are less regulated except for the access to technicians and 'Meisters' qualifications. That allows firms to achieve greater flexibility as a response to their specific needs.

As the basic features of the 'dual' training system are well known, we will concentrate on recent developments. Nevertheless, before doing that, we can recall two specific aspects of the German system that can be more generally linked to what Hall and Soskice (2001) call a coordinated market economy (CME). One point is that the link between vocational training and competence certification and recognition makes sense in reference to a particular occupation. The other point is that this link leads to cooperative forms of work organization and of technology transfers favouring incremental processes of innovation. The first point favours deepening the comparison with the French case, and the second point favours a comparison with the British case.

13.3.2.1. A Coordinated Process of Training and Innovation

In both France and Germany, vocational credentials have a national and standardized dimension, but the logic of standardization is different (Möbus et Verdier 1997). Indeed, in Germany, the construction of vocational credentials integrates all the actors concerned by the training issue within an occupation, whereas, in France, the state plays a central role both in the definition of training curricula and in certification. That comes from the fact that French vocational training takes place mainly within school and is more certificate orientated in reference to a single nomenclature of certification levels. The certification of vocational competencies does not correspond to a precise job but rather to a job level with the possibility of further education. As a consequence, a more important weight is given to theoretical aspects according to a learning model following on from the general to the particular.

In Germany, the more important role played by firms in training leads to a construction of vocational credentials taking into account more practical aspects of the particular occupation. The certification of vocational competencies is not conceived as opening access to further education. The absence of a single nomenclature of certification levels does not mean that any form of certification hierarchy applies. It is a horizontal logic of differentiation, more based on different categories of occupation than a single scale of competency levels. There is no equivalence between dual vocational credentials and general education diplomas in spite of the recurrent claims of 'social partners'.

Another specificity of the German dual system is that the work organization is strongly constrained by training conditions. We have already noted (see above) that this is also a characteristic of the traditional British apprenticeship system.[14] A big difference is that the latter is more task-centred than the former in which work is organized in reference to functions integrating broad skills. That confers to blue-and white-collar workers a much greater degree of autonomy at work and mobility within the vocational 'channel'. Therefore, technicians or *Meister* share with their subordinates the same professional knowledge. That leads to forms of work organization that are more cooperative and more consistent with incremental product and process innovations.

In a dynamical perspective, the German dual training system has exhibited a high degree of reactivity to both technological transformations and changes in the general educational attainment of youngsters by the way of collective bargaining and the tied links between all actors of training within an industry. That can explain the fact that German apprenticeship system has continued to function in contrast to the British system which had not the same possibilities of adaptation.

At a more macroeconomic level, inter-firm cooperation concerning vocational training schemes, relayed by powerful employer associations, provide high levels of industry-specific skills. That in turn encourages inter-firm collaboration that promotes technology transfer. Hall and Soskice (2001) show that such an institutional setting tends to support an incremental process of innovation which characterizes certain industries (metallurgy, machine tools, etc.). This kind of CME can be opposed to a liberal market economy (LME), which facilitates a more radical innovation process such as one finds in high-technology industries (biotechnology, software, etc). The UK gives a good illustration of this configuration in which technology transfers relies on individuals taking their competencies from one firm to another. It is compatible with the individualization of employment relationship and fluid labour markets. But apart from these high-tech industries, one can wonder whether the British labour market is not rather characterized by a 'low-skill equilibrium' which is antithetical to competition based on quality or on innovation. Within a configuration in which neither the work organization of firms, nor inter-firm relationships are cooperative, the competence certification of the less skilled workers, including intermediate qualifications, is problematic and their vocational mobility relies on individual initiative.

13.3.2.2. German Dual System Changes

The dual system is changing in order to cope with new challenges, in particular flexibility constraints and rapid technical changes. Coupled with the orientation of youth towards higher education levels, that has led firms (the larger ones) to change their recruitment policy, by hiring students coming from upper secondary vocational schools or universities, and to reduce their training cost by lowering the number of apprenticeship positions. One of the problems of the dual system is that it prepares apprentices for quite narrowly defined occupations. Such narrow specialization is now considered inappropriate when the trend is towards flexibility and multi-skilling. The result has been a trend towards broader training programmes, including key competencies, to overcome the discontinuities between school-based study and learning in the workplace. As shown by the reform in the metallurgy industry (1978), which is a leading industry in Germany, the training programmes are more and more based on general 'functions' rather than the use of particular techniques or equipment. More specifically, in the German car industry, training programmes co-produced by the 'social partners' try to achieve a better articulation between 'theory' and 'practice', such that trained workers have a more global apprehension of the work process and a better capacity for solving problems. This 'work process knowledge', according to the expression of Boreham, Samurcay, and Fisher (2002), allows apprentices to make their work experiences more explicit and reflexive thus facilitating the sharing of professional knowledge. But 'knowledge sharing' has some limits linked to the fact that professional knowledge also serves to create occupational identities.

The creation of new occupations has been a response to a decrease in the number of apprenticeship positions.[15] In 1997, the creation of four new dual credentials in the ICT domain gives a good illustration of this kind of change. This new development was promoted by the German government to cope with manpower shortages in this new technological field and with the difficulties of coordination encountered by firms belonging to different industries (Sheuer et al. 2003). These new dual credentials conserve the reference to the notion of 'occupation' (*Beruf*) while conceiving training programmes with a strong degree of openness in order to integrate further technical changes. This tends to reinforce the tendencies mentioned above concerning the definition of new training curricula and to undermine the categories which structure both the traditional professional fields and the education system.

One of the major consequences of this innovation is that these new dual credentials, added to the existing dual credentials within the ICT field, constitute the basis of a certification scale going from dual credentials all the way to university diplomas. The passage from one training track to another, including continuous training for adults, is both anticipated and encouraged by relying on a system of horizontal equivalence between different routes of qualification. The new continuing IT training system (since June 2002) provides qualifications for jobs which so far have mostly been held by university graduates. In fact, this innovation introduces different certification levels within a same technological field[16] and ensures a more modular conception of training and certification. On the one hand, this permeability and equivalence of vocational education and training allows students who have abandoned their university studies to have access to dual training. On the other, it opens up possibilities for blue- and white-collar workers to gain more ready access than before to *Meisters*, specialist, or engineer level certifications by the way of continuing training programmes and the validation of work experience.[17] The objective is to make continuing training the second major route to top-level qualifications (BMBF, rapport 2003). To ensure the transparency and quality of continuing training, the Federal government has strived to establish a nationwide certification system for this kind of training and to increase the competition on this market.

These recent evolutions make the German education and training system closer to the British and the French ones, even if the reference to the notion of 'occupation', implicating strong institutional links between the actors, still structures that system and guarantees the recognition of vocational competence certification. This restructuring is connected to German employment public policy supporting disadvantaged young people and low-skilled adults, associated with the employment policy guidelines of the EU. It also responds to the objective of the Federal government to make Germany a competitive place for vocational education and training at the European level.

13.4. CONCLUSION

The establishment of new forms of certification of competencies is a response to changes in how work is organized and evaluated in firms. The British NVQ system can be seen as a reform designed to overhaul the education and training system in order to facilitate these changes. However, the UK experience attests to the difficulty of developing standards for training and competency that are recognized by all actors in an industry. This difficulty can be linked to the tensions between 'innovation' and 'codification'. On the one hand, both fast-moving knowledge and new forms of work organization imply competence flexibility. This constraint of flexibility makes the codification of competencies difficult. On the other hand, the codification process is important to the labour market in so far as it allows transferability of competencies. The main solution adopted by the NVQ system for resolving these tensions has been to increase the reference to general aptitudes, which are traditionally developed and valued in school. This might explain the fact that the adoption of this system has been far more extensive in the area of post-school education than within firms, despite the fact that the framework was originally supposed to respond to the needs of industry.

Another factor in explaining the lack of employer participation in the NVQ system is the greater transparency of competencies. There is a problem of cost sharing when skills are made more transparent, and easier for other employers to 'poach'. That reinforces the need for an institutional framework (Marsden 1998).

More generally, the British experience illustrates the fact that, in the absence of institutional links, the implementation of a new system of competence certification is limited. Such a process of certification would require collective agreements between all actors within an industry. In the UK, this is not compatible with employment contracts that are less and less regulated by collective bargaining (Brown et al. 2000) and with the lack of institutional structures encouraging the formation of employer networks. All these factors explain why the NVQ system has developed most extensively at the lowest competence levels, corresponding to standard jobs, which contribute little to innovation.

In France and in Germany, the attempts to change the system of competence certification have been less far-reaching and have not had as large an impact on the educational and training system as in the UK. This is mainly because their vocational training systems are more developed. Nevertheless, we can identify certain important evolutions in each country.

In the French case, one observes the development of certification procedures which renew, like the British case, traditional modes of apprenticeship (the French CQPs). But, the development of this new procedure of certification is still relatively weak; mostly it is used to solve recruitment problems in particular occupations. The introduction of an intermediate form of certification of vocational competencies, between the national degree/diploma and company certifications, is still far from established. Although the role played by the French state is less and less important for the regulation of the vocational education and training system, the rise of an institutional logic allowing for a strong social recognition of competence certification is far from achieved. The risk is that the single nomenclature of certification levels will lead to an accelerated degree of 'credential inflation' and, therefore, to the exclusion from the labour market of those lacking any degree or certificate.

The German dual training system runs a lower risk of generating credential inflation because of the strong involvement of the employers in the definition of training programmes and the value they confer on credentials in their human resources policy. Nevertheless, this system is changing in order to provide broad training programmes compatible with competence flexibility, including sectors characterized by fast-moving knowledge, like the IT industry.

Its recent restructuring, relying on the permeability and the equivalence of vocational education and training, has been widely ensured by the German Federal State seeking to adopt EU standards, above all concerning continuing education and training. Although the logic and the institutional framework are different, there is a relative convergence between the three educational and training systems we have studied. One can see in this convergence a direct effect of the European directives on education and training. In particular, the 'principle of equivalence' of the different routes to 'qualification' (or certification) throughout a person's life has been largely adopted by the member states of EU, including the Netherlands and Spain.

Although this principle based on the transferability of competencies may very well be suited to lifelong learning, it can also result in a perpetual race for training, with implicit risks of exclusion. It therefore seems necessary to raise normative doubts concerning the premises upon which European education and training policy has been based since the early 1980s. First, the objective of raising levels of education is implicitly based on a learning model valorizing academic training which follows on from the general to the particular.[18] A priori, the development of systems based on the validation on experience-based competencies should serve to counter this tendency. But, ironically, as the UK case shows, such a system can have a contrary effect when it is implemented without the wide support of professional and employer communities.

Second, as we have shown, in each country, the restructuring of the education and training system, although to different degrees, brings into competition all training providers, including firms. The risk is that such a restructuring will lead to selection to the detriment of the most underprivileged categories of employees. From the social point of view this risk can largely offset the positive results obtained for entrants in training programmes, due to the service provider's incentives to ensure their success by favouring the most general capability. Finally, there is a certain ambiguity in the European strategy on 'competence and mobility', which ensures professional (inter-industry) and geographic (national and international) mobility of workers, on the one hand, and cooperative relationships between all actors in matters of training, on the other hand. This recommendation underestimates the fact that professional mobility supposes the solution to the collective goods problem of sharing the costs of training investments. This cooperation is difficult as soon as you cross the boundaries between particular occupations and between different geographical areas or countries. In this latter respect, the construction of a quasi-market of training, at the national or at the European level, presents important stakes for the private sector. The argument of this chapter is that this transformation of the system of competence certification cannot be based on an exclusively market logic.

NOTES

1. The notions of 'intrinsic' and 'institutional' logic make reference to the work of Young (2001) on this subject. We used them in a more extensive sense for integrating the conception of competence associated to each mode of certification. On the issue of taking into account the plurality of criteria for evaluating competencies, see Bessy and Eymard-Duvernay (1997) and Eymard-Duvernay and Marchal (1997). An in-depth analysis of these tools applied in the identification of equivalence in the job market was made in a study for the French Commissariat Général au Plan, on recruitment institutions in France and the UK (Bessy et al. 2001). The research presented in this article was part of that study. The first section of this article presents the main elements of a text devoted to the British case (Bessy 2000).
2. On this issue see Marsden (1998) and Rainbird (1995). One factor in particular, underlined by Marsden, was multi-unionism, which meant that the broadening of skills and the development of multi-disciplinary apprenticeships conflicted with long-standing organizational boundaries between the spheres of influence of different unions in the same workplace. Although the trade unions have little influence on the definition of NVQs, they nevertheless supported the system in exchange for recognition of qualifications.
3. On this point see the recommendations of the European Commission White Paper on Education and Training (1995).
4. Gospel (1998) cites the example of SMEs in this sector which, as part of a collective programme, registered at a local training institute responsible for imparting initial education and training and coordinating additional training at the local high school.
5. This reform entailed the privatization of government training programmes. Development of general education in the private sector was encouraged and sources of income for public sector schools and universities were extended.
6. In this perspective, Affichard (1983) shows how this nomenclature is the sphere of 'classifying struggles' between different French administrations.
7. The 1992 law instituting procedures for the recognition of occupational skills followed a series of measures that departed from the traditional process of obtaining a diploma/degree (modularity, credit accumulation, ongoing assessments, etc.) and aimed to validate occupational experience, knowledge and capabilities acquired outside any training system (law of 1985). This new apparatus made it possible to obtain exemption from examinations if the candidate had five years of experience on the job, and provided for recognition of practical training courses in industry. This law can be compared to that of December 1991 on 'leave for personal competency appraisal' (especially in contexts of corporate restructuring), the aim of which was to promote employees' internal and external mobility. More recently, the 17 January 2002 law reinforced procedures of validation of occupational competencies by giving experience the same value as a training course to obtain a diploma, degree, title, or certificate of qualification.

8. In this perspective, the greater importance granted to representatives of local employers in steering occupational training initiatives can be compared to the operational mode of the British TECs.

9. The role of the National Joint Commissions for Employment (*Commissions Paritaires Nationales pour l'Emploi*—CPNE), whose function was defined by the national inter-occupational agreement of 10 February 1969 on job security and its 21 November 1974 amendment, was reinforced in the fields of employment, training, and occupational insertion of young people. These commissions were, to a large extent, associated with the creation of qualification contracts and the development of CQP (definition and recognition in occupational hierarchies). The 1991 inter-occupational agreement extended the missions of the CPNE by giving them a key role in the definition of policies on continuous education and training, and qualifications: individual leave for training, leave for competency appraisal, training plan, measures for the youth, etc.

10. These contracts propose sandwich courses for young people, financed partly by the state. The content and structure of these courses are more flexible than in the case of preparation for a degree/diploma. This measure can be compared to the British 'Modern Apprenticeship' programme.

11. That represents around 1 per cent of the total number of 'certificates' (including diplomas and other titles) delivered in 1997. This is equivalent to the number of diplomas acquired by the new way of 'validation of experience'.

12. The study by Charraud, Personnaz, and Veneau (1998) provides a clear illustration based on a comparison of the construction of CQPs in different industries. The history of the plastics and metallurgy industries, and especially of their modes of organization of representation and involvement in initial and continuous education and training, leads to different construction processes.

13. The example of the French plastics sector shows that because of the large number of SMEs working for other firms, training caters for employees so that these firms can meet increasingly strict product standards. In this case certification of competencies fits into quality assurance procedures.

14. For the differences between the two systems, see Marsden (1998).

15. Since 1999, eighteen new 'occupations' have been creating (BMBF, rapport 2003).

16. This distinction between different certification levels had been attempted within the dual initial training system, but without really reaching its objective. This model establishing different levels of certification within a same occupation, coming from the 'Vocational Training Law of 1969', has not succeeded because of the absence of a consensus between the 'social partners'. Nevertheless, such a differentiation has been accepted in certain industries in order to offer training opportunities to young people in difficulty (Koch 1997).

17. Such a modification has been already made in the craft trades.

18. This is particular the case in France where academic education is overvalorized in the secondary schools.

REFERENCES

Affichard, J. (1983). 'Nomenclatures professionnelles et pratiques de classement', *Formation et Emploi*, 4: 47–61.

Bessy, C. (2000). 'La certification des compétences en Grande-Bretagne, les risques d'exclusion induits par la valorisation d'aptitudes générales', *Formation-Emploi*, 71: 21–35.

—— and Eymard-Duvernay, F. (1997). *Les intermédiaires du marché du travail.* Paris: Presses universitaires de France, Cahiers du Centre d'Etudes de l'Emploi, n°36.

—— Eymard-Duvernay, F., de Larquier, G., and Marchal, E. (2001). *Des marchés du travail équitables? Approche comparative France/Royaume-Uni.* Bruxelles: P.I.E. Peter Lang.

Brown, W., Deakin, S., Nash, D., and Oxenbridge, S. (2000). 'The Employment Contract: From Collective Procedures to Individual Rights', *British Journal of Industrial Relations*, 38(4): 611–29.

Bundes Ministerium für Bildung unf Forshung (2003). *Rapport on Vocational Training.*

Buechtemann, C. and Verdier, E. (1998). 'Education and Training Regimes Macro-Institutional Evidence', *Revue d'Economie Politique*, 108(3): 292–320.

Boreham, N., Samurçay, R., and Fisher, M. (2002). *Work Process Knowledge.* London: Routledge.

Charraud, A. M., Personnaz, E., and Veneau, P. (1998). 'Les 'Certificats de qualification professionnelle: Diversité de construction et contextes de branche', *Cahiers lillois d'économie et de sociologie*, 31: 71–82.

Colardyn, D. (1996). *La gestion des compétences.* Paris: PUF.

Commission Européenne (1995). *Livre blanc sur l'éducation et la formation: enseigner et apprendre. Vers la société cognitive*, Bruxelles.

Dreyfus, H. L. and Dreyfus, S. E. (1986). 'Expert Systems versus Intuitive Expertise', in H. L. Dreyfus and S. E. Dreyfus (eds.), *Mind over Machine—The Power of Human Intuition and Expertise in the Era of the Computer.* New York: Free Press.

Eymard-Duvernay, F. and Marchal, E. (1997). *Façons de recruter, Le jugement des compétences sur le marché du travail.* Paris: Métailié.

Gospel, H. (1998). 'Le renouveau de l'apprentissage en Grande-Bretagne', *Formation et Emploi*, 64: 25–41.

Hall, P. A. and Soskice, D. (2001). *Varieties of Capitalism: The Institutional Foundations of Comparative Advantage.* Oxford: Oxford University Press.

Jessup, G. (1990). 'National Vocational Qualifications: Implications for Further Education', in M. Becs and M. Swords (eds.), *National Vocational Qualifications and Further Education.* London: Kogan.

Jobert, A. and Tallard, M. (1995). 'Diplômes et certifications de branches dans les conventions collectives', *Formation et Emploi*, 52: 133–49.

—— —— (1997). 'Politiques de formation et de certification des branches professionnelles en France', in M. Möbus and E. Verdier (eds.), *Les Diplômes professionnels en Allemagne et en France.* Paris: L'Harmattan.

Koch, R. (1997). 'La rénovation des formations professionnelles réglementées: instrument majeur de modernisation du système dual depuis les années 1970', in M. Möbus and E. Verdier (eds.), *Les Diplômes professionnels en Allemagne et en France*. Paris: L'Harmattan.

Lindley, R. M. (1996). 'Le passage de l'école à la vie active au Royaume-Uni', *Revue Internationale du Travail*, 135(2): 170–95.

Marsden, D. (1998). 'Apprentissage: Le Phénix renaît-il de ces cendres? La formation professionnelle en Grande-Bretagne', *Formation et Emploi*, 61: 35–57.

—— (1999). *A Theory of Employment Systems*. Oxford: Oxford University Press.

Merle, V. (1997). 'L'évolution des systèmes de validation et de certification—Quels modèles possibles et quels enjeux pour la France?', *Formation Professionnelle-Revue Européenne*,12: 37–49.

Möbus, M. and Verdier, E. (1997). *Les diplômes professionnels en Allemagne et en France*. Paris: l'Harmattan.

NCVQ (1999). *Data News*. Winter.

Rainbird, H. (1995). 'La construction sociale de la qualification', in M. Jobert and L. Tanguy (eds.), *Education et Travail en Grande-Bretagne, en Allemagne et en Italie*. Paris: Armand Colin.

Ryan, P. (1995). 'Education et formation professionnelle au Royaume-Uni, Changements institutionnels', *Formation et Emploi*, 50: 41–62.

Scheuer, M., Dehio, J., Graskamp, R., and Rothgang, M. (2003). 'Allemagne, pénurie de spécialistes en nouvelles technologies: la nécessaire réforme de la formation professionnelle'. *Formation et Emploi*, 82: 33–45.

Steedman, H. and Hawkins, J. (1994). 'Shifting Foundations: The Impact of NVQs on Youth Training for the Building Trades', London: National Institute Economics Review.

West, A., Pennell, H., and Edge, A. (1998). 'L'introduction des principes de l'économie de marché dans le système de formation en Angleterre et au Pays de Galles', *Formation Professionnelle-Revue Européenne*, 13: 42–9.

Wolf, A. (1994). 'La mesure des "compétences": l'expérience du Royaume-Uni', *Formation Professionnelle-Revue Européenne*, 1: 31–8.

Young, M. (2001). 'Certification et formation tout au long de la vie: deux approches contradictoires', *Formation et Emploi*, 76: 205–10.

Part IV

Multi-level Governance and Policy Options

14

Innovation Systems and Institutional Regimes: The Construction of Different Types of National, Sectoral, and Transnational Innovation Systems

Richard Whitley

14.1. INTRODUCTION

The existence and nature of distinct systems of innovations have been extensively discussed over the past few decades (see e.g. Lundvall 1992; Nelson 1993; Edquist 1997, 2005; Braczyk, Cooke, and Heidenreich 1998). However, there has been much debate about whether they are predominantly national, regional, or sectoral, and the relative importance of societal institutions and technological regimes in generating them (Malerba and Orsenigo 1993; Breschi and Malerba 1997; Guerrieri and Tylecote 1997; Whitley 2000b). This is partly because many authors have been reluctant to specify precisely the nature of innovation systems, their key components, and variable characteristics (Carlsson et al. 2002; Edquist 2005).

In addition to there being considerable uncertainty about the boundaries, central features and mode of organization of innovation systems, further important issues arise from the increasing internationalization of competition, investment, and regulation. Growing economic and political integration across national borders has been seen by some as heralding the decline of nationally distinctive governance structures and economic systems. This is especially so in the EU where the pooling of state sovereignty and the creation of pan-European competition regimes and other economic institutional arrangements has created a supranational tier of governance (see e.g. Sandholtz and Sweet 1998) that may affect the many different kinds of national and sectoral innovation systems that have developed in Europe (Borras 2004; Kaiser and Prange 2004).

In order to understand how different patterns of innovation in Europe and their governing institutions are changing, it is important to identify the varied nature of key components of innovation systems and explore how these combine to constitute distinctive types that become established in different institutional environments. Such systems develop nationally or regionally depending on: (*a*) the strength of key institutions at those levels of collective organization and (*b*) their complementarity in reinforcing particular features and rationalities of economic actors. Their coherence and distinctiveness will be affected by EU integration to the extent that transnational organizations and regulations across Europe become significant relative to national ones.

As a contribution to exploring the changing nature of European innovation systems, this chapter suggests: (*a*) a way of distinguishing between systems of innovation in terms of three key dimensions, (*b*) how these characteristics can be expected to vary across distinctive institutional regimes, and (*c*) how different types of innovation systems become established and reproduced at national, sectoral, and international levels of socio-economic organization. First, I shall outline the key characteristics of innovation systems that stem from variations in how economic actors develop and diffuse innovations, and suggest how these combine to form six distinct ideal types. Next, I shall suggest how these six types of innovation systems are likely to become established in particular kinds of institutional regimes governing economic activities, especially capital and labour markets. Finally, I shall consider the institutional conditions that can be expected to produce distinctive national innovation systems and the implications of this analysis for the establishment of a separate European innovation system.

Essentially, I argue that coherent and distinctive kinds of innovation systems only become established when strong and complementary institutions develop at transnational, national, or regional levels, and so the relative weakness, and often contradictory nature, of many European institutions and policies limit their impact on well-established national patterns of innovative activity. In so far as they have institutionalized a particular approach to economic coordination, this tends to focus on deregulation and liberalization in a comparable manner to liberal market economies (LMEs). As a result, a highly standardized European system of innovation is unlikely to develop.

14.2. THE NATURE AND CHARACTERISTICS OF DIFFERENT INNOVATION SYSTEMS

Much of the literature on systems of innovation emphasizes the importance of different processes of knowledge production and dissemination, as well as varied patterns of interactive learning between groups and organizations in developing and commercializing new processes, products, and services (e.g. Carlsson et al. 2002; Lundvall et al. 2002). Additionally, a common theme in many comparisons of national innovation systems concerns the nature of state science and technology policies, and of the organization of university and other publicly supported research. Any consideration of the nature of innovation systems needs, then, to identify the main types and characteristics of knowledge developers and users in different contexts and how they are coordinated to generate distinctive kinds of innovations (Kaiser and Prange 2004).

The key components of innovation systems are usually taken to include private companies of different kinds, their organization into research consortia, business associations, etc. public and private research organizations, education and training systems and various providers of infrastructural services such as venture capitalists and lawyers, as well as the major institutions governing their behaviour. Variations in their central characteristics, such as governance structures and organizational capabilities, and in how their activities are coordinated lead to the constitution of distinctive systems of innovation.

The critical innovative agent in market economies is the private company. They generate new knowledge from current operations by employees through 'learning-by-doing', as well as from directed search for new processes and products through dedicated research and development activities (Coriat and Weinstein 2002). However, as numerous comparisons of business systems, social systems of production and varieties of capitalism have demonstrated, the nature and behaviour of firms varies greatly between countries, regions and cultures (Hollingsworth and Boyer 1997; Whitley 1999; Hall and Soskice 2001a; Amable 2003). In considering how different innovation systems develop and change, then, it is especially important to identify the central differences in how firms learn and develop new knowledge. Two characteristics dealing with the sources of new knowledge and how it is integrated into the organization are especially important.

First, there is the extent to which owners and managers learn from various groups of employees, business partners, and other organizations within and beyond their industry, and develop organization specific routines for integrating new knowledge from these groups. These differences affect the kinds of collective capabilities they develop and how they use them to produce new goods and services (Whitley 2003a). The extent to which companies involve employees in problem-solving activities and actively incorporate their knowledge—as well as that of business partners and other external organizations—into the development of new products, processes, and services constitutes, then, a major differentiating characteristic of systems of innovations in market economies. It can be termed the degree of *authority sharing* between economic actors because it implies a willingness to delegate authority over, and actively encourage involvement in, innovation development and problem solving activities.

This characteristic distinguishes firms that rely considerably upon the skills and activities of their skilled workforce to improve production technologies and introduce new products from those that rely primarily on technologists' and managers' learning, both about current processes and new opportunities. Many 'artisanal' enterprises in Italian industrial districts, parts of Denmark and elsewhere appear to resemble the former, while Taylorist and Fordist firms resemble the latter (Chandler 1990; Andersen and Kristensen 1999; Crouch et al. 2001). Additionally, of course, many large companies in continental European countries and Japan integrate shop-floor learning with that of engineers and managers (see e.g. Fujimoto 2000). They thus effect greater levels of knowledge integration within the firm than either artisanal or Fordist companies.

Such 'internal' authority sharing and involvement of skilled staff in collective problem-solving is often, but not always, combined with 'external' cooperation and knowledge sharing with other companies and organizations in particular kinds of socio-political environments. This can involve collaboration with competitors in dealing with industry-specific issues, such as training, union negotiations, and standards setting. Such sectoral cooperation is a feature of the more coordinated market economies (CMEs), in which institutional arrangements constrain opportunism and encourage continuing commitment to collective problem-solving across firms (Soskice 1999). Knowledge development and learning in these kinds of regions and countries occur repeatedly among owners, managers, and technical experts of separate companies as well as within them.

In contrast, the kinds of technology alliances and similar inter-firm collaborations that are becoming more widespread in particular industries, such as the biotechnology sector, in some LMEs, tend to be narrower in scope, restricted in time, and subject to more rapid shifts in partners (Powell 2001). Inter-firm learning here is therefore more limited in scope and longevity, and based more upon individual agreements and labour mobility than collective ones, as in much of Silicon Valley and Silicon Alley (Angel 2000; Almeida and Kogut 2001; Christopherson 2002; Grabher 2002).

Second, innovative firms differ in the extent to which, and how, they learn from the formal knowledge production systems of their domestic economy and, more recently, those of other countries. While most rely on the education and training system to provide them with skilled staff, and many use the scientific and technological literature to access research results for their own search activities, the extent to which they become directly involved in knowledge production processes in the public research system varies considerably. The public research system is here understood as the set of organizations whose employees are primarily engaged on research for publication together with the institutional arrangements governing their funding, direction, and evaluation (Whitley 2000*a*, 2003*b*). Differences in the extent of such involvement obviously affect the speed with which companies are able to use new knowledge, as well as their ability to understand the relevance and implications of new research techniques and processes. The more dependent is technical development on the knowledge and skills produced by the public sciences, the more significant these linkages become. At least three forms of such connections can be distinguished.

First, relatively *passive* and indirect forms of involvement in public science systems occur where innovative companies rely on universities and similar educational organizations to select and train scientists and technologists in particular skills and disciplines for initial employment, but do not actively participate in research development or recruit staff in mid-career. Any use of the knowledge and techniques produced by the public science system tends to be at arm's length and relatively remote, with a strong reliance on codified forms. While such firms may employ researchers as private consultants to deal with specific problems, they rarely seek to incorporate publicly oriented research projects and skills in their technological problem-solving activities. Many large Japanese companies appear to prefer this autarkic mode of knowledge development with respect to the formal research system (Kneller 2003), as do most artisanal companies.

Second, more direct and *active* engagement with formal knowledge production outside the firm is encouraged where state agencies and associations of companies support technologically focused research activities in public or semi-public institutions that are closely connected to current problems, products, and markets. Here, both SMEs and large firms are encouraged to participate in co-funding and guiding knowledge production in public–private organizations, such as the German Fraunhofer Institutes, and often employ their staff on a part-time or full-time basis (Abramson et al. 1997). External knowledge production and skill development is thus linked to companies' learning and search activities, but these remain within current technological and market trajectories and so are continuous with existing competences rather than being radically different.

Third, even greater levels of active involvement in the production of new knowledge and techniques occur when companies develop close links with universities and other research organizations engaged on the study of generic processes and phenomena. Perhaps the best-known instance of such direct connections with the public sciences is in the biotechnology industry, but it has also occurred where other emerging technologies depended greatly on new knowledge and skills developed by academic scientists, such as the German dyestuffs industry towards the end of the nineteenth century and the US computer software industry. Such involvement is more focused on the processes by which new knowledge is produced and problems are solved than the use of codified results, and so encompasses advanced training of researchers, co-development, and management of research projects, recruitment of mid-career scientists and technologists, as well as secondment of employees to academic posts and sharing facilities.

In addition to these differences in the extent to which firms obtain and use new knowledge from different kinds of sources, a third major contrast between innovation systems concerns the extent to which knowledge production, transfer, and use, and innovative activities in general, are coordinated through ad hoc, anonymous, market transactions, or more continuous and cooperative relationships between economic actors governed by common authority commitments. Low levels of authoritative coordination of innovative activities occur where most transactions between companies and other actors are similar to those in spot markets and there is little continuous commitment to maintaining particular relationships between them. Learning across organizational boundaries here tends to be short-term, ad hoc, and built around individuals rather than being sustained, partner specific, and organized into routines.

Greater levels of authoritative integration of innovative activities occur in societies where there are stronger constraints on opportunistic behaviour, and both public and private agencies are involved in generating and disseminating new technologies and techniques. Such integration can be achieved either through state commitment to, and support for, particular innovation goals and/or through inter-firm alliances, business groups and research consortia, often involving public research organizations. Sharing knowledge and collaborating in the development of innovations is easier and less risky in these kinds of economies than in more arm's length ones. However, such collaboration may inhibit more radical innovations that are discontinuous with, or disruptive for, established technologies and customers.

Combining these three broad dimensions of innovative firm characteristics and the coordination of their activities enables us to identify six ideal types of innovation systems that resemble many of the examples discussed in the literature. These types also differ in three further respects: (*a*) the firm specificity of innovative capabilities, (*b*) their likelihood of producing radical, discontinuous innovations, and (*c*) their ability to generate systemic as opposed to modular innovations.

Two more ideal types of innovation systems could, in theory, be distinguished in these terms. However, it seems unlikely that active involvement in the public science system will be combined with low levels of internal authority sharing since an openness to new formal knowledge and research skills implies a willingness and ability to deal with considerable technical uncertainty. This in turn encourages delegation of control to technologists who are most able to judge and make use of new knowledge. Authority thus has to be shared if innovations are to benefit from close links to the formal knowledge production system of a society.

Equally, the combination of high non-market coordination, low authority sharing, and passive involvement with the public science system seems improbable because alliance-based knowledge sharing and coordination encourages employer–employee commitment by restricting economic opportunism. Where such coordination is more based upon state-led technology policies, it is likely to involve closer connections between the formal research system and companies, although probably limiting the level of delegation of authority within firms. The key features of the six more likely ideal types of innovation systems are summarized in Table 14.1 and will now be further discussed.

There are three distinct kinds of innovation systems with limited authoritative, non-market coordination of innovative activities between knowledge producers and users. First, those where learning and development of innovations take place largely within the upper echelons of managerial and technical hierarchies can be termed *highly autarkic* because they rely mostly on the internally generated knowledge produced by engineers and managers. Firms here do not make much use of either skilled workers' knowledge or research activities in the public science system. Collaboration and information sharing across formal authority boundaries is low in such systems and inter-firm relations are essentially adversarial and governed by short-term market logics. Authority sharing in general is limited in this kind of innovation system, as is the systemic integration of innovative activities across organizations.

Innovations are therefore quite firm specific, closely dependent on managers' and engineers' knowledge as well as on their ability and willingness to incorporate publicly available, codified knowledge into developmental activities. As technological 'paradigms' and innovative styles become institutionalized within large companies, their capacity for integrating different kinds of knowledge and pursuing novel kinds of innovations that do not readily fit with them reduces. This means that learning new skills and ways of dealing with technical and market problems becomes difficult for such firms without substantial changes in personnel.

Table 14.1 Characteristics of six ideal types of innovation systems

Characteristics	Type of Innovation System					
	Autarkic	Artisanal	Technological teams	State-led	Group-based	Highly collaborative
Authority sharing	Limited	Considerable	Considerable	Limited	Considerable	Considerable
Involvement with public science systems	Passive	Passive	Active	Active	Passive	Active
Non-market coordination	Limited	Limited	Limited	Considerable	Considerable	Considerable
Firm-specificity of innovations	High	Limited	Limited	High	High	Considerable
Discontinuity of innovations	Limited	Limited	Potentially high	Varies	Limited	Limited
Systematic nature of innovations	Considerable	Low	Low	Considerable	Considerable	Considerable

Second, where coordination of innovative activities across organizations remains predominantly market based through contracting and labour mobility, but owners and managers share considerable authority over problem definition, work organization, and technical development with engineers and other experts inside companies, two distinct kinds of innovation systems can be distinguished. These can be termed *technological team* and *artisanal* systems of innovation.

In the former, involvement with formal knowledge production in the public science system and rapid acquisition of new ideas and skills through buying firms and/or researchers is considerable. However, technology alliances or risk sharing agreements tend to be short term and limited for particular purposes. Commitments between investors, managers, and workers are restricted in scope and time, but employee discretion over work performance and involvement in problem-solving is much greater than in the previous type of innovation system, partly because of the considerable level of technical uncertainty. Innovations here are often quite radical in terms of technological or market discontinuities because of the rapid integration of new and different kinds of knowledge and skills, but are more modular than systemic because of the high levels of technical and market uncertainty involved and limited organizational coordination (Casper 2000; Casper and Whitley 2004).

Third, artisanal innovation systems combine similar levels of authority sharing inside companies with greater cooperation between firms in developing and applying new technologies and knowledge. Competition between companies is less adversarial and zero-sum than in the previous two cases, and supplier–customer relationships are more collaborative, often encouraged by local and regional governments, consulting agencies, banks, and marketing cooperatives. However, direct involvement with research projects in the public science system tends to be relatively limited, and new formal knowledge that is both generic across technologies and product families and different from that currently being used rarely impinges upon firms' innovative activities. Innovation is here driven more by the incremental and separate improvements of relatively small companies in industrial districts than by systematically coordinated investments and developments across them. It is more continuous within current technological trajectories than radical and disruptive.

There are also three kinds of innovation systems that are more coordinated through non-market relationships. These vary in how such authoritative coordination is achieved, particularly whether this is primarily by the state or through inter-firm alliances, and in the extent to which companies are actively involved in the formal knowledge production system. In *state-led* systems of innovation, authority sharing both within and between companies tends to be limited by the high level of dependence of many firms on state agencies, but central coordination encourages considerable integration of projects in the public research system with corporate innovation development. The risks involved in developing major systemic technological change are here shared between the state and private companies, often through the provision of cheap credit and state subsidized and/or conducted research. Innovations can be correspondingly large scale and complex in terms of the variety of scientific and technological knowledge involved, but are unlikely to rely extensively on skilled workers' contributions to the incremental improvement of operational procedures.

Greater levels of internal and external authority sharing occur in *group-based* innovation systems. Here, large firms develop relatively stable networks of commitments and collaborations within and across sectoral boundaries to share knowledge and opportunities within distinct groups of companies. These are often cemented by mutual shareholdings, as in the Japanese inter-market groups and some vertical *keiretsu*, as well as exchange of managers and common banking relationships (Gerlach 1992). Long-term employment commitments encourage firm-specific problem-solving and competence building amongst the core workforce, so that organizational learning becomes continuous and broad in scope.

However, companies in these kinds of innovation systems tend to have rather passive connections with the formal research system, except through the recruitment of new graduates, and in that sense are relatively separate from generic knowledge production, as Kneller (2003) has claimed is the case for many large Japanese pharmaceutical companies. Innovations here build on continuous, group learning in and between network members, and so tend to follow particular technological trajectories that do not devalue current organizational capabilities.

Finally, there are *highly collaborative* innovation systems that combine considerable authority sharing within and between companies with more active involvement in the public science system, especially that part focused on the development of technologically and industrially specific knowledge. Innovations are here based on learning within the firm, within industry and trade associations and within research associations and similar public–private collaborative institutions connecting formal knowledge production with technical development. National and local state bodies are often directly involved in encouraging such links, through joint funding of projects and the establishment of public research organizations dedicated to technological innovation, such as the Fraunhofer institutes in Germany.

Insofar as new formal knowledge becomes integrated into firms' innovative activities, these may be less limited to firms' current knowledge and capabilities than those in group-based innovation systems, but the extensive cooperation within and between companies means that radically different innovations are unlikely to be a major feature of these kinds of innovation systems. In new industries, such as software and biotechnology, companies here tend to focus on more incremental and technologically continuous kinds of innovations (Casper 2000; Casper and Whitley 2004).

14.3. INSTITUTIONAL CONDITIONS FOR THE CONSTRUCTION OF DIFFERENT INNOVATION SYSTEMS

Having distinguished six ideal types of innovation systems, I now consider the circumstances in which they are most likely to develop and become repro-duced as distinct ways of generating new products, processes, and services, particularly the role of different institutional regimes. Different sets of insti-tutions governing property rights, capital, and labour markets lead owners and managers to delegate authority to skilled workers and involve them in collective learning to varying extents (Tylecote and Conesa 1999; Whitley 2003a). Combined with different state science and technology policies and kinds of public science systems, these kinds of institutions also lead to varying patterns of firm involvement in public research organizations and coordin-ation of innovative activities (Whitley 2002, 2003b).

Considering first the institutional arrangements affecting variations in authority sharing, these include the norms governing trust and authority relationships in a society as well as the institutions encouraging commitment between economic actors. Trust in the formal institutions governing economic transactions, and economic activities more generally, is critical to investors and other economic actors delegating control over assets. In societies where it so low that owners feel unable to rely on the legal system, accounting conventions and formal systems for assessing competence and contractual compliance to control the behaviour of customers, suppliers, and employees in predictable ways, they are unlikely to share substantial amounts of authority with relative strangers with whom they do not have strong personal bonds of loyalty and reciprocity. Additionally, in paternalist political cultures that justify leadership more in terms of elites' superior abilities to look after the best interests of the population than through their formally credentialed expertise or by success in formally governed electoral competi-tions (Beetham 1991), owners tend to consider employees as unqualified to exercise discretion.

In contrast, where the dominant institutions governing economic activities are more reliable and patterns of authority in a society are less paternalistic, owners may well share authority with some employees and business partners and establish organizational careers. Some trust in formal institutions and development of contractarian or communitarian political cultures are, then, necessary, but not sufficient, conditions for owners and managers to share authority within and between firms. How much they do so, though, and with whom, varies considerably, between market economies with different political, financial, and labour market institutions affecting economic opportunism. In general, the more financiers, managers, and skilled workers are locked-in to each others' destinies, the less likely they are to act opportunistically and seek short-term advantages through changing business partners. Institutional frameworks that encourage such lock-in therefore reduce the risks associated with long-term commitments and so facilitate authority sharing.

Key institutional features that constrain short-term opportunism include: (*a*) coordinating and risk sharing state policies, (*b*) strong business associations and union federations—often encouraged by state corporatist policies and, (*c*) insider dominated financial systems. Where active, 'promotional' (Evans 1994: 77–81) states play major roles in the development of new industries and skills as direct producers, midwives, and supporters, firms are likely to work together in developing new technologies and to plan long-term investments. Coordinating and risk-sharing states here reduce the likelihood of opportunistic behaviour by firms and, because, such states encourage cooperation and mutual commitment between companies, they are likely to feel able to enter into relatively long term commitments with many employees.

In contrast, where more *arm's-length* states focus on establishing clear rules of the competitive game within which economic actors are free to pursue their objectives as they wish and to develop new technologies as separate, competing entities, incentives to share authority with employees and business partners tend to be less (Whitley 2005). Such states often consider collaboration between companies in developing new technologies to be anti-competitive and discouraged, except in a few areas of direct state concern such as defence.

However, it is important to point out that *dominant developmental* states in which owners and managers depend greatly on political and bureaucratic elites who work closely together to pursue state-led economic development polices may also limit authority sharing. In these kinds of institutional regimes, the state actively and directly promotes the improvement and success of particular firms and sectors, but in a directive rather than a collaborative manner. Firms here develop close connections to state policymakers rather than with each other, as the state discourages horizontal alliances and the establishment of independent collaborative organizations that could threaten their dominance of the economic system.

Second, strong business associations help to control opportunistic behaviour by member companies, and so encourage longer-term investments in developing new technologies and training employees. They also restrict employee opportunism, whether individual or collective through unions. Particularly if wage rates and other aspects of employment relationships are agreed centrally, either at the industry or national level, and firms are constrained from poaching skilled staff by offering higher wages, employers are encouraged to develop quite long-term commitments to employees. This is enhanced by strong regulatory frameworks governing employment relations in many of the more CMEs of Continental Europe.

In addition to strong business associations affecting authority sharing between and within firms, powerful labour unions and federations are also important, especially when they collaborate with employers' groups in managing effective public training systems, as in the German 'skills machine' (Culpepper and Finegold 1999). The more highly skilled is the workforce, particularly when employers recognize the high quality of these skills, and the greater is the bargaining power of unions, the more employers are encouraged to share authority with skilled workers, and involve them in problem-solving activities.

Third, the nature of the financial system, especially whether it facilitates a strong market for corporate control, affects authority sharing both between companies and between employers and employees. Where capital markets are small and illiquid and shareholder control over large companies is relatively concentrated, it is difficult to transfer ownership through the market and large owners are often locked-in to particular companies, especially if significant proportions of firms' shares are held by strategic investors and/or are effectively controlled by top managers, as is the case in many European countries (Barca and Becht 2001) and Japan (Sheard 1994). This enables employers to make credible long-term commitments to skilled staff.

In contrast, the combination of liquid capital markets, legal and other restrictions on managers' ability to develop strong defensive measures against hostile takeovers, and fragmented shareholdings in more 'liberal' kinds of market economy can result in a strong market for corporate control that limits investor–manager commitments and reduces the credibility of long-term career incentives. Where capital is impatient and volatile it is difficult to convince skilled employees to become committed to the long-term development of a particular firm's organizational capabilities. While employers may delegate considerable autonomy over work procedures to skilled staff and be willing to enter into short-term alliances with other companies in such societies, long term collaboration and organizational learning through continuing employee involvement in problem-solving are inhibited by the ease and frequency of ownership changes. Such financial markets can, however, facilitate the provision of venture capital for highly risky investments that can be aggregated into portfolios, and also enable firms to offer relatively high-powered incentives for skilled staff to work intensively and cooperatively on specific projects.

These sorts of institutional differences also affect the extent and mode of non-market coordination of innovative activities in an economy. Where the state is actively involved in coordinating economic development, whether directly or through business associations and other groupings, we would expect firms to cooperate more in achieving technological change than in societies where the state prohibits collaboration. Similarly, industry and trade associations that are accustomed to coordinating economic activities and resolving disputes seem likely to promote joint R&D projects, collective setting of technical standards, and sharing of new knowledge. Promotional state policies, strong business associations and corporatist arrangements, then, should be associated with considerable non-market coordination of innovation, while societies with states pursuing arm's-length regulatory policies and weak business associations will not.

Turning to consider next the institutional features influencing business involvement with the public research system, the role of the state is again critical, not least because most of these systems are funded and directly controlled by nation states. In the case of dominant developmental states that take the leading role in managing economic development, we would expect them to ensure that firms in favoured sectors were able to access the results of publicly supported research activities. Active involvement in the public science system is here more facilitated and coordinated by state agencies around public objectives and missions than the result of strategic investments by autonomous companies. It will, therefore, tend to be restricted to particular areas of economic activities favoured by the state rather than generalized throughout the economy.

More collaborative state coordination of technological development with firms and industry associations can be expected to generate different kinds of company involvement in parts of the public science system. Where the state provides funding for a range of applied research organizations and encourages firms, both individually and collectively, to organize and fund research in them, as in Germany (Abramson et al. 1997), companies often cooperate with public research organizations in developing and diffusing new technological knowledge. By underwriting much of the costs associated with technological research and involving industry associations in its management, states here facilitate both inter-firm cooperation and the widespread involvement of firms in part of the public science system. An important feature of many such 'diffusion-oriented' technology policies is their involvement of small and medium sized enterprises, as well as large ones, in technical improvements, and their extension over many sectors of the economy (Ergas 1987; Morris-Suzuki 1994).

This kind of involvement in publicly oriented research is, though, usually limited to work on technologies and materials that are closely connected to current problems and trajectories rather than with more generic research that could lead to quite different technologies. Because the primary goal is to enhance and improve existing industrial competences, such state policies are unlikely to encourage strong connections with researchers engaged upon more remote topics intended to produce general explanations of phenomena, especially in academic systems that are strongly structured around discrete disciplines, and where the incentives for senior researchers to move into the private sector are restricted by employment regulations.

In addition, how the state and other actors organize the public research system greatly affects the degree and form of company involvement. Particularly important in this respect is the extent to which formal research systems are organized into a strong and stable hierarchy of prestige and resources dominated by a small number of elite research organizations (Whitley 2003*b*). In highly concentrated and hierarchical academic systems, the best researchers are not only recruited and trained in the leading organizations, but are also likely to remain in them for most of their careers because of their superior status and resources. More peripheral universities are rarely able to improve their standing through attracting leading scientists, or by acquiring better facilities through competitive processes. Open competition between research organizations in such societies, therefore, is quite limited, as is mobility between employers in the course of scientific careers. Where, in contrast, there are a number of competing research universities that are funded in different ways by a variety of agencies pursuing different objectives, together with different kinds of research organizations also competing for scientific prestige, it will be more difficult for such groups to monopolize intellectual goals and standards. In the case of the post-war US research system, for instance, the variety of state funding agencies, and of Congressional committees overseeing them, has probably encouraged intellectual competition and pluralism (Stokes 1997). More generally, the variety of institutional forms, high level of decentralization and institutionalization of competition for prestige and resources in the US academic system have encouraged universities and colleges there to compete with leading institutions in a way that is unusual in much of Europe and Japan (Graham and Diamond 1997; Feller 1999).

Generally speaking, the greater the rate of competition between research organizations for prestige and resources, and the more mobile are scientists in seeking promotions, the more ideas and skills circulate between departments, and the more likely intellectual change and novelty will increase. Such mobility is affected by broader patterns of labour market organization that vary across market economies, as well as by the nature of competition between universities for leading researchers.

A second important feature of the organization of public research systems that affects their flexibility and pluralism is the segmentation of goals, careers, and resources between different employment units. By this I mean the strength of the separation and division of labour between research universities, applied research institutes, technology transfer agencies, research association laboratories, and private companies. Where these have quite distinct goals, funding arrangements and control procedures, so that researchers in them are trained in different ways, do different kinds of work and have separate career paths, the degree of organizational segmentation is high. In such systems, researchers are discouraged from undertaking a wide variety of types of research, including that focused on technological and commercial objectives, within universities, and from moving between different kinds of employers without suffering a great loss of intellectual credibility.

Knowledge and skill transfer between types of research organizations will be relatively slow and difficult in highly segmented public science systems. Rapid technological responses to new research results are unlikely to occur here, and technological trajectories will continue to develop largely in isolation from radical intellectual innovations. For example, the separation of much biological research from medical schools and hospitals in France, Japan, and perhaps Germany, has been seen as inhibiting the development of biotechnology firms in these countries (Thomas 1994; Henderson, Orsenigo, and Pisano 1999; Kneller 1999).

In contrast, where organizational segmentation is lower, research organizations have overlapping goals, contain a variety of kinds of research activity and have overlapping labour markets, funding arrangements, and control procedures. As a result, knowledge and skills flow more easily between them and the development of joint projects between researchers from different employment units and fast adaptation to new knowledge is facilitated. Low segmentation can also allow academic scientists to pursue a variety of objectives more easily, and thus transfer their results directly to the development of new products and processes, than in more segmented environments. As Stokes (1997: 45) points out, it has long been a feature of the US research system that many organizations, such as research universities and Bell Labs, have provided a home for researchers pursuing both theoretical and applied goals. The founding and development of Genentech exemplify these low levels of organizational and goal segmentation in the emergence of the US biotechnology industry (McKelvey 1996).

These features of public science systems affect the ease with which scientists and engineers are able to develop new intellectual goals, fields, and approaches, such as software engineering and molecular biology. Where objective and strategies are varied and changeable, as distinct from being tightly integrated around established disciplinary goals, frameworks, and expertise, it should be easier to extend and apply new ideas and techniques for technological purposes. The boundaries between theory-driven scientific research and more instrumental knowledge production are more fluid, permeable, and overlapping in such public science systems than in those where intellectual, skill, and organizational boundaries are structured around separate disciplines.

Here, firms should find it relatively easy to become involved in research networks that combine theory-driven research with more instrumental projects and organizations. Such fluidity and adaptability of intellectual goals and skills in public science systems also generates a high level of change in ideas and expertise, which in turn enables firms to hire new kinds of skills relatively easily, especially where research training is closely integrated with current projects. Because labour markets in such systems are typically not highly segmented around separate kinds of intellectual goals, employing organizations and performance standards, researchers are able to move relatively easily between universities, other research organizations and private companies without losing status and long-term career opportunities.

Overall, then, more flexible and pluralistic public science systems should enable innovative firms to become more involved in research projects and incorporate new knowledge and skills into their developmental activities more rapidly than those organized into strong prestige hierarchies with stable disciplinary and organizational boundaries and separate labour markets. When combined with mission-oriented state science and technology policies (Ergas 1987), these kinds of research systems should encourage fluidity of research goals and skills as researchers adapt their projects to state priorities within the overall peer review system and facilitate close connections between firms and researchers in sectors favoured by such policies. Where research training is also tied to current research projects, firms are able to recruit high-skilled researchers in these areas, and so adapt rapidly to new knowledge and expertise.

These connections between authority sharing, involvement in the public research system and non-market coordination and institutional environments enable us to identify the key conditions in which the six ideal types of innovation systems are likely to occur and become institutionalized. These are summarized in Table 14.2 and will now be discussed.

Considering first innovation systems relying mostly on market forms of coordination of innovative activities, these will tend to develop in societies with fluid external labour markets, limited state coordination and promotion of industrial development, limited segmentation of product markets, relatively weak industry associations policing entry and exit and generally few constraints on economic opportunism, at least at the national level. In the case of autarkic innovation systems, these are particularly likely to become established where: (*a*) an arm's-length state outlaws inter-firm cooperation, (*b*) liquid capital markets facilitate an active market in corporate control and, (*c*) there are few restrictions on hiring and firing employees. They additionally rely on an education and training system that provides relatively generic and codified skills for key roles, and sufficient organizational stability to encourage managerial staff to build firm specific innovative capabilities.

Innovation systems relying on professional teams can also develop in such institutional environments, but usually depend on some state support for the development of new technologies, often through the funding of novel research skills and fields in universities, as in the case of computer science groups in the US (Mowery 1996), and some relaxation of anti-trust rules for pre-competitive collaboration. Strong technical communities facilitate the evaluation and improvement of technical skills in such systems, as well as reducing search costs for both employers and employees. In addition, these kinds of innovation systems are helped by flexible and pluralistic public science systems that enable new fields and intellectual goals to become institutionalized in the academic system relatively quickly and new organizations to compete effectively with existing elite groups. Organizational segmentation and prestige hierarchies are thus not strong or stable in societies that encourage such innovation systems to become established and reproduced.

Artisanal innovation systems also rely on some institutional infrastructure to encourage inter-firm cooperation in improving technologies, exploring new markets, and acquiring resources, albeit often at the local or regional levels of organization. Rather than arising in regulatory states that implement a firmly arm's-length approach to economic development throughout the economy, however, these kinds of innovation systems seem more likely to become established in societies where the central state acts interdependently with strong business associations and unions who are able to exercise considerable influence on the development of distinctive rules of the game. Such *interdependent* states are not necessarily weak in the sense discussed by Migdal (1988) but rather have limited autonomy in organizing civil society.

Table 14.2 Institutional conditions encouraging the establishment and reproduction of different innovation systems

	Type of Innovation System					
Institutional conditions	Autarkic	Artisanal	Technological teams	State-led	Group-based	Highly collaborative
Type of State	Arm's-length	Interdependent	Arm's-length	Dominant developmental	Business corporatist	Inclusive corporatist
State science and technology policy	Mission	Weak	Mission	Mission	Diffusion	Diffusion
Strength of independent business associations	Low	Some	Low	Low	Considerable	Considerable
Strength of independent labour unions	Low	Some	Low	Low	Considerable	Considerable
Financial system	Capital market	Local bank-based	Capital market	State credit based	Credit based	Credit based
Scope and strength of collaborative public training system	Low	Considerable	Limited	Low	Limited	Considerable
Strength of prestige hierarchy of universities and research organization	Limited	Varies	Limited	Considerable	Considerable	Limited
Competitive and pluralist public science system	Varies	Varies	Yes	No	Limited	Some
Segmentation of research organizations and careers	Some	Varies	Limited	Some	Some	Some

In the case of countries like Denmark, major intermediary groups include local and national employers' associations, industry groups, and craft associations (Kristensen 1992, 1994; Karnoe 1999). Such groups are also often involved in the establishment and running of technical schools and other support facilities that enable skilled staff to continue to improve their expertise without becoming tied to any particular employer. Strong technical communities, whether local, regional, or national, provide the basis for effective reputational evaluation and control of expertise, as well as incentives to enhance technical competences, in these kinds of innovation systems (Kristensen 1996, 1999).

A further important feature of the institutional environments of artisanal innovation systems is the lack of a strong market for corporate control, and a relatively decentralized banking system in which connections between local savings and municipal banks and SMEs are close (Hopner 1999). Together these local and regional institutional arrangements facilitate the establishment of loosely cooperative networks between small firm owners and managers that enable learning to be continuous within and between them (Lundvall et al. 2002).

The last three types of innovation system manifest greater reliance on non-market forms of coordination of innovative activities. In the case of state-led systems, this is mostly achieved through dominant developmental states coordinating investment strategies, risk sharing, and technical problem-solving, as well as often underwriting credit provision and guaranteeing sales. Such states typically pursue mission-oriented science and technology policies with substantial funding and coordination of research supporting their developmental objectives, often in state laboratories attached to individual ministries as well as in universities. The ability of public research organizations to pursue independent strategies and obtain resources from different kinds of agencies and groups is often limited in such societies.

Group-based and highly collaborative innovation systems are also assisted by considerable state coordination, but usually this involves much greater reliance on business associations and decentralization of control over resources to scientific and technological elites. More corporatist states seek to play a leading role in economic and technological development but in, and through, employers' groups, industry associations and, sometimes, with the support of unions and other representational groups (Streeck and Schmitter 1985; Crouch 1999: Chapter 12). They develop and implement diffusionist science and technology policies in collaboration with trade associations, often supporting their use of public research faculties to improve technologies and solve technical problems.

They differ, however, in their involvement of labour unions in economic policy making and implementation, in developing and managing public training systems and in the extent to which unions are able to play a coordinating role in technical change at local, regional, and national levels (Whitley 2005). *Business corporatist* states collaborate with business associations and individual companies in developing new technologies and improving existing ones, but rarely encourage unions to become involved in such activities and typically do not establish national public skill formation and certification systems in collaboration with union federations. In countries like Japan, business–state relations have been characterized as being governed by norms of 'reciprocal consent' (Samuels 1987), and unions restricted mostly to enterprise-based roles in much of the post-war period. Inter-firm cooperation in technological development is thus encouraged by these kinds of states, but without industrial or national union groups being involved.

Inclusive corporatist states, in contrast, encourage the development of more collaborative innovation systems by institutionalizing the role of national and regional union federations in economic policymaking and implementation and establishing cooperative skill formation systems that encompass a wide range of skills with employers' groups and unions. The relatively important role of independent unions in these activities, and their continuing negotiations with employers' groups and other organizations in managing labour relations issues, encourage the development of more cooperative norms governing relations between economic actors and enables unions to coordinate technical improvements in some industries, as Herrigel and Wittke (2005) have shown in the German car industry.

Group-based innovation systems are additionally more likely to develop in societies with stable and strong prestige hierarchies of public science research organizations whose goals and labour markets are quite segmented. In these kinds of public science systems, firms are likely to find it difficult to gain access to current research projects and to influence their objectives. This is especially likely where academics are civil servants who are restricted in the kinds of external activities they may pursue, and cannot easily move between universities and private business without losing prestige and other benefits. In general, strongly hierarchical public science systems in which competition between universities and other research organizations is limited are likely to encourage autarkic innovation strategies (Kneller 2003).

More collaborative innovation systems in which companies become more actively involved in the public science system are likely in countries where there is greater competition between research organizations and they are not ordered into a stable strong hierarchy of social and intellectual prestige. They will also be encouraged by the existence of different kinds of research laboratories with distinct goals and means of support, especially non-state ones, and the institutionalization of transorganizational career paths for researchers that enable them to move between these types without greatly losing status. Organizational pluralism, flexibility, and permeability in terms of recruitment and cooperation are likely to encourage such innovation systems when combined with the other characteristics of CMEs outlined above.

14.4. INSTITUTIONAL CONDITIONS FOR THE CONSTRUCTION OF NATIONAL INNOVATION SYSTEMS AND THEIR IMPLICATIONS FOR EUROPEAN INNOVATION SYSTEMS

Many of these conditions favouring the establishment of different kinds of innovation systems are characteristic of nation states and suggest that such distinctive types are most likely to become established and reproduced at the national level of collective organization, rather than at sectoral, regional, or transnational ones. However, this does not necessarily mean that each nation state develops its own kind of innovation system, nor that distinctive systems cannot be established at regional, international, or sectoral levels of collective organization. Both the national specificity and distinctiveness of these key institutions, and the extent to which they standardize the nature of economic actors and their strategies across industries and regions, differ between countries.

In particular, the development of nationally distinctive and homogenous innovation systems is contingent upon three key features of national institutional regimes. First, the strength of national institutions compared to those governing economic activities at regional and international levels. Second, the extent to which they are complementary in reinforcing particular strategies and patterns of behaviour and, third, the extent to which they standardize the organization of socio-economic groups, and the ways that they compete and cooperate, across industries and regions.

Considering first the national strength of institutional arrangements, this reflects the relative importance of national 'rules of the game' governing economic activities in, say, capital and labour markets as compared to those operative regionally or across national borders or within particular industries. The more that national norms and regulations governing economic competition and cooperation, the constitution of economic actors and their access to key resources, and the organization of public science systems, dominate those at other levels, the more likely that patterns of innovation will vary between countries rather than between regions and sectors.

Second, institutional complementarity at the national level refers here to the extent to which national institutions governing different aspects of innovation systems encourage similar kinds of behaviour, or, on the other hand, conflict in their implications for actors' rationalities and strategies. For example, public science systems with fluid boundaries between different kinds of research organizations, high tolerance of varied intellectual goals and performance criteria in the higher education and research system, and high levels of competition within and between universities and similar organizations, can be said to be complementary to highly fluid labour markets with few constraints on employer and employee opportunism in their encouragement of labour mobility and the rapid transfer of new knowledge and skills between academia and business in research intensive industries.

On the other hand, highly segmented research organizations and strongly hierarchical higher education systems can be seen as complementary to relatively constrained labour markets that limit mobility between employers through their encouragement of firm-specific innovation strategies and capabilities. To a considerable extent, this kind of complementarity has characterized much of the post-war Japanese economy (Kneller 2003; Whitley 2003*b*).

The more such complementarities between key institutions occur nationally rather than regionally or transnationally, the more likely that distinctly national innovation systems become established and reproduced. Where dominant national institutional regimes are complementary in encouraging particular patterns of: (*a*) authority sharing, (*b*) involvement in the public science system and, (*c*) overall coordination of innovative activities, innovation systems will tend to be nationally cohesive and distinctive rather than regional or sectoral. Where they are relatively weak and/or conflicting in their implications for economic actors, distinctive kinds of regional and/or industrial innovation systems may develop within nation states.

Third, states, financial systems, and labour market institutions differ in how much they organize and standardize the nature of legitimate economic actors and interest groups, how these collective agents can acquire and use resources, and how they can change them (Whitley 2005). The more homogenous are the rules of the game specifying appropriate actors and norms of economic behaviour throughout a country, the less likely distinctive sectoral innovation systems will become established around particular technological regimes (Malerba and Orsenigo 1993; Malerba 2002). In contrast, where such specification is restricted to the establishment of formal rules within which a variety of kinds of groups can pursue different strategies with different resources, and are able to shift direction relatively easily, the more sectoral and regional differences in innovation patterns could become significant.

In a country like the US, for instance, the combination of particular kinds of capital and labour market institutions, national state structures and policies and legal institutions has produced a distinctive framework for innovative activities that has encouraged the development of a particular kind of innovation system at the national level (Casper, Lehrer, and Soskice 1999; Hall and Soskice 2001*b*). However, this framework does not greatly restrict: (*a*) the kinds of collective entities that can be constituted as economic actors and interest groups, (*b*) how they are to be organized, or (*c*) how they can acquire, dispose of, and reallocate key resources between activities and sectors. It therefore permits greater variety of innovative actors and organizations than do more corporatist frameworks that standardize the nature and organization of economic actors and interest representation across sectors, and their interaction, to a greater extent. Within the broad set of capital and labour market institutions dominating the US economy, then, there is scope for regional and sectoral patterns of innovation and economic organization to vary considerably.

In seeking to understand the conditions in which distinctive kinds of innovation systems become established at the national level rather than the regional or sectoral ones, it is important, then, to consider how much, and in which ways, different kinds of states organize economic actors and the rules of the games they engage in. Along similar lines to the types of state outlined above, we can distinguish four distinct sets of state structures and policies in terms of how much they standardize the constitution of economic actors and interest groups, and their interaction, at the national level (Whitley 2005).

First, in interdependent states political and bureaucratic elites are quite constrained in their attempts to construct national competitive advantages by powerful, relatively autonomous and varied social groupings, as perhaps is the case in Denmark (Kristensen 1992, 1994; Karnoe 1999). As a result, such countries are unlikely to develop nationally specific and homogenous innovation systems with similar characteristics throughout the country and across all sectors (Edquist and Lundvall 1993; Maskell 1998). The likelihood of such societies standardizing the key institutions governing economic activities across regions and sectors is correspondingly low.

Second, arm's-length states with complementary institutions limiting commitments between economic actors establish formal rules of competition and cooperation without greatly restricting and standardizing the nature of economic actors, the organization of interest groups, or the movement of resources and skills between markets. Such rules are usually generic across markets. They impose few limits on the kinds of owners or managers that can enter particular kinds of markets, or on the kinds of strategies they follow and how they implement them. Equally, the structure and boundaries of interest groups, as well as their relationships with their members, are typically not specified, so that employers' groups, unions, and professions are heterogeneous in their governance and operations. This means that the relative influence of such groups on firms' priorities and strategies can vary within and between such countries, as can their pursuit of growth or profit goals and investment in developing different kinds of organizational capabilities.

Consequently, while the overall extent of authority sharing between business partners, employers, and most employees tends to be limited in such societies, sectoral differences as well as changes over time in particular industries, can be considerable. This is especially likely when different technological regimes encourage contrasting patterns of managerial behaviour and the state pursues particular policy 'missions' in areas such as defence and health care. Even within the same sorts of industries, distinct differences in economic organization can develop between regions with contrasting histories and environments, as Saxenian (1994) has emphasized in her discussion of Route 128 firms and Silicon Valley (see, also, Kenney 2000).

Third, in dominant developmental states companies in favoured sectors are often able to obtain cheap credit for expansion in line with state objectives, and so to grow without diluting owners' control, while others usually have to rely on their own resources and so typically are unable to compete in capital-intensive sectors. Similarly, while the state may assist the former to obtain licenses for new technologies and import scarce components, the latter are likely to experience much greater difficulty in accessing key resources for entering new industries. As a result, state supported firms and sectors will probably grow faster in the more capital-intensive and innovation-based industries, be able to attract better educated staff and invest in developing distinctive organizational capabilities. They will therefore tend to be larger, more diversified, and have stronger coordinating abilities than less favoured companies.

Fourth, more corporatist states encourage firms to join business associations and to form federations that unite major interest groups. As a result, these associations are usually able to exert considerable influence over their members and to constrain opportunistic behaviour. Their organization tends to be more systematic and standardized across sectors than in arm's-length states. The more inclusive corporatist states often, but by no means always, encourage positive union attitudes and delegate certain welfare functions to them, as well as systematically organize labour representation at the national level. By establishing formal mechanisms to coordinate wage bargaining and economic policy development, many European states have consequently developed quite nationally cohesive and distinctive patterns of labour organization that encourage firms to work together as well as to engage in continuous discussions with unions and state agencies. Employment and labour relations more generally are, then, quite systematically organized throughout the economy in ways that encourage cooperation within the overall framework of competitive markets.

Some such states have also developed relatively homogenous skill formation systems that integrate state schools with employer-provided training, usually with the active participation of labour unions and workplace representatives. While the extent of employer-provided training varies between, say, Germany and Sweden, it is usually cooperatively planned and monitored by representatives of employers, unions, and state agencies. Skills are therefore quite highly standardized and well understood by firms and unions (Hinz 1999). Such cooperation may limit the speed of response to market changes but does ensure rapid introduction of new standards and courses once they have been agreed.

Overall, then, the more inclusive corporatist is the political system, the more owners, managers and employees are likely to be organized in similar ways and deal with each other according to relatively standardized procedures. Firms in highly corporatist environments will be more constrained to follow institutionalized conventions and should vary less in their innovation strategies than those in less organized societies. Sectoral, regional, and size differences between companies should be less marked in these kinds of regimes than in other ones. Because the institutions governing labour and capital markets typically encompass small- and medium-sized firms as well as large ones here, more companies are likely to follow similar policies and practices—and so develop similar kinds of organizational capabilities than where states focus on larger firms and do not establish stable mechanisms for managing labour relationships.

In considering the implications of growing multi-levelled governance in the EU for national and sectoral innovation systems, these points suggest that we need to compare: (*a*) the relative strength of EU institutions governing innovative activities, (*b*) their complementarity in encouraging particular patterns of innovative behaviour, and (*c*) their impact on the nature and behaviour of economic actors and interest groups across the EU, with national and regional institutions.

The strength of EU institutions relative to national ones has usually been discussed in terms of the ability of the European Commission (EC) and related agencies such as the European Court of Justice (ECJ) to act autonomously in establishing and implementing EU-wide rules of the game. The conflicts between 'inter-governmentalists' and 'supranationalists' concerning the powers and purposes of European supranational organizations have focused on the relative independence of their goals and strategies from national governments, and their capacity to exert autonomous causal influence on policy outcomes (Pierson 1998; Pollack 1998; Schmidt 2002: 52–7).

For example, Pollack (1998) suggests that four factors are critical: (*a*) the distribution of preferences between national governments and such agents, (*b*) the nature of the institutional decision rules governing the delegation of powers, (*c*) the distribution of information, and (*d*) their ability to mobilize transnational constituencies in support of their policies. Variations in these help to explain differences in the success of the EC and other agencies in creating 'more Europe' in different areas. While he concludes that the 'Commission enjoys considerable autonomy and influence on its implementation of Commission policies' (1998: 248), he also suggests that this should not be overstated and it depends very much on the preferences and coordination of member states, the behaviour of the ECJ and the interests of associated transnational actors in different issue areas.

As part of a multi-tiered governance structure, then, the EU is less sovereign and autonomous in terms of establishing its own 'constitutional choice' rules that affect who determines, and how they do, the 'collective choice' and 'operational' rules governing innovative activities in Amable's hierarchy of institutions, than most, if not all, European governments, and is more subject to lower level rules and agreements (2003: 68). Despite the emergent powers and path-dependent competences of many supranational agencies arising from the combination of large fixed costs, learning effects, coordination effects, and adaptive expectations (Pierson 1998), they remain relatively weak in this sense.

This can be seen in the area of science and technology policies, and public science systems in general, across Europe. For the EU to develop and implement an effective pan-European innovation policy, it would have to be able to establish distinctive rules of the game for firms and other groups that dominated national ones. This would require, amongst other things, the support of key transnational actors such as strong European industrial associations and research organizations who could dominate national ones. Just as the weakness of employers' groups and unions in France contributed to the failure of the attempt to reshape existing patterns of skill formation around 'German' collaborative institutions in the 1980s (Culpepper 1999, 2001; Hancke 2002: 32; Hancke and Goyer 2005), so too the lack of strong supporting groups at the European level limits the likely success of attempts at implementing an effective technology policy across the EU.

Additionally, insofar as the EC has been able to pursue distinctive public policy 'missions' that involve substantial scientific and technological development, such as those in the IT industry, these have rarely been as substantial in terms of resources committed, or as centrally integrated and directed, as those implemented by some national governments, and their success may be questioned. Furthermore, much EU support for European research networks and collaborations appears to have reinforced existing national prestige hierarchies and 'short-term' objectives rather than reduce inequalities and improve social cohesion in the longer term (Garcia-Fontes and Geuna 1999; Geuna 1999). This suggest that the ability of the EC to achieve long-term objectives involving the restructuring of national and international hierarchies is limited.

Similarly, the institutions governing capital markets and banking activities in Europe continue to diverge considerably between member countries, including many accounting standards and prudential regulations, despite the efforts of the EC to create a 'level playing field' for financial transactions across Europe. Especially with regard to the market for corporate control, voting rights and minority shareholder protection, few European rules have become dominant and national variations remain very significant (Barca and Becht 1999). As Amable emphasizes (2003: 60), the Vodafone takeover of Mannesman so stimulated German business opposition to the EC's attempt to develop a Europewide market for corporate control that would have made them vulnerable to hostile takeovers, that they effectively ensured the continuance of nationally fragmented merger and takeover regimes in Europe.

Finally, there is little evidence that strong European institutions governing public science systems have become established. The funding, organization, and control of universities and other research organizations remain concentrated in the hands of national and regional governments, with little pan-European regulation or specification of research roles, skills, or authority structures. Research evaluation methods, strategies and outcomes, for example, vary considerably across national systems and are clearly developed and implemented in different ways by national governments (Geuna and Martin 2003). Despite the 'Bologna' agreement on degree courses—which seems likely to be implemented differently across Europe—the transnational harmonization of academic structures remains limited and few European institutions have become established that could greatly influence the organization of national systems.

Considering next the complementarity of EU institutions governing economic activities, these reflect two contrasting political projects that differ on a left–right axis. According to Amable (2003: 228–30), the first is a neoliberal project aimed at creating an arm's-length regulatory regime for a liberal European market economy, while the second, exemplified perhaps by the Delors Commission, is intended to create a regulated social market form of capitalism at the European level. As he points out, much of the impetus behind the process of European integration since the Rome treaty has been focused on liberalizing and deregulating markets, and so was neoliberal from the start.

More recently, the combination of right wing, and non-traditional social democratic, governments in many countries in the 1990s, with antagonism in some towards 'Brussels' assuming greater powers, has ensured that the neoliberal approach continues to predominate. Thus, despite the social chapter and related regulatory steps in favour of social protection and employee voice, as well as the Common Agricultural Policy, the prevalent approach adopted by the EU towards economic development has been concerned to standardize competition rules, abolish state subsidies and similar developmental strategies, prohibit cartels and other forms of collaboration between companies, and generally encourage a deregulated, liberal and transparent European market (Djelic and Bensendrine 2001; Lilja and Moen 2003; McKenna, Djelic, and Ainamo 2003).

The prevalence of an arm's-length regulatory style at the European level is additionally encouraged by the lack of democratic legitimacy of many EU institutions, particularly the EC. Without the authority derived from competitive pan-European elections between integrated European political parties, it is difficult for them to implement active promotional policies in favour of specific sectors or projects, encouraging inter-firm collaboration and/or monopolistic forms of interest group representation, especially in the face of resistance from nationally elected governments and groups supported by them. It should be much easier for the EC as an unelected agency to legitimize liberalization of markets as a way of opening up opportunities for all European companies and reducing the influence of special interests than to segment markets, promote European champions, and support particular groups amidst democratically elected governments.

However, the existence of the regulated capitalism project, and the groups supporting it, together with the strong emphasis on social cohesion and integration in many European states since the war, have hindered the strength and complementarity of EU arm's-length institutions and regulatory policies, so that they do not consistently encourage LME logics and innovation strategies. Pan-European labour markets organized along US lines, for instance, scarcely exist, and there seems little EC pressure to remove the strong employment protection regulations entrenched in a number of states. Consequently, transnational professional team-based innovation systems seem unlikely to develop in Europe.

Insofar as the EU does establish a distinctive and complementary set of regulatory institutions and governance norms dealing with innovative activities at the European level, then, these tend to permit considerable variation in how innovation systems are organized, whether at the national, sectoral, or regional levels. The standardization of a single 'European' type of innovation system is most improbable. However, the prevalence of an arm's-length transnational regulatory approach in the EU may constrain the national specificity and homogeneity of state-coordinated and collaborative kinds of innovation systems in some European states, especially when combined with pressures from external investors.

This has already been seen in countries where the state has taken a leading role in coordinating innovative activities, especially if direct subsidies were involved. Given the importance of competition policy in the EU, and its broadly liberal market character, it seems unlikely that a cohesive state-led innovation system will become established and reproduced as a national, cross-sectoral type within the EU. Additionally, the predominant emphasis on liberalizing markets and preventing collusion can reinforce pressures from national economic actors to reconstruct collaborative relationships, as Djelic and Quack (2005) have suggested happened in the German banking system in the 1990s.

In general, the effects of the EU regulatory approach are going to be most evident when it coincides with, and complements, other efforts to restructure commitments between companies, employers, and employees. It is probably too weak and contradictory to develop new kinds of innovation systems at the European level, but when combined with broader international, national, and regional pressures to limit constraints on economic opportunism, it may well reduce the national specificity, complementarity, and standardization of group-based and highly collaborative innovation systems in some European countries. In so doing, it could encourage the strengthening of sectorally specific innovation systems around different technological regimes within national boundaries (Breschi and Malerba 1997; Malerba 2002). However, the continued diversity of labour market institutions, skill formation systems, and public science systems will limit the extent to which these become established across Europe.

Turning finally to consider the relative strength and standardization of interest group representation at the European level, these seem quite limited compared to those established in many member states. Despite the growth of lobby groups and trade association agents in Brussels over the past few decades, there are few if any European peak associations that can credibly act as central bargaining organizations on behalf of all major companies throughout western Europe, resolve disputes between members, constrain opportunism and sanction deviance. As Plehwe and Vescovi (2003) point out, European market integration in the transport industry has led to considerable fragmentation and polarization of interest group representation at the transnational level, and many associations have opened separate offices in Brussels to lobby for their sectional goals. In this field, 'supranational and national public authorities are confronted and cooperate with a growing number of competing business associations' (Plehwe and Vescovi 2003: 211), although in some other industries companies have been more successful in developing 'interface actor associations'.

Similarly, labour organization and representation at the European level tends to be more a matter of coordinating national groups than integrating them into a cohesive transnational association that could negotiate centrally. As Amable suggests (2003: 253):

'the European Trade Unions Confederation (ETUC) has no power over its national union members and must rely on their voluntarism and their active participation .... voluntarism is in fact a more general problem for Continental Europe. Its generalization leads to the spread of the "contract culture" ... and collective bargaining runs the risk of turning into ... a vehicle for market coordination and competition.'

The EU-interest groups' interrelationships seem, then, to be closer to the US pattern of sponsored pluralism than the many varieties of national corporatism in Europe (Streeck and Schmitter 1985; Crouch 1999). As Schmidt (2002: 246) puts it: 'a wide range of policy actors, governmental as well as non-governmental, negotiate the construction of policy programmes through an elaborate coordinative discourse .... negotiations involve complex system of Commission-organized discussion among experts, interest groups, governmental representatives, lobbyists and the like.' Even though such groups have developed distinctive epistemic communities in some sectors, with European coordinating discourses, they often have little legitimacy at the national level (Schmidt 2002: 248). Similarly, the key institutions governing skill formation and certification remain nationally specific in Europe, with extremely limited harmonization across the EU, and not much mutual recognition of qualifications.

14.5. CONCLUDING REMARKS

In this chapter I have suggested how three key features of innovation systems could be combined to constitute six distinct ways of organizing innovative activities, and outlined the institutional circumstances in which different types are likely to become established and reproduced at different level of collective organization. In conclusion, it is perhaps worth emphasizing four main points arising from this discussion.

First, the development and reproduction of particular ways of inventing and commercializing new processes, products, and services as coherent systems of innovation depends greatly on the strength and complementarity of key institutions at particular organizational levels. Because of this institutional dependence, different kinds of learning, cooperation, and competition take place in different institutional contexts. While many institutions governing innovative activities are associated with the nation state, not all are, and the extent to which they do indeed complement each other in encouraging particular logics of action varies considerably between countries and over historical periods. Insofar as we are in a post-Westphalian state era (Held et al. 1999: 37–8; Schmidt 2002: 17–57), the dominance of national institutions may be weakening and their construction of distinctively national innovation systems becoming less autarkic and cohesive, especially within the EU.

Second, the homogeneity and standardization of economic actors and other socio-economic groups, as well as of the norms governing their behaviour, within any particular set of complementary institutions varies according to the kind of institutions and organizations that dominate a given social system, and the policies that key agents, especially states, pursue. In so far as technological regimes are significant in the construction of different kinds of sectoral innovation systems, these are more likely to become established in arm's-length institutional environments than in highly corporatist ones in which interest groups, and the regulation of their interaction, are organized in similar ways across industries.

Given the considerable variety of institutions, agencies, and policies between European countries, this means that innovative activities organized in different ways in different industries in one country may be less separately structured in other ones, so that pan-European sectoral innovation systems are relatively rare. British, German, and Swedish biotechnology firms, for instance, differ considerably in their competences and strategies as a result of major variations in state policies, financial systems, and labour markets (Casper 2000; Casper and Kettler 2001; Casper and Whitley 2004).

Third, the development of transnational rules of the competitive game and supranational forms of governance in the EU has created a new tier of institutional constraints and opportunities for innovative activities in Europe without necessarily leading to the demise of existing ones at national and regional levels. This is because of the limited ability of central EU organizations to act independently from national ones as authoritative agents in establishing constitutional choice rules across Europe, as well as the often contradictory policies followed in different areas. Additionally, political parties, interest groups, and other socio-political actors remain more focused on national than on European competitions, and these are quite heterogeneously organized. While the EU may have created a new kind of transnational political and legal space within which firms have to operate, this seems to function in addition to, rather than instead of, existing national ones, and it is not obvious why this should change greatly in the medium term.

Finally, insofar as this additional tier of governance has followed a particular approach to economic organization and behaviour in a consistent manner, it resembles the institutions and logic of LMEs rather than those of more coordinated ones. As such, it permits considerable variability in the kind of firms that compete in different markets, how they do so, and how they adapt to changing circumstances. It is unlikely, then, to encourage much standardization of patterns of innovation across the EU, although it may reduce the level of homogeneity within some national innovation systems by providing alternative opportunities for strategic managers. Overall, then, while the strength and cohesion of collaborative innovation systems may decline in the EU, and state-led ones seem unlikely to be viable, the variety of different ways of organizing innovative activities, and of the kinds of innovations successfully produced, in Europe seems likely to remain considerable, and perhaps to increase.

REFERENCES

Abramson, H., Encarmacao, J., Reid, P., and Schmoch, U. (eds.) (1997). *Technology Transfer Systems in the United States and Germany.* Washington, DC: National Academy Press.

Almeida, P. and Kogut, B. (1999). 'Localization of Knowledge and the Mobility of Engineers in Regional Networks', *Management Science,* 45: 905–17.

Amable, B. (2003). *The Diversity of Modern Capitalism.* Oxford: Oxford University Press.

Andersen, P. H. and Kristensen, P. H. (1999). 'The Systemic Qualities of Danish Industrialism', in P. Karnoe et al. (eds.), *Mobilising Resources and Generating Competencies.* Copenhagen: Copenhagen Business School Press, pp. 299–331.

Angel, J. P. (2000). 'High Technology Agglomeration and the Labor Market: The Case of Silicon Valley', in M. Kenney, (ed.), *Understanding Silicon Valley.* Stanford, CA: Stanford University Press, pp. 124–40.

Barca, F. and Becht, M. (eds.) (2001). *The Control of Corporate Europe.* Oxford: Oxford University Press.

Beetham, D. (1991). *The Legitimation of Power.* London: Macmillan.

Borras, S. (2004). 'System of Innovation Theory and the European Union', *Science and Public Policy,* 31: 425–33.

Braczyk, H.-J., Cooke, P., and Heidenreich, M. (eds.) (1998). *Regional Innovation Systems: The Role of Governances in a Globalized World*. London: UCL Press, republished by Routledge in 2003.

Breschi, S. and Malerba, F. (1997). 'Sectoral Innovation Systems: Technological Regimes, Schumpeterian Dynamics, and Spatial Boundaries', in C. Edquist, (ed.), *Systems of Innovation: Technologies, Institutions and Organizations*. London: Pinter, pp. 130–55.

Carlsson, B., Jacobsson, S., Holmen, M., and Rickne, A. (2002). 'Innovation Systems: Analytical and Methodological Issues', *Research Policy*, 331: 233–45.

Casper, S. (2000). 'Institutional Adaptiveness, Technology Policy, and the Diffusion of New Business Models: The Case of German Biotechnology', *Organization Studies*, 21: 887–914.

—— and Kettler, H. (2001). 'National Institutional Frameworks and the Hybridization of Entrepreneurial Business Models: The German and UK Biotechnology Sectors', *Industry and Innovation*, 8: 5–30.

—— and Whitley, R (2004). 'Managing Competences in Entrepreneurial Technology Firms: A Comparative Institutional Analysis of Germany, Sweden and the UK', *Research Policy*, 33: 89–106.

—— Lehrer, M., and Soskice, D. (1999). 'Can High-Technology Industries Prosper in Germany: Institutional Frameworks and the Evolution of the German Software and Biotechnology Industries', *Industry and Innovation*, 6: 6–23.

Chandler, A. (1990). *Scale and Scope*. Cambridge, MA: Harvard University Press.

Christopherson, S. (2002). 'Project Work in Context: Regulatory Change and the New Geography of Media', *Environment and Planning A*, 34: 2003–15.

Coriat, B. and Weinstein, O. (2002). 'Organizations, Firms and Institutions in the Generation of Innovation', *Research Policy*, 31: 273–90.

Crouch, C., le Gales, P., Trigilia, C., and Voelzkow, H. (2001). *Local Production Systems in Europe: Rise or Demise?* Oxford: Oxford University Press.

Culpepper, P. D. (1999). 'Individual Choice, Collective Action, and the Problem of Training Reform: Insights from France and Eastern Germany', in P. Culpepper and D. Finegold (eds.), *The German Skills Machine: Sustaining Comparative Advantage in a Global Economy*. New York: Berghahn Books, pp. 269–325.

—— (2001). 'Employers' Associations, Public Policy and the Politics of Decentralised Cooperation,' pp. 275–306 in P. Hall and D. Soskice (eds.), *Varieties of Capitalism*.

Djelic, M.-L. and Bensedrine, J. (2001) 'Globalization and Its Limits: The Making of International Regulation', in G. Morgan, P. H. Kristensen, and R. Whitley (eds.), *The Multinational Firm: Organizing Across Institutional and National Divides*. Oxford: Oxford University Press, pp. 253–80.

—— and Quack, S. (eds.) (2003). *Globalization and Institutions: Redefining the Rules of the Economic Game*. Cheltenham, UK: Edward Elgar.

—— —— (2005). 'Rethinking Path Dependency from an Open Systems Perspective: The Crooked Path of Institutional Change in Postwar Germany', pp. 137–166 in Morgan, Whitley, and Moen (eds.), *Changing Capitalisms?*

Edquist, C. (ed.) (1997). *Systems of Innovation: Technologies, Institutions and Organizations.* London: Pinter, pp. 265–98.

—— (2005). 'Systems of Innovation: Perspectives and Challenges', in J. Fagerberg, D. Mowery, and R. Nelson (eds.), *The Oxford Handbook of Innovation.* Oxford: Oxford University Press, pp. 181–208.

—— and Lundvall, B.-A. (1993). 'Comparing the Danish and the Swedish Systems of Innovation', in R. Nelson (ed.), *National Innovation Systems.*

Ergas, H. (1987). 'Does Technology Policy Matter?', in B. R. Guile and H. Brooks (eds.), *Technology and Global Industry: Companies and Nations in the World Economy.* Washington, DC: National Academy Press.

Evans, P. (1994). *Embedded Autonomy: States and Industrial Transformation.* Princeton, NJ: Princeton University Press.

Feller, I. (1999). 'The American University System as a Performer of Basic and Applied Research', in L. M. Branscomb F. Kodama, and R. Florida (eds.), *Industrializing Knowledge: University-Industry Linkages in Japan and the United States.* Cambridge, MA: MIT Press, pp. 65–101.

Fujimoto, T. (2000). 'Evolution of Manufacturing Systems and *ex post* Dynamic Capabilities', in G. Dosi, R. Nelson, and S. Winter (eds.), *The Nature and Dynamics of Organizational Capabilities.* Oxford: Oxford University Press, pp. 244–80.

Garcia-Fontes, W. and Geuna, A. (1999). 'The Dynamics of Research Networks in Europe', in A. Gambardella and F. Malerba (eds.), *The Organization of Economic Innovation in Europe.* Cambridge: Cambridge University Press, pp. 343–66.

Gerlach, M. (1992). *Alliance Capitalism.* Berkeley, CA: University of California Press.

Geuna, A. (1999). *The Economics of Knowledge Production: Funding and the Structure of University Research.* Cheltenham, UK: Edward Elgar.

—— and Martin, B. (2003). 'University Research Evaluation and Funding: An International Comparison', *Minerva,* 41: 277–304.

Grabher, G. (2002). 'Fragile Sector, Robust Practices: Project Ecologies in New Media', *Environment and Planning A.,* 34: 1911–26.

Graham, H. and Diamond, N. (1997). *The Rise of the American Research Universities.* Baltimore, MD: Johns Hopkins University Press.

Guerrieri, P. and Tylecote, A. (1997). 'Interindustry Differences in Technical Changes and National Patterns of Technological Accumulation', pp. 107–29 in C. Edquist (ed.), *Systems of Innovation.*

Hall, P. and Soskice, D. (2001*a*) 'Introduction', in P. Hall and D. Soskice (ed.), *Varieties of Capitalism.*

—— —— (eds.), (2001*b*). *Varieties of Capitalism: The Institutional Foundations of Comparative Advantage.* Oxford: Oxford University Press.

Hancke, R. (2002). *Large Firms and Institutional Change.* Oxford: Oxford University Press.

—— and Goyer, M. (2005). 'Degrees of Freedom: Rethinking the Institutional Analysis of Economic Change', pp. 53–77, in Morgan, Whitley, and Moen (eds.), *Changing Capitalisms?*

Held, D., McGraw, A., Goldblatt, D., and Perraton, J. (1999). *Global Transformations.* Cambridge: Polity Press.

Henderson, R., Orsenigo, L., and Pisano, G. (1999). 'The Pharmaceutical Industry and the Revolution in Molecular Biology', in D. C. Mowery and R. R. Nelson (eds.), *Sources of Industrial Leadership.* Cambridge: Cambridge University Press.

Herrigel, G. and Wittke, V. (2005). 'Varieties of Vertical Disintegration: The Global Trend Towards Heterogeneous Supply Relations and the Reproduction of Difference in US and German Manufacturing', pp. 312–51, in Morgan, Whitley, and Moen (eds.), *Changing Capitalisms?*

Hinz, T. (1999). 'Vocational Training and Job Mobility in Comparative Perspective', in P. D. Culpepper and D. Finegold (eds.), *The German Skills Machine.* New York: Berghahn Books pp. 159–88.

Hollingsworth, R. and Boyer, R. (eds.) (1997). *Contemporary Capitalism: The Embeddedness of Institutions.* Cambridge University Press.

Hopner, J. (1999). 'The Danish Banking System: Concentration, Local Autonomy and the Financing of Small and Medium-Sized Enterprises', pp. 113–35, in Karnoe et al. (eds.), *Mobilizing Resources and Generating Competencies.*

Kaiser, R. and Prange, H. (2004). 'The Reconfiguration of National Innovation Systems: The Example of German Biotechnology', *Research Policy,* 33: 395–408.

Karnoe, P. (1999). 'The Business Systems Framework and Danish SMEs', pp. 7–72, in P. Karnoe, P. H. Kristensen, and P. H. Andersen (eds.), *Mobilizing Resources and Generating Capabilities.*

—— Kristensen, P. H., and Andersen, P. H. (eds.) (1999). *Mobilizing Resources and Generating Capabilities.* Copenhagen: Copenhagen Business School Press.

Kenney, M. (ed.) (2000). *Understanding Silicon Valley: The Anatomy of an Entrepreneurial Region.* Stanford, CA: Stanford University Press.

Kneller, R. (1999). 'University-Industry Cooperation in Biomedical R&D in Japan and the United States: Implications for Biomedical Industries', in Lewis Branscomb et al. (eds.), *Industrializing Knowledge: University-Industry Linkages in Japan and the United States.* Cambridge, MA: MIT Press, pp. 410–38.

—— (2003). 'Autarkic Drug Discovery in Japanese Pharmaceutical Companies', *Research Policy,* 32: 1805–27.

Kristensen, P. H. (1992). 'Strategies Against Structure: Institutions and Economic Organization in Denmark', in R. Whitley (ed.), *European Business Systems.* London: Sage, pp. 117–36.

—— (1994). 'Strategies in a Volatile World', *Economy and Society,* 23: 305–34.

—— (1996). 'On the Constitution of Economic Actors in Denmark: Interacting Skill Container and Project Coordinators', in R. Whitley and P. H. Kristensen (eds.), *The Changing European Firm: Limits to Convergence.* London: Routledge, pp. 118–58.

Lilja, K. and Moen, E. (2003). 'Coordinating Transnational Competition: Changing Patterns of International Business Transactions', pp. 137–60, in Djelic and Quack (eds.), *Globalization and Institutions.*

Lundvall, B.-Å. (ed.) (1992). *National Systems of Innovation.* London: Pinter.

—— Johnson, B., Andersen, E. S., and Dalum, B. (2002). 'National Systems of Production, Innovation and Competence Building', *Research Policy*, 31: 213–31.

Malerba, F. (2002). 'Sectoral Systems of Innovation and Production', *Research Policy*, 31: 247–64.

—— and Orsenigo, L. (1993). 'Technological Regimes and Firm Behaviour', *Industrial and Corporate Change*, 2: 45–71.

McKelvey, M. (1996). *Evolutionary Innovations: The Business of Biotechnology.* Oxford: Oxford University Press.

McKenna, C., Djelic, M. L., and Ainamo, A. (2003). 'Message and Medium: The Role of Consulting Firms in Globalization and Its Local Interpretation', pp. 83–107, in Djelic and Quack (eds.), *Globalization and Institutions.*

Migdal, J. S. (1988). *Strong Societies and Weak States.* Princeton, NJ: Princeton University Press.

Morgan, G., Whitley, R., and Moen, E. (eds.) (2005). *Changing Capitalisms? Internationalization, Institutional Change and Systems of Economic Organization.* Oxford: Oxford University Press.

Morris-Suzuki, T. (1994). *The Technological Transformation of Japan.* Cambridge: Cambridge University Press.

Mowery, D. C. (1999). 'The Computer Software Industry', in D. Mowery and R. Nelson (eds.), *Sources of Industrial Leadership.* Cambridge: Cambridge University Press, pp. 133–68.

Nelson, R. (ed.) (1993). *National Innovation Systems.* Oxford: Oxford University Press.

OECD (2002). *Benchmarking Industry-Science Relations.* Paris: OECD.

Pierson, P. (1998). 'The Path to European Integration: A Historical-Institutionalist Analysis', pp. 27–58, in W. Sandholtz and A. Stone Sweet (eds.), *European Integration and Supranational Governance.*

Plehwe, D. and Vescovi, S. (2003). 'Europe's Special Case: The Five Corners of Business-State Interactions', pp. 193–219, in M.-L. Djelic and S. Quack (eds.), *Globalization and Institutions.*

Pollack, M. A. (1998). 'The Engines of Integration? Supranational Autonomy and Influence in the European Union', pp. 217–49, in Sandholtz and Stone Sweet (eds.), *European Integration and Supranational Governance.*

Powell, W. (2001). 'The Capitalist Firm in the Twenty-First Century: Emerging Patterns in Western Perspective', in Paul DiMaggio (ed.), *The Twenty-First Century Firm.* Princeton, NJ: Princeton University Press, pp. 33–68.

Samuels, R. J. (1987). *The Business of the Japanese State.* Ithaca, NY: Cornell University Press.

Sandholtz, W. and Stone Sweet, A. (1998). *European Integration and Supranational Governance.* Oxford: Oxford University Press.

Saxenian, A. (1994). *Regional Advantage: Culture and Competition in Silicon Valley and Route 128.* Cambridge, MA: Harvard University Press.

Sheard, P. (1994). 'Interlocking Shareholdings and Corporate Governance in Japan', in M. Aoki and R. Dore (eds.), *The Japanese Firm: The Sources of Competitive Strength.* Oxford: Oxford University Press, pp. 310–49.

Schmidt, V. A. (2002). *The Futures of European Capitalism*. Oxford: Oxford University Press.

Soskice, D. (1999). 'Divergent Production Regimes: Coordinated and Uncoordinated Market Economies in the 1980s and 1990s', in H. Kitschelt et al. (eds.), *Continuity and Change in Contemporary Capitalism*. Cambridge: Cambridge University Press.

Stokes, D. E. (1997). *Pasteur's Quadrant: Basic Science and Technological Innovation*. Washington, DC: Brookings Institution Press.

Streeck, W. and Schmitter, P. (eds.) (1985). *Private Interest Government: Beyond Market and State*. London: Sage.

Thomas, L. G. III (1994). 'Implicit Industrial Policy: The Triumph of Britain and the Failure of France in Global Pharmaceuticals', *Industrial and Corporate Change*, 3: 451–89.

Tylecote, A. and Conesa, E. (1999). 'Corporate Governance, Innovation Systems and Industrial Performance', *Industry and Innovation*, 6: 25–50.

Whitley, R. (1999). *Divergent Capitalisms: The Social Structuring and Change of Business Systems*. Oxford: Oxford University Press.

—— (2000*a*). *The Intellectual and Social Organization of the Sciences*. Oxford: Oxford University Press 2nd edn. first edition, 1984).

—— (2000*b*). 'The Institutional Structuring of Innovation Strategies', *Organization Studies*, 21: 855–86.

—— (2002). 'Developing Innovative Competences: The Role of Institutional Frameworks', *Industrial and Corporate Change*, 11: 497–528.

—— (2003*a*). 'The Institutional Structuring of Organizational Capabilities: The Role of Authority Sharing and Organizational Careers', *Organization Studies*, 24: 667–95.

—— (2003*b*). 'Competition and Pluralism in the Public Sciences: The Impact of Institutional Frameworks on the Organization of Academic Science', *Research Policy*, 32: 1015–29.

—— (2005). 'How National Are Business Systems? The Role of States and Complementary Institutions in Standardising Systems of Economic Coordination and Control at the National Level', pp. 190–231, in Morgan et al. (eds.), *Changing Capitalisms?*

15

For National Strategies of Transition
to a Knowledge Economy in the European
Union—Learning, Innovation, and the Open
Method of Coordination

Maria João Rodrigues

15.1. KNOWLEDGE ECONOMY AND KNOWLEDGE POLICIES

15.1.1. On the Transition to the Knowledge-Intensive Economy

We are going through a great transformation which can be called a transition to knowledge-intensive economies. We can say that we are entering a new mode of knowledge creation, diffusion, and use due to three main factors: the acceleration of information and communication technologies; the increasingly sophisticated procedures to codify, learn, and manage knowledge; and the social perception of knowledge as a strategic asset of companies, nations, and people.

These three factors are gradually transforming:

- knowledge creation by professional groups, such as researchers, artists, engineers as well as by the different social communities, developing different forms of life in working life, family life, leisure, public space;
- knowledge diffusion by telecommunications networks, content industries, media, education and training;
- knowledge use by companies, public services, local authorities, the different actors of civil society, and people at large.

This broad transformation involves new patterns of behaviour, values, social relationships, and institutional forms. The financial markets were the first markets to be transformed by the new opportunities opened by cyberspace. With just-in-time interaction becoming possible, the global interdependency of these markets and the mobility of capital has increased dramatically. The same does not happen with their regulation, which still has many shortcomings—hence, the greater risks of systemic crisis.

More recently, we have been witnessing a new dimension of the process of globalization (Soete 2001) with the rise of the intangible transactions at the international level encompassing not only services, but also transfers of technology, information, and knowledge connected with manufacturing. Just-in-time interaction and coordination at the global level is also becoming possible for manufacturing. The production chains are being reorganized at the global level. Multinational corporations are focusing the most value-added production based on trademarks and building, wide networks of outsourcing, and delocalization. With the diffusion of e-commerce, more particularly with business-to-business, new e-market places are emerging and speeding up global transactions which can involve not only big but also small and medium companies that are discovering completely new opportunities.

Within companies, it is not only the production process which is becoming more intensive in information and knowledge, but also the content of the products and the services themselves, as we can understand by driving a car, using a TV set, a washing machine, or looking for a personal banking, health, or entertainment service (Tapscott 1995). Hence, knowledge management is becoming a key factor of competitiveness, leading to a fundamental recon-sideration of the principles of strategic management (Wikström and Norman 1994). The goal of knowledge management is to build and exploit intellectual capital effectively and gainfully (Despres and Chauvel 2000).

Against this background, there are companies reshaping their organization towards a learning organization, with multitasking, more flexible arrange-ments, more open communication, more scope for initiative and creativity, and more opportunities for lifelong learning. More sophisticated procedures are introduced in HRM based on competence assessment (Le Boterf 1998). New types of workers are spreading, called knowledge workers by Robert Reich (1991), categorized by Manuel Castells (1996) in different occupational profiles such as innovators, connectors, and captains.

In the meantime, new risks of social downgrading or social exclusion— a digital divide—involve the workers who cannot keep up with this pace of change. Labour markets tend to new forms of segmentation between workers with voluntary mobility based on updated skills and workers with involuntary mobility due to outdated skills. New types of labour contracts and collective agreements are being experimented in order to take into account the time and the financial resources invested in lifelong learning by the companies, the workers, and the public authorities. New forms of security regarding training or social protection are being defined in order to facilitate the occupational mobility of workers and their choices between working, learning, and family life throughout the life cycle.

The institutional framework of labour markets is being reshaped in order to combine competence building, employability, and adaptability with basic conditions of security and citizenship (e.g. Esping-Anderson 1996; Fitoussi and Rosanvallon 1996). Labour market services are being more focused on active employment policies, social protection systems on activating social policies, industrial relations on negotiating new trade-offs between flexibility, security, and competence building. Finally, education and training systems are facing the challenge of developing a learning society, improving their access to knowledge to the different kinds of users taking advantage of the different kinds of media.

These trends are still in conflict with other trends coming from the past, the previous mode of development, but they might be fostered by a new generation of policies, which can be called knowledge policies.

15.1.2. Knowledge Policies

Knowledge is becoming the main source of wealth for nations, companies, and people, but it can also become the main factor of inequality. Therefore, public policies should be more concerned in facilitating the access to knowledge and enhancing learning capacities (Lundvall 2001). This is why we can also speak about knowledge policies.

Knowledge policies can be defined as policies aiming at fostering and shaping this transition to a knowledge-based society.

Regarding knowledge creation, these policies support basic research, applied research, as well as culture industries, encouraging dialogue among different cultures, social groups, and generations. Regarding knowledge diffusion, these policies develop broadband networks, spread the access to Internet, promote content industries and their dissemination by different media, and reform education and training towards what we can call a learning society.

Regarding knowledge utilization, these policies foster innovation in products and processes, knowledge management, and learning organizations in companies and social services, as well as local and international partnerships for innovation.

Against this background, we can highlight a more far-reaching role for the policies concerning notably research, culture, media, innovation, information society, education and training, and their implications for other issues such as employment, social inclusion, and regional development. Moreover, some implications should also be drawn for macroeconomic policies and their impact on structural change. Budgetary policies should give a stronger priority to knowledge policies and even tax policies should encourage new patterns of behaviour in line with these policies.

All this was at stake, when a strategy for the transition to a knowledge economy was defined in the EU.

15.2. A EUROPEAN STRATEGY FOR THE TRANSITION TO THE KNOWLEDGE ECONOMY

15.2.1. In Search of a European Way[1]

In the preparations for the Lisbon Summit (23–4 March 2000), we faced the following main question: is it possible to update Europe's development strategy so that we can rise to the new challenges resulting from globalization, technological change, and population ageing, while preserving European values? In the new emerging paradigm, knowledge and innovation are the main source of both wealth and divergence between nations, companies, and individuals. Europe is losing ground to the US, but this does not mean we have to copy them.

The purpose was to define a European way to evolve into a new innovation- and knowledge-based economy, using distinctive attributes ranging from the preservation of social cohesion and cultural diversity to the very technological options. A critical step would be to set up a competitive platform that can sustain the European social model, which should also be renewed.

Answering this question requires institutional innovations, if we want to tap into the potential of this new paradigm while avoiding risks of social divide. Innovation, for example, of norms regulating international trade and competition, of social models, or of education systems. Moreover, in each and every Member State of the EU, institutional innovation has to internalize the level of integration accomplished through the single market and the single currency. This means that some level of European coordination is required to carry out institutional reforms, while respecting national specificity. A multi-level governance system is needed that enables its various levels (i.e. European, national, and local) to interact.

In order to find an answer to the initial question, we had to commit to an extensive intellectual and political undertaking of reviewing Europe's political agenda and the main Community policy documents in the light of the latest advances in the social sciences. European intellectuals with broad experience in these fields were involved in this task (Rodrigues 2002). Our purpose was to ascertain which institutional reforms could change the way in which European societies are currently regulated, so as to pave the way for a new development trajectory towards a knowledge-intensive economy.

15.2.2. The Lisbon Strategy[2]

A new strategic goal and an overall strategy was defined by Lisbon European Council on 23–4 March 2000. Quoting its own conclusions:

to become the most competitive and dynamic knowledge-based economy in the world capable of sustainable economic growth with more and better jobs and greater social cohesion. Achieving this goal requires an overall strategy aimed at:
- *preparing the transition to a knowledge-based economy and society by better policies for the information society and R&D, as well as by stepping up the process of structural reform for competitiveness and innovation and by completing the internal market;*
- *modernising the European social model, investing in people and combating social exclusion;*
- *sustaining the healthy economic outlook and favourable growth prospects by applying an appropriate macro-economic policy mix.*

This quotation is important to clarify that, contrary to some vulgarizations, the strategic goal defined in Lisbon is not 'to become the most competitive' but to achieve this particular combination of strong competitiveness with the other features. This should make clear the specificity of the European way (see Table 15.1).

15.2.3. Strategy and Governance

The actual implementation of any strategy requires a political engine, that is, a governance centre at the European level with the power to coordinate policies and adapt them to each national context. The Lisbon decisions made this governance centre stronger, in three ways:

- first, the European Council would play a stronger role as coordinator of the economic and social policies, henceforth devoting its Spring Council to the monitoring of this strategy, based on a synthesis report presented by the European Commission;
- second, the broad economic policy guidelines would improve the synergy between macroeconomic policies, structural policies, and employment policy;

Table 15.1 The main political orientations of the Lisbon Strategy

The Lisbon Strategy set the following main political orientations:
  a. a policy for the information society aimed at improving the citizens' standards of living, with concrete applications in the fields of education, public services, electronic commerce, health, and urban management; a new impetus to spread information technologies in companies, namely e-commerce and knowledge management tools; an ambition to deploy advanced telecommunications networks and democratize the access to the Internet, on the one hand, and produce contents that add value to Europe's cultural and scientific heritage, on the other;
  b. an R&D policy whereby the existing community programme and the national policies converge into a European area of research by networking R&D programmes and institutions. A strong priority for innovation policies and the creation of a Community patent;
  c. an enterprise policy going beyond the existing community programme, combining it with a coordination of national policies in order to create better conditions for entrepreneurship—namely administrative simplification, access to venture capital, or manager training;
  d. economic reforms that target the creation of growth and innovation potential, improve financial markets to support new investments, and complete Europe's internal market by liberalizing the basic sectors while respecting the public service inherent to the European model;
  e. macroeconomic policies which, in addition to keeping the existing macroeconomic stability, vitalize growth, employment and structural change, using budgetary and tax policies to foster education, training, research, and innovation;
  f. a renewed European social model relying on three key drivers, that is, making more investment in people, activating social policies, and strengthening action against old and new forms of social exclusion;
  g. new priorities defined for national education policies, that is, turning schools into open learning centres, providing support to each and every population group, using the Internet and multimedia; in addition, Europe should adopt a framework of new basic skills and create a European diploma to embattle computer illiteracy;
  h. active employment policies intensified with the aim of making lifelong training generally available and expanding employment in services as a significant source of job creation, improvement of the standards of living, and promotion of equal opportunities for women and men. Raising Europe's employment rate was adopted as a key target in order to reduce the unemployment rate and consolidate the sustainability of the social protection systems;
  i. an organized process of cooperation between the Member States to modernize social protection, identifying reforms to answer to common problems such as matching pension systems with population ageing;
  j. national plans to take action against social exclusion in each and every dimension of the problem (including education, health, housing) and meeting the requirements of target groups specific to each national situation;
  k. improved social dialogue in managing change and setting up of various forms of partnership with civil society, including the dissemination of best practices of companies with higher social responsibility.

Sources: Council of European Union (2000, 2001*a*).

– third, in order to complement the legislative instruments, the Union adopted an open method for inter-Member State coordination, which began being applied to various policy fields, stepping up the translation of European priorities into national policies.

The open method of coordination was elaborated after a reflexion on governance aiming at defining methods for developing European dimension. The political construction of Europe is a unique experience. Its success has been dependent on the ability to combine coherence with respect for diversity and efficiency with democratic legitimacy. This entails using different modes of governance depending on the problems to be solved and involving specific instruments and institutions. For good reasons, various methods have been worked out which are placed somewhere between pure integration and straightforward cooperation (see Table 15.2).

15.2.4. The Open Method of Coordination

Three years after its first implementation by the Luxembourg process on employment, the definition of the open method of coordination was expressly undertaken during the preparation of Lisbon European Council in order to develop the European dimension in new policy fields, namely information society, research, innovation, enterprise policy, education, and fighting social exclusion. After in-depth discussions led by the Presidency with governments, the European Commission, the European Parliament, and social partners, this Summit formally adopted this method in the following terms (Presidency Conclusions 2000):

Implementing a new open method of coordination

1. *Implementation of the strategic goal will be facilitated by applying a new open method of coordination as the means of spreading best practices and achieving greater convergence towards the main EU goals. This method, which is designed to help Member States to progressively developing their own policies, involves:*

   − *fixing guidelines for the Union combined with specific timetables for achieving the goals which they set in the short, medium, and long terms;*
   − *establishing, where appropriate, quantitative and qualitative indicators and benchmarks against the best in the world and tailored to the needs of different Member States and sectors as a means of comparing best practices;*
   − *translating these European guidelines into national and regional policies by setting specific targets and adopting measures, taking into account national and regional differences;*
   − *periodic monitoring, evaluation and peer review organized as mutual learning processes.*

2. *A fully decentralized approach will be applied in line with the principle of subsidiarity in which the Union, the Member States, the regional and local levels, as well as the social*

Table 15.2 Policies, modes of governance, and instruments

Modes of governance Policies	>Instruments	Monetary policy	Trade policy	Single market policy	Fiscal policy	Employment labour policies	Research policy	Social protection and social inclusion policies	Education and training policies	Enterprise and innovation policies	Environment
Single policy	Delegation in European bodies, laws	X	X	X							
Harmonization of national policies	Framework laws			X		X		X			X
Coordination of national policies	Framework laws, decisions				X		X				
Open coordination of national policies	Decision on recommendations with monitoring and opinions					X	X	X	X	X	X
Cooperation of national policies	Recommendations						X	X	X	X	X
Supporting national policies	Community programmes					X	X	X	X	X	X

partners and civil society, will be actively involved, using varied forms of partnership. A method of benchmarking best practices on managing change will be devised by the European Commission networking with different providers and users, namely the social partners, companies and NGOs.

A last issue should be addressed. How could the implementation of the open method of coordination in the different policy fields be coordinated? The European Council should regularly guide and monitor the outcomes achieved by the open method of coordination in its different fields, based on regular initiatives taken by the European Commission. This requires two different capacities from the Members of the European Council:

– to define general orientations for the different policy fields in order to organize the work of the different formations of the Council upstream and downstream;
– to ensure their implementation at the European and national levels.

The open method of coordination has already been subject to many discussions at the political level, and it is also raising some first contributions coming from social sciences researchers. This emerging debate leads me to contribute with some *ex post* elaboration and clarification. These remarks also take into account recent theoretical developments in political science, economics, and management sciences.

Some general remarks seem necessary in order to clarify the method itself:

a. the purpose of the open method of coordination is not to define a general ranking of Member States in each policy, but rather to organize a learning process at the European level in order to stimulate exchange and the emulation of best practices and in order to help Member States improve their own national policies.
b. the open method of coordination uses benchmarking as a technique, but it is more than benchmarking. It creates a European dimension and makes political choices by defining European guidelines, and it encourages management by objectives by adapting these European guidelines to national diversity.
c. the open method of coordination is a concrete way of developing modern governance renewing the principle of subsidiarity.
d. the open method of coordination can foster convergence on common interests and on some agreed common priorities while respecting national and regional diversities. It is an inclusive method for deepening European construction.
e. the open method of coordination is to be combined with the other available methods, depending on the problem to be addressed. These methods can range from harmonization to cooperation. The open method

of coordination itself takes an intermediate position in this range of different methods. It goes beyond inter-governmental cooperation, and it is an instrument of integration to be added to a more general set of instruments.

f. The European Commission can play a crucial role as a catalyst in the different stages of the open method of coordination namely by: presenting proposals on European guidelines, organizing the exchange of best practices, presenting proposals on indicators, and supporting monitoring and peer review.

g. The open method of coordination can also become an important tool to improve transparency and democratic participation.

Finally, the open method of coordination is called 'open' for several reasons:

a. because European guidelines and their relative priority can be adapted to the national level, because best practices should be assessed and adapted in their national context;

b. because there is a clear distinction between reference indicators to be adopted at the European level and concrete targets to be set by each Member State for each indicator, taking into account their starting point. For example, the common indicators can be the ratio between investment in R&D and the GDP, or the women participation rate, but the target should be different for each Member State. It means that monitoring and evaluation should mainly focus on progressions or relative achievements;

c. because monitoring and evaluation should take the national context into account in a systemic approach; and

d. last, but not least, because the development of this method in its different stages should be open to the participation of the various actors of civil society. Partnership is a tool of modern governance.

15.3. WHERE ARE WE NOW?

15.3.1. The Phases of the Implementation

The implementation of the Lisbon strategy should be envisaged in different phases with the horizon of 2010. A first phase of the implementation of the Lisbon Strategy is now almost completed. This phase was focused on:

a. specifying the Lisbon Summit Conclusions into policy instruments of the EU (directives, community programmes, action plans, recommendations, see Table 15.3);
b. adding the environmental dimension and building the approach on sustainable development;
c. preliminary implementation in the Member States (still very imbalanced among areas and Member States);
d. introducing the basic mechanisms for implementation (Spring European Council, reorganization of the Council formations and schedules, involvement of the European Parliament and other European institutions, social partners, and organized civil society at the European level, development of the open method of coordination tools); and
e. introducing stronger mechanisms in the upcoming European Constitution (e.g. the General Affairs Council, coordination between economic and social policies, the instrument mix in each policy, the basic tools of the open method of coordination).

A second phase is now beginning, putting the focus on implementation at the national level, including new Member States. This new focus will require a stronger interface between the European and the national levels of governance, with implications for the behaviour of the main actors, notably:

a. Governments should be invited to increase the coherence and consistency between the instruments they adopt at the European level with the instruments they implement at the national level. In this implementation they should enhance the involvement of relevant stakeholders of civil society at the national level;
b. the European Commission should consider new ways of improving its internal coordination and direct work with each Member State (a more comprehensive and holistic approach to each national case is now needed);
c. the European Parliament should consider new ways to develop the interface with the National Parliaments by more actively providing the relevant information on the European agenda as well as opportunities for joint discussion on their implications for national policies; and
d. in organized civil society (social partners, NGOs, other bodies), the European organizations should be invited to develop a collaborative work of information, debate, and implementation and monitoring with its counterparts at the national level.

15.3.2. Assessing and Improving the Governance Instruments

The implementation of the Lisbon strategy is being based on a wide range of policy instruments: directives, community programmes, and action plans using the open method of coordination (see Table 15.3).

Nevertheless, the mix of policy instruments is different according to each policy field: the single market policy is more based on directives, whereas the research policy on a community programme and the social protection policy are based on the open method of coordination. Now, when most of the instruments are already defined, the priority should go to improve the consistency and synergy of the instrument mix in each policy field. For instance, the community programmes should support the common objectives already defined to develop the open method of coordination in the education field.

The open method of coordination has been introduced in eleven policy fields. In spite of some peculiarities concerning its use in each of them, some general improvements should be introduced:

a. the discussion on the common guidelines and indicators or on the monitoring should be based not only on institutional meetings, but also on more informal working meetings involving experts and other stakeholders. This leads to a richer exchange of experience and reduces the bureaucratic bias. The European Commission could play a more active role in fostering this process; and

b. the adoption of national plans should be based not only on reports summing up national progress but on real plans engaging all the relevant stakeholders. This is a main responsibility of the Governments.

It is also important to improve the coordination of the policies included in the Lisbon strategy at both the European and national levels. One of the main problems of the present situation is that most of the Member States remain unable to have an overview of the implementation of the Lisbon agenda at the national level and to define their own strategy for this purpose. What seems to be at stake now is to turn the European Lisbon agenda into national agendas.

Hence, the coordination of this process should be improved according to the following lines:

– to invite each Member State to prepare its own national programme for the implementation of the Lisbon Strategy;

– to invite the European Commission to prepare the Strategic Report buiding on national programmes. It should include the Lisbon scoreboard assessing both relative performance and progress and a Lisbon roadmap with concrete priorities;

Table 15.3 The instrument mix of the various policies

		Types of Instruments		
	Directives	Open method of coordination	Community programmes
Information society	- Directive on a common regulatory framework for electronic communications networks and services - Directive on electronic commerce - Directive on privacy and electronic communications - Universal Service Directive - Authorization Directive - Access Directive - Directive on electronic commerce - Directive on a community framework for electronic signatures	Europe Action Plan	Programme to encourage the development, distribution and promotion of European audio-visual works (MEDIA Plus) (2001–5) - Multi-annual programme to promote the linguistic diversity of the community in the information society
Enterprise policy	Technical harmonization directives	European charter for small enterprises	Multi-annual programme for enterprise and entrepreneurship
Innovation policy Research policy		Framework of common objectives European research area towards 3% of GDP action plan for research	6th Framework Programme
Single market	Harmonization directives	- Financial services action plan - Risk-capital action plan	
Education	Directive establishing a mechanism for the recognition of qualifications in respect of the professional activities covered by the Directives on liberalization and transitional measures and supplementing the general systems for the recognition of qualifications	- eLearning - Common objectives and targets - Bologna process for high level education - Copenhagen declaration for lifelong learning Action plan for skills and mobility	Community programmes 'Socrates' and 'Leonardo'

(Continued)

Table 15.3 (*Continued*)

	Types of Instruments		
	Directives	Open method of coordination	Community programmes
Employment	- Directive on the abolition of restrictions on movement and residence within the Community for nationals of Member States with regard to establishment and the provision of services - Directive on the introduction of measures to encourage improvements in the safety and health of workers at work - Directive on the organization of the working time of persons performing mobile road transport activities - Directive concerning the framework agreement on fixed-term work concluded by ETUC, UNICE, and CEEP - Directive concerning certain aspects of the organization of working time - Directive supplementing the measures to encourage improvements in the safety and health at work of workers with a fixed-duration employment relationship or a temporary employment relationship - Directive on the approximation of the laws of the Member States relating to the application of the principle of equal pay for men and women	European employment strategy: Joint employment report, Employment guidelines and recommendations for Members States' employment policies	Community programme 'Equal'

Social protection	Directive on the implementation of the principle of equal treatment for men and women in occupational social security schemes	- Common objectives for pension provision - Integrated approach for safe and sustainable pensions
Social inclusion		- Common objectives - Framework strategy on gender equality Programme of Community action to encourage cooperation between Member States to combat social exclusion
Environment	Directives on the protection and improvement of the environment -Directive on the assessment of the effects of certain public and private projects on the environment	- EU strategy for sustainable development -Community Eco-label working plan - Council resolution on corporate social responsibility Sixth Community Action Programme for environment

– to keep the Spring European Council in March as the main focal point, but to reorganize working methods in order to have a discussion on political assessments and choices, based on the Strategic Report and national programmes.

Finally, it seems important to create a framework of positive incentives to foster the implementation of the Lisbon agenda. For that purpose, a specific connection should be set between this implementation and:

– the assessment of national programmes of stability and growth in the framework of the Stability Pact;
– the assessment of the Community Support Frameworks, regarding the structural funds;
– the selection of applications to the Community programmes.

Let us focus now on two critical policies for the preparation of the Lisbon national programmes, if these are designed as national strategies to step up the transition to a knowledge economy: lifelong learning and innovation policies.

15.4. ON EUROPEAN POLICIES FOR LIFELONG LEARNING[3]

Lifelong learning plays a central role in order to explore the full potential of a knowledge-intensive economy for competitiveness, growth, and job creation with social inclusion. The analysis of the present situation in EU shows very important bottlenecks, in spite of an increasing public awareness of this issue. Following recent policy developments at the European level, all Member States are about to define their national strategies to develop lifelong learning.

Some elements of this broader strategy seem to be emerging everywhere such as: lifelong learning as an issue concerning the population as a whole, the importance of basic competences, the role of multiple stakeholders, new funding instruments, the development of multiple pathways and the need to remove obstacles, the potential of e-learning, the need to improve guidance and recognition. By contrast, others topics still seem underdeveloped: the critical role of early childhood learning, the potential of work organization, the role of collective bargaining, the budgetary implications of the targets for investment in lifelong learning.

15.4.1. From the Learning System to the Strategy for Lifelong Learning

There is a clear gap between the European ambition to become a dynamic, competitive, and inclusive knowledge-based economy and the present scope of the learning activities involving both public and private initiatives. In order to overcome this gap we need a more systematic approach to the development of a *learning system*, which should build on the following principles (see Figure 15.1):

a. this approach should take into account the general context of a knowledge-based society;

b. lifelong learning is a central activity in a knowledge society because it disseminates the knowledge which is produced to those who might use it. Therefore, lifelong learning plays a central role in the chain of knowledge production, dissemination, and utilization;

c. in order to analyse the outcome of the autonomous initiatives of the actors of knowledge dissemination versus the actors of knowledge utilization, it is useful to speak about the *supply of learning services* versus the *demand for learning services*. As matter of fact, we are considering a specific sector of services which is expanding and becoming more complex and sophisticated;

d. the supply of learning services is evolving according to the types, places, and instruments of learning: schools and training centres might evolve to open learning centres; companies can create more sophisticated learning organizations; e-learning is developing by using websites, CD-ROMS, DVDs, and data basis; digital TV can play an increasing role;

e. the demand for learning services is very heterogeneous according to the various target groups, from high-skilled staff to skilled craftsmen or to marginalized groups and according to their concrete economic, social, and cultural activities;

f. the demand for learning services depends on some framework conditions, such as working time flexibility and family care facilities. This demand also depends on the prospects to get incentives in terms of productivity gains and of personal or professional development, or in terms of salary or promotion to be defined by labour contract or collective agreement;

g. the interaction between the supply of and demand for learning services depends on forecasting and guidance procedures, the validation and recognition of learning activities, and funding mechanisms; in simpler words, well known to economists, interactions between supply and demand depend on information, value, and money;

h. finally, all the interactions in this chain can be more strongly developed on the basis of a more powerful infrastructure of telecommunications (broadband) and logistics.

These seem to be the main components of what we can call a *learning system* which will have concrete specificities in each national case. A national strategy for lifelong learning should therefore aim to dynamize this system in order to develop lifelong learning taking into account these national specificities. Nevertheless, beyond these specificities it is possible to identify some general strategic priorities to be taken into account in each national case:

a. to define the goals for lifelong learning in terms of not only educational levels but also new job profiles and competences;
b. to develop a new infrastructure for lifelong learning;
c. to create a diversified supply of learning opportunities able to provide more customized solutions:
   - to develop new instruments of e-learning and explore the potential of digital TV;
   - to turn schools and training centres into open learning centres;
   - to encourage companies to adopt learning organizations;
   - to shape the appropriate learning mode for each target group;
   - to spread new learning solutions for the low-skilled workers.
d. to foster the various demands for learning and to create a demand-led system:
   - to improve the framework conditions for lifelong learning;
   - to develop a dynamic guidance system over the life course;
   - to renew the validation and recognition system;
   - to create compensations for the investment in learning.
e. to spread new financial arrangements in order to share the costs of lifelong learning;
f. to improve governance for lifelong learning, involving all the relevant public departments and stakeholders of civil society.

15.4.2. To Define the Goals for Lifelong Learning

The goals of lifelong learning should be defined first of all in terms of education levels and educational attainments. The EU has recently adopted a short list of common targets, assuming that the upper secondary level seems nowadays the minimal level to provide a solid foundation for lifelong learning. These targets (see Table 15.4) aim at focusing investment in education

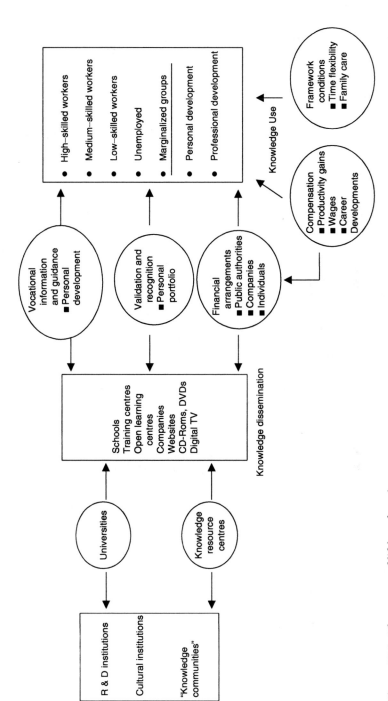

Figure 15.1. The system of lifelong learning

Table 15.4 Education targets in the European Union

---

1 By 2010, an EU average ratio of no more than 10% of early school leavers should be achieved;

2 The total number of graduates in mathematics, science, technology in the EU should increase by at least 15% by 2010, while at the same time the gender imbalance should decrease;

3 By 2010, at least 85% of 22-year olds in the EU should have completed upper secondary education;

4 By 2010, the percentage of low-achieving 15 year olds in reading, mathematical and scientific literacy will be at least halved;

5 By 2010, the EU average participation in lifelong learning should be at least 12.5% of the adult working population (25–64 age group).

---

and training in areas with clear value added, in terms of economic growth and employability. This additional effort should combine targeted public investments and higher private contributions (Com 2002: 779).

Moreover, according to the above presented analysis, two other targets should be added:

– a specific target concerning the education and training of the adult population who only has basic education;
– a general target concerning the pre-schooling education for all children, as it is proved it can play a crucial role in their cognitive development and their subsequent educational and professional performance; this target might be connected with the other already adopted targets, dealing with the generalization of childcare services.

In the meantime, the EU also agreed on a short list of basic skills which, in addition to literacy and numeracy, should include ICT skills, foreign language, entrepreneurship, and social skills.

Lifelong learning activities are very often hindered by a lack of relevant information and awareness about skill needs. Companies complain about education institutions not being able to cope with their needs, and education institutions argue they should not be completely subordinated to short-term economic needs. Nevertheless, behind the success cases of European regions and clusters, we will find new patterns of interaction between skill demand and supply (Stahl 2001).

Drawing some lessons from this experience, the goals of lifelong learning should also be defined in terms of occupational profiles and their specific competences. The purpose is not coming back to traditional models of forecasting, setting a mechanical and unidirectional relationship between the industrial pattern of growth on the one hand and the skills need on the other. On the contrary, the purpose should be to develop a permanent interaction between skills and the growth pattern at the European, national, sectoral, and local levels, involving the relevant actors and taking into account both long- and short-term needs. The recently created *Skillsnet* should be enhanced in order to provide basic references for this process at the European level, building on the already very diversified work across Member States, which combines very different techniques: enterprise and labour force surveys, case studies, expert inquiries, analyses of jobs advertisements, forecasting and scenarios, observatories on skills developments (Descy and Tessaring 2001).

In a knowledge-based society, lifelong learning can play a central role in paving the way to new areas of job creation. Job creation is increasingly intertwined with innovation in all its dimensions: innovations not only in processes but in products and services; not only in technologies but in organization, marketing, and design. At the core of innovation there is the capacity to turn knowledge into more added value, and this requires skilled people with specific occupational profiles such as designers, engineers, differ- ent specialists of marketing, management, logistics, telecommunications.

15.5. ON THE EUROPEAN POLICY FOR INNOVATION[4]

Turning knowledge into added value is a central process in the transition to a knowledge-intensive economy. This is the role of innovation in its various forms, technological or organizational, in products or in services. Innovation policies aim at fostering this process within companies, by developing the innovation system and interactions between knowledge production, diffusion, and utilization. Hence, innovation policies should be considered as a major catalyst of a strategy of transition to a knowledge economy.

Therefore, in the context of the Lisbon agenda, it is important to improve national policies for innovation, taking advantage and respecting the differences across Member States, but it is also important to enhance the European dimension by defining common objectives or guidelines at the European level by developing networks, partnerships, and joint initiatives at the European level.

Nevertheless, innovation policy seems to have a very important specificity regarding other policies, working with their interfaces. It seems to be a kind of 'meta-policy,' the purpose of which is twofold:

- to improve the coordination among different policies, regarding namely enterprise, competition, research, information society, education and training, financial markets, labour markets, and social policy;
- to improve the focus of each of these policies on supporting innovation.

The contribution of these various policies for innovation is already being improved by their political reorientation defined by the Lisbon strategy, but some steps forward seem possible using the open method of coordination and the coordination cycle defined by the Spring European Council, notably:

- to define a framework of specific common objectives or guidelines at European level for innovation policy, using the open method of coordination;
- to translate these common objectives or guidelines into national policies for innovation itself, respecting the specificities of each Member State, and involving the governments and civil society;
- the Council of Ministers for Competitiveness might be reinforced as central platform to improve the coordination between different policies with impacts on innovation;
- a group of senior officials representing the Member States can provide a regular follow-up of these developments, using other elements already available such as the Trend Chart and the scoreboard for innovation;
- the European Council might make a general follow-up of the innovation policy, due to its very horizontal nature and its central role towards the Lisbon strategic goals;
- the 7th FP for RTD, the Community Programme for Competitiveness and Innovation, the instruments of regional policy, and the European Investment Bank might give a stronger priority to building European networks for innovation.

If we take into account a list of activities which are relevant for innovation (Equist 2004: 188), as well as the common objectives which were already agreed at the European level for other policies, the following guidelines might be identified to be adapted at the national level:

a. provision of R&D: increasing public investment in R&D; creating conditions to foster private investment in R&D; reduce the cost of patenting;
b. competence building: training resources for R&D; spreading skills for innovation; developing national strategies for lifelong learning;
c. financial innovation: access to ventures capital; reorientation of public investment to R&D and innovation; tax incentives with the same purpose; new priorities for structural funds;
d. provision of consultancy services: developing the support services for innovation and diffusion;
e. improving quality and paving the way to new products and services: competition policy; dissemination of quality standards; improving the criteria of public procurement; targeting sophisticated markets;

f. changing organizations: national programmes for organizational development in companies; reforming university management; modernizing public services;

g. incubating activities: developing incubators; supporting high-tech start-ups;

h. networking: promoting clusters and partnerships for innovation; extending access to broadband; developing e-business.

This range of guidelines should be supported by some important initiatives at the European level such as:

a. the Framework Programme for RTD and the development of the European Research Area;

b. the reform of the Stability and Growth Pact, the new Financial Perspectives and the reduction and reorientation of state aids more in line with the Lisbon agenda;

c. the integration of European financial markets and the development of new venture capital schemes;

d. the Community Programme for Competitiveness and Innovation and the development of European networks for innovation;

e. opening new sectors to the competition of the European single market;

f. opening new markets in the framework of WTO negotiations and other trade agreements.

As pointed out in Table 15.5, some of these activities are not yet adopted as concrete measures in this building process of the European innovation policies.

15.6. THE DIVERSITY OF THE NATIONAL STRATEGIES OF TRANSITION TO A KNOWLEDGE INTENSIVE ECONOMIES

The national programmes to implement the Lisbon strategy can offer a unique opportunity to define national strategies of transition to knowledge-intensive economies. As mentioned above, this European agenda introduces new priorities in research policy, education and training policy, information society policy, and innovation policy, which are crucial to develop a more systematic and creative process of knowledge production, diffusion, and utilization. The key question for each Member State is how to develop this process, adapting the European agenda and, more precisely, the guidelines already adopted at the European level, to its specificities. Some of these

Table 15.5 Building the European innovation policy

Innovation Policy Components	European level	National level
Provision of R&D	FP6/7 for RTD Networks of excellence Era-nets European Research Council* Technology Platforms Community Patent*	Actions Plans "Investing in Research" Developing public research Creating conditions for private research Fast track visa for Researchers* Reduce the cost of patenting*
Competence building	Marie Curie Research Fellowships Common objectives for education and training European framework for lifelong learning	Developing human resources for research Developing skills for innovation* National strategies for lifelong learning*
Financial innovation	Integration of financial markets European framework for venture capital European framework of State Aid Reform of Stability and Growth Pact – Quality of public finances* EIB and EIF initiatives New financial perspectives more in line with Lisbon* Reform of Structural Funds	Venture capital New priorities for public expenditure Tax incentives for Research and Innovation National strategic frameworks for structural funds
Provision of consult-ancy services Improving quality	Business Innovation Support Scheme* Developing competition in the single European Market New agreements WTO negotiations	Enhancing the support services for innovation and diffusion Competition policy Diffusion of quality standards Targeting sophisticated markets Improving public procurement*
Formation of new products and services	Developing competition in the single European Market WTO negotiations Identifying new markets trends	Competition policy Diffusion of quality standards Targeting sophisticated markets Improving public procurement
Changing organizations	European network for organizational development*	National programmes for organizational development* Reforming universities management* Modernizing public services

Incubating activities	European network of BIC (Business Innovation Centres)	Developing incubators Supporting high-tech startups
Networking	Developing European networks for innovation* Supporting Innovation Regions Interoperability of standards of ICT	Promoting clusters and partner ships for innovation Extending access to broadband Developing e-business
Governance of the Innovation systems	Council of Ministers for Competitiveness	Council of Ministers for Innovation* Innovation Board* Mr./Ms. Lisbon*

Measures still not adopted in formal terms.

specificities should be particularly underlined to explain and justify the diversity of national strategies to a knowledge-intensive economy:

- the industrial specialization patterns, the relationship with the global economy and the position in the international division of labour;
- the institutional framework regarding, in particular, corporate organization, the education and training system, the research system, the financial system, and labour markets regulations;
- the quality of infrastructures;
- the educational levels and specific skills of the labour force;
- the organization of civil society and instruments to manage change.

Apart from improving the general conditions, the national strategy of transition to a knowledge-intensive economy should be itself adapted to specific circumstances of each concrete region or cluster within the country. For example, the approach based on clusters should aim at developing partnerships for innovation, jobs creation, and competence building, involving all the relevant actors: companies, research institutions, education and training institutions, financial bodies. A critical path can be discovered by asking how is it possible to add more value to the already existing competence. For instance, if we take general human needs as a broad reference for associating clusters of economic activity (see Figure 15.2):

- competences in tourism should be combined with competences in cultural activities, sport, and environment in order to develop the area of *leisure*;
- competences in construction, furniture, electronics, urban management should be combined in order to develop the area of *habitat*;

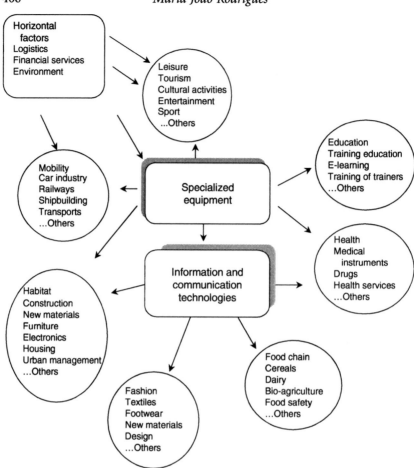

Figure 15.2. Innovation and competence building

- competences in clothing, footwear, new materials and design should be combined in order to develop the *fashion* area;
- competences in the car industry, transport and logistics should be combined, in order to develop the area of *mobility*.

In the meantime, other horizontal competences are required to develop all the clusters of activities, such as electromechanic equipment, information and communication activities, and biotechnologies.

Finally, let us conclude with a thesis to be tested by cross-country empirical research. Recent experiences suggest there is a critical path to develop an innovation policy as a catalyst to the transition to a knowledge-intensive economy:

1. to use the European agenda as leverage to introduce this strategic goal in the national agenda;
2. to spread a richer concept of innovation, taking into account its different dimensions: technological and organizational, in processes or in products and services, based on science or in learning-by-doing, using, or interacting;
3. highlighting the implications of the innovation system approach for the coordination of policies;
4. to define the priority areas of an innovation policy and prepare a tool box of operational measures;
5. to open access to this tool box in order to support innovating projects and companies whatever the sector;
6. to focus on some clusters in order to illustrate the advantages of developing partnerships for innovation, as a good practice which can be followed by other clusters;
7. to make dynamic the national innovation system by focusing the missions and the interactions among its bodies;
8. to reform public services with implications for innovation;
9. to spread skills for innovation and to train innovation managers;
10. to improve governance for innovation, by improving the internal coordination of the government and relevant public departments, by creating public awareness and by developing specific consultation and participation mechanisms with civil society.

There is no open method of coordination which can help to solve this problem of finding the critical path. This will be 'history in the making' in each of the EU Member States.

NOTES

1. For an overview of European policies for a knowledge economy, see Rodrigues (2003*a*).
2. Relevant European documentation on the Lisbon Strategy include: Council of the European Union (2000, 2003, 2004); European Commission (2001*b*, 2002*a*, 2002*b*, 2003*c*); and European Parliament (2001).
3. Relevant European documentation on lifelong learning include: Council of the European Union (2001*b*, 2002*a*, 2002*b*, 2004); European Commission (2001*a*, 2001*c*, 2002*a*, 2003*a*); and CEDEFOP (2002, 2004*a*, 2004*b*).

4. Relevant European documentation on innovation policy include: European Commission (2000, 2003*b*, 2003*c*); and European Investment Bank (2000*a*, 2000*b*, 2001).

REFERENCES

Archibugi, D. and Lundvall, B.-Å. (eds.) (2001). *The Globalizing Learning Economy.* Oxford: Oxford University Press.

Castells, M. (1996). *The Information Age: Economy, Society and Culture,* reprinted 1999. Oxford: Blackwell.

CEDEFOP (2002). *Consultation Process on the European Commission's Memorandum on Lifelong Learning—Analysis of National Reports.* Luxembourg: Office for Official Publications of the European Communities.

—— (2004*a*). *Getting to Work on Lifelong Learning—Policy, Practice & Partnership.* Luxembourg: Office for Publications of the European Communities.

—— (2004*b*). *Learning for Employment—Second Report on Vocational Education and Training Policy in Europe.* Luxembourg: Office for Publications of the European Communities.

Council of the European Union (2000). *Conclusions of the Lisbon European Council,* Council of the European Union SN 100/00, 23–4 March 2000.

—— (2001*a*). *Conclusions of the Stockholm European Council,* Council of the European Union SN 100/01, 23–4 March 2001.

—— (2001*b*). *Report from the Council (Education) to the European Council on the concrete future objectives of education and learning systems,* 5680/01 EDUC23, 12.02.2001.

—— (2002*a*). *Council Resolution—Education and Lifelong Learning,* Ref. 8944/02, 30.05.2002.

—— (2002*b*). *Declaration of the European Ministers of Vocational Education and Training, and the European Commission, convened in Copenhagen on 29 and 30 November 2002, on enhanced European cooperation in vocational education and training—'The Copenhagen Declaration',* Copenhagen, 30.11.2002.

—— (2003). *Conclusions of the Brussels European Council,* Council of the European Union SN 100/03, 20–1 March 2003

—— (2004). *Draft Council Resolution on Guidance Throughout Life in Europe,* Ref. 8448/04, 16.04.2004.

Descy, P. and Tessaring, M. (2001). *Training and Learning for Competence.* Luxembourg: Office for Official Publications of the European Communities and Cedefop.

Despres, C. and Chauvel, D. (2000). *Knowledge Horizons—The Present and the Promise of Knowledge Management.* Oxford: Butterworth-Heinemann.

Edquist, C. (2005). 'Systems of Innovation— Perspectives and Challenges', in J. Fagerberg, D. Mowery, and R. Nelson, (eds.), *The Oxford Handbook of Innovation.* New York: Oxford University Press, pp. 181–208.

Esping-Andersen, G. (ed.) (1996). *Welfare States in Transition—National Adaptations in Global Economics*, reprinted 1998. London: Sage.

European Commission—Directorate-General for Education and Culture (2003). *Implementing Lifelong Learning Strategies in Europe: Progress Report on the Follow-up to the Council Resolution of 2002—EU and EFTA/EEA countries*, 17.12.2003.

European Commission (2000). *Communication: Innovation in a Knowledge-Driven Economy*, COM (2000) 567, 20.09.2000.

—— (2001*a*). *Communication from the Commission - Making a European Area of Lifelong Learning a Reality*, COM (2001) 678 final, 21.11.2001.

—— (2001*b*). *Communication from the Commission: Realising the European Union's Potential: Consolidating and Extending the Lisbon Strategy*, COM (2001) 79, 08.02.2001.

—— (2001*c*). *Report on the Future Objectives of Education Systems*, COM (2001) 59 final, 31.01.2001.

—— (2002*a*). *Communication from the Commission—European Benchmarks in Education and Training: Follow-up to the Lisbon European Council*, COM (2002) 629 final, 20.11.2002.

—— (2002*b*). *Contribution to the Spring European Council in Barcelona: The Lisbon Strategy—Making Change Happen*, COM (2002) 14 final, 15.01.2002.

—— (2003*a*). *'Education & Training 2010'—The Success of the Lisbon Strategy Hinges on Urgent Reforms*, (Draft joint interim report on the implementation of the detailed work programme on the follow-up of the objectives of education and training systems in Europe), COM(2003) 685 final, 11.11.2003.

—— (2003*b*). *Communication: Choosing to Grow: Knowledge, Innovation and Jobs in a Cohesive Society— Report to the Spring European Council, 21 March 2003 on the Lisbon Strategy of Economic, Social and Environmental Renewal*, COM (2003) 5 final, 14.01.2003.

—— (2003*c*). *Communication from the Commission Innovation Policy: Updating the Union's Approach in the Context of the Lisbon Strategy*, COM (2003) 112 final, 11.03.2003.

European Commission (2005). *Commission Staff Working Document in Support of the Report from the Commission to the Spring European Council, 22–23 March 2005, on the Lisbon Strategy of Economic, Social and Environmental Renewal*, SEC (2005) 160, 28.01.2005.

European Investment Bank (2000). *From Lisbon to Santa Maria da Feira—Progress in Implementing the EIB's 'Innovation 2000 Initiative'*, June 2000.

—— (2000*b*). *Innovation 2000 Initiative*, Council of the European Union 6442/00, 15.03.2000.

—— (2001). *Innovation 2000 Initiative: From Lisbon to Stockholm: The EIB's i2i One Year After—Progress and Perspectives in Implementation*, March 2001.

European Parliament (2001). *Report on the Spring 2001 European Council: The Lisbon Process and the Path to be Followed*, A5-0034/2001, 30.01.2001.

Fitoussi, J.-P. and Rosanvallon, P. (1996). *Le nouvel âge des inégalités*. Paris: Seuil.

Le Boterf, G. (1998). *L'Ingénierie des compétences*. Paris: Éditions d'Organization.

Méhaut, P. and Delcourt, J. (1995). *The Role of the Company in Generating Skills: The Learning Effects of Work Organization—Synthesis Report.* Luxembourg: Office for Official Publications of the European Communities and CEDEFOP.

Presidency Conclusions (Barcelona European Council) (2000). Ref. Council of the European Union SN 100/02.

Presidency Conclusions (Stockholm European Council). Ref. Council of the European Union SN 200/01.

Presidency of the European Union (2000*a*). *Document from the Presidency—'Employment, Economic Reforms and Social Cohesion—Towards a Europe Based on Innovation and Knowledge',* Council of the European Union 5256/00, 12.01.2000.

—— (2000*b*). *Future Challenges and Objectives of Education Systems in the Learning Society: Follow-up to the Lisbon European Council (Background paper for debate),* Council of the European Union 8880/00, 26.05.2000.

—— (2000*c*). *Revised Presidency Proposal for a Draft Council Resolution on Establishing a European Area of Research and Innovation,* 15.05.2000.

Reich, R. B. (1991). *The Work of Nations.* Vintage Books.

Rodrigues, M. J. (ed.), with the collaboration of Robert Boyer, Manuel Castells, Gøsta Esping-Andersen, Robert Lindley, Bengt-Åke Lundvall, Luc Soete and Mario Telò (2002). *The New Knowledge Economy in Europe—A Strategy for International Competitiveness and Social Cohesion.* Cheltenham, UK: Edward Elgar.

—— (2003*a*). *European Policies for a Knowledge Economy.* Cheltenham, UK: Edward Elgar.

Soete, L. (2001). 'The new economy: A European perspective', in Archibugi, D. and Lundvall, B.-Å. (eds.), *The Globalizing Learning Economy,* Oxford: Oxford University Press.

Stahl, T. (2001). 'The Learning Region and Its Potential Roles in Lifelong Learning', in Colardyn Danielle (ed.), *Lifelong Learning: Which Ways Forward?* Bruges: College of Europe.

Tapscott, D. (1995). *The Digital Economy: Promise and Peril in the Age of Networked Intelligence,* Verspagen, B. (2005). New York: McGraw-Hill. 'Innovation and Economic Growth', in J. Fagerberg, D. Mowery, and R. Nelson, (eds.), *The Oxford Handbook of Innovation.* New York: Oxford University Press, pp. 487–513.

Wikström, S. and Normann, R. (eds.) (1994). Barbro Anell, Göran Ekvall, Jan Forslin, Per-Hugo Skärvad, *Knowledge and Value.* London: Routledge.

16

Welfare and Learning in Europe—How to Revitalize the Lisbon Process and Break the Stalemate

Bengt-Åke Lundvall and Edward Lorenz

16.1. INTRODUCTION

In this book we have demonstrated that firms and people in Europe's economies learn in different ways. We have seen the contours of groupings of countries in this respect where some countries depend more on hierarchical organizations and flexible markets while others rely more on regulated markets with less distance between management and workers. We have also demonstrated that such differences are systemic and rooted in the history of the nation states.

In this concluding chapter we pursue further specificities for groups of national economies with a focus on the link between economic welfare and learning. In this light we discuss how Europe can exit from the current stalemate. So far, there has been a tendency in the EU Commission to downplay national differences in welfare systems within Europe and how the role of state and market is valued differently in different national political cultures. We believe that being explicit about these differences and rethinking them in the context of the learning economy might be one way to reestablish the dynamics of the Lisbon process.

It is true that the Lisbon process set the focus not only on economic growth but also on social cohesion. But it appears as if, for the Commission, the social dimension has been added as something outside the innovation process—sometimes seen even as a kind of historical burden that Europe is obliged to carry when competing with the US, Japan, and China. Agreement on the nebulous concept 'structural reform' has substituted for an open debate on the strength and weaknesses of different types of national welfare systems in Europe. Our comparison of national systems of innovation and competence-building makes it clear that this view is mistaken since national welfare regimes are structurally interrelated to modes of learning and innovation. Not only do people work and learn differently under different welfare regimes. The welfare they experience from specific modes of working and learning reflects such differences.

On this basis we argue that recognition of the national *systemic* differences in these respects should be a first step in defining a revised agenda for European integration. A revitalization of the Lisbon process should take the national learning systems and their interrelated welfare regimes as point of departure for defining a new set of policy strategies. A policy package that aims at promoting the learning economy and takes into account national systemic differences and preferences may be a way to break the current stalemate in Europe. This implies that the Commission's current practice of benchmarking specific policy areas separately in the search for local 'best-practice' in for instance competition policy or innovation policy needs to be subordinated to an integrated understanding of the national system as a whole.

We begin with a brief section on the fundamental ideological cleavages that get in the way of the integration process in Europe. In the second section we argue that there is a need to rethink fundamentally *what constitutes welfare in the learning economy.* This opens up a new perspective where the basis of the polar positions in the current ideological conflict tends to be dissolved. In the third section we argue that neither neoliberal nor neoprotectionist positions in Europe are tenable in the new context of the learning economy. What is needed is a process of convergence towards a new institutional set-up that combines the flexibility aimed at in the neoliberal universe with the security aimed at in the neoprotectionist universe. In the fourth section we show that some of the small European countries have come much closer towards such an institutional constellation and at the end of the chapter we use 'the Danish model' as a possible benchmark for European *systemic convergence.* At the end of the chapter we point to the need for a new more ambitious agenda for Europe, including the construction of a European Welfare State.

16.2. THE EUROPEAN STALEMATE

After the 2005 majority, no-vote on the European constitution in France and Netherlands Europe seems to be in disarray and torn between classical ideological poles of pro-state and pro-market. The British do not like the way the Commission imposes state regulation on their economy and they regard 'jobless growth' in Germany and France as rooted in rigid labour markets and overambitious social security systems. In France, on the right as on the left side of the political spectrum, the EU is seen as an institution that carries privatization and liberalization on its back. National state regulations that the EU commission regards as rigidities are in France seen as safeguards against the negative social consequences of globalization. This was the rational background for the French majority no-vote to the European Constitution in June 2005.[1]

Behind the conflict are historically rooted national ideologies regarding the role of state and market as well as actual differences in how state and market combine in the governance of the economy respectively in the UK and France. At the core of these differences are different conceptions of the socio-economic roles of work and consumption. To caricature: in the ideal market-dominated state the consumer is king and the professional worker his adaptive servant. In the French version of the republican state, the professional worker is king and the client/consumer is expected to adapt to the needs of the professional. This applies both to private and public sector activities. In the neoliberal ideal state, the consumer gets what he wants at low prices and the more flexible the supply side, including the workforce, the better. In the neoprotectionist ideal state, it is the duty of government to protect the producers and the workers in order to avoid pauperization and insecurity.

In what follows we demonstrate that the institutional set-up that promotes learning and competitiveness in the current era cannot be captured by any of these two models. At the core of the learning economy are *consumers* who are active as producers and innovators, and *workers* who are involved in processes of technical and organizational change. This implies an institutional set-up where consumers *interact with* producers and workers. For most important transactions neither pure markets nor pure hierarchies promote learning and competitiveness. Social capital becomes a key to economic dynamics and to the working of the economic system. A common European focus on building a *learning economy* may therefore be helpful in overcoming the current divisions in Europe.

16.3. WELFARE IN THE LEARNING ECONOMY

16.3.1. The Learning Economy as Working Hypothesis

Widening the perspective in this way reflects a specific hypothesis regarding a set of emerging trends that we bring together under the heading 'the learning economy'. The assumption is that globalization, deregulation, and information technology have resulted in an acceleration of economic change. Competition in OECD countries has changed so a growing share of workers and consumers are required to participate in frequent processes of learning and forgetting.

This hypothesis is one out of several competing ideas about what is 'new' in the current era. For example, there are proposals that we have entered the 'information society', 'the knowledge-based society', 'the network society', and 'the new economy'. Common to several of these is the focus on globalization, deregulation, and radical technological change. At the level of management, outsourcing, reengineering, and governance based on shareholder value have become more generally diffused. In labour markets, globalization weakens contractual obligations, polarization in job opportunities, and growth in the amount of precarious work. At the same time, the more rapid pace of technological change and the need for greater flexibility are often seen as calling for new organizational forms based on participation and continuous learning and problem-solving on the part of employees.

The learning economy may be seen as an attempt to *summarize these different tendencies in one single concept*. Seen from the point of view of a national economy we might see the learning economy as implying a growing transformation pressure for the population of domestic firms and by analysing how the population of firms responds we can say important things about 'how the national economy learns'. This is the perspective applied in the following sections.

16.3.2. A New Perspective on the Welfare of Workers and Consumers

The economic policy discourse is certainly deeply influenced by the tenets of standard economics including its theory of economic welfare. The clear distinction between the interest of the producer and the consumer is one illustrating example, and this is reflected in the ideological divide between pro-work and pro-consumption ideologies. In what follows we discuss how some of these classical perceptions need to be fundamentally changed in the current context of the learning economy. The 'true interests' of consumers as well as professional workers are not the ones that 'their representatives' in the policy community tend to respond to and propagate. Rather than putting one of the two categories in command of the other, the learning economy thrives when there is a process where they interact and learn from each other.

The standard view of neoclassical welfare economics is that individual welfare is an increasing function of the amount of consumption and decreasing with the amount of work. The indicators used are quantities (vectors) of consumption goods and hours worked. The analysis compares different *states*. The *processes* of consumption and work remain hidden in black boxes. In this section we introduce alternative perspectives on economic welfare and discuss how the standard view needs to be rethought when we focus on the activity of learning. We argue that the alternative view calls for a revision of basic tenets in the Commission's policy strategy.

16.3.3. The View of Amartya Sen

Amartya Sen, famous for his critical analysis of traditional theory of inequality and income distribution, presents an alternative view of individual welfare (Sen 1999; Robeyns 2000). The individual operates, according to Sen, in different *functions* with different *capabilities* and the welfare experienced from a given resource vector will depend on the functions engaged in as well as on the capabilities to engage in each specific function. Having a bicycle in a village without roads or having one without mastering the art of cycling or having one and not being allowed to use it (belonging to the wrong caste or gender) is of limited utility and does not give much satisfaction. The freedom and capability to transform a resource to an *achievement* fundamental for individual welfare is thus *context-dependent* according to Sen.

The idea that *capabilities* are important makes it natural to relate his approach to 'knowledge', but it is paradoxical that 'the capability to learn' does not appear as central in Sen's analytical scheme and that 'learning' does not appear among achievements. Below we will show that adding these dimensions might enhance the value of his model and make it more suitable to analyse *the dynamics of welfare in the learning economy*.

16.3.4. A Dynamic and Evolutionary View of Welfare

In principle, we might think about what an individual owns and knows as two vectors. With 'knowing' we refer both to *information about the world* and *capabilities to change the world*. At any point of time the two vectors can be seen as defining a state. But we might also refer to the *processes* that change the two vectors. The 'have-vector' will be the outcome of processes of acquiring, receiving, consuming, and exchanging resources. The 'know-vector' will reflect processes of learning and forgetting. Some learning will come through formal education and from separate search activities while other elements will come as side effects of the processes where acquiring, receiving, consuming, and exchanging resources take place.

We follow Sen and argue that welfare emanates not from states but from processes. According to Amartya Sen, it is only in connection with the act of utilizing resources or the potential for utilizing resources that we can judge welfare. Having access to resources is less important than the experience of acquiring and using them. To this we now add some reflections on the intrinsic value of acquiring and forgetting knowledge.

16.3.5. Welfare Aspects of Learning

In the psychological and social psychological literature there are different perspectives on how learning affects the well-being of individuals. Learning might be seen primarily as the normal route for personal development from childhood to becoming an adult. Seen from this perspective, to learn might be seen as a *fundamental human right* and the deprivation of the possibility to learn may be seen as a most cruel form of suppression of the individual. Not all learning is enjoyable. Learning that implies fundamental change in the understanding of the world has been described as constituting a painful personal crisis. Some rote learning is boring. Learning to play games or advancing from being a novice to become professional—joining a community of practise—may on the other hand may be fun and most satisfactory. It is obvious that learning may be both joy and pain depending on incentives, context, and rewards. Not to learn at all would, however, for most modern individuals signify a boring life. Learning does not fit well into standard economics. If it appears at all it is basically regarded as a cost since it takes time to learn, and time is a scarce resource for the economic agent. In human capital theory it is seen as investment. The learning economy hypothesis challenges the basic structure of welfare economic theory in these respects. I am here also referring to the distinction between consumers and producers and to the respective socio-economic role assigned to them.

The basic assumption that consumption is pleasure and work is pain is too simplistic in the learning economy. Consumers need to engage in learning processes that are more or less painful while workers that are excluded from learning appear to be less satisfied in the short run and much more vulnerable in the long run. For the dynamic performance of the economy it is fundamental that workers and consumers engage in learning.

16.4. ON THE UTILITY OF LEARNING AT THE WORK PLACE

The basic assumption that *work is pain* needs to be reconsidered. It is well known that work gives identity and that access to interaction to others is valued. There is a need for a new welfare theory of work that includes other benefits from work than the salary. The 'recognition' experienced may be seen as one welfare element. 'Social capital' accumulated in an interaction with colleagues is another element. Work is social consumption as well as social investment.

When the job implies learning to do new things it involves further benefits. The outcome may be an increase in the knowledge vector but we also need to consider the intrinsic pain and pleasure of learning discussed above. There are different opinions on how to make up the balance between the pain and pleasure of taking part in a modern working life characterized by relentless change. Some scholars emphasize that rapid change undermines the professional identity and the security of workers (Sennett 1998). Other scholars emphasize the positive consequences of a reduction of routine work and a delegation of decision-making to the lower level of the organization.

The net impact of these changes on 'aggregate welfare' may be difficult to assess. What appears to be the case is that benefits and costs are unequally distributed across sectors and functions. Those learning most are managers and experts while women and unskilled workers are the ones least involved in learning in their work life situation (for the UK, see Tomlinson 2002). If this is combined with results showing that unskilled workers tend to have more secure jobs in learning organizations (see below and Christensen and Lundvall 2004), one might end up with a hypothesis that insecurity in the learning economy is an increasing function of *exclusion from processes of learning*. Put differently: having access to learning opportunities in working life has become a key source of economic welfare for the individual worker.

16.4.1. Worker Learning and Welfare in Different National Contexts

The fact that employees value opportunities to learn and do so in a reasonably autonomous situation—without too much control from the management—can be demonstrated using the taxonomy of organizational forms developed by Lorenz and Valeyre (this volume). Responses to the third European Survey of Working Conditions, which were used to construct the taxonomy include a measure of job satisfaction.[2] Table 16.1 below shows the percentage distribution of employees in each organizational class according to their degree of job satisfaction. It demonstrated that workers in Europe value different forms of work organization differently.

On average, discretionary learning promotes job satisfaction while Taylorism is the worst alternative. The difference between simple production and lean production is negligible. This shows that while having a job may be a positive value in itself, how happy you are with being employed will reflect

Table 16.1 Organizational forms and levels of job satisfaction—EU-15

	Discretionary learning	Lean production	Taylorism	Simple production
Highly satisfied	34.2	20.2	13.3	22.3
Largely satisfied	55.9	57.9	55.8	57.1
Largely unsatisfied	7.7	16.6	23.8	14.4
Highly unsatisfied	2.2	5.3	7.1	6.2

Note: Percentage of employees in each organizational class.
Source: Lorenz, Lundvall, and Valeyre (2004).

how work is organized in terms of learning opportunities and autonomy. Discretionary learning is attractive since it gives the employee opportunities to learn with some freedom. That simple production is valued more highly than Taylorism may reflect that simple production includes many activities where workers interact directly with customers while Taylorism gives the least opportunity for interaction with others: the worker is closely linked to a machine. In general, we see the results as confirming that workers value positively interactive learning, while absence of learning and loss of autonomy is the worst possible combination.

This demonstrates that welfare does not emanate exclusively from consumption. Perhaps the part emanating from working life is as important. One important way to enhance welfare in our societies is thus to transform workplaces so that employees get more autonomy and more opportunities for learning. As illustrated later on in the chapter, this is also a way of making firms more innovative and thereby to promote economic growth in the economy.

16.4.2. Different Patterns of Work Organizations in Different Parts of Europe

While consumption patterns may be converging with the single market, working life remains dramatically different in different parts of Europe and again we can distinguish significant groupings of European countries. The comparative analysis of Lorenz and Valeyre (this volume) shows that the forms of work organization are quite different between different parts of Europe. The learning forms of work organization are most widely diffused in the Netherlands (65 per cent), the Nordic countries and to a lesser extent Germany and Austria, while they are little diffused in Ireland and the southern European nations (18.7 per cent in Greece). The lean model is most in evidence in the UK (40.6 per cent), Ireland and Spain and to a lesser extent in France, while it is little developed in the Nordic countries as well as in Germany (19.6 per cent), Austria, and the Netherlands. The Taylorist forms of work organization show almost the reverse trend compared to the learning forms, being most developed in the southern European nations and Ireland (20.7 per cent). Finally, the simple forms of work organization are most in evidence in Greece and Italy and to a lesser extent in Germany, Sweden, Belgium, Spain, and Portugal.

This implies that a process of transformation moving workplaces towards the discretionary learning model must take place from very different starting positions in different groupings of countries. While the transformation of taylorist organization might be of little importance in the Netherlands, where it now is marginal, it remains a major issue in Greece. This is one of many instances where it is necessary to take into account the national differences as they reflect different levels of economic development and income levels in different parts of Europe. To set up similar benchmarks and objectives for establishing learning organizations in the North and the South is not very helpful. There is a great potential for enhancing welfare through reforming working life in Europe but the process must take into account that the original differences are huge.

16.4.3. National Differences in the Effect of Organizational Forms on Job Satisfaction

But it is also important to note how differences in organizational forms and learning opportunities affect welfare differently in different institutional settings (Lorenz, Lundvall, and Valeyre 2004). In Table 16.2 below we have excluded the four southern European nations in order to focus on countries with comparable levels of economic and technological development. The UK and Ireland are grouped together under the deregulated labour market label. The Nordic countries, the Netherlands, Belgium, Germany, and Austria characterized by relatively high levels of employment and/or unemployment protection are grouped under the heading of regulated labour market economies. The dependent variable is the job satisfaction score presented in Table 16.1.

The results show that the employees in the regulated labour market countries are considerably more satisfied with the discretionary learning forms of organization than they are with the lean forms, while this is not the case in the UK and Ireland. While there is a need for more analysis here, one possible interpretation of the pattern observed is that given adversarial industrial relations and low levels of employment protection in the UK and

Table 16.2. Ordered logit regression estimates of job satisfaction: deregulated vs. regulated labour market economies[1]

	Deregulated labour market countries	Regulated labour market economies
Discretionary learning	0.586**	0.819**
Lean production	0.437*	0.170
Simple production	0.034	0.327**
Taylorism	Reference category	
Pseudo R2	0.113	0.971
No.	1,240	5,285

Notes: * = significant at the 0.05 level; ** = significant at the 0.01 level
[1] The estimates control for age, sex, occupation, sector, the duration of training offered by the employer, and the type of payment system. See Lorenz, Lundvall, and Valeyre (2004).

Ireland, the higher levels of autonomy characteristic of the discretionary learning forms generate as much stress as they do satisfaction.

This contrasts with the regulated labour market countries characterized by relatively high level of employment or unemployment protection and well-developed systems of employer coordination around vocational training. In these countries, the dominant reaction to lean production would appear to be dissatisfaction due to the relatively low levels of control exercised by employees over work pace and methods. The preference for simple production in these countries may reflect that service workers have professional standing and pride to a much higher degree than in the deregulated labour market economies where 'the consumer is king'. The results imply that Sennett's negative assessment (1998) of the new trends in working life may be less applicable in countries where power is delegated in the work place and where there are more ambitious social security systems than in the Anglo-Saxon countries.

16.5. ON THE UTILITY OF CONSUMER LEARNING

While welfare theory has little to say about working life besides assuming that working is pain, it has a lot to say about consumption but again very little to say about consumer learning. Pasinetti (1981) stands out as one of the few economists who have pointed to consumer learning as being of critical importance for structural change and economic growth. When 'consumer learning' appears in the literature it normally refers to trivial processes of getting more information about brands or prices and qualities. The fact that many products sold to consumers are difficult to use and require competences and a change in lifestyle when they are used is completely neglected.

Box 16.1. Welfare effects from learning organizations through job opportunities and job security—the Danish case

---

We have shown that elements of welfare come out of learning in the workplace—that is, that work may be more or less appreciated with discretionary learning as the preferred alternative. In a related study, Lundvall and Nielsen (1999) show how learning organizations give rise to welfare for workers—including unskilled workers—by offering them more job security and job opportunities.

Using a combination of survey data and register data from Denmark, we have demonstrated that job security and job opportunities are much better in dynamic firms (combining learning organization characteristics with pursuing product innovation) than in static firms (doing neither). Interestingly, our results indicate that *unskilled workers* are the ones that have most to gain from belonging to a dynamic organization.

The study finds that *there are massive job losses for workers without professional training in firms that are exposed to intensified competition, but are not well prepared in terms of the organizational set-up and innovative capability.* This contrasts with the result that, on average, workers belonging to dynamic organizations will not be affected negatively by an increase in the competition pressure.

In terms of policy, the results emphasize the need to give workers without professional training privileged access to upgrading their skills and to enhance the possibilities for 'traditional' firms to engage in incremental innovation and organizational change. The other major policy should be one diffusing good organizational practices and promoting innovation.

But not all firms will be able to successfully engage in change when exposed to stronger pressure and in such cases firms will stagnate and close down. This may reflect that *opportunities* for technical and organizational change are very limited in certain industries. To move resources out of firms into more promising activities at a rhythm that keeps social and human costs at a reasonable level is an important task for competition and industrial policy.

This is remarkable in an era where whole generations of consumers have had to learn to drive cars, use complex household machines, and more recently to use advanced information and communication products. In the current era the welfare of the consumer is as much dependent on thecompetence to master new products as having access to them. Another important phenomenon is that consumers increasingly appear as co-producers and co-innovators in specific areas. In high-income countries *passive consumption* is not regarded as attractive. To lie down on the couch, eat, drink, and watch soap operas is not associated with an interesting life. At best it can be seen as 'relaxation' after a concentrated work effort. In rich countries people increasingly engage in formal or informal 'clubs' and 'communities' where members specialize in the consumption of wine, surfing, mountain

---

Box 16.2. Use of the Internet by individuals (OECD Science and Technology Scoreboard 2003)

- In many countries over half of all adults use the Internet from home, work, or another location. Countries with the highest rates of Internet use by adults are Sweden (70%), Denmark (64%), and Finland (62%). However, Internet use is growing more slowly in these countries than other OECD countries—a sign that they are reaching saturation.
- Men make greater use of the Internet than women in all countries for which data are available. The gap is largest in Switzerland where one-half of men but only one-third of women use the Internet.
- The Internet is used for different purposes in different countries. More than eight out of ten Internet users in Switzerland, Austria, the USA, Denmark, and Sweden use e-mail. It is also commonly used to find information about goods and services, particularly in Sweden, Denmark, and Finland—small countries with high Internet penetration rates.
- E-business is also an important area for Internet use. In the USA, almost 40% of Internet users buy online, as do many users in Denmark, Sweden, and Finland. In Sweden and the USA, almost two-thirds of individuals use the Internet to read and/or download online newspapers or news magazines.
- In Portugal and Sweden, about half of all Internet users play games online and/or download games and music. In Sweden and Denmark, more than half of all Internet users utilize e-banking and in Finland, one-third do so.

---

climbing, safari hunting, and computer gaming. The pleasure derived from these activities has little to do with the material things or the market services consumed. More important is the social interaction in connection with the consumption.

Sometimes there are markets for such activities (cf. charter tourism and safari services) but there is a lot of self-production going on in terms of planning and executing expeditions and events. Tangible things are acquired in order to get an excuse to interact with other people in a more or less challenging context. Sometimes these free time activities are more risky and require more effort and skill than what is required at the ordinary workplace. Using terms from earlier work on user–producer interaction more and more consumers take on characteristics of 'professional users'—and they increasingly become engaged in an interaction with producers as co-innovators and co-producers (Lundvall 1985). The most important illustration of this phenomenon may be the 'open-source'-software community where the scale of the activity is such that it has a major impact on the working of the formal economy (von Hippel 2002).

A case where a lot of user-learning is called for is in obtaining the skill to use the Internet. In Box 16.2 we have summarized the results of an OECD survey of international differences in frequency and form of use of the Internet. It is interesting to note that the small Nordic countries— Sweden, Denmark, and Finland appear at the top in both dimensions. This is remarkable since the dominant language on the Net is English and therefore one would expect users in English-speaking countries to be far ahead. Some of the same factors that make these countries intensive in terms of discretionary learning in working life seem to support consumer learning as well. Societies characterized by high degrees of equality and social security result in an even distribution of learning capabilities and of access to the infrastructure. This may be the major factors explaining this pattern.

16.5.1. Consumer Preferences and Consumer Learning

One of the major implications of the above is that the fundamental starting point of all welfare analyses that individuals are assumed to make decisions that maximize their preference functions becomes problematic. If we assume that the individual at any point of time has a preference function, this function would need to include *the intended change in the preference function* as argument in the function.

The point is that consumers will engage in consumption that results in processes of learning with the aim of changing their preference functions. Learning may result in 'a refined taste' for music or wine or in a more attractive use of the Internet. Learning might also result in a capability to engage in complex activities such as mountain climbing or software development. The very act of learning cannot be reduced to 'investment' since it involves pleasure as well as (self-inflicted) pain.

These considerations lead to a different understanding of what it means to make the individual consumer the king of the economy and also a different understanding of the importance of lifelong learning. A first conclusion is that the distribution of competence and of learning capabilities will be crucial for what satisfaction growing income and 'free markets' can offer. Increasing access to material assets without enhancing the learning capability of consumers may have a very limited impact on welfare. Since investment in learning capabilities—lifelong learning schemes for instance—often calls for public investment, the truth of the proposition that 'money is best placed in the pockets of the private consumer' can be disputed, even from a narrow consumer welfare perspective.

It also has implications in determining the kind of producers with whom consumers want to interact. A decreasing proportion of the household budget will be allocated to standard commodities where low price is most important.

More and more of the budget is used for advanced services where what is required is professional and competent producers with whom the consumer may interact in processes of learning and service development. In the learning economy neither consumer nor producer should be king. Rather they should be partners in permanent interaction (and sometimes in conflict) with each other.

16.6. TRANSFORMATION PRESSURE AND REDISTRIBUTION OF COST AND BENEFITS—NATIONAL POLICY MODELS

In the introduction we pointed out that there is path dependency both in the national political discourse and in the actual design of policy. Some of these national differences can be illustrated by defining four positions related to transformation pressure and the redistribution of cost and benefits of change respectively (see the Introduction). In real life all models are mixed and the categories are less pronounced than the labels indicate. International collaboration has brought some convergence but there are clear differences in underlying political culture.

These differences will be reflected both in political discourse and in practical implementation of policy. They may have an impact on what arguments—including economic theoretical arguments—are seen as relevant and legitimate. They may even imply that certain policies can be ruled out in advance because they are incompatible with basic political principles.[3] It is a major challenge for European integration and policy coordination to find ways to build upon these differences while constructing of a more coherent

Table 16.3. National policy regimes in terms of transformation pressure and redistribution of costs and benefits of change

	Increase transformation pressure	Reduce transformation pressure
Leave distribution of costs and benefits to the market	Liberalism UK	Protectionism Portugal
Compensate losers in the game of change	Neoreformism Nordic countries	Neoprotectionism France

European economy. Here we propose that realizing the new reality of the learning economy may be helpful in making progress in this respect.

16.6.1. National Welfare Regimes

In the modern welfare state the public sector absorbs taxes and insurance fees from its citizens. Some of the taxes are used to enhance the capability to cope with change (science, education, and infrastructure). Another part is used to compensate the victims of change (unemployment, sickness, and social problems). This might be called a *state-dominated welfare regime.*

But state intervention is not the only way to redistribute the costs and benefits of change. In Japan, the big corporation has worked as a kind of welfare institution with guaranteed lifelong learning as well as lifelong employment. If the demand for some specific function inside the firm disappeared the workers affected were trained and moved to another function within the company or possibly to another company in the network. This might be called a *company-dominated welfare regime.*

In the south of Europe the extended family shares the costs and benefits of change. Young and old still live together for longer periods of their lifespan. Young unemployed stay with their parents who help them until they can get a new job. This might be called a *family-dominated welfare regime.*

The fourth possibility is of course a *market-dominated welfare regime.* Here the individual is expected to take care of himself. Family obligations in terms of saving for the education of children and for the care of parents, as they grow older may be combined with an extended system of private insurance. In such regimes, taxes are lower but income inequality may be bigger.

It is striking that all four of the forms may be seen as crisis-ridden. The Japanese system seems to have difficulties with coping with rapid change. The family model in Southern Europe is undermined by the fact that women enter the labour market. In the state-dominated systems the costs of the welfare state have come into focus because of the assumed negative impact on location of firms. In the learning economy the market-dominated regime tends to establish degrees of inequality so extreme that they undermine social cohesion.

16.6.2. National Labour Market Systems

As can be seen from the last two sections there are systemic links between national policy regimes and welfare regimes. Both of these can be analysed in connection with the workings of the labour market. Here two different dimensions are crucial for the mode of innovation. One has to do with the welfare regime—are there collective security nets for the worker who falls between jobs. The other has to do with 'flexibility'—how difficult is it for employers to fire workers that are no longer seen as profitable. In Table 16.4 we have grouped countries according to these two dimensions.

In the Anglo-Saxon countries there are few restrictions on hiring and firing and there is a reluctance to compensate the unemployed. This gives a high degree of flexibility but also an uncertain and insecure situation for workers who will be reluctant to take active part in or initiate change.

In Mediterranean countries such as Portugal, Greece, and Spain the support level for unemployed is still low but there are limits on firing of workers. Workers are insecure but they have a strong incentive to engage in change if it aims at survival of the firm. The limited mobility of labour may slow down structural change.

In the big continental European systems and in Sweden, high substitution rates for unemployed are combined with contractual limits on firing. It is expected that the state takes responsibility when big workplaces are closed down. Here workers are secure. They might neither resist nor promote change. Industrial transformation may be slowed down by the lack of mobility.

The Danish model is actually rather unique in combining a very high rate of mobility in the labour market with high substitution rates also for workers that remain unemployed for a longer period. One interesting aspect of the model is that it might be helpful in combining more long-term participatory learning at the workplace with 'learning by moving around'. In a context of rapid change this combination might be especially important.

The current debate on 'flexicurity' is interesting because it points at a possible compromise between different political regimes and different welfare regimes. Gradually introducing more substantial support for the unemployed in some European countries and less restrictions on hiring and firing in others might be a more realistic strategy than the current emphasis on 'structural reform' where the agenda seems to be focused exclusively on increasing flexibility.

Table 16.4. Redistribution systems and flexibility of labour markets

	Limited contractual protection	High contractual protection
Leave distribution of costs and benefits to the market	Precarious flexibility UK/Ireland	Precarious security Portugal/Spain
Compensate losers in the game of change	Flexible security Denmark	Rigid security France/GermanyFrance/Germany

16.6.3. Different Welfare Systems Support Different Modes of Innovation

The implications of this analytical perspective are that the institutional set-up determining the dynamic performance of national systems is much broader than normally assumed when applying the innovation system concept. The redistribution policies and institutions are of fundamental importance for how innovation and interactive learning is organized. This is especially true for welfare and labour market institutions. There are alternative ways to build 'high performance innovation systems' and different innovation systems tend to organize work and distribute welfare differently among citizens.

We might identify two different innovation modes. In the egalitarian society with a strong social security net we would expect the ordinary worker not only to accept but also to be willing to promote change. The risk of getting into serious problems if change results in job loss is not seen as dramatic. This will not be the case in a 'self-made society' and here we would expect most innovation to emanate from the top, including from research and development laboratories with workers either passively adapting to or actually resisting change.[4]

Therefore, the choice between different welfare regimes cannot be decoupled from the workings of the learning and innovation system. Mismatches may become a major problem because old norms and new incentives do not support the kind of behaviour that is aimed at. More generally the transition from one welfare regime to another and from one historical political stance to another would always be painful and difficult.

16.7. THE DANISH MODEL AS A BENCHMARK FOR INSTITUTIONAL CONVERGENCE?

It is interesting to note that the normally pro-market weekly, *The Economist*, through its analytical unit, in May 2005 pointed to Denmark as the most attractive country in the world for investment. The liberal version of 'structural reform' is based on the idea that a small public sector, weak trade unions, and a high degree of income inequality are prerequisites for economic growth. Denmark seems to negate this idea and therefore calls for giving 'structural reform' a different and much broader content.

There are no single best ways to organize the national socio-economic systems. What works well today did not do so yesterday and today's ideal will be proven to be highly problematic tomorrow. The fascination of the Japanese model a decade ago is one reminder of this but there are many others, including the fascination of the German Wirtschaftswunder.

So when we introduce 'the Danish model' it is to be taken as a heuristic device rather than literally as a 'best practice' to be copied by others.[5] The point to be made here is that the Danish social and economic system has developed some characteristics that indicate possible solutions to the European tension between market and state regulation. Also, we argue that the Danish innovation system has developed institutions that are well-adapted to the current era—'the learning economy'.

This is most obvious in relation to the labour market. It is not difficult to fire workers in Denmark and the mobility in the labour market is as high or higher than in the US. But the common social security net financed by unemployment insurance and direct taxes is designed in such a way that employees on average express less insecurity than their colleagues in, for instance, Germany and France where there is more contractual security. There is a willingness to move between organizations and professions and the public investment in adult training has made this kind of mobility less difficult for the individual worker.

16.7.1. Citizen Participation and Local Democracy—An Alternative to Consumer Power?

Another area where the Danish model gives an alternative to the European stalemate is that of competition policy and state ownership. According to the pro-market ideology, the only way to make producers listen and adapt to the needs of the consumer is to install private ownership and competition.

This is not completely wrong. When Air France, France Telecom, and other French major state companies get more exposed to international competition, employees at all levels will be affected and experience a speed up of change. Those who are not able to respond quickly enough will lose their jobs. Others have to become more service-minded and flexible. As a positive result, the services delivered might become less expensive and better adapted to users. It is not obvious that being employed by a state-owned monopoly firm automatically should give the employee authority over customers and allow for rigid behaviour when confronted with user problems. But if the change means that professional pride and skills are undermined and flexibility becomes the only dimension promoted, the consequence may be lower quality in the services delivered. There is a reason why most Europeans prefer French restaurants and hospitals to British ones, even if the British were less expensive.

But the pro-market ideology goes further than dismantling public mon-opolies. There is a tendency for the European court to gradually extend the rule of competition law to more and more activities that historically have been seen as 'legitimate' core public sector activities. Among the more controversial are health and education. In Denmark, these activities still remain in public hands and the need to give consumers/clients/users a say has been solved not by the market but by local democracy (especially in the school system where parents have a voice in discussions with the education professionals). It is well known that the market (exit) is less effective in enhancing the quality of services than direct democracy (voice) in areas such as education.

16.8. A EUROPEAN INNOVATION SYSTEM WITHOUT A EUROPEAN WELFARE STATE?

There are increasing efforts in Europe to establish a 'European Innovation System'. The Framework programmes link knowledge producers and users in different European countries closer together. One motivation for the Euro-pean Research Area is to make research efforts more Coordinated. The Open Method of Coordination and benchmarking exercises (see Rodrigues, this volume) have been especially intense in relation to innovation related policies and institutions. But to develop coordination and to promote convergence in these fields neglecting fundamental differences in welfare regimes may prove counterproductive. Speeding up change while neglecting the distribution of the costs and benefits of change is not sustainable.

The increase in the transformation pressure puts the social cohesion of member countries under pressure. This is problematic since it is a key factor underlying economic progress in the learning economy. Whether this cohe-siveness can be re-established at a transnational regional level (the EU) when the national welfare system becomes weakened is an open question. The question was actually raised forty-five years ago by Svennilson, an outstand-ing expert on economic transformation in Europe, who pointed out the deep historical roots of the existing national welfare regimes.

... the institutions of the highly organized welfare state gives an indication of how many national ties need to be complemented by corresponding international ties in order to approach international integration. The welfare idea is so deeply rooted that its manifestations within the national framework can be superseded only by corre-sponding institutions of an international welfare community. How this can be made is an important subject for investigation. (Svennilson 1960: 9–10)

Forty-five years later, difficulties in establishing a consensus on strengthening the social dimension of the European project indicates that finding out how welfare state can be built and how social capital be reproduced at the transnational European level is still an important and very difficult task to achieve. Jacques Delors always insisted on the need to build a strong social dimension into the construction of a united Europe but there are big differences among the dominating nation states in this respect and so far there is little to suggest that the burden of redistributing the cost and benefits of change will be lifted away from national institutions.

In this chapter, we have tried to demonstrate that the learning economy if properly analysed and understood offers the European project a unique chance to establish a common movement towards a new set of institutions where welfare is seen as wider than maximizing growth and consumption. But in order to go into such a process it is necessary to challenge traditional economic wisdom about what constitutes welfare and it is necessary to recognize that the starting point for the process is very different in different parts of Europe. These differences in ideology and practice need to be recognized and not hidden behind loose concepts such as 'structural reform'. Especially in the current impasse, people need to be informed about what choices they have for the future and the problems need to be presented in a clear and transparent way.

We see it as a major problem that the Commission and the Lisbon process have not given sufficient recognition to systemic national differences. The idea that the policy learning process could advance in parallel to, for instance, innovation policy and welfare state reform without linking the two is not sound. The current crisis makes it impossible to neglect systemic national differences.

NOTES

1. Several other factors were at play but we believe that without the wide perception in France of the Commission as primarily pushing towards market solutions, the outcome would have been different.
2. Respondents were asked whether they were very satisfied, rather satisfied, rather unsatisfied, or not at all satisfied with their main paid job.
3. As part of an OECD-delegation visiting policymakers and top managers in Silicon Valley, Lundvall asked them about the fact that, on average, schoolchildren in Silicon Valley had much less easy access to computers than children in Denmark. Even the most sophisticated among them pointed to the need for low taxes as the explanation without finding this in any way scandalous.

4. In recent work we have made an attempt to develop the distinction between a DUI-mode (referring to learning by Doing, Using, and Interacting) and a STI-mode referring to (Science, Technology, and Innovation) on the basis of Danish survey data (Jensen, Johnson, Lorenz et al. 2004). We would assume that the DUI-mode might be used more intensively in egalitarian welfare regimes while the STI-mode would be more dominant in Anglo-Saxon welfare regimes.
5. See Lundvall (2002) for a fuller discussion of the Danish model.

REFERENCES

Christensen, J. L. and Lundvall, B.-Å. (eds.) (2004). *Product Innovation, Interactive Learning and Economic Performance.* Amsterdam: Elsevier.

Jensen, M. B., Johnson, B., Lorenz, E., and Lundvall, B.-Å. (2004). 'Absorptive Capacity, Forms of Knowledge and Economic Development', Paper presented at the *Second Globelics Conference.* Tsinghua University, Beijing.

Lorenz, E., Lundvall, B.-Å., and Valeyre, A. (2004). 'The Diffusion of New Forms of Work Organisation and Worker Outcomes: Lessons from the European Case', Paper presented at the *Second Globelics Conference.* Tsinghua University, Beijing.

Lundvall, B.-Å. (1985). *Product Innovation d User-Producer Interaction.* Aalborg, Denmark: Aalborg University Press.

—— (2002). *Innovation, Growth and Social Cohesion—The Danish Model.* London: Elgar.

—— and Nielsen, P. (1999). 'Competition and transformation in the learning economy—the Danish case', *Revue d'Economie Industrielle,* 88: 67–90.

OECD Science and Technology Score Board (2003). Paris: OECD.

Pasinetti, L. (1981). *Structural Change and Economic Growth.* Cambridge: Cambridge University Press.

Robeyns, I. (2000). 'An Unworkable Idea or Promising Alternative: Sen's Capability Based Approach', Working Paper, Wolfson College.

Sen, A. (1999). *Development as Freedom.* New York: Knopf.

Sennett, R. (1998), *The Corrosion of Character: The Personal Consequences of Work in the New Capitalism.* NewYork: Norton.

Svennilson, I. (1960). 'The Concept of the Nation and its Relevance to Economic', in E. A. G. Robinson (ed.), (1960). *Economic Consequences of the Size of Nations.* Proceedings of a Conference held by the International Economic Association, London: Macmillan.

Tomlinson, M. (2002). 'Measuring competence and knowledge using employee surveys: evidence using the British skills survey of 1997', CRIC Discussion Paper no. 50, Manchester.

von Hippel, E. (2002), Open Source Projects and User Innovation Networks, *MIT Sloan School* Working Paper 4366–02, June.

Index